Tek Raj Chhetri

Improving Decision Making Using Semantic Web Technologies

Springer Vieweg

Tek Raj Chhetri
Massachusetts Institute of Technology &
Center for Artificial Intelligence (AI)
Research Nepal
Cambridge, MA, USA

ISBN 978-3-658-45876-8 ISBN 978-3-658-45877-5 (eBook)
https://doi.org/10.1007/978-3-658-45877-5

This research was conducted at the University of Innsbruck, Austria, as part of a doctoral study and was successfully defended on October 11 2023, with excellent grades. Additionally, the work was generously supported by the European Union's Horizon 2020 research and innovation program through the smashHit project (grant number: 871477) and by the European Interreg Austria-Bavaria project KI-Net (grant number: AB292).

This Springer Vieweg imprint is published by the registered company Springer Fachmedien Wiesbaden GmbH, part of Springer Nature.
The registered company address is: Abraham-Lincoln-Str. 46, 65189 Wiesbaden, Germany

In memory of my beloved late mother

And

To my father

Preface

Decision making is by human nature. We make decisions daily. In recent decades, however, the influence of technology, particularly computing technology such as artificial intelligence (AI) and the Internet of Things (IoT), has changed the way we make decisions. An example is the use of IoT data and AI techniques to support decision making in the case of smart cities. This technological revolution has not only changed our decision making processes but also our lifestyles. Smart homes are one example of how IoT can be used to improve life quality. Focus is placed on data-driven AI technologies such as machine learning (ML) for making decisions or supporting decision making. Even though data-driven ML techniques have excellent pattern-learning capabilities, they exclude domain knowledge (or human experience or contextual information), which is fundamental to human decision making. As righteously said by the Greek philosopher Plato: *"A good decision is based on knowledge and not on numbers"*. This is precisely the subject of this dissertation: improving decision making through domain knowledge and context information using knowledge graphs that capture knowledge in human and machine-comprehensible formats, which numeric methods like ML lack. In particular, this dissertation will show how semantic technology (or Semantic Web technology), through ontologies and knowledge graphs, can lead to improved decision making, facilitating aspects such as explainability and complementing numerical methods like machine learning by providing answers to questions such as: (i) how to incorporate domain knowledge using semantic technology?; (ii) can semantic technology and machine learning be combined to achieve the best of both worlds and if so, how?

In addition, this dissertation will demonstrate how semantic technology can improve data sharing by addressing privacy issues in complex environments such as smart cities. A statement by Tim Cook, Apple's chief executive officer, exemplifies the indisputable importance of privacy, which is, *"If those of us in positions of responsibility fail to do everything in our power to protect the right to privacy we risk something far more valuable than money—we risk our way of life."* GDPR (General Data Protection Regulation) is a legal requirement considered within the scope of this study. Nonetheless, the approach presented in this dissertation is generalisable to other laws. Specifically, the work on data sharing addresses the challenges introduced by the new requirements of GDPR, such as the need for consent prior to data processing, which impede the progress and potential benefits that could be realised through cross-sectorial data sharing, answering questions such as (i) is it possible to translate the legal requirements into a code?; (ii) can we use semantic technology to address the data quality issues in a privacy-aware manner; if so, how?

Tek Raj Chhetri

Acknowledgements

As I walk to the end of this long and arduous journey of my PhD studies, I want to express my gratitude to everyone who has supported me throughout this journey. First and foremost, I would like to express my gratitude to my mentor, Professor Anna Fensel, for her supervision. I am particularly grateful for her willingness to assist me beyond academic supervision. Additionally, I appreciate the open discussions we have had. Like a mother, her genuine care and concern for personal and professional well-being have been a constant source of encouragement. Once again, I extend my heartfelt thanks to Professor Anna Fensel for her unwavering support, mentorship, and guidance. I owe her an enormous debt.

I would also like to take this opportunity to express my gratitude to Anelia Kurteva, Sareh Aghaei, Amar Tauqeer, Rainer Hilscher and Dennis Sommer for their discussions and thank you for being part of my PhD journey as co-authors and colleagues; it is nice working with you. I would also like to use this chance to thank Jubril Gbolahan Adigun for the discussion and especially for coming to the University of Innsbruck for his PhD. In addition, I would like to acknowledge the smashHit (grant number 871477) and KI-Net (grant agreement AB 292) projects, respectively, of which this work is a part, and particularly, express my gratitude to Ana Teresa Correia from ATB-Bremen, Rance J. DeLong from The Open Group and Nick Walker from LexisNexis Risk Solutions for their support.

I would also like to thank Robert Schimpf of Inncubator for his startup mentoring. Similarly, I would like to thank Viktoria Tollinger of the Institute for Entrepreneurship Cambridge-Tirol -Hermann Hauser (I.E.C.T. -Hermann Hauser) for all the assistance she provided and for enabling me to attend I.E.C.T. summer school and Tiroler Sparkasse bank for sponsorship. Additionally, I would like to thank all other co-authors, particularly Professor Satish Narayana Srirama from the University of Hyderabad, Assistant Professor Chinmaya Kumar Dehury from the University of Tartu and Reader (Associate Professor) Blesson Varghese from the University of St Andrews, for accepting my collaboration invitation and their support. I would also like to thank Associate Professor Amnir Hadachi from the University of Tartu for generously allowing me to contribute to the Intelligent Transportation Systems (ITS) Lab during my time there. Within this dynamic environment, I honed invaluable skills and gained crucial experience that significantly enriched my PhD research journey.

In addition, I extend my heartfelt gratitude to JP Koirala, Tekendra Timsina, Shishir Bhattarai, Prashant Acharya and all others whose names may not be listed here but whose contributions are equally appreciated.

I am profoundly grateful to my parents, twin brother (Tek Singh Chhetri), and sister (Kabita Chhetri) for their unwavering love, support, and encouragement throughout my academic journey. In particular, I would like to pay homage to my cherished mother whom I lost during my PhD, my initial guide in life whose absence I keenly feel. Her enduring love, boundless compassion, and support have transcended mere academics, shaping me into the individual I am today. I am also indebted to my father, who, like my mother, has played an integral role in shaping the person I have become, standing by my side throughout life's journey. I would also like to extend my heartfelt thanks to my wife, Bipana Acharya, for her endless love, encouragement, and support. Their faith in me and confidence in my abilities have been a constant source of inspiration, and their selfless sacrifices have enabled me to pursue my ambitions. I am truly fortunate to have such remarkable parents and siblings who have stood by me through thick and thin. Without their steadfast support, I could not have achieved what I have, and for that, I will remain eternally grateful. This work is dedicated to them as a token of my deepest appreciation for their love and sacrifices.

Passion is the genesis of genius. (Galileo Galilei)

I never lose. Either I win or learn. (Nelson Mandela)

Our greatest glory is not in never falling, but in rising every time we fall. (Confucius)

Integrity is about pursuing bigger goals that are beyond your personal success. If people see you only for yourself, they will not trust you. And, without trust, no growth and success are possible. (Jaggi Vasudev)

Abstract

As the pervasiveness of technology in our lives increases, so does its use in decision making tasks. For example, the use of machine learning to support data-driven decision making and the use of the Internet of Things to support decision making in smart cities and manufacturing. Moreover, as these technologies become ever more ubiquitous, they are becoming increasingly significant in the present day, with applications in crucial sectors such as healthcare. However, there are constraints. Machine learning, for example, lacks context awareness and does not incorporate domain expertise. Furthermore, specific challenges exist, such as the one posed by GDPR (General Data Protection Regulation), which includes compliance verification, for example, when processing and sharing sensitive (or personal) data. Semantic Web technology, specifically knowledge graphs and ontologies, has the potential to provide solutions to these problems of lack of context awareness and data quality, thereby aiding in the improvement of decision making due to its ability to model real-world relationships and provide reasoning support. However, there are a number of challenges with Semantic Web technology. Processing at scale in heterogeneous environments such as smart cities, supporting cyber-physical systems such as Internet of Things are just a few examples. There are also challenges in combining knowledge graphs and machine learning. For example, how should these two distinct technologies be combined, or what approaches should be taken to combine knowledge graphs and machine learning while simultaneously improving the results, such as prediction accuracy? Therefore, this dissertation investigates the techniques for addressing these challenges of Semantic Web technology in order to improve (or support) decision making in three distinct use case scenarios, namely data sharing, manufacturing, and agriculture. The data sharing use case focuses on addressing the challenges, such as scalable processing, as well as the use case-specific challenges, such as the GDPR challenges. Similarly, the focus of the remaining two use cases is on use case-specific challenges and the challenge of combining Semantic Web technology and machine learning. With our work in three distinct application scenarios, this thesis demonstrates how to support scalable processing in heterogeneous environments, such as smart cities, and the techniques for combining knowledge graphs and machine learning to improve decision making.

Contents

Abbreviations

AI	Artificial Intelligence
ASCII	American Standard Code for Information Interchange
BN	Bayesian Network
CCPA	California Consumer Privacy Act
CNN	Convolutional Neural Network
CPU	Central Processing Unit
DAG	Directed Acyclic Graph
DL	Deep Learning
DPD	Data Protection Directive
EU	European Union
GCN	Graph Convolutional Networks
GDPR	General Data Protection Regulation
GNN	Graph Neural Network
IoT	Internet of Things
IRI	Internationalised Resource Identifier
ISO	International Organisation for Standardisation
KG	Knowledge Graph
ML	Machine Learning
MLP	Multilayer Perceptron
OWL	Web Ontology Language
PII	Personally Identifiable Information
RDF	Resource Description Framework
RDFS	RDF Schema
RGCN	Relational Graph Convolutional Networks

RL	Reinforcement Learning
RO	Research Objective
RQ	Research Question
SDG	Sustainable Development Goals
SOSA	Sensor, Observation, Sample, and Actuator
SPARQL	Simple Protocol and Resource Description Framework Query Language
SQL	Structured Query Language
SW	Semantic Web
SWRL	Semantic Web Rule Language
TOMs	Technical and Organisational Measures
UN	United Nations
URI	Uniform Resource Identifier
US	United States
USD	United States Dollar
W3C	World Wide Web Consortium

List of Figures

List of Tables

Listings

List of Algorithms

Part I
Introduction

Introduction

1

This chapter provides an introduction to the thesis as well as an overview of why this research was conducted. Section 1.1 provides a general introduction, whereas Sect. 1.2 explains the impetus behind our work. Section 1.3 describes the challenges, while Sect. 1.4 describes RQs. Sect. 1.5 provides an overview of our ROs to answer RQs, and Sect. 1.6 provides an overview about the research methodology. Finally, Sect. 1.7 provides the outline of the thesis. All the abbreviations used in this chapter are introduced in the List of Abbreviations.

1.1 Introduction

Decision making is innate to the human species, and we make decisions on a daily basis. Choosing what to wear is one example of the daily decisions we make. An additional illustration of decision making is selecting between an apple and an orange. While choosing between an apple and an orange is relatively easy and can be done quickly, selecting an outfit is somewhat more difficult due to the need to consider additional external factors, such as the weather. The illustrative examples highlight a number of key points that align with Wang and Ruhe's [1] definition of decision making that is present in Definition 1.1.1.

Definition 1.1.1 *Decision making is defined as the process of selecting a decision (see* Definition 1.1.2*) from a set of alternatives based on a set of predetermined criteria for a given decision goal.*

T. R. Chhetri, *Improving Decision Making Using Semantic Web Technologies*,
https://doi.org/10.1007/978-3-658-45877-5_1

Definition 1.1.1 highlights three key points. The first point is that decision making involves selecting a decision from among the alternatives. The decision itself involves selecting one alternative from a set of alternatives based on a set of criteria. Definition 1.1.2 [1] provides the formal definition of the term decision. The second important point is the complexity of decision making, which grows with the increase in the number of alternatives or the set of criteria. This is because decision making requires selecting a decision, which is the function of the Cartesian product of the available alternatives and the set of criteria. For instance, even the simple case of choosing between an apple and an orange can become complex if the number of criteria (or conditions) is increased or if the number of available alternatives is expanded beyond apple and orange.

Definition 1.1.2 *Decision, d, is defined as a selected alternative $a \in A$ from non-empty set of alternative A based on the given criteria C, represented as $d = f(A, C) = f : A \times C \rightarrow A, A \subseteq U$ and $A \neq \phi$, where U is the universal set and $\times$ is the Cartesian product.*

The third important point is that decision making is always goal-oriented and the goal (or decision goal) is the result of the decision we make [1]. In our example of selecting an outfit, the objective is to select the best outfit for the given criteria, such as weather and events, from the available alternatives. Finally, the other important point is that there needs to be an alternative available to be able to make decisions.

Today, however, with the advancement of computing technologies such as AI and IoT, the process of decision making (or simply decision making) has shifted largely towards technology-driven decision making, both automated and semi-automated. By technology-driven, we refer to the use of technology in decision making. Autonomous vehicles are one of the prime examples of the use of technology for decision making [2]. The other examples include the use of AI to support clinical decision making [3] and the use of IoT in manufacturing and healthcare, together with other technologies such as AI, to support (or enhance) decisions related to manufacturing and healthcare [4, 5].

As we rely more and more on technology for decision making today, it is imperative that we address the current limitations in order to improve decision making, such as the lack of context-awareness in ML [6], an AI technique. Decision making can be improved in many ways. One can improve decision-making by enhancing the applied methods or assistive technology, which in turn enhances the applied methods and, in turn, decision making. One such example is the case of data, in which an improvement in data (or data quality) can result in an improvement in decision making. This is because the quality of the data can improve the final results of the applied techniques, such as prediction results in the case of ML. Similarly, the other example is the case of the IoT, which indirectly contributes to the improvement of decision making.

The field of decision making is vast and it is impossible to cover every aspect of improving decision making in all areas. Therefore, in this dissertation, we investigate the use of SW technology to to improve decisions related to data sharing, with an emphasis on smart city and insurance use cases. Similarly, this dissertation investigates techniques to combine (or use of) SW technology and ML to improve (or support) decision making, with an emphasis on manufacturing and agriculture use cases. The work on data sharing is part of the smashHit [7] project. Similarly, the work on manufacturing and agriculture use cases is part of the KI-Net [8] project.

The data sharing use case focuses on addressing challenges posed by GDPR [9], a data protection and privacy regulation under EU law, in tasks such as compliance verification. In addition to addressing GDPR challenges in compliance verification, the data sharing use case also focuses on other aspects of data, such as data quality and accuracy (i.e. data has not been tampered with). In the context of compliance verification, as described in [6], the focus is on decisions such as whether data exchange should be permitted, and performing verification to determine if there is any violation of GDPR. In addition, the other decisions in the context of the data sharing use case correspond to other aspects of data, such as determining whether or not the data is of defined quality.

The focus of the manufacturing use case is predictive maintenance and product failure. Likewise, the agriculture use case emphasises disease prediction. The improvement of decisions within the context of the manufacturing and agriculture use cases focuses on enhancing the accuracy of predictions. In addition, the emphasis is placed on providing explainability as opposed to enhancing prediction accuracy. This is because sometimes even the high accuracy of predictions can be misleading due to factors such as data imbalances [10, 11], and having additional information (or explanations) allows one to make better decisions than accuracy alone. For instance, in the case of manufacturing product failure, it is more advantageous to know the influence of different manufacturing steps on a product failure than to have just the prediction.

1.2 Motivation

Today, as a result of the pervasiveness of technology and the presence of more than 4 billion active internet users, there is an exponential increase in the amount of data generated by various sources, such as Twitter and Facebook [12]. Furthermore, with the expansion of IoT connectivity, which is expected to reach 83 billion by 2024 from 35 billion in 2020, an unprecedented increase in data can be expected [13]. This big data, generated by the pervasiveness of technology and IoT connectivity, has unlocked numerous opportunities and benefited numerous industries and individuals, including those in the manufacturing and healthcare sectors. The same data that benefits individuals and industries is also causing harm due to its misuse. The level of harm can vary depending on the level of misuse. The harm can be as severe as undermining fundamental rights such as privacy and democracy [14]. One such instance is the case of Cambridge Analytica, which is reported to have manipulated the US presidential election and the Brexit referendum by misusing Facebook user data [15].[1] GDPR [9] went into effect in 2018 to prevent the misuse of PII data and the potential harm such misuse may cause. The GDPR defines a set of requirements, such as obtaining consent and implementing data protection by design, which is also the focus of this thesis, that one must fulfil in order to share and process PII data in a lawful manner. GDPR's implementation has resulted in a shift in the data protection paradigm and ushered in new challenges for businesses, such as compliance verification (or automated compliance verification) [16]. Among the implementation roadblocks are dealing with dynamic consent, interoperability issue, and the realisation of data protection by design principles [16, 17].

GDPR is one of the strictest data protection laws and *violations are punishable by fines of up to 20 million euros or 4% of a company's global annual revenue in the preceding fiscal year, whichever is greater (Art. 83)*. Several companies, such as Google, Facebook, and Enel Energia, have already been fined for GDPR violations [18, 19]. Various studies have been conducted. For example, Pandit's [20] research focuses on the representation of consent and personal data using the SW, and Rhahla et al. [21] have proposed a framework for compliance verification. While these studies address a subset of the challenges, there are still limitations, such as in dealing with consent in complex environments such as in smart city and insurance sectors and the realisation of other GDPR principles, data protection by design, which is not addressed in compliance verification [16]. As shown in Fig. 1.1, the increasing number of fines highlights this: despite efforts, challenges persist in

[1] ⚠ **Terminological note:** In our research, the term PII refers to personal data under the GDPR; therefore, when using the term PII, it should be referred to as personal data.

ensuring GDPR compliance. Of the different types of fines, the majority, i.e., 676 of 2179, are due to insufficient legal basis for data processing. For example, processing PII data without appropriate legal bases, such as consent, constitutes fines, followed by non-compliance with GDPR, which results in 560 fines. The other categories include inadequate TOMs and inadequate fulfillment of data subject rights, accounting for 374 and 201 fines, respectively. Similarly, the other categories of fines include insufficient data processing agreement (11), lack of cooperation with the supervisory authority (76), and the lack of involvement of the data protection officer (16). Eighteen fines are unknown, i.e., no information can be obtained regarding the types of GDPR violations.

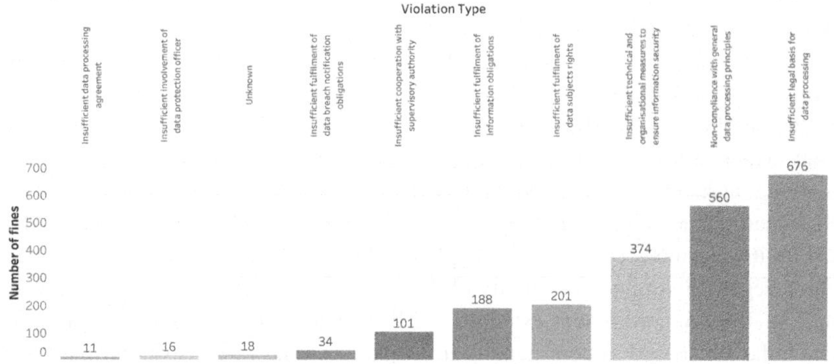

Fig. 1.1 The total number of GDPR fines categorized by type, as of January 7th, 2024. (Data source: GDPR Enforcement Tracker)

Existing limitations in GDPR compliance verification and the current industrial demand for GDPR-compliant solutions to enable the data economy's potential are the primary drivers for this work. In addition, these limitations and the current industrial needs are the impetus behind projects such as smashHit [7], which this work is also part of.

Additionally, as the IoT expands, so do the challenges and the growth in the amount of data being produced. For example, with the proliferation of heterogeneous IoT devices and the generation of massive amounts of data, the issue of data quality and accuracy (also known as veracity) has become more prevalent [22–25]. According to Bansal et al. [22], three-quarters of IoT projects are failing due to the data quality issue alone. In addition, as the IoT data is being used in critical sectors such as healthcare to support decision making; it is, therefore, imperative to address data issues like data quality and veracity problems, in addition to privacy concerns. Similar to the case of compliance verification, studies have been conducted on IoT data sharing; however, there are limitations, such as interoperability and context[2] awareness. Moreover, limitations, like the lack of context awareness, severely impact the quality of the decision making process [27]. For example, temperature is measured in different units, and if there is no information on the units of measurement, it will negatively impact a decision [27]. This is because the same temperature value on different temperature scales has different meanings, and depending on where the observation is made, the repercussions can be catastrophic, such as in the monitoring of nuclear reactors or patient monitoring in hospitals. Furthermore, existing studies do not account for fog computing and edge computing, which are considered next-generation IoT technical solutions for supporting real-time decisions in sectors like smart cities and autonomous vehicles [28–31].

The advancement in ML and its subfields have changed the landscape of computing, especially the way we solve problems by learning from the data. Due to this ML has applications across science, technology, and business. This has resulted in more evidence-based decision making in many fields, such as healthcare, manufacturing, agriculture, education, and modelling [32]. Almost everyone today uses ML, whether knowingly or not [33]. Numerous studies have demonstrated that ML, despite its enormous progress, has explainability, bias, and interpretability issues, which negatively impact the quality of decisions and, consequently, decision making [34–36]. One prominent example of ML bias is in the US judicial system, in which the ML-based system penalised people of colour more severely than their counterparts (i.e. white people), despite the severity of the crimes of the latter being greater [37]. Moreover, the ML lacks context awareness, which is essential in the improvement of decision making [38]. An instance of this is sentiment analysis, in which accurate decision-making requires context, or the set of facts or circumstances surrounding the events [39]. For instance, if we want to determine whether movie reviews are positive or negative, we need to consider the context of the reviews. Elements such as the genre of the movie, cultural nuances, and the demographics of the reviewer should be taken into account; failure to do so would result in an incorrect classification by the ML model. The same, i.e., importance of context holds true in other situations, such as computer vision [40]. In addition to a lack of context

[2] Any information that can be used to describe the situation (i.e. whether a person, place, or object) of an entity is referred to as context [26]. In the case of data sharing, by context (or contextual information), we refer to the set of interrelated conditions that describe the data, such as sensor information, units of measurement, and the observed property.

awareness, ML does not incorporate the domain expertise (or human experience) of domain experts, which can be extremely useful for decision making [41, 42]. This also helps to include humans in the loop, which contributes to the development of trust, the third motivation for our work.

Similarly to other technological advancements, manufacturing has also advanced. However, despite significant manufacturing advancements, product and equipment failure remains a major concern, and a substantial amount is spent on maintenance. Maintenance, for example, accounts for 15 to 60 percent of the total manufacturing costs in industries such as oil and gas [43]. Moreover, the repeated occurrence of the failure results in reputation damage, which is an intangible asset that accounts for approximately 85 percent of the value of a business today [44, 45]. This has resulted in a high demand for predictive solutions for both product and equipment failures, with a projected market value of USD 21.20 billion by 2027 [46]. Studies have been conducted and the focus is mostly on the use of ML [47]. Therefore, limitations, such as context awareness and interpretability, exist. In addition, other rule-based studies [48] are incapable of learning complex patterns. Existing limitations and the need for predictive solutions, which have led to projects like KI-Net [8], of which this work is a part, constitute our fourth motivation.

The other use case is agriculture, which also addresses the ML limitations, such as explainability for non-experts and other ML limitations discussed before, and focuses on improving disease classification. This is because being able to predict diseases early helps to take appropriate on time action and also limits the negative consequences. For example, if you can accurately predict the disease, you do not need to apply pesticides to the entire field, reducing the negative impact of the pesticides on the climate and soil. This use case is further motivated by the current food security challenges that have arisen as a result of factors such as climate change, the occurrence of diseases, and population growth, which is expected to reach 10-billion by 2050 [49]. Moreover, according to a UN report [50], one-third of the world's population (2.37 billion) suffers from a moderate-to-severe food security problem, making it one of the most urgent issues that must be addressed immediately.

SW technologies such as ontology and KG can model real-world relationships [6]. In addition, SW technologies, supporting the reasoning for decision making, can aid in the incorporation of domain knowledge and support interoperability and knowledge representation [51–54]. The use of SW technologies in this study is motivated by their potential to address current issues such as interoperability, lack of context awareness, explainability in ML, and the incorporation of missing domain knowledge in ML in order to improve decision making.

1.3 Problem Statement

As broad as the decision making process is, so too are the challenges. As a result, based on our objective, which is to address the issue of enhancing decision making, we have identified a number of significant obstacles, which are discussed in the sections that follow. The identified difficulties are a result of the scope of this dissertation. Moreover, the challenges identified within the scope of this dissertation are consistent with the results of other studies, such as [55–57], as well as the Dagstuhl Seminar report [58], which discusses the challenges and new directions for SW technologies, such as KGs. Depending on the type of work, the identified challenges have been categorised into two groups: (i) data sharing and (ii) combining KGs and ML. The sections that follow discuss the discovered challenges.

1.3.1 Data Sharing

Due to heterogeneous IoT sensors and distinct computing paradigms, data sharing is considerably more complex today. Figure 1.2 shows a high-level overview of today's data sharing environment with heterogeneous IoT sensors and different computing paradigms such as edge, fog, and cloud computing. In addition, Fig. 1.2 illustrates the current challenges in data sharing, which are discussed below.

CHALLENGE 1: INTEROPERABILITY

Due to the heterogeneity of IoT sensors and their applications, interoperability is currently one of the major challenges for data sharing. Numerous studies have shed light on the interoperability challenges [22, 23]. McKinsey predicts that the IoT will have an annual economic impact of $11.1 trillion by 2025, with interoperability accounting for approximately 40% of the total benefits [59]. This further emphasises the significance of the problem. Moreover, with the growing use of automated systems in various sectors, such as the manufacturing industry, healthcare, and smart cities, interoperability becomes even more important. This is because interoperability enables the common understanding, and failure to do so can have negative consequences. Interoperability challenges also exist in the regulatory context, i.e. the GDPR case [60]. For example, heterogeneous and dynamic consent information originating from a variety of sources must be processed in order to successfully put GDPR principles into practice and enable the data economy, which existing solutions appear to be lacking [16].

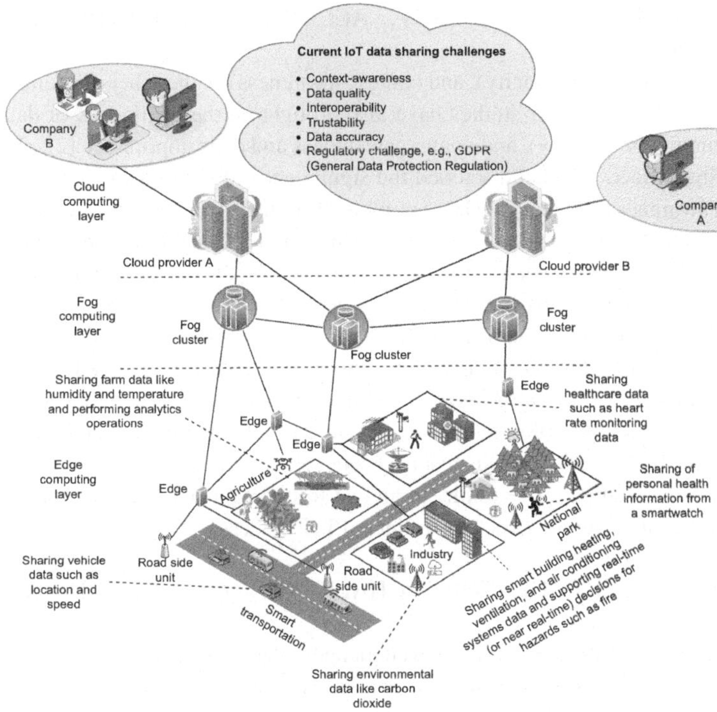

Fig. 1.2 IoT data sharing environment with an edge/fog scenario and the associated challenges. (This source of the figure is the publication [27])

Challenge 2: Scalability

The other challenge is scalability, especially given the expanding use of IoT in heterogeneous sectors such as smart cities [61]. In particular, the scalability challenge is also highlighted by Harth et al. and Groth et al. in the Dagstuhl Seminar report [58], especially for knowledge-driven applications that use KGs, and has been regarded as a key challenge. In addition, other requirements, such as GDPR, have also contributed to the scalability challenge. This is because existing technologies must be carefully evaluated; otherwise, they may become a bottleneck. Blockchain, for instance, offers immutability features and can be used to enable the secure sharing of IoT data. However, blockchain suffers from scalability issues [62] and conflicts with the "right to be forgotten" requirement of the GDPR.

Challenge 3: Data Quality, Accuracy and Context-Awareness

Data quality, accuracy (or veracity), and context-awareness are the other challenges in data sharing. Several other studies have also brought up the challenges of data quality, accuracy (or veracity), and context awareness and their importance [22–25, 63]. In addition, Sect. 1.2 also discussed the significance of data quality, veracity, and context awareness. Moreover, a large number of studies (over 50, at the moment) have been conducted on data quality using statistical and ML techniques following a post-hoc approach [63]. Byabazaire et al. [25] emphasise the need for an intrinsic data quality approach as post-hoc approaches using ML are costly. Data quality, despite significant efforts, remains an issue and a cause for the failure of $3/4^{th}$ of IoT projects [22]. In addition, Byabazaire et al. [25] emphasise the need for the assessment of context information as component of the data quality, and they assert that there are no available solutions. Similar to the case of data quality and context awareness, the challenge also lies in ensuring data veracity (or accuracy) along with other criteria like GDPR, for example, in an end-to-end data sharing environment with consideration of the resource constraints of IoT devices.

Challenge 4: Regulatory Challenge and Trustworthiness

Data sharing in the IoT presents additional challenges related to privacy and trust [17, 64–66], leading to the implementation of data privacy regulations such as GDPR. The following regulatory challenges exist in particular: (i) implementation of the data protection by design and data protection by default principles; (ii) implementations of TOMs; (iii) translation of legal regulations into code; and (iv) compliance verification based on dynamic informed consent to enable GDPR compliant data sharing and processing [16]. Just like in the case of data quality, a number of studies have been done on trust management [25, 64, 67]. However, despite significant studies, there is a lack of studies that focus on intrinsic trust metrics (or scores) for shared data. Byabazaire et al.'s [67] work is a good example of this because it focuses on getting trust metrics (or scores) from shared data using data analysis approach and not intrinsically. This is particularly important in data sharing, considering its use in sectors such as healthcare and smart homes, because having a trust score helps one decide to what extent one can rely on data. The benefits of the trust score have already been proven in other contexts, for example, in Google search [68], which rank trustworthy sources highly.

Challenge 5: Instantaneous Translation of Knowledge into Practise

As highlighted by Groth et al. in the Dagstuhl Seminar report [58], there is a disconnect between theory and practise, particularly regarding the translation of knowledge into the KGs representation from cyber-physical systems such as IoT, and the vision is to eliminate this gap. The difficulty stems from the resource-constrained nature of IoT and other external factors, such as GDPR and the requirement to support emerging computing paradigms. For example, in the case of IoT data sharing, how to translate incoming high velocity and heterogeneous data into the KG representation in order to facilitate decision making tasks in real-time or near real-time while supporting the new distributed computing paradigms, e.g. edge and fog computing. Similarly, in the manufacturing and agricultural scenarios, there is a question about how this translation should be made so as to facilitate reasoning to support decision making in combination with other techniques such as ML.

1.3.2 Combining Knowledge Graphs and Machine Learning

As per Staab et al. in the Dagstuhl Seminar report [58], KGs are an asset for ML and provide grand opportunities such as the generation of consistent and coherent predictions, as well as aiding in explainability. Other researchers, including Sabou et al. and Claudia d'Amato in the Dagstuhl Seminar report [58], have also identified comparable opportunities. As Groth et al. [58] noted in the case of instantaneous translation of knowledge, a similar gap between theory and practise exists when combining KGs and ML. In addition, according to Groth et al. [58], the task of combining the KGs and ML is one of the grand challenge tasks. For instance, how to combine ML and KGs such that the result improves rather than decreases in a complex environment such as manufacturing and agriculture, dealing with various types of data including image and textual (or sensor) data. Similarly, how should mappings be performed to generate concise explanations while simultaneously improving the accuracy of prediction?

1.4 Research Questions

Despite numerous challenges (see Sect. 1.3), the SW has the potential to improve decision making in environments as complex, distributed, and heterogeneous as manufacturing and smart cities. Therefore, based on the potential of the SW, we argue that by using SW technologies, we can improve decision making. In accordance with our argument, we hypothesise the same, which is outlined below.

Hypothesis
SW TECHNOLOGIES CAN IMPROVE DECISION MAKING IN DISTRIBUTED AND HETEROGENEOUS ENVIRONMENTS.

We must test our hypothesis in order to evaluate our claim. In order to test our hypothesis, we seek answers to the RQs. By answering the RQs, we intend to confirm our hypothesis. Listed below are the RQs that our work intends to answer to validate our hypothesis. The first two RQs are concerned with the data sharing case, while the third RQ is focused on the other case, which involves combining KGs and ML with an agriculture and manufacturing-focused use case.

RQ1
HOW TO CREATE A SCALABLE AND INTEROPERABLE APPLICATION THAT USES SW TECHNOLOGY TO IMPROVE DATA SHARING AND PROCESSING DECISIONS, SUCH AS WHETHER OR NOT TO ALLOW DATA SHARING OR PROCESSING, WHILE ALSO ADDRESSING THE REGULATORY CHALLENGE POSED BY GDPR IN A HETEROGENEOUS ENVIRONMENT LIKE SMART CITIES?

RQ2
CAN WE TRANSLATE DATA FROM CYBER-PHYSICAL SYSTEMS, SUCH AS IOT, INTO KNOWLEDGE REPRESENTED BY KGS TO ENABLE REAL-TIME (OR NEAR REAL-TIME) DECISIONS WHILE ALSO SUPPORTING EMERGING DISTRIBUTED COMPUTING PARADIGMS, SUCH AS EDGE AND FOG COMPUTING, AND ENSURING OTHER ASPECTS OF DATA, SUCH AS DATA QUALITY AND DATA VERACITY IN A SCALABLE MANNER?

RQ3
How to combine KGs and ML to improve decision making in sectors such as manufacturing and agriculture while also facilitating explainability?

1.5 Research Objectives

The major objective of this study is to validate our hypothesis, which is that by using SW technology, we can improve decision making in complex environments like smart cities. Therefore, our ROs is to validate our hypothesis by answering our RQs. Following our RQs (see Sect. 1.4), we have three ROs, which we discuss below.

Our first two ROs are focused on data sharing use cases. Our first two ROs seek an answer to the two RQs, namely, RQ1 and RQ2, and address the corresponding challenges outlined in Sect. 1.3.1. These two ROs, RO1 and RO2, are tasked with identifying necessary requirements, such as GDPR TOMs, and designing the optimal architecture based on requirements such as scalability. In addition to the investigation and design of the new (or improve existing) methods, RO1 and RO2 focus on the implementation and evaluation to determine if it meets the requirements, such as scalable processing, to answer our RQs. Our RO1 is particularly focused on addressing GDPR-related challenges to unlock the potential of the data economy, such as by implementing data protection by design principles and demonstrating how to translate legal regulation into code. As a result, our first RO is as follows:

RO1
To investigate, design, implement, and evaluate a scalable and interoperable methods and application that uses SW technology to improve data sharing and processing decisions, such as whether or not to allow data sharing or processing, while also addressing the regulatory challenge posed by GDPR in a heterogeneous environment such as smart cities.

Our second RO focuses on other challenges in data sharing and responding to the second RQ. For example, our second RO focuses on data quality while taking into account newer computing paradigms such as edge computing and fog computing to support real-time (or near real-time) decision making. Thus, our second RO can be stated as follows:

RO2
TO INVESTIGATE, DESIGN NEW (OR IMPROVE EXISTING) METHODS, IMPLEMENT, AND EVALUATE AN END-TO-END PROTOTYPE THAT SUPPORTS REAL-TIME (OR NEAR REAL-TIME) DECISIONS IN THE EDGE (OR EDGE COMPUTING) AND EDGE/FOG (OR EDGE AND FOG COMPUTING COMBINED) SCENARIO AND ENSURES OTHER ASPECTS OF DATA HANDLING, SUCH AS DATA VERACITY (ACCURACY), PRIVACY, AND QUALITY.

Similar to the previous two ROs, our third RO focuses on answering the third RQ. In contrast to the other two ROs, which focuses on use cases involving data sharing, this RO focuses on manufacturing and agriculture use cases. This RO investigates techniques for combining KGs and ML to improve decision making, as well as techniques for enabling explainability. In addition, this RO focuses on the design of new (or improving existing) methods and implementation of either a proof-of-concept or a prototype of the technique that combines KGs and ML, as well as performing evaluation. Therefore, our third and final RO is as follows:

RO3
TO INVESTIGATE, DESIGN NEW (OR IMPROVE EXISTING) METHODS, IMPLEMENT A PROOF-OF-CONCEPT OR PROTOTYPE, AND EVALUATE TECHNIQUES FOR COMBINING KGs AND ML TO IMPROVE DECISION MAKING AND FACILITATE EXPLAINABILITY.

1.6 Research Methodology

This section provides an overview of the research methodology that was followed. Section 1.6.1 provides a methodology that was followed for the literature review. Section 1.6.2 provides an overview of the methodology that was followed for the implementation of the prototype (or conducting an experiment). Section 1.6.3 provides an overview of how the evaluation was conducted.

1.6.1 Literature Review

As with any other task that we do, the first thing is to understand the problem and what has been done so far. Therefore, to understand the problem and the work that has been done, appropriate literature was reviewed. The review of the literature was as per the scope of the work that was being performed. For example, in the case of data sharing, one of the objectives is to enable GDPR-compliant data sharing. The literature reviewed in this case concentrated on works on GDPR, both with and without the use of SW technology. In the other case, combining ML and SW technology, the literature reviews included the reviews of the papers using both ML and SW technology, following the scope of the work, such as failure prediction. In addition to reviewing the scientific literature, the documents describing the project requirements were also examined. This is because the work presented in this dissertation is a component of smashHit [7] and KI-Net [8], and the projects have delivered most up-to-date state of the art and requirements.

1.6.2 Design and Implementation

After the review of the literature and understanding of the project requirements, the next step is to design the architecture (or experiment) and perform the implementation. The design and implementation are driven by the use cases of the projects, smashHit [7] and KI-Net [8], that our work is part of, the ROs, and our initial analysis [6]. For example, in the case of the RO1, one of the concerns is scalability, whereas in the case of the RO3, scalability is not a concern. Additionally, as our ROs highlighted, the legal requirements, i.e. GDPR, in addition to the use case requirements, also influenced the design and implementation of our work in data sharing. Similarly, in our work on combining KG and ML, the design and implementations were influenced by the users, such as in our work on explainability. Moreover, the agile development methodology was followed during the design and implementation to maintain agility throughout the entire development process [69].

The fundamental criteria or mandatory functional requirements that influenced the design decisions and implementation of our data-sharing-related work are outlined as follows:

1. The design and implementation must use SW technology, such as KGs and SPARQL.
2. The design and implementation should be scalable, i.e. scalable enough to meet the industrial use case requirements.
3. The design and implementation should follow the legal, i.e. GDPR, requirements, such as data minimisation and ability to revoke the given consent in an easy manner. Furthermore, the design and implementation should prioritise measures to ensure security and privacy.
4. The design and implementation should also take into account the auditability features, i.e. logging all the information (or decisions) made, which are required to demonstrate GDPR compliance to the authority.
5. In the case of the GDPR, the system should automatically perform compliance checking and be able to trigger the notification.
6. The implementation must permit easy integration with other systems and be interoperable. In addition, the implementation should be extendable to other use cases.
7. The design and implementation should support the resource constrained IoT devices that are used in smart cities for data collection and sharing with minimal overhead in terms of system resource utilisation.
8. In the case of IoT data sharing, the design and implementation should also ensure that predefined quality criteria are met to enable the collection and sharing of high-quality data and the trustworthiness of shared data.

In a manner analogous to the case of data sharing, we describe below the fundamental requirements that influenced our design and implementation of the work on combining KG and ML.

1. The design and implementation should account for the requirements of the use case, such as manufacturing.
2. Design and implementation of the proposed method must always employ KGs in conjunction with ML techniques.
3. The combination of KGs and ML should result in either an improvement in performance or in the result's interpretability and explainability.
4. Regarding interpretability and explainability, it should be geared towards non-experts and, as a result, be easily understandable.
5. As the prevalence of vision-based techniques rises, the design and implementation must also consider multimodal data, which includes both images and text.

6. The design of the proposed method must be sufficiently generalisable to be applicable to other domains or use cases.

In Part II, Publications, which consists of scientific publications, the design of the architecture or proof-of-concept experiments and their respective implementations are described in detail.

1.6.3 Evaluation

Similar to the cases of design and implementation, our ROs and the design and implementation criteria (see Sect. 1.6.2) that are based on use cases serve as the driving forces behind our evaluation. The details about the evaluations conducted are provided in Part II, Publications, of this dissertation, which consists of the scientific publications. Moreover, in addition to the ROs, our evaluation follows the standard evaluation approaches. In the case of scalability, for example, the evaluation was carried out by determining whether the implemented applications can scale to handle an increasing (or decreasing) number of incoming requests, whereas in the case of works involving ML, the prediction accuracy was evaluated and compared to the state-of-the-art.

1.7 Thesis Outline

The whole thesis is split into three parts, namely: (i) Part I, introduction; (ii) Part II, publications; and (iii) Part III, the conclusion, and each part is followed by the corresponding chapters. Figure 1.3 provides an overview of the outline for the thesis.

Part I includes three chapters, namely, Chap. 1, Chap. 2 and Chap. 3. Chapter 1 (this chapter) introduced the decision making, the overall motivations for this research, the problem statements, the RQs, and the ROs with which we aim to answer the RQs. Chap. 2 provides an information about the research contributions. In particular, Chap. 2 serves as a bridge, linking the ROs and contributions made in the form of scientific publications that are organised into chapters in Part II. Similarly, Chap. 3 provides a summary of the technologies, such as ontologies and RDF, utilised in this thesis. Furthermore, Chap. 3 discusses the concepts, such as ML that is utilised in our work.

Part II, as shown in Fig. 1.3, consists of a total of five chapters and describes our scientific contributions. Chap. 4, Chap. 5 and Chap. 6 provide detail about the contributions that focus on our RO3, which is about combining SW technology and

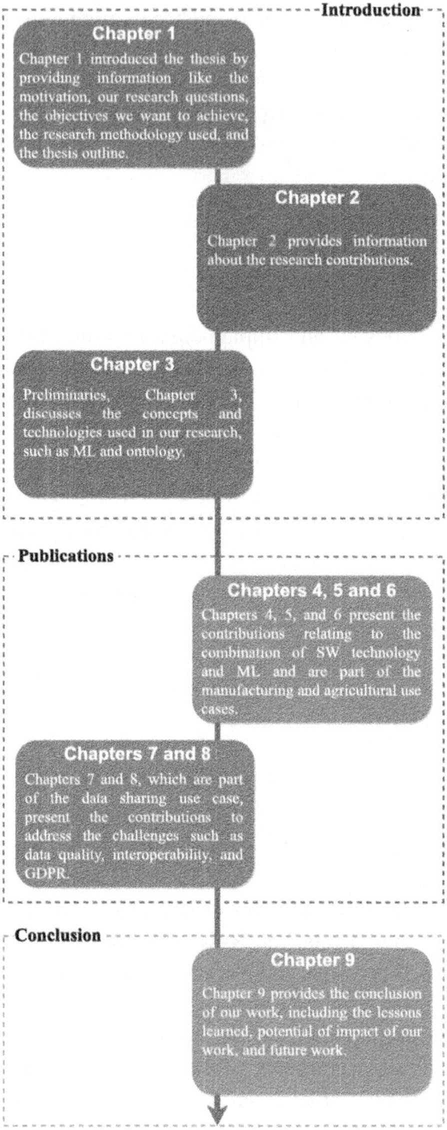

Fig. 1.3 Thesis outline

ML as part of the manufacturing and agricultural use cases. Similarly, Chap. 7 and Chap. 8 provide information on our contributions relating to the data sharing use case. Further details on our contributions are present in Chap. 2.

Part III, which consists of one chapter, Chap. 9, provides the conclusion.

Bibliography

1. Yingxu Wang and Guenther Ruhe. 'The Cognitive Process of Decision Making'. In: Novel Approaches in Cognitive Informatics and Natural Intelligence. Hershey, PA, USA: IGI Global, 2009, pp. 130–141. https://doi.org/10.4018/978-1-60566-170-4.ch009.
2. Liangzhi Li, Kaoru Ota, and Mianxiong Dong. 'Humanlike Driving: Empirical Decision-Making System for Autonomous Vehicles'. In: *IEEE Transactions on Vehicular Technology* 67.8 (2018), pp. 6814–6823. https://doi.org/10.1109/TVT.2018.2822762.
3. Faiq Shaikh, Jamshid Dehmeshki, Sotirios Bisdas, Diana Roettger-Dupont, Olga Kubassova, Mehwish Aziz, and Omer Awan. 'Artificial Intelligence-Based Clinical Decision Support Systems Using Advanced Medical Imaging and Radiomics'. In: *Current Problems in Diagnostic Radiology* 50.2 (2021), pp. 262–267. https://doi.org/10.1067/j.cpradiol.2020.05.006.
4. Yuan Guo, Nan Wang, Ze-Yin Xu, and Kai Wu. 'The internet of things-based decision support system for information processing in intelligent manufacturing using data mining technology'. In: *Mechanical Systems and Signal Processing* 142 (2020), p. 106630. https://doi.org/10.1016/j.ymssp.2020.106630.
5. Pantea Keikhosrokiani. 'IoT for Enhanced Decision-Making in Medical Information Systems: A Systematic Review'. In: *Enhanced Telemedicine and e-Health: Advanced IoT Enabled Soft Computing Framework*. Ed. by Gonçalo Marques, Akash Kumar Bhoi, Isabel de la Torre Díez, and Begonya Garcia-Zapirain. Cham: Springer International Publishing, 2021, pp. 119–140. https://doi.org/10.1007/978-3-030-70111-6_6.
6. Tek Raj Chhetri. 'Improving Decision Making Using Semantic Web Technologies'. In: *The Semantic Web: ESWC 2021 Satellite Events*. Ed. by Ruben Verborgh, Anastasia Dimou, Aidan Hogan, Claudia d'Amato, Ilaria Tiddi, Arne Bröring, Simon Mayer, Femke Ongenae, Riccardo Tommasini, and Mehwish Alam. Cham: Springer International Publishing, 2021, pp. 165–175.
7. *smashHit*. https://smashhit.eu/. Last accessed on 01 October 2022.
8. *KI-NET*. https://ki-net.eu/. Last accessed on 01 October 2022.
9. European Parliament and Council. 'Regulation (EU) 2016/679 of the European Parliament and of the Council of 27 April 2016 on the protection of natural persons with regard to the processing of personal data and on the free movement of such data, and repealing Directive 95/46/EC (General Data Protection Regulation)'. In: *Official Journal of the European Union, L119* (2016), pp. 1–88.
10. Mohammad Hossin and MN Sulaiman. 'A review on evaluation metrics for data classification evaluations'. In: *International Journal of Data Mining & Knowledge Management Process* 5.2 (2015), p. 1.

11. Brendan Juba and Hai S Le. 'Precision-recall versus accuracy and the role of large data sets'. In: *Proceedings of the AAAI Conference on Artificial Intelligence*. Vol. 33. 01. Honolulu, HI, USA, 27 January–1 February, 2019, pp. 4039–4048.
12. Kaneez Fizza, Prem Prakash Jayaraman, Abhik Banerjee, Dimitrios Georgakopoulos, and Rajiv Ranjan. 'Age of Data Aware Internet of Things Applications'. In: *2022 IEEE 19th Annual Consumer Communications Networking Conference (CCNC)*. 2022, pp. 399–404. https://doi.org/10.1109/CCNC49033.2022.9700640.
13. Marco Centenaro, Cristina E. Costa, Fabrizio Granelli, Claudio Sacchi, and Lorenzo Vangelista. 'A Survey on Technologies, Standards and Open Challenges in Satellite IoT'. In: *IEEE Communications Surveys Tutorials* 23.3 (2021), pp. 1693–1720. https://doi.org/10.1109/COMST.2021.3078433.
14. Maja Brkan. 'EU fundamental rights and democracy implications of data-driven political campaigns'. In: *Maastricht Journal of European and Comparative Law* 27.6 (2020), pp. 774–790.
15. Carole Cadwalladr and Emma Graham-Harrison. 'Revealed: 50 million Facebook profiles harvested for Cambridge Analytica in major data breach'. In: *The guardian* 17 (2018), p. 22.
16. Tek Raj Chhetri, Anelia Kurteva, Rance J. DeLong, Rainer Hilscher, Kai Korte, and Anna Fensel. 'Data Protection by Design Tool for Automated GDPR Compliance Verification Based on Semantically Modeled Informed Consent'. In: *Sensors* 22.7 (2022). https://doi.org/10.3390/s22072763.
17. Anelia Kurteva, Tek Raj Chhetri, Harshvardhan J. Pandit, and Anna Fensel. 'Consent through the lens of semantics: State of the art survey and best practices'. In: *Semantic Web* Preprint (2021). Preprint, pp. 1–27. https://doi.org/10.3233/SW-210438.
18. Commission nationale de lînformatique et des libertés (CNIL). *Cookies: the CNIL fines GOOGLE a total of 150 million euros and FACEBOOK 60 million euros for non-compliance with French legislation*. https://www.cnil.fr/en/cookies-cnil-fines-google-total-150-million-euros-and-facebook-60-million-euros-non-compliance. Last accessed on 07 October 2022. 2022.
19. European Data Protection Board (EDPB). *Aggressive telemarketing: Italian SA fines Enel Energia eur 26.5 million*. https://edpb.europa.eu/news/national-news/2022/aggressive-telemarketing-italian-sa-fines-enel-energia-eur-265-million_en. Last accessed on 07 October 2022. 2022.
20. Harshvardhan J Pandit. 'Representing activities associated with processing of personal data and consent using semantic web for GDPR compliance'. In: *Trinity College Dublin, School of Computer Science & Statistics* (2020).
21. Mouna Rhahla, Sahar Allegue, and Takoua Abdellatif. 'A Framework for GDPR Compliance in Big Data Systems'. In: *Risks and Security of Internet and Systems*. Ed. by Slim Kallel, Frédéric Cuppens, Nora Cuppens-Boulahia, and Ahmed Hadj Kacem. Cham: Springer International Publishing, 2020, pp. 211–226.
22. Maggi Bansal, Inderveer Chana, and Siobhán Clarke. 'A Survey on IoT Big Data: Current Status, 13 V's Challenges, and Future Directions'. In: *ACM Comput. Surv*. 53.6 (2020). https://doi.org/10.1145/3419634.
23. Muhammad Naeem, Tauseef Jamal, Jorge Diaz-Martinez, Shariq Aziz Butt, Nicolo Montesano, Muhammad Imran Tariq, Emiro De-la Hoz-Franco, and Ethel De-La-Hoz-Valdiris. 'Trends and Future Perspective Challenges in Big Data'. In: *Advances in Intel-*

ligent Data Analysis and Applications. Ed. by Jeng-Shyang Pan, Valentina Emilia Balas, and Chien-Ming Chen. Singapore: Springer Singapore, 2022, pp. 309–325.
24. Li Cai and Yangyong Zhu. 'The challenges of data quality and data quality assessment in the big data era'. In: *Data science journal* 14 (2015).
25. John Byabazaire, Gregory O'Hare, and Declan Delaney. 'Data Quality and Trust: Review of Challenges and Opportunities for Data Sharing in IoT'. In: *Electronics* 9.12 (2020), p. 2083. https://doi.org/10.3390/electronics9122083.
26. Anna V Zhdanova, Josip Zoric, Marco Marengo, Herma van Kranenburg, Niels Snoeck, Michael Sutterer, Christian Räck, Olaf Droegehorn, and Stefan Arbanowski. 'Context acquisition, representation and employment in mobile service platforms'. In: *Proceedings of the 15th IST Mobile & Wireless Communications Summit*. Vol. 53. Myconos, Greece, 4–8 June, 2006.
27. Tek Raj Chhetri, Chinmaya Kumar Dehury, Blesson Varghese, Anna Fensel, Satish Narayana Srirama, and Rance J. DeLong. 'Enabling privacy-aware interoperable and quality IoT data sharing with context'. In: *Future Generation Computer Systems* 157 (2024), pp. 164–179. https://doi.org/10.1016/j.future.2024.03.039.
28. Joern Ploennigs, John Cohn, and Andy Stanford-Clark. 'The Future of IoT'. In: *IEEE Internet of Things Magazine* 1.1 (2018), pp. 28–33. https://doi.org/10.1109/IOTM.2018.1700021.
29. Keyan Cao, Yefan Liu, Gongjie Meng, and Qimeng Sun. 'An Overview on Edge Computing Research'. In: *IEEE Access* 8 (2020), pp. 85714–85728. https://doi.org/10.1109/ACCESS.2020.2991734.
30. Mohammed Laroui, Boubakr Nour, Hassine Moungla, Moussa A. Cherif, Hossam Afifi, and Mohsen Guizani. 'Edge and fog computing for IoT: A survey on current research activities future directions'. In: *Computer Communications* 180 (2021), pp. 210–231. https://doi.org/10.1016/j.comcom.2021.09.003.
31. Shanhe Yi, Cheng Li, and Qun Li. 'A Survey of Fog Computing: Concepts, Applications and Issues'. In: *Proceedings of the 2015 Workshop on Mobile Big Data*. Mobidata '15. Hangzhou, China: Association for Computing Machinery, 2015, 37–42. https://doi.org/10.1145/2757384.2757397.
32. M. I. Jordan and T. M. Mitchell. 'Machine learning: Trends, perspectives, and prospects'. In: *Science* 349.6245 (2015), pp. 255–260. https://doi.org/10.1126/science.aaa8415.
33. Batta Mahesh. 'Machine learning algorithms-a review'. In: *International Journal of Science and Research (IJSR).[Internet]* 9 (2020), pp. 381–386.
34. Cynthia Rudin. 'Stop explaining black box machine learning models for high stakes decisions and use interpretable models instead'. In: *Nature Machine Intelligence* 1.5 (2019), pp. 206–215.
35. Rachel KE Bellamy, Kuntal Dey, Michael Hind, Samuel C Hoffman, Stephanie Houde, Kalapriya Kannan, Pranay Lohia, Sameep Mehta, Aleksandra Mojsilovic, Seema Nagar, et al. 'Think your artificial intelligence software is fair? Think again'. In: *IEEE Software* 36.4 (2019), pp. 76–80.
36. Mariya I Vasileva. 'The Dark Side of Machine Learning Algorithms: How and Why They Can Leverage Bias, and What Can Be Done to Pursue Algorithmic Fairness'. In: *Proceedings of the 26th ACM SIGKDD International Conference on Knowledge Discovery & Data Mining*. 2020, pp. 3586–3587.

37. Osonde A Osoba and William Welser IV. *An intelligence in our image: The risks of bias and errors in artificial intelligence*. Rand Corporation, 2017 (cited on page 10).
38. Upkar Varshney. 'Context-awareness in Healthcare'. In: *Pervasive Healthcare Computing: EMR/EHR, Wireless and Health Monitoring*. Boston, MA: Springer US, 2009, pp. 231–257. https://doi.org/10.1007/978-1-4419-0215-3_11.
39. Yun Zeng. 'Context Aware Machine Learning'. In: *CoRR* abs/1901.03415 (2019).
40. Mengmi Zhang, Claire Tseng, and Gabriel Kreiman. 'Putting Visual Object Recognition in Context'. In: *Proceedings of the IEEE/CVF Conference on Computer Vision and Pattern Recognition (CVPR)*. 2020.
41. Tek Raj Chhetri, Anelia Kurteva, Jubril Gbolahan Adigun, and Anna Fensel. 'Knowledge Graph Based Hard Drive Failure Prediction'. In: *Sensors* 22.3 (2022), p. 985. https://doi.org/10.3390/s22030985.
42. Tek Raj Chhetri, Armin Hohenegger, Anna Fensel, Mariam Aramide Kasali, and Asiru Afeez Adekunle. 'Toward improving prediction accuracy and user-level explainability using deep learning and knowledge graphs: A study on cassava disease'. In: *Expert Systems with Applications* (2023), p. 120955. https://doi.org/10.1016/j.eswa.2023.120955.
43. Tiago Zonta, Cristiano André da Costa, Rodrigo da Rosa Righi, Miromar José de Lima, Eduardo Silveira da Trindade, and Guann Pyng Li. 'Predictive maintenance in the Industry 4.0: A systematic literature review'. In: *Computers & Industrial Engineering* (2020), p. 106889.
44. KPMG. *Protecting intangible assets: Preparing for a new reality*. https://assets.kpmg/content/dam/kpmg/uk/pdf/2020/08/lloyds-intangibles-6-aug-2020-.pdf. Last accessed on 10 October 2022.
45. Samer Ajour El Zein, Carolina Consolacion-Segura, and Ruben Huertas-Garcia. 'The Role of Sustainability in Brand Equity Value in the Financial Sector'. In: *Sustainability* 12.1 (2020), p. 254.
46. Reports and Data. *Predictive Maintenance Market, By Component (Solutions, Services), By Deployment (On-premise, Cloud), By Technique (Infrared Thermography, Fluid Analysis), By Industry Vertical (Manufacturing, Healthcare), and By Region Forecast to 2030*. https://www.reportsanddata.com/report-detail/predictive-maintenance-market. Last accessed on 10 October 2022. 2022.
47. Jovani Dalzochio, Rafael Kunst, Edison Pignaton, Alecio Binotto, Srijnan Sanyal, Jose Favilla, and Jorge Barbosa. 'Machine learning and reasoning for predictive maintenance in Industry 4.0: Current status and challenges'. In: *Computers in Industry* 123 (2020), p. 103298. https://doi.org/10.1016/j.compind.2020.103298.
48. Nazakat Ali and Jang-Eui Hong. 'Failure detection and prevention for cyber-physical systems using ontology-based knowledge base'. In: *Computers* 7.4 (2018), p. 68.
49. Rohit Sharma, Sachin S Kamble, Angappa Gunasekaran, Vikas Kumar, and Anil Kumar. 'A systematic literature review on machine learning applications for sustainable agriculture supply chain performance'. In: *Computers & Operations Research* 119 (2020), p. 104926.
50. United Nations. *The Sustainable Development Goals Report 2021*. https://unstats.un.org/sdgs/report/2021/The-Sustainable-Development-Goals-Report-2021.pdf, note = Last accessed on 10 October 2022, year=2021.

51. Salwa Muhammad Akhtar, Makia Nazir, Kiran Saleem, Hafiz Mahfooz Ul Haque, and Ibrar Hussain. 'An Ontology-Driven IoT based Healthcare Formalism'. In: *Int. J. Adv. Comput. Sci. Appl* 11.2 (2020), pp. 479–486.
52. Natasha Noy, Yuqing Gao, Anshu Jain, Anant Narayanan, Alan Patterson, and Jamie Taylor. 'Industry-scale knowledge graphs: lessons and challenges'. In: *Queue* 17.2 (2019), pp. 48–75.
53. Ming Tao, Kaoru Ota, and Mianxiong Dong. 'Ontology-based data semantic management and application in IoT-and cloud-enabled smart homes'. In: *Future generation computer systems* 76 (2017), pp. 528–539.
54. Ilaria Tiddi and Stefan Schlobach. 'Knowledge graphs as tools for explainable machine learning: A survey'. In: *Artificial Intelligence* 302 (2022), p. 103627. https://doi.org/10.1016/j.artint.2021.103627.
55. Luigi Bellomarini, Emanuel Sallinger, and Sahar Vahdati. 'Reasoning in Knowledge Graphs: An Embeddings Spotlight'. In: *Knowledge Graphs and Big Data Processing*. Springer, Cham, 2020, pp. 87–101.
56. Truong Khanh Duy, Josef Küng, and Hoang Huu Hanh. 'Survey on IoT Data Analytics with Semantic Approaches'. In: *The 23rd International Conference on Information Integration and Web Intelligence*. iiWAS2021. Linz, Austria: Association for Computing Machinery, 2021, 199–204. https://doi.org/10.1145/3487664.3487785.
57. Hafizur Rahman and Md Iftekhar Hussain. 'A comprehensive survey on semantic interoperability for Internet of Things: State-of-the-art and research challenges'. In: *Transactions on Emerging Telecommunications Technologies* 31.12 (2020), e3902.
58. Piero Andrea Bonatti, Stefan Decker, Axel Polleres, and Valentina Presutti. 'Knowledge Graphs: New Directions for Knowledge Representation on the Semantic Web (Dagstuhl Seminar 18371)'. In: *Dagstuhl Reports* 8.9 (2019). Ed. by Piero Andrea Bonatti, Stefan Decker, Axel Polleres, and Valentina Presutti, pp. 29–111. https://doi.org/10.4230/DagRep.8.9.29.
59. James Manyika, Michael Chui, Peter Bisson, Jonathan Woetzel, Richard Dobbs, Jacques Bughin, and Dan Aharon. 'The internet of things: mapping the value beyond the hype'. In: *McKinsey Global Institute* (2015).
60. Paul Ryan, Martin Crane, and Rob Brennan. 'Design Challenges for GDPR RegTech'. In: *Proceedings of the 22nd International Conference on Enterprise Information Systems - Volume 2: ICEIS, Prague, Czech Republic, 5–7 May 2020*. INSTICC: Milan, Italy. SciTePress: Setubal, Portugal, 2020, 2020, pp. 787–795. https://doi.org/10.5220/0009464507870795.
61. Sheeraz Kirmani, Abdul Mazid, Irfan Ahmad Khan, and Manaullah Abid. 'A Survey on IoT-Enabled Smart Grids: Technologies, Architectures, Applications, and Challenges'. In: *Sustainability* 15.1 (2022), p. 717. https://doi.org/10.3390/su15010717.
62. Amit Kumar Tyagi, Sathian Dananjayan, Deepshikha Agarwal, and Hasmath Farhana Thariq Ahmed. 'Blockchain—Internet of Things Applications: Opportunities and Challenges for Industry 4.0 and Society 5.0'. In: *Sensors* 23.2 (2023), p. 947. https://doi.org/10.3390/s23020947.
63. Ahmed Abdulhasan Alwan, Mihaela Anca Ciupala, Allan J. Brimicombe, Seyed Ali Ghorashi, Andres Baravalle, and Paolo Falcarin. 'Data quality challenges in large-scale cyber-physical systems: A systematic review'. In: *Information Systems* 105 (2022), p. 101951. https://doi.org/10.1016/j.is.2021.101951.

64. Avani Sharma, Emmanuel S. Pilli, Arka P. Mazumdar, and Poonam Gera. 'Towards trustworthy Internet of Things: A survey on Trust Management applications and schemes'. In: *Computer Communications* 160 (2020), pp. 475–493. https://doi.org/10.1016/j.comcom.2020.06.030.
65. Lo'ai Tawalbeh, Fadi Muheidat, Mais Tawalbeh, and Muhannad Quwaider. 'IoT Privacy and Security: Challenges and Solutions'. In: *Applied Sciences* 10.12 (2020), p. 4102. https://doi.org/10.3390/app10124102.
66. Giancarlo Fortino, Lidia Fotia, Fabrizio Messina, Domenico Rosaci, and Giuseppe M. L. Sarné. 'Trust and Reputation in the Internet of Things: State-of-the-Art and Research Challenges'. In: *IEEE Access* 8 (2020), pp. 60117–60125. https://doi.org/10.1109/ACCESS.2020.2982318.
67. John Byabazaire, Gregory O'Hare, and Declan Delaney. 'Using Trust as a Measure to Derive Data Quality in Data Shared IoT Deployments'. In: *2020 29th International Conference on Computer Communications and Networks (ICCCN)*. 2020, pp. 1–9. https://doi.org/10.1109/ICCCN49398.2020.9209633.
68. Ramanathan Guha. *Search result ranking based on trust*. US Patent 7,603,350. 2009.
69. Ashley Aitken and Vishnu Ilango. 'A Comparative Analysis of Traditional Software Engineering and Agile Software Development'. In: *2013 46th Hawaii International Conference on System Sciences*. 2013, pp. 4751–4760. https://doi.org/10.1109/HICSS.2013.31.

Contributions 2

This chapter provides a summary of the contributions made and details about the list of publications. Sect. 2.1 details the list of publications, while Sect. 2.2 describes the contributions. List of Abbreviations defines the abbreviations used in this chapter.

2.1 Publications

Below is a list of peer-reviewed publications produced during the PhD. The publications are arranged according to their publication venues, such as journal and conference papers. The journal papers are marked with the word **JP** and the number that indicates the publication count. Similarly, the conference papers are marked with the word **CP** and the conference poster and demo papers with the word **CDP** and a number.[1]

Journal Papers

JP8. **Tek Raj Chhetri**📘, Blesson Varghese, Chinmaya Kumar Dehury, Anna Fensel, Satish Narayana Srirama, Rance J. DeLong. 'Enabling privacy-aware interoperable and quality IoT data sharing with context'. In: Future Generation Computer Systems (2024), https://doi.org/10.1016/j.future.2024.03.039. → Chap. 8

[1] ℹ **Note**
📘 indicates that the publication has been incorporated into this thesis as a chapter.
★ indicates that the publication partially contributes to our ROs but is not included as a chapter in this dissertation.

T. R. Chhetri, *Improving Decision Making Using Semantic Web Technologies*, https://doi.org/10.1007/978-3-658-45877-5_2

JP7. **Tek Raj Chhetri**, Armin Hohenegger, Anna Fensel, Mariam Aramide Kasali, and Asiru Afeez Adekunle. 'Toward an Explainable Artificial Intelligence Using Deep Learning and Knowledge Graphs: A Study on Cassava Disease'. In: Expert Systems With Applications (2023), https://doi.org/10.1016/j.eswa.2023.120955 → Chap. 6

JP6. Anelia Kurteva, **Tek Raj Chhetri**★, Rainer Hilscher, Amar Tauqeer, Anna Fensel, Kevin Nagorny, Ana Correia, Albert Zilverberg, Stefan Schestakov, Thorben Funke, and Elena Demidova. 'The smashHitCore ontology for GDPR-compliant data sharing in smart cities'. In: Sensors 23.13 (2023). https://doi.org/10.3390/s23136188

JP5. Amar Taquer, Anelia Kurteva, **Tek Raj Chhetri**★, Albin Ahmeti, and Anna Fensel. 'Automated GDPR Contract Compliance Verification Using Knowledge Graphs'. In: Information 13.10 (2022), p. 447. https://doi.org/10.3390/info13100447

JP4. **Tek Raj Chhetri**, Chinmaya Kumar Dehury, Artjom Lind, Satish Narayana Srirama, and Anna Fensel. 'A Combined System Metrics Approach to Cloud Service Reliability Using Artificial Intelligence (Editor's choice)'. In: Big Data and Cognitive Computing 6.1 (2022), p. 26. https://doi.org/10.3390/bdcc6010026

JP3. **Tek Raj Chhetri**, Anelia Kurteva, Rance J. DeLong, Rainer Hilscher, Kai Korte, and Anna Fensel. 'Data Protection by Design Tool for Automated GDPR Compliance Verification Based on Semantically Modeled Informed Consent'. In: Sensors 22.7 (2022). https://doi.org/10.3390/s22072763 → Chap. 7

JP2. **Tek Raj Chhetri**, Anelia Kurteva, Jubril Gbolahan Adigun, and Anna Fensel. 'Knowledge Graph Based Hard Drive Failure Prediction'. In: Sensors 22.3 (2022), p. 985. https://doi.org/10.3390/s22030985 → Chap. 4

JP1. Anelia Kurteva, **Tek Raj Chhetri**★, Harshvardhan J. Pandit, and Anna Fensel. 'Consent through the lens of semantics: State of the art survey and best practices'. In: Semantic Web Preprint (2021). Preprint, pp. 1–27. https://doi.org/10.3233/SW-210438

Conference Papers

CP4. **Tek Raj Chhetri**, Sareh Aghaei, Anna Fensel, Ulrich Göhner, Sebnem Gül-Ficici, and Jorge Martinez-Gil. 'Optimising Manufacturing Process with Bayesian Structure Learning and Knowledge Graphs'. In: Proceeding of the 18th International Conference on Computer Aided Systems Theory. Las

Palmas de Gran Canaria, Spain, 2023, 1–9. https://doi.org/10.1007/978-3-031-25312-6_70 → Chap. 5

CP3. Sareh Aghaei, Sepide Masoudi, **Tek Raj Chhetri**, and Anna Fensel. 'Question Answering over Knowledge Graphs: A Graph-Driven Approach'. In: Proceeding of the 21st IEEE/WI-C/ACM International Conference on Web Intelligence and Intelligent Agent Technology. forth- coming. Niagara Falls, Canada, 2022. https://doi.org/10.1109/WI-IAT55865.2022.00050

CP2. **Tek Raj Chhetri**★. 'Improving Decision Making Using Semantic Web Technologies'. In: The Semantic Web: ESWC 2021 Satellite Events. Ed. by Ruben Verborgh, Anastasia Dimou, Aidan Hogan, Claudia d'Amato, Ilaria Tiddi, Arne Bröring, Simon Mayer, Femke Ongenae, Riccardo Tommasini, and Mehwish Alam. Cham: Springer International Publishing, 2021, pp. 165–175. https://doi.org/10.1007/978-3-030-80418-3_29

CP1. Junyi Gu and **Tek Raj Chhetri**. 'Range Sensor Overview and Blind- Zone Reduction of Autonomous Vehicle Shuttles'. In: IOP Conference Series: Materials Science and Engineering 1140.1 (2021), p. 012006. https://doi.org/10.1088/1757-899x/1140/1/012006

Conference Demo & Poster Paper

CDP1. Marco Kainzner, Christoph Klösch, Dominik Filipiak, **Tek Raj Chhetri**★, Anna Fensel, and Jorge Martinez-Gil. 'Towards reusable ontology alignment for manufacturing maintenance'. In: CEUR Workshop Proceedings. Vol. 2941. SEMANTiCS 2021 EU: Amsterdam, The Netherlands, 2021. url: http://ceur-ws.org/Vol-2941/paper9.pdf

2.2 Contributions

Section 2.1 contains a list of publications and their respective chapter assignments. These mapped chapters represent our core contributions that fulfil our RO and provide the answer to our RQ in order to validate our hypothesis. The relationships between the mapped chapters, RO, RQ, and our hypothesis are depicted in Fig. 2.1. In addition, Fig. 2.1 outlines the relationships between the individual chapters and the use cases other than the RO and RQ. Moreover, Fig. 2.1 demonstrates that some publications contribute partially or entirely to multiple RO and RQ, with the dotted arrow representing the partial contributions. Fig. 2.1 does not, however, contain any information about the non-chapter publications that partially contributed to our RO, information about which is provided in Sect. 2.1. These articles contribute to both the synthesis of previous research and the identification of research gaps.

Below is a brief discussion of the contributions made by the chapters depicted in Fig. 2.1.

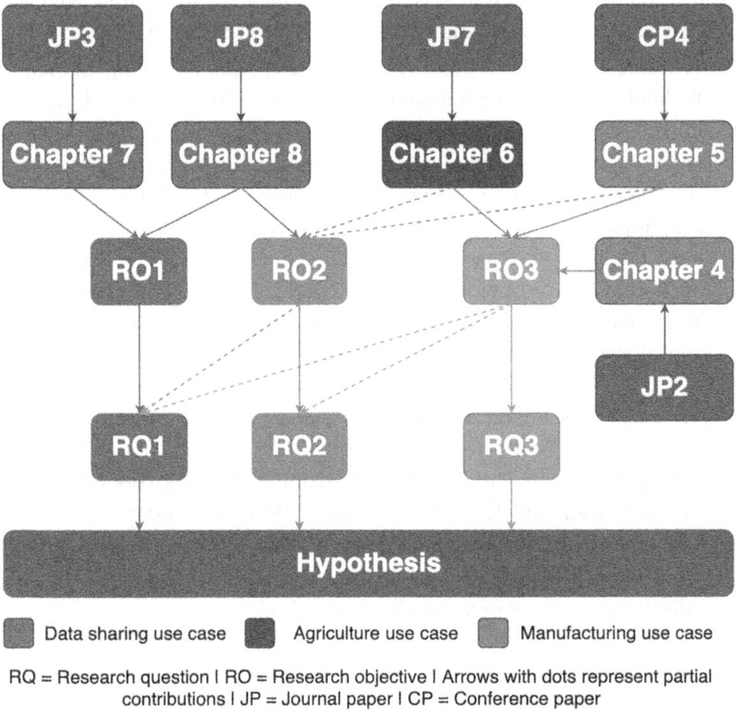

Fig. 2.1 The mapping between publications, individual contribution chapters and the RO, RQ, and hypothesis

Chapter 4, Chapter 5 and Chapter 6: The chapters, Chap. 4, Chap. 5 and Chap. 6, contribute to our third RO, which is to combine KGs and ML to improve decision making. Chap. 5 and Chap. 6, however, partially contribute to the second RO, translating IoT data into the KG representation to support decision making in combination with ML. The focus of Chap. 4 is the utilisation of KGs and ML for predictive maintenance. In a similar fashion, Chap. 5 focuses on the application of KGs and ML in the event of product failure, whereas Chap. 6 focuses on agriculture. In contrast to the work on predictive maintenance and agricultural disease classification use cases, the work on product failure focuses on learning tabular data using Bayesian structure learning and transforming it into KGs for supporting decision making tasks. Similarly, the disease classification work is geared toward non-experts and focuses on explainability in addition to improving prediction accuracy. To fulfil the RO, a proof-of-concept and prototypical implementation have been made and evaluated accordingly, details of which are provided in their constituent chapters.

Chapter 7: This chapter, Chap. 7, as indicated in Fig. 2.1, contributes to our first RO. Information regarding the publications that correspond to this chapter is provided in Sect. 2.1. As described in Sect. 1.5 of Chap. 1, RO1 aims to develop a scalable knowledge-driven software application based on SW technology to facilitate data sharing and decision making in heterogeneous environments, such as smart cities. To fulfil this RO, a scalable software application has been developed. The application represents knowledge (i.e. consent) with KG. The application supports both scalable processing and integration with other third-party software components. In addition, the application addresses the GDPR-specific challenges associated with data sharing.

Chapter 8: This chapter, Chap. 8, is also associated with data sharing use cases, similar to Chap. 7. Sect. 2.1 contains information about the corresponding publications that represent this chapter. Work on this chapter, as indicated in Fig. 2.1, corresponds to both RO1 and RO2, details of which are presented in Sect. 1.5 of Chap. 1. This work on this chapter builds on Chap. 7's scalable architecture and applies it to the case of IoT, supporting the emerging distributed computing paradigms of fog and edge computing while at the same time addressing other aspects of data, such as quality and veracity. To achieve our objectives, an end-to-end prototype, that translates the data from the cyber-physical system into the knowledge represented by KGs, has been designed and implemented. In addition, the prototype is evaluated in edge and edge/fog scenarios, which are described in detail in Chap. 8.

Preliminaries 3

This chapter offers a concise summary of the concepts and technologies utilised in our research. Sect. 3.1 provides information about GDPR, whereas Sect. 3.2 presents an overview of AI paradigms. Sect. 3.3 of this chapter discusses SW related technology and Sect. 3.4 provides an overview of ML. Similarly, Sect. 3.5 describes GNN, a DL technique, and finally, Sect. 3.6 describes Bayesian structure learning. The abbreviations used in this chapter are defined in List of Abbreviations.

3.1 General Data Protection Regulation

GDPR [1] is the EU regulation for data protection that went into effect in May 2018, replacing DPD [2], a directive for data protection in effect since 1995. With a total of 99 articles and 173 recitals, the GDPR is one of the strictest data protection regulations ever introduced to safeguard personal privacy. For the processing of PII data to be lawful, one of the GDPR's six legal bases must be met. The six legal bases of GDPR (Art. 6) are: (i) informed consent (ii) legitimate interests; (iii) legal obligation; (iv) protection of vital interests of the data subject; (v) tasks performed in the public interest or in the exercise of official authority vested in the controller; and (vi) performance of a contract. GDPR is applicable to anyone, regardless of location, who collects and processes the PII data of EU citizens [3]. Given that our on GDPR depends on consent, we will concentrate our discussion on GDPR on

T. R. Chhetri, *Improving Decision Making Using Semantic Web Technologies*,
https://doi.org/10.1007/978-3-658-45877-5_3

legal basis of consent. However, before delving into the specifics of consent, we will first review the key terminology that is used for consent, as follows.[1]

Definition 3.1.1 *A data subject in the* GDPR *is defined as "a natural person".*

Definition 3.1.2 *Personal data (Art. 4(1)), which is also referred to as* PII *in our research, is defined as "any information relating to an identified or identifiable natural person ('data subject'–see Definition* 3.1.1*) directly or indirectly, by reference to an identifier such as a name, location data, identification number, or physical, genetic, and cultural factors".*

Definition 3.1.3 *Processing (Art. 4(2)) is defined as "any operation or set of operations that are performed on* PII *data (see Definition* 3.1.2*), whether or not by automated means, such as collection, storing, adaptation, alteration, and retrieval".*

Consent according to GDPR (Art. 4(11)) is defined as "*any freely given, specific, informed and unambiguous indication of the data subject's (see Definition* 3.1.1*) wishes by which he or she, by a statement or by a clear affirmative action, signifies agreement to the processing (see Definition* 3.1.3*) of personal data (see Definition* 3.1.2*) relating to him or her*". In addition to providing definitions of consent, the GDPR has introduced additional requirements for consent (or obtaining consent), including specifics for each term used in the definitions. Before going deeper into the specifics, however, we will first examine some of the key terms necessary to comprehend the consent's stipulations. The definitions of the key terms are provided below.

[1] **Terminological note** • In our research, the term PII refers to personal data under the GDPR; therefore, whenever the term PII is used, it means personal data. • Consent will henceforth refer to informed consent and will be used interchangeably. • The controller and data controller are synonymous in our work and used interchangeably. Similarly, processor and data processor refer to the same concept.

Definition 3.1.4 *The controller (Art. 4(7)) is defined as "the natural or legal person, public authority, agency, or other body which, alone or jointly with others, determines the purposes and means of processing personal data; where the purpose and means of processing are determined by Union or Member State law, the controller or the specific criteria for its nomination may be provided for by Union or Member State law".*

Definition 3.1.5 *The processor (Art. 4(8)) is defined as "a natural or legal person, public authority, agency or other body that processes personal data on behalf of the controller (see Definition* 3.1.4*)".*

The details of the additional requirements for consent are as follows:

- **Informed:** The data subject must be aware of both the identity of the controller (see Definition 3.1.4) and the processing purpose (Rec. 42).
- **Unambiguous:** Information should be presented in a clearly distinguishable manner and in an understandable and easily accessible form using plain and clear language without any unfair terms (Art. 7, Rec. 42).
- **Freely given:** The data subject has a genuine or free choice, with the option to refuse or revoke (or withdraw[2]) consent, and the option to provide separate consent for different personal data processing (Art. 7, Rec. 42 and 43).
- **Specific:** Consent should be requested for the use of specific data for a particular purpose (Art. 6 and 7).

In order to begin processing the personal data, the data processor (see Definition 3.1.5) or data controller (see Definition 3.1.4) must comply with all consent criteria. Moreover, the data processor or controller should keep track of all processing activities in order to demonstrate compliance and make the records available to the supervisory authority upon request (Rec. 82). In addition to keeping records of processing details, GDPR requires the controller or processor to implement appropriate TOMs, such as encryption, to ensure the security of processing (Art. 32).

[2] The withdrawal of the consent should be as easy as giving the consent (Art. 7).

3.2 Artificial Intelligence and its Paradigms

John McCarthy coined the term "AI" in 1955 and also provided its definition [4], which is shown in Definition 3.2.1.

> **Definition 3.2.1** AI *is defined as "the science and engineering of creating intelligent machines".*

AI has a long history. Nonetheless, the majority of individuals associate AI with ML and its subfields, including DL. ML and its subfields, such as DL, are not the only AI paradigms; there are other AI paradigms as well. Therefore, this section discusses the different paradigms of AI in an effort to provide a concise overview of AI paradigms. This is also noteworthy due to the recent emergence of a new AI paradigm, which we will discuss later, that combines DL, specifically, the neural network, with other symbolic AI paradigms.

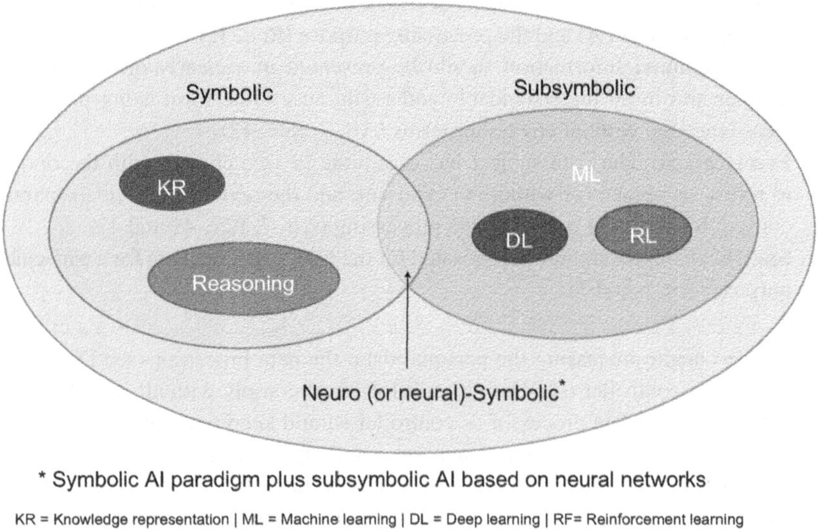

Fig. 3.1 A high-level overview of AI paradigms

Figure 3.1 shows the high-level overview of the different AI paradigms. As shown in Fig. 3.1, there are three AI paradigms: *symbolic AI*, *subsymbolic AI*, and, most recently, *neuro (or neural) symbolic AI*. Subsymbolic AI encompasses methods that use statistical methods and weighted connections between a large number of neurons, such as DL [5]. Furthermore, subsymbolic AI (aside from RL) is data-based, meaning that data is an indispensable component that is, for example, used to train ML and DL algorithms. In contrast, symbolic AI is based on the explicit representation of knowledge using formal languages and the manipulation of symbols, including formal logic [5, 6]. Techniques like knowledge representation and reasoning are examples of symbolic AI techniques. Expert systems are an excellent illustration of AI-based symbolic systems. Expert systems are one of the prime example of AI-based symbolic systems. SW technologies (e.g. OWL), which provide formal knowledge representation and reasoning and are based on logic (i.e. description logic) [7, 8], are therefore a paradigm of symbolic AI. Neuro (or neural) symbolic AI, a more recent paradigm, is on the rise, complementing the limitations of each of the AI paradigms; the lack of commonsense reasoning in symbolic AI, for example. Neuro (or neural) symbolic AI combines symbolic AI with subsymbolic AI-based neural network methods such as DL [5, 6, 9]. Cambria et al. [10], for example, use symbolic and subsymbolic AI to construct a new commonsense knowledge base for sentiment analysis.

3.3 Semantic Web Technologies

The "Semantic Web" is a term coined by Sir Tim Berners-Lee in 2001 for the web of data that enables capabilities such as automated logical reasoning [11]. In addition, "Semantic Web" refers to the W3C's linked data vision, which is enabled by the SW technologies such as RDF.[3] Today, SW technologies are used for a variety of tasks in a variety of application areas in conjunction with other technologies. Fig. 3.2 illustrates some of the tasks and application areas where SW technologies are used alone or in conjunction with other technologies such as ML. In manufacturing, SW technologies are used for tasks such as predictive maintenance [12]. In healthcare, semantic technology is used for tasks such as supporting clinical decision making [13] and increasing the interpretabiliy of clinical data [14]. Similarly, in data governance, semantic technology is used to enable interoperability and to perform

[3] ⚠ **Terminological note** In this thesis, SW technologies and semantic technology are used interchangeably.

tasks such as GDPR compliance verification [15]. In the sections that follow, we will look into some of the key SW technologies.

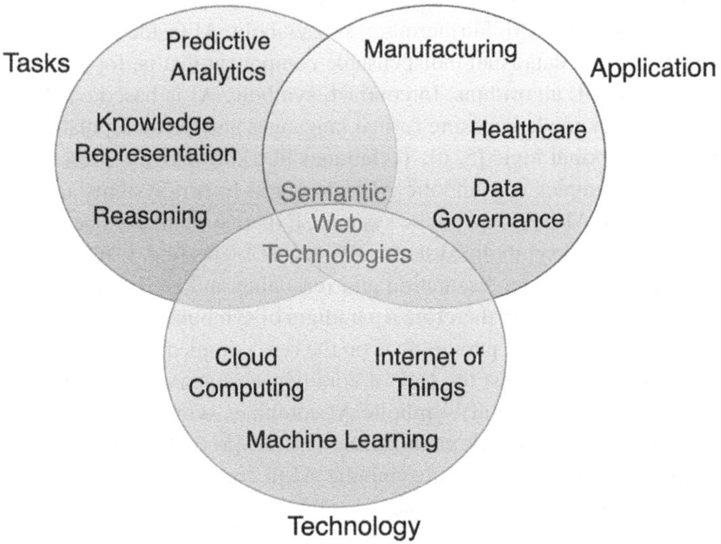

Fig. 3.2 A high-level overview of the SW technologies, as well as some of their application areas and tasks that they are used to perform in conjunction with other technologies

3.3.1 Ontology and Knowledge Graphs

The SW emerged to enable machine-comprehensible, meaningful information transitioning from a web centred on documents to a web centred on data [11]. Moreover, the aim of the SW is also to enable common semantics so that every machine and software agent understand the same shared meaning. This enabling of common semantics is achieved by the use of ontology, which is one of the basic and most important components of the SW [11]. The most prominent definition is by Studer et al. [16], which extends the other two well-known definitions by Gruber [17] and Borst [18] and is shown in Definition 3.3.1.

Definition 3.3.1 *Ontology is defined as "a formal, explicit specification of shared conceptualisation".*

The term "formal" in the ontology definition refers to the defined syntax and semantics for enabling machine readability, whereas "explicit" indicates that all concepts and constraints must be defined explicitly. Similarly, the definition of "conceptualisation" refers to an abstract representation of real-world entities. Classes and properties are utilised by an ontology to define the conceptualisation of a particular domain. In addition, an ontology provides the necessary formalisation for machine-readability and reasoning through the use of constraints between classes and properties. Ontology enables us, for instance, to specify the types of values (e.g. range) we anticipate for a property. In addition, ontology permits the definition of a class and property hierarchy (e.g. subclass) as well as property characteristics such as transitivity and symmetry[4].

Figure 3.3 illustrates a segment of the SOSA ontology [20] that models sensor observation. In Fig. 3.3 , the $sosa : Sensor$ and $sosa : Observation$ classes represent the concepts associated with sensor observation. Similarly, the properties $sosa : sub$, $sosa : hasSimpleResult$, and $sosa : resultTime$ are used to define additional constraints, such as the relationship between these two distinct classes and the types of values they can or should contain. The property $sosa : madeObservation$, also known as the object property, defines the relationship between the classes $sosa : Sensor$ and $sosa : Observation$. The property $sosa : madeObservation$ establishes the connection (or defines the relationship) through domain and range constraints, where the domain is a class $sosa : Sensor$ and the range is a class $sosa : Observation$. Similarly, the properties $sosa : hasSimpleResult$ and $sosa : resultTime$ are referred to as data properties (or data type properties) and are used to define the data type that an instance of a class can must have (e.g. literal and date time). The $sosa$ in Fig. 3.3 is a prefix that represents the URI, which is used to uniquely identify the ontology [21]. In a nutshell, we can say that the ontology provides a necessary formal structure

[4] **Terminological note** Classes are sometimes also called concepts. Similarly, properties are sometimes also called slots, or roles, and restrictions on properties (or slots) are called facets, or role restrictions [19].

(e.g. for KGs) and also enables the common semantics. We refer readers to [19, 22] for additional information on ontology topics such as ontology development.[5]

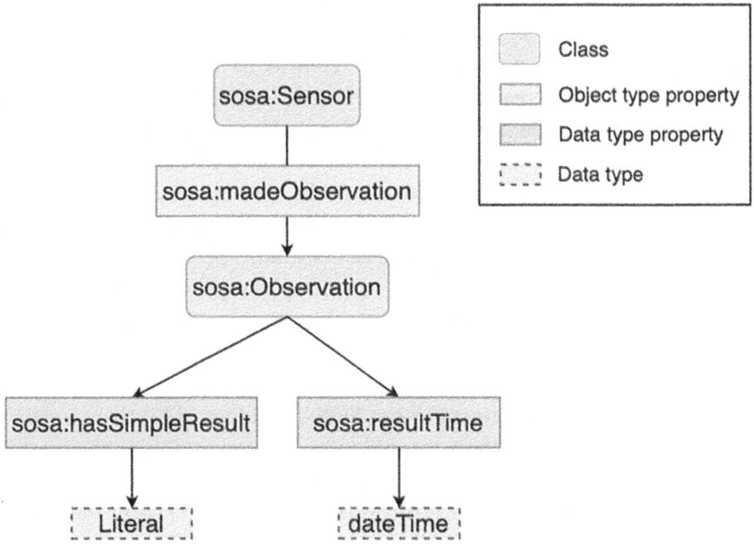

Fig. 3.3 Snippet of SOSA ontology

KGs, on the other hand, contain the actual data. Similar to ontology, the KGs have multiple definitions. The most recent one was published by Hogan et al. [24] in 2021, and it is shown in Definition 3.3.2.

Definition 3.3.2 KG *is defined as "a graph of data intended to accumulate and convey knowledge of the real-world, whose nodes represent entities of interest and whose edges represent potentially different relations between these entities".*

[5] ⚠ **Terminological note** An IRI is an update to URI, which only contain the ASCII character set, in order to include the missing Unicode/ISO 10646 character set [23]; both serve the same purpose. In this thesis, URI and IRI are used interchangeably to describe semantic technology, similar to [21], which uses the term URI to ensure compatibility between OWL 1.0 and 1.1.

The ontology provides the formal structure for KGs and also makes it more interoperable [24]. Listing 1 displays a snippet of KG in RDF (see Sect. 3.3.2 for details) format based on the ontology depicted in Fig. 3.3. Similarly, Fig. 3.4 illustrates the visual representation of the KG presented in Listing 1. As shown in Listing 1 (and Fig. 3.4), the KG contains the sensor observation data, which in our case is the temperature sensor observation. The KG contains data about the sensor, DHT11, a temperature and humidity sensor. In addition, the KG includes information regarding the temperature and time at which it was recorded.

Listing 1: A sample KG for sensor observation represented in RDF format.

```
@prefix sosa: <http://www.w3.org/ns/sosa#> .
@prefix xsd: <http://www.w3.org/2001/XMLSchema#> .
@prefix : <https://tekrajchhetri.com/phd#>.
:TemperatureSensorObservationRoom2W01
    a sosa:Observation ;
    sosa:hasSimpleResult "30"^^xsd:float;
    sosa:resultTime "2022-06-06T12:16:13Z"^^xsd:dateTime .
:DHT11 a sosa:Sensor;
    sosa:madeObservation :TemperatureSensorObservation .
```

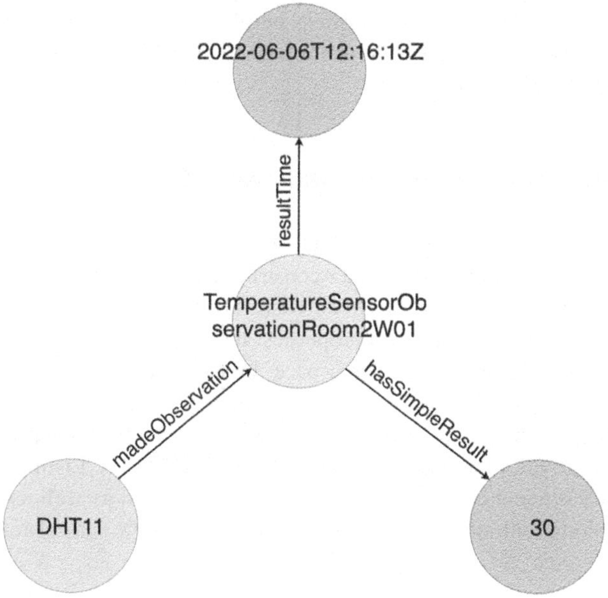

Fig. 3.4 Visualisation of the KG from Listing 1

3.3.2 Resource Description Framework

RDF, which addresses the fundamental issue of the SW, managing distributed data, is the foundation of the SW and is used to represent web data [25, 26]. Subject, predicate, and object represent the triple, which is the fundamental building block of RDF [25]. The predicate describes the relationship between the subject and object, which represents the resources. If we were to represent the natural language statement "Tek Raj lives in Austria" using RDF triple, "Tek Raj" would correspond to the subject, "lives in" would correspond to the predicate, and "Austria" would correspond to the object. The formal representation of this triple would also include an IRI. The IRI helps resolve the identity problem for RDF on the web [25]. Listing 1 from Sect. 3.3.1 displays the serialised formal RDF representation in Turtle [27] format. JSON-LD [28] and N-Triples [29] are some other serialisation formats of RDF. The subject, predicate, and object can all be an IRI and, in the case of the object, a literal data value. However, the subjects and objects can also be represented by a blank node. This is usually done when we do not have identity information (i.e. we know something exists but do not have the identity information). For example, we know that Shakespeare had a mistress but do not have any information about the mistress's identity. To represent this information in RDF, we use a blank node, which is also called a *bnode*.

3.3.3 Resource Description Framework Schema

RDFS, which is an extension of RDF, is a schema language [30, 31]. The RDFS provides the necessary RDF descriptor constructs. For example, $rdfs : subClassOf$ describes the relationship between classes, while $rdfs : subPropertyOf$ describes the relationship between properties. In $rdfs : subClassOf$ and $rdfs : subPropertyOf$, the $rdfs$ is a namespace. In addition, RDFS provides the necessary constructs, such as $rdfs : domain$ and $rdfs : range$, for describing the relationship between classes and properties (e.g. data or object property). In summary, RDFS provides the necessary vocabulary for RDF [31]. Listing 2 displays a simple RDFS schema consisting of a class and a property, as well as the domain and range, along with other RDFS constructs such as $rdfs : label$ for describing the book.

Listing 2: An illustrative example of RDFS.

```
@prefix rdf: <http://www.w3.org/1999/02/22-rdf-syntax-ns#> .
@prefix rdfs: <http://www.w3.org/2000/01/rdf-schema#> .
@prefix schema: <http://schema.org/> .
@prefix xsd: <http://www.w3.org/2001/XMLSchema#> .
@prefix : <https://tekrajchhetri.com/phd#>.
:Book rdf:type rdfs:Class ;
        rdfs:label "Book" ;
        rdfs:subClassOf schema:Thing .
:bookName a rdf:Property ;
        rdfs:domain :Book ;
        rdfs:range xsd:string .
```

3.3.4 Web Ontology Language

RDFS provides advanced constructs that RDF lacks, such as how classes or properties are related. However, RDFS's capacity to express the vocabulary is quite limited. For example, using RDFS does not have constructs that can tell if two different concepts (or resources) are the same or if the two classes should be disjoint [32]. OWL, which addresses the limitations of RDFS, provides a rich set of vocabulary and restrictions to describe the classes and properties, such as: cardinality, equality, and characteristics of properties (e.g. symmetry) [33, 34]. OWL is an ontology language containing formally defined meaning [35].

3.3.5 SPARQL Protocol and RDF Query Language

SPARQL, similar to SQL for relational databases, is a query language for RDF [36]. A SPARQL query similar to SQL matches the data specified in the WHERE condition, which in our case is a triple pattern, executes the intended query, binds the variables, and returns the triples. SPARQL allows us to manipulate the RDFS data (or KG) in various ways, such as updating and deleting it. Listing 3 illustrates a sample SPARQL query. The SPARQL query listed in Listing 3 is used to query the sensor observation KG data shown Listing 1 from Sect. 3.3.1, represented in RDF format. The query returns all KG triples with an observation value that is greater than or equal to 20.

Listing 3: A sample SPARQL query to select sensor observations whose value (i.e. $sosa : hasSimpleResult$ value) exceeds 20. The s, p, and o components of the SPARQL query represent the subject, predicate, and object of a triple, respectively.

```
PREFIX sosa: <http://www.w3.org/ns/sosa#>
PREFIX : <https://tekrajchhetri.com/phd#>
select ?s ?p ?o where {
        ?s a sosa:Observation;
    ?p ?o.
    FILTER(?o >= 20)
}
```

3.4 Machine Learning

ML is a subfield of AI. The term "ML" was coined by Arthur Samuel, who defined ML as *"field of study that gives computers the ability to learn without being explicitly programmed"* [37]. Tom Mitchell, lately, provided a more formal definition [38] that has proven to be more beneficial to engineering setup [39], which is presented in Definition 3.4.1.

Definition 3.4.1 *A computer program is said "to learn from experience E with respect to some class of tasks T and performance measure P, if its performance a tasks in T, as measured by P, improves with experience E".*

The experience in the case of a machine, as indicated in Definition 3.4.1, is the data-driven learning. Therefore, in this context, experience is the knowledge gained from the data. As an example, if we consider a simple classification task (such as cat and dog classification), we provide the necessary training data so that our ML model (or, in simpler terms, computer program) can learn, and we make predictions based on this learning, which in this case would be to perform the classification task to distinguish cat and dog. The following are the key points pertaining to the Definition 3.4.1:

- The experience E is the **learning** about cats and dogs based on the training data provided as input.
- Task T is the classification task, which is further narrowed to the classification of cats and dogs.

- The performance measure P of the learning for the task T with experience E is the prediction accuracy.
- The improvement of experience E is achieved by **optimisation** of the **loss function**.

The example illustrates several important aspects of ML. The first is learning itself, as defined in Definition 3.4.1, followed by the loss function and optimisation. We will begin by discussing the loss function. In ML, the loss function indicates how bad (or good) the prediction is. In brief, the loss function provides a clear contrast between reality (also known as ground truth) and predictions. Equation 3.1 shows the cross entropy loss function, whereas Equation 3.2 shows the variants of the cross entropy loss function, specifically, the binary cross entropy loss function [40]. The loss function varies depending on the tasks. For the classification and regression tasks, different loss functions are utilised. The demonstrated loss functions, cross entropy and its variants, are applied to classification tasks. For regression tasks, loss functions such as root mean square error are used. We refer the reader to the recent (2020) study by Wang et al. [41] on loss function for more information on the various types of loss functions. The other aspect of ML is optimisation. Optimisation is at the core of the ML.

$$loss(\hat{y}, y) = -\sum_{i=1}^{n} y_i log(\hat{y_i}) \tag{3.1}$$

$$loss(\hat{y}, y) = -\frac{1}{n}\sum_{i=1}^{n} \left(y_i log(\hat{y} + (1 - y_i)log(1 - \hat{y_i})\right) \tag{3.2}$$

where in Equation 3.1 and Equation 3.2,

- n is the number of iterations (or training samples).
- y_i is the true label.
- $\hat{y_i}$ is the predicted label (or model prediction).

The optimisation is performed to optimise the objective function (or loss function) to fit the data. It is the optimisation that helps to map the inputs to the expected output accurately. Stochastic gradient descent [42], a variant of gradient descent, is one of the optimisation techniques used in ML algorithms such as logistic regression [43] and support vector machine [44]. Learning is the other dimension of ML. On the basis of the learning mechanism, ML can be broadly classified into three types: (i) supervised; (ii) unsupervised; and (iii) RL. Supervised learning is a machine learning technique in which specific tasks are taught to a machine by providing guidance. In this instance, the guidance would be to provide information about the target label during training. This means that the supervised learning methods acquire knowledge from data of type $\{x_i, y_i\}_{i=1}^{n}$, where x_i is the input and y_i is the corresponding output value. Examples of supervised learning include classification and regression tasks in which the target label is specified (e.g. cat and dog in the case of classifying cat and dogs from the image dataset). Unsupervised learning , as its name implies, is not supervised. This indicates that we do not provide any information (i.e. unsupervised learning contains the data of type $\{x_i\}_{i=1}^{n}$ – only input, no output), as in the case of supervised learning, the target label for information. Using techniques such as distance measures, the unsupervised algorithm learns patterns. Examples of unsupervised learning include clustering [45] and principal component analysis [46]. RL is an additional learning paradigm in ML that is entirely distinct from supervised and unsupervised learning. In RL, an agent learns the desired behaviour through trial-and-error in a dynamic environment.

Each time an agent performs an action by interacting with the environment, the state is updated and the corresponding reward is granted. A successful action is rewarded positively, while an unsuccessful action is punished negatively. The agent modifies its behaviour and continues the action based on the rewards. Fig. 3.5 depicts an overview of the RL and its interaction with the environment. In addition, other variants of ML learning exist, such as semi-supervised learning [47], in which labelled and unlabelled data are provided.[6]

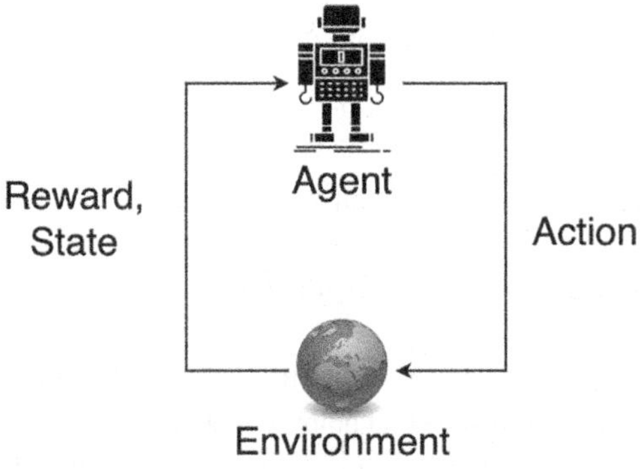

Fig. 3.5 An Overview of the Interaction between the RL Agent and the Environment

[6] **Conceptual note** Graphs are a type of data structure consisting of a collection of vertices (or nodes) connected by edges (or links). The edges of a graph represent the relationships between nodes [48] and can be either directed or undirected.

3.5 Graph Neural Networks

GNN is a DL method that enables the representation and learning from graphs [48]. The GNN, which directly applies learning to (or learns from) graphs, is very useful for solving real-world problems, as graphs are the most natural way to depict real-world phenomena. For instance, social networks are used to represent and capture intergroup relationships, and in chemistry, graphs are used to represent the relationships between molecules. GNNs can be utilised for tasks including node classification, edge classification, and graph classification. Fig. 3.6, specifically, Fig. 3.6a and Fig. 3.6b, illustrate the distinction between the conventional neural network (or DL) and the GNN, respectively. In addition, Fig. 3.6b, GNN, illustrates the similarity between DL (i.e. Fig. 3.6a) and GNN (i.e. Fig. 3.6b), as GNN is also a DL method that is specialised for graphs.[7]

The MLP shown in Fig. 3.6 is one of the most common neural networks [49]. The MLP, as indicated by its name, has multiple hidden layers. The MLP has two phases of operation for learning (i.e. training). During the initial phase, the forward pass is performed by updating the weight parameters from the input layer to the output layer, traversing the hidden layers, and applying activation functions. The second phase, also known as backpropagation, involves adjusting the weights and bias based on the error and performing an inward traversal from the output to the input layer. Backpropagation is an algorithm used to fine-tune the weights and enhance the precision of neural networks (or MLP in this context) [50]. Fig. 3.7 shows a MLP with two hidden layers.

As illustrated in Fig. 3.6a and Fig. 3.6b, the primary distinction between a conventional neural network and a GNN is the message passing layer, which serves as the GNN's central processing unit. The message passing (or graph update) layer is what enables direct graph-based learning and performs tasks such as neighbourhood aggregation and updating. Equation 3.3 shows the general message passing scheme [51, 52].

$$x_i^l = \gamma^l \left(x_i^{l-1}, \square_{j \epsilon N} \phi^l \left(x_i^{l-1}, x_j^{l-1}, e_{j,i} \right) \right) \tag{3.3}$$

The x_i in Equation 3.3 represents the features of node i and $e_{j,i}$ represents the edge feature of node j and i from node j to i. The l in Equation 3.3 represents

[7] ⚠ **Terminological note** The neural network (or artificial neural network) is the core of the DL. The "deep" in DL refers to the depth of the neural network. When referring to neural networks in the context of this thesis, we are referring to neural networks with multiple hidden layers, also called deep neural networks or DL.

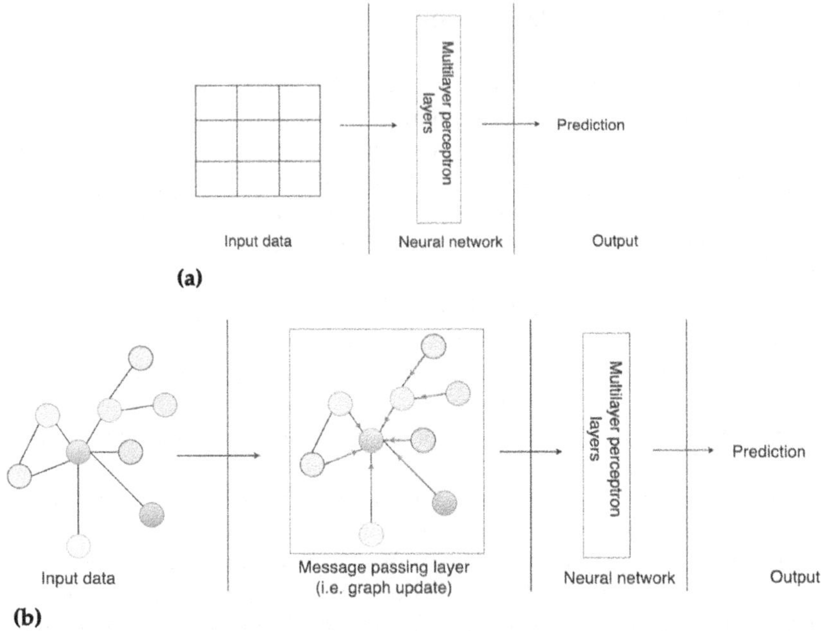

Fig. 3.6 Comparison of conventional neural network to GNN. (**a**) A neural network-based learning strategy that uses tabular data as input. (**b**) A GNN-based learning technique that utilises graph data as input

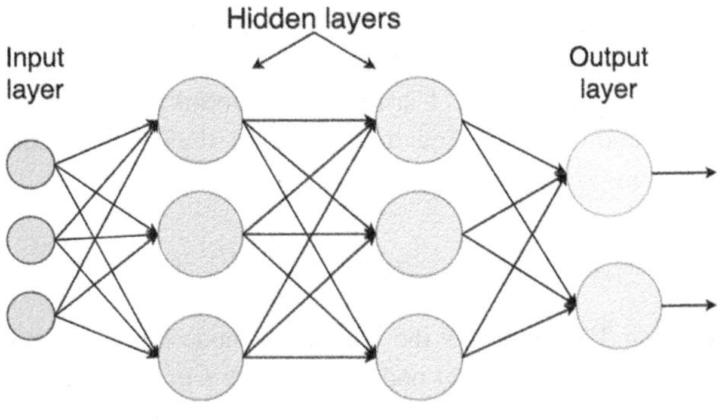

Fig. 3.7 An overview of the MLP

the layers and □ represents the aggregation function, such as sum. ϕ denotes the differentiable functions (or message function), such as MLP and γ denotes the final transformation (or update aggregation) function. Similarly, N in Equation 3.3 denotes the neighbour.

There are various GNN variants based on how they implement message passing. GCN [53], which can be viewed as a subset of differential message passing [54], is one of the GNN variants that uses a convolution filter (or CNN). The RGCN, which is an extension of the GCN, is another variant [55]. Fig. 3.8 shows the GCN and RGCN weight update mechanisms. As can be seen in Fig. 3.8a and Fig. 3.8b, the GCN and RGCN take into account the neighbourhood information, as indicated by the arrow, when performing a weight update (or aggregation). Moreover, if we look closely at Fig. 3.8a and Fig. 3.8b, we notice a difference in the relationships. In Fig. 3.8a (or GCN), we do not find any indication of the relationships (or edge labels), while in Fig. 3.8b, we find different types of relationships (or edge labels). This is because GCN only operates on graphs with homogeneous relationships. RGCN, on the other hand, is capable of operating on graphs with heterogeneous relationships, which are indicated by the different labels.

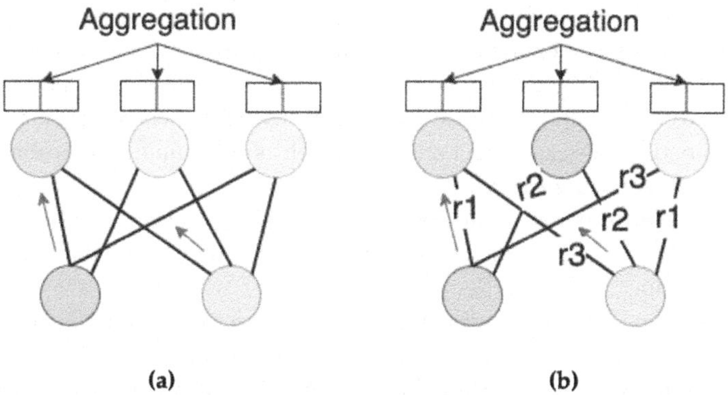

Fig. 3.8 Comparison of GCN and RGCN. (**a**) GCN weight update and aggregation with only a homogeneous relationship. (**b**) RGCN weight update and heterogeneous relationship aggregation

In addition, 3.4 and 3.5 demonstrate the mathematical representation of the weight update employed by GCN and RGCN, respectively [53, 55]. The σ in Equations 3.4 and 3.5 represents the activation function, c is the problem specific normalisation constant, W denotes the weight matrix and h is the hidden unit. The N_i^r in Equation 3.5 represents the neighbourhood of node i under relation r.[8]

$$\sigma\left(\sum_{j\varepsilon N_i}\frac{1}{c_{ij}}h_j^l W^l\right) \tag{3.4}$$

$$\sigma\left(\sum_{r\varepsilon R}\sum_{k\varepsilon N_i^r}\frac{1}{c_{ir}}W_r^l h_k^l + W_o^l h_i^l\right) \tag{3.5}$$

The GCN primarily provides advantages by incorporating neighbour information and also addresses the permutation invariant problem[9] [57]. Within the context of the KGs, RGCN is suitable. This is the case because KGs represent heterogeneous relationships (see Definition 3.3.2) and RGCN can manage such relationships.

3.6 Bayesian Structure Learning

Bayesian structure learning is the process of discovering a BNs from data. A BNs [58] are the class of graphical models that are used to model the uncertainty and causality [59] that is represented by a DAG, $G(V, E)$, where V is the node and E is the directed edge (or arc). For example, BNs are used for uncertainty situations and for causality (i.e. cause and effect relations), such as determining the **probability** of rain given the **conditions** that it is windy and cloudy. Fig. 3.9 depicts the same, i.e. the cause and effect relationships of windy, cloudy, and rainy conditions in DAG. The causes in this case are the cloudy and windy conditions, and the effect of this cause is the rain.

The preceding example illustrates the most important aspect of BNs and Bayesian structure learning, namely the conditional probability and conditional independence. The conditional probability (or conditional probability distribution) is the essence of BNs and is constructed based on the Bayes theorem, which facilitates the expression of the conditional probability distribution as shown in Equation 3.6 [60]. Similarly, Equation 3.7 represents the condensed representation of the the joint probability

---

[8] **Conceptual note** Activation functions are the core of neural networks, which by means of non-linear transformations help to learn complex mappings, and without activation functions, the neural network would not be able to learn non-linear relationships [56]. There exist different types of activation functions, such as $Tanh$ and $Sigmoid$.

[9] The order of the inputs has an effect on the output (or end result).

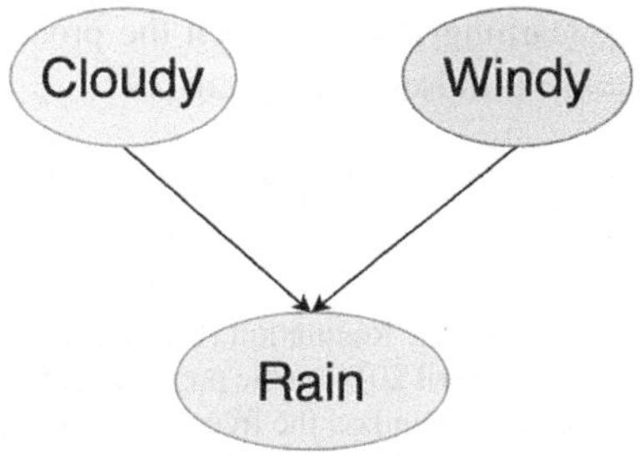

Fig. 3.9 A DAG (or BN) representing the occurrence of rain due to the independent causes of cloudy and windy conditions

distribution (or conditional probabilities) that satisfies the Markov condition[10] and is used in practise because it minimises the exponential space complexity requirements [61]. In addition, the joint probability distribution factors into a series of conditional probability distributions. The $x_1, x_2, x_3, ..., x_n$ in Equation 3.7 represents the random variables and p denotes the probability.

$$p\,(A|B) = p(B|A) \bullet \frac{p(A)}{p(B)} \tag{3.6}$$

Similarly, A and B in Equation 3.6 denote the events. The $p(A|B)$ is called the posterior probability, $p(B|A)$ the likelihood, and $p(A)$ and $p(B)$ are called the prior probability.

$$p\,(x_1, x_2, x_3, ..., x_n) = \Pi_i\, p\,(x_i|parent(x_i)) \tag{3.7}$$

There are various approaches to learning BNs. The algorithms, hill climbing and tabu search, are examples of score-based learning. Also examples of constraint-based learning are the grow-shrink and PC (Peter and Clark) algorithms. Score-based learning uses scores such as the Bayesian information criterion, also known as the BIC [62], to determine the goodness of fit, whereas constraint-based learning uses tests such as the Chi-squared test [63] to determine independence. The problem of learning BN structures is an NP-hard combinatorial problem, and there has recently

[10] According to the Markov condition, nodes in BNs are conditionally independent from their non-descendant, given their parents.

been a new approach to learning BNs in which the problem of learning BNs is formulated as a continuous optimisation problem [64].

Bibliography

1. European Parliament and Council. 'Regulation (EU) 2016/679 of the European Parliament and of the Council of 27 April 2016 on the protection of natural persons with regard to the processing of personal data and on the free movement of such data, and repealing Directive 95/46/EC (General Data Protection Regulation)'. In: *Official Journal of the European Union, L119* (2016), pp. 1–88.
2. European Parliament and Council. 'Directive 95/46/EC of the European Parliament and of the Council of 24 October 1995 on the protection of individuals with regard to the processing of personal data and on the free movement of such data'. In: *Official Journal of the European Union, L281* (1995), pp. 31–50.
3. Vincenzo Mangini, Irina Tal, and Arghir-Nicolae Moldovan. 'An Empirical Study on the Impact of GDPR and Right to Be Forgotten—Organisations and Users Perspective'. In: *Proceedings of the 15th International Conference on Availability, Reliability and Security*. ARES '20. Virtual Event, Ireland: Association for Computing Machinery, 2020. https://doi.org/10.1145/3407023.3407080.
4. Christopher Manning. *Artificial Intelligence Definitions*. https://hai.stanford.edu/sites/default/files/2020-09/AI-Definitions-HAI.pdf. Last accessed on 17 September 2022. Sept. 2020.
5. Md Kamruzzaman Sarker, Lu Zhou, Aaron Eberhart, and Pascal Hitzler. *Neuro-Symbolic Artificial Intelligence: Current Trends*. 2021. https://doi.org/10.48550/ARXIV.2105.05330.
6. Pascal Hitzler, Aaron Eberhart, Monireh Ebrahimi, Md Kamruzzaman Sarker, and Lu Zhou. 'Neuro-symbolic approaches in artificial intelligence'. In:*National Science Review* 9.6 (Mar. 2022). nwac035. https://doi.org/10.1093/nsr/nwac035.
7. Thomas Eiter, Giovambattista Ianni, Thomas Lukasiewicz, and Roman Schindlauer. 'Well-Founded Semantics for Description Logic Programs in the Semantic Web'. In: *ACM Trans. Comput. Logic* 12.2 (2011). https://doi.org/10.1145/1877714.1877717.
8. Anni-Yasmin Turhan. 'Description Logic Reasoning for Semantic Web Ontologies'. In: *Proceedings of the International Conference on Web Intelligence, Mining and Semantics*. WIMS '11. Sogndal, Norway: Association for Computing Machinery, 2011. https://doi.org/10.1145/1988688.1988696.
9. Roberta Calegari, Giovanni Ciatto, Enrico Denti, and Andrea Omicini. 'Logic-Based Technologies for Intelligent Systems: State of the Art and Perspectives'. In: *Information* 11.3 (2020), p. 167. https://doi.org/10.3390/info11030167.
10. Erik Cambria, Yang Li, Frank Z. Xing, Soujanya Poria, and Kenneth Kwok. 'SenticNet 6: Ensemble Application of Symbolic and Subsymbolic AI for Sentiment Analysis'. In: *Proceedings of the 29th ACM International Conference on Information amp; Knowledge Management*. CIKM '20. Virtual Event, Ireland: Association for Computing Machinery, 2020, 105–114. https://doi.org/10.1145/3340531.3412003.

11. Tim Berners-Lee, James Hendler, and Ora Lassila. 'The semantic web'. In: *Scientific american* 284.5 (2001), pp. 34–43.
12. Tek Raj Chhetri, Anelia Kurteva, Jubril Gbolahan Adigun, and Anna Fensel. 'Knowledge Graph Based Hard Drive Failure Prediction'. In: Sensors 22.3 (2022), p. 985. https://doi.org/10.3390/s22030985.
13. Xiayu Xiang, Zhongru Wang, Yan Jia, and Binxing Fang. 'Knowledge Graph-Based Clinical Decision Support System Reasoning: A Survey'. In: *2019 IEEE Fourth International Conference on Data Science in Cyberspace (DSC)*. 2019, pp. 373–380. https://doi.org/10.1109/DSC.2019.00063.
14. Alberto Santos, Ana R. Colaço, Annelaura B. Nielsen, Lili Niu, Maximilian Strauss, Philipp E. Geyer, Fabian Coscia, Nicolai J. Wewer Albrechtsen, Filip Mundt, Lars Juhl Jensen, and Matthias Mann. 'A knowledge graph to interpret clinical proteomics data'. In: *Nature Biotechnology* 40.5 (2022), pp. 692–702. https://doi.org/10.1038/s41587-021-01145-6.
15. Tek Raj Chhetri, Anelia Kurteva, Rance J. DeLong, Rainer Hilscher, Kai Korte, and Anna Fensel. 'Data Protection by Design Tool for Automated GDPR Compliance Verification Based on Semantically Modeled Informed Consent'. In: *Sensors* 22.7 (2022). https://doi.org/10.3390/s22072763.
16. Rudi Studer, V. Richard Benjamins, and Dieter Fensel. 'Knowledge engineering: Principles and methods'. In: *Data Knowledge Engineering* 25.1 (1998), pp. 161–197. https://doi.org/10.1016/S0169-023X(97)00056-6.
17. Thomas Robert Gruber. 'A translation approach to portable ontology specifications'. In: *Knowledge Acquisition* 5.2 (1993), pp. 199–220. https://doi.org/10.1006/knac.1993.1008.
18. Willem Nico Borst. 'Construction of engineering ontologies for knowledge sharing and reuse.' PhD thesis. The Netherlands: Institute for Telematica and Information Technology, University of Twente, Enschede, 1997.
19. Natalya F Noy and Deborah L McGuinness. *Ontology development 101: A guide to creating your first ontology*. 2001.
20. Krzysztof Janowicz, Armin Haller, Simon J.D. Cox, Danh Le Phuoc, and Maxime Lefrançois. 'SOSA: A lightweight ontology for sensors, observations, samples, and actuators'. In: *Journal of Web Semantics* 56 (2019), pp. 1–10. https://doi.org/10.1016/j.websem.2018.06.003.
21. World Wide Web Consortium (W3C) Member. *OWL 1.1 Web Ontology Language Structural Specification and Functional-Style Syntax*. https://www.w3.org/Submission/owl11-owl_specification/#2.2. Last accessed on 12 September 2022. 2006.
22. Nicola Guarino, Daniel Oberle, and Steffen Staab. 'What Is an Ontology?' In: *Handbook on Ontologies*. Ed. by Steffen Staab and Rudi Studer. Berlin, Heidelberg: Springer Berlin Heidelberg, 2009, pp. 1–17. https://doi.org/10.1007/978-3-540-92673-3_0.
23. Network Working Group. *RFC3987 Internationalised Resource Identifiers (IRIs)*. https://www.rfc-editor.org/info/rfc3987. Last accessed on 12 September 2022. July 2005.
24. Aidan Hogan, Eva Blomqvist, Michael Cochez, Claudia D'amato, Gerard De Melo, Claudio Gutierrez, Sabrina Kirrane, José Emilio Labra Gayo, Roberto Navigli, Sebastian Neumaier, Axel-Cyrille Ngonga Ngomo, Axel Polleres, Sabbir M. Rashid, Anisa Rula, Lukas Schmelzeisen, Juan Sequeda, Steffen Staab, and Antoine Zimmermann. 'Knowledge Graphs'. In: *ACM Comput. Surv.* 54.4 (2021). https://doi.org/10.1145/3447772.

25. Dean Allemang and James Hendler. *Semantic Web for the Working Ontologist*. 2nd Edition. Chapter 3. RDF–The basis of the Semantic Web. Morgan Kaufmann, 2011.
26. Guus Schreiber and Yves Raimond. RDF 1.1 Primer. https://www.w3.org/TR/rdf11-primer/. 2014.
27. David Beckett, Tim Berners-Lee, Eric Prud'hommeaux, and Gavin Carothers. *RDF 1.1 Turtle*. https://www.w3.org/TR/turtle/. Last accessed on 16 September 2022. Feb. 2014.
28. Manu Sporny, Dave Longley, Gregg Kellogg, Markus Lanthaler, Pierre-Antoine Champin, and Niklas Lindström. JSON-LD 1.1. https://www.w3.org/TR/json-ld11/. Last accessed on 16 September 2022. July 2020.
29. David Beckett. RDF 1.1 N-Triples. https://www.w3.org/TR/n-triples/. Last accessed on 16 September 2022. Feb. 2014.
30. Dean Allemang and James Hendler. *Semantic Web for the Working Ontologist*. 2nd Edition. Chapter 7. RDF Schema. Morgan Kaufmann, 2011.
31. Brian McBride. *RDF Schema 1.1*. https://www.w3.org/TR/rdf-schema/. Last accessed on 16 September 2022. Feb. 2024.
32. Aidan Hogan. 'Web Ontology Language'. In: *The Web of Data*. Cham: Springer International Publishing, 2020, pp. 185–322. https://doi.org/10.1007/978-3-030-51580-5_5.
33. Dean Allemang and James Hendler. *Semantic Web for the Working Ontologist*. 2nd Edition. Chapter 11. Basic OWL. Morgan Kaufmann, 2011.
34. W3C. *OWL Web Ontology Language Overview*. https://www.w3.org/TR/2004/REC-owl-features-20040210/. Last accessed on 16 September 2022. Feb. 2004.
35. W3C. *OWL 2 Web Ontology Language Document Overview (Second Edition)*. https://www.w3.org/TR/owl2-overview/. Last accessed on 16 September 2022. Dec. 2012.
36. W3C. *SPARQL 1.1 Protocol*. https://www.w3.org/TR/sparql11-protocol/. Last accessed on 16 September 2022. Mar. 2013.
37. A. L. Samuel. 'Some Studies in Machine Learning Using the Game of Checkers'. In: *IBM Journal of Research and Development* 3.3 (1959), pp. 210–229. https://doi.org/10.1147/rd.33.0210.
38. Tom Mitchell. *Machine learning*. Vol. 1. 9. McGraw-hill New York, 1997.
39. Jafar Alzubi, Anand Nayyar, and Akshi Kumar. 'Machine Learning from Theory to Algorithms: An Overview'. In: *Journal of Physics: Conference Series* 1142 (2018), p. 012012. https://doi.org/10.1088/1742-6596/1142/1/012012.
40. Iffat Zafar, Giounona Tzanidou, Richard Burton, Nimesh Patel, and Leonardo Araujo. *Hands-on convolutional neural networks with TensorFlow: Solve computer vision problems with modeling in TensorFlow and Python*. Chapter 2. Packt Publishing Ltd, 2018.
41. Qi Wang, Yue Ma, Kun Zhao, and Yingjie Tian. 'A Comprehensive Survey of Loss Functions in Machine Learning'. In: *Annals of Data Science* 9.2 (2022), pp. 187–212. https://doi.org/10.1007/s40745-020-00253-5.
42. Tong Zhang. 'Solving Large Scale Linear Prediction Problems Using Stochastic Gradient Descent Algorithms'. In: *Proceedings of the Twenty-First International Conference on Machine Learning*. ICML '04. Banff, Alberta, Canada: Association for Computing Machinery, 2004, p. 116. https://doi.org/10.1145/1015330.1015332.
43. Alfred DeMaris. 'A Tutorial in Logistic Regression'. In: *Journal of Marriage and Family* 57.4 (1995), pp. 956–968. (Visited on 09/21/2022).
44. William S. Noble. 'What is a support vector machine?' In: *Nature Biotechnology* 24.12 (2006), pp. 1565–1567. https://doi.org/10.1038/nbt1206-1565.

45. Absalom E. Ezugwu, Abiodun M. Ikotun, Olaide O. Oyelade, Laith Abualigah, Jeffery O. Agushaka, Christopher I. Eke, and Andronicus A. Akinyelu. 'A comprehensive survey of clustering algorithms: State-of-the-art machine learning applications, taxonomy, challenges, and future research prospects'. In: *Engineering Applications of Artificial Intelligence* 110 (2022), p. 104743. https://doi.org/10.1016/j.engappai.2022.104743.
46. Basna Mohammed Salih Hasan and Adnan Mohsin Abdulazeez. 'A Review of Principal Component Analysis Algorithm for Dimensionality Reduction'. In: *Journal of Soft Computing and Data Mining* 2.1 (2021), 20–30.
47. Jesper E. van Engelen and Holger H. Hoos. 'A survey on semi-supervised learning'. In: *Machine Learning* 109.2 (2020), pp. 373–440. https://doi.org/10.1007/s10994-019-05855-6.
48. Jie Zhou, Ganqu Cui, Shengding Hu, Zhengyan Zhang, Cheng Yang, Zhiyuan Liu, Lifeng Wang, Changcheng Li, and Maosong Sun. 'Graph neural networks: A review of methods and applications'. In: *AI Open* 1 (2020), pp. 57–81. https://doi.org/10.1016/j.aiopen.2021.01.001.
49. H. Taud and J.F. Mas. 'Multilayer Perceptron (MLP)'. In: *Geomatic Approaches for Modeling Land Change Scenarios*. Ed. by María Teresa Camacho Olmedo, Martin Paegelow, Jean-François Mas, and Francisco Escobar. Cham: Springer International Publishing, 2018, pp. 451–455. https://doi.org/10.1007/978-3-319-60801-3_27.
50. Raúl Rojas. 'The Backpropagation Algorithm'. In: *Neural Networks: A Systematic Introduction*. Berlin, Heidelberg: Springer Berlin Heidelberg, 1996, pp. 149–182. https://doi.org/10.1007/978-3-642-61068-4_7.
51. Justin Gilmer, Samuel S. Schoenholz, Patrick F. Riley, Oriol Vinyals, and George E. Dahl. 'Message Passing Neural Networks'. In: *Machine Learning Meets Quantum Physics*. Ed. by Kristof T. Schütt, Stefan Chmiela, O. Anatole von Lilienfeld, Alexandre Tkatchenko, Koji Tsuda, and Klaus-Robert Müller. Cham: Springer International Publishing, 2020, pp. 199–214. https://doi.org/10.1007/978-3-030-40245-7_10.
52. PyTorch Geometric. *CREATING MESSAGE PASSING NETWORKS*. https://pytorch-geometric.readthedocs.io/en/latest/notes/create_gnn.html. Last accessed on 25 September 2022.
53. Thomas N. Kipf and Max Welling. *Semi-Supervised Classification with Graph Convolutional Networks*. 2016. DOIurlhttps://doi.org/10.48550/ARXIV.1609.02907.
54. Minjie Wang, Da Zheng, Zihao Ye, Quan Gan, Mufei Li, Xiang Song, Jinjing Zhou, Chao Ma, Lingfan Yu, Yu Gai, Tianjun Xiao, Tong He, George Karypis, Jinyang Li, and Zheng Zhang. 'Deep Graph Library: A Graph-Centric, Highly-Performant Package for Graph Neural Networks'. In: *arXiv preprint* arXiv:1909.01315 (2019).
55. Michael Schlichtkrull, Thomas N. Kipf, Peter Bloem, Rianne van den Berg, Ivan Titov, and Max Welling. 'Modeling Relational Data with Graph Convolutional Networks'. In: *The Semantic Web*. Ed. by Aldo Gangemi, Roberto Navigli, Maria-Esther Vidal, Pascal Hitzler, Raphaël Troncy, Laura Hollink, Anna Tordai, and Mehwish Alam. Cham, Switzerland: Springer International Publishing, 2018, pp. 593–607.
56. Mohit Goyal, Rajan Goyal, P. Venkatappa Reddy, and Brejesh Lall. 'Activation Functions'. In: *Deep Learning: Algorithms and Applications*. Ed. by Witold Pedrycz and Shyi-Ming Chen. Cham: Springer International Publishing, 2020, pp. 1–30. https://doi.org/10.1007/978-3-030-31760-7_1.

57. Nicolas Keriven and Gabriel Peyré. 'Universal Invariant and Equivariant Graph Neural Networks'. In: *Advances in Neural Information Processing Systems*. Ed. by H. Wallach, H. Larochelle, A. Beygelzimer, F. d'Alché-Buc, E. Fox, and R. Garnett. Vol. 32. Curran Associates, Inc., 2019.
58. Daphne Koller and Nir Friedman. *Probabilistic graphical models: principles and techniques*. MIT press, 2009.
59. Kevin Murphy. *A Brief Introduction to Graphical Models and Bayesian Networks*. https://www.cs.ubc.ca/~murphyk/Bayes/bnintro.html. Last accessed on 27 September 2022.
60. Michal Horný. 'Bayesian networks'. In: *Boston University School of Public Health* 17 (2014).
61. Mauro Scanagatta, Antonio Salmerón, and Fabio Stella. 'A survey on Bayesian network structure learning from data'. In: *Progress in Artificial Intelligence* 8.4 (2019), pp. 425–439. https://doi.org/10.1007/s13748-019-00194-y.
62. Andrew A. Neath and Joseph E. Cavanaugh. 'The Bayesian information criterion: background, derivation, and applications'. In: *WIREs Computational Statistics* 4.2 (2012), pp. 199–203. https://doi.org/10.1002/wics.199.
63. Rakesh. Rana and Richa. Singhal. 'Chi-square test and its application in hypothesis testing'. In: *Journal of the Practice of Cardiovascular Sciences* 1.1 (2015), pp. 69–71. https://doi.org/10.4103/2395-5414.157577.
64. Xun Zheng, Bryon Aragam, Pradeep K Ravikumar, and Eric P Xing. 'DAGs with NO TEARS: Continuous Optimization for Structure Learning'. In: *Advances in Neural Information Processing Systems*. Ed. by S. Bengio, H.Wallach, H. Larochelle, K. Grauman,N. Cesa-Bianchi, and R. Garnett. Vol. 31. Curran Associates, Inc., 2018.

Part II
Publications

Knowledge Graph Based Hard Drive Failure Prediction

4

Abstract

The hard drive is one of the important components of a computing system, and its failure can lead to both system failure and data loss. Therefore, the reliability of a hard drive is very important. Realising this importance, a number of studies have been conducted and many are still ongoing to improve hard drive failure prediction. Most of those studies rely solely on machine learning, and a few others on semantic technology. The studies based on machine learning, despite promising results, lack context-awareness such as how failures are related or what other factors, such as humidity, influence the failure of hard drives. Semantic technology, on the other hand, by means of ontologies and knowledge graphs (KGs), is able to provide the context-awareness that machine learning-based studies lack. However, the studies based on semantic technology lack the advantages of machine learning, such as the ability to learn a pattern and make predictions based on learned patterns. Therefore, in this paper, leveraging the benefits of both machine learning (ML) and semantic technology, we present our study,

This chapter is a copy of the previously published article: **Tek Raj Chhetri**, Anelia Kurteva, Jubril Gbolahan Adigun, and Anna Fensel. 'Knowledge Graph Based Hard Drive Failure Prediction'. In: Sensors 22.3 (2022), p. 985. https://doi.org/10.3390/s22030985

Contribution as a first author: The scientific contributions include the following: (i) conceptualisation of the study; (ii) design of the methodology; (iii) implementation of the proposed methodology and execution of experiments; (iv) performing formal analysis and validation of the experiments; (v) data curation and data visualisation; and (vi) writing the manuscript.

T. R. Chhetri, *Improving Decision Making Using Semantic Web Technologies*, https://doi.org/10.1007/978-3-658-45877-5_4

knowledge graph-based hard drive failure prediction. The experimental results demonstrate that our proposed method achieves higher accuracy in comparison to the current state of the art.

4.1 Introduction

In recent years, advancements in fields such as machine learning (ML) have led the shift towards the fourth industrial revolution, also referred to as Industry 4.0 [1]. Its main objective is to *"bring an increase in productivity in both production and management systems"* [2] by focusing on analytics-driven insight development such as predictive maintenance (PdM) [3]. The transition to Industry 4.0 is driven by the Internet of Things (IoT) and the amount of generated data, which has increased exponentially, requiring large data centres being used to meet companies' storage demands [4]. The data itself is stored on hard drives (HDs), which are one of the most commonly used data storage devices [5]. However, HDs are often prone to different failures. The most common failures can be categorised as logical, mechanical, or firmware failures (https://www.salvagedata.com/common-causes-of-hard-drive-failure/ (accessed on 6 June 2021)). Such failures can result in system unavailability or even permanent data loss, which can have a negative impact due to system downtime and can lead to monetary losses for companies [6]. For example, 78% of hardware replacements in Microsoft (https://www.microsoft.com/de-at/ (accessed on 10 June 2021)) data centres were due to HD failure [7]. HD reliability is key and the research for solutions that can predict such failures is an ongoing endeavour.

Through the years, various ML and reasoning approaches based on algorithms such as Decision Trees (DT) [8], k-Nearest Neighbour [9], Classification Trees (CT) [10], and Regression Trees (RT) [11] have been adopted successfully for PdM (i.e., the failure prediction accuracy rates have improved) [12–14]. State of the art solutions such as [7, 15–18] have shown to achieve more than 90% accuracy in failure prediction. However, ML on its own lacks context awareness [19] and therefore, lacks the benefits that comes with it. The term context refers to any information that can be used to characterise an entity's situation (i.e., whether a person, place, or object) [20]. For example, let us consider the following knowledge graph (KG) facts as triples *("Humans", "are", "mortal")* and *("Socrates", "is a", "human")*. Now, using these triples we can deduce the fact that *("Socrates", "is", "mortal")*. This is made possible by the context-awareness generated as a result of the connected relationships. However, as machines do not inherently have the deductive capability, we need to formalise the logical consequences based on entailment regimes (https://www.w3.org/TR/sparql11-entailment/ (accessed on 12 August 2021)) to make such deductions, which ontologies and KGs are capable of due to their ability to model relationships [21]. In the case of the hard drive failure prediction we can have similar benefits of KGs. For example, let us consider the following KG triples *("Hard drive", "smart5", "10"), ("Hard drive", "has humidity", "89"), ("Hard drive", "storage has average temperature", "65")*. Now, using these KG triples we can deduce the fact that *("Hard drive", "status", "fail")* (i.e., hard drive will fail). This is due to the fact that high humidity and temperature deteriorate hardware, particularly electronic devices [22]. In ML, we can leverage such advantages of the KGs using the nodes (or entities) representation and taking features of a local neighbourhood coupled with relationships (details in Sect. 4.4) to improve the prediction. Therefore, considering the benefits of using KGs and extending our initial idea (see [23]), we hypothesise that by combining KGs and ML, we can achieve even greater benefits in failure prediction and present our work on hard drive failure prediction. The proposed approach takes the benefits of both: KGs' context-awareness and ML pattern learning and predictability capabilities. It also eliminates the limitations of rule-based approaches, which requires us to have all the rules defined beforehand and also lacks predictability like ML. Recent studies, such as [24], have also highlighted such limitations.

KG, which Fensel et al. [25] define as *"very large semantic nets that integrate various and heterogeneous information sources to represent knowledge about certain domains"*, have the ability to transform data into information and information into knowledge by creating meaningful relationships between entities [21, 25]. With the help of relationships, a KG is able to provide context to ML. Other benefits of semantic technology such as data interopretability, connectivity of data across domains and faster and easier knowledge discovery, have been further discussed in more detail in [26–30]. Because of the benefits of semantic technology, we can find its application in domains such as predictive maintenance [31, 32] and recommender systems [33] that utilise ontologies [34] and KGs. Additionally, Kainzner et al. [35] demonstrate the potential benefits of semantic technology in relevant domains such as manufacturing. Other than the relationships, KGs also offer a simple and adaptable way to include additional information. For example, humidity can have a significant impact on HD failure [22]. However, such environmental data is not available in SMART (Self-Monitoring, Analysis, and Reporting) (https://www.ibm.com/support/pages/define-smart-used-smartcollect (accessed on 13 June 2021)) attributes. SMART attributes are obtained from SMART technology [36], which enables monitoring of the hard disk's status (see [7]) and reporting of various reliability indicators.

In this paper, we demonstrate the value of combining KGs and ML for predicting HD failures. Our proposed approach uses KGs and relational graph convolutional networks (RGCN), a ML technique for failure prediction (details in Sect. 4.4.4). The KG used in this study is based on data from SMART attributes.

The paper is structured as follows. Section 4.2 presents an overview of related works on hard drive failure prediction. Section 4.3 provides information on the following methodology. A detailed description of the proposed solution in the paper is presented in Sect. 4.4, while its performance evaluation is described in Sect. 4.5. Conclusions can be found in Sect. 4.6.

4.2 State of the Art

This section summarises the related work. The use of both ML techniques and semantic technology can be found in various domains such as failure prediction in manufacturing. However, because our study is focused on the prediction of HD failure, we restrict our review of related work to HD. Schoenfisch et al. [37], for example, used semantic technology (ontology) and Markov logic networks (see [38]) to conduct a study on the root cause analysis of information technology (IT) infrastructure. Such studies are not included in our analysis because they do not address HD failure prediction directly. The first section, Sect. 4.2.1, summarises the study using semantic models, while the second section, Sect. 4.2.2 focuses on the studies with ML techniques. Finally, Sect. 4.2.3 summarises the related work presented in Sects. 4.2.1 and 4.2.2.

4.2.1 Semantic Model-Based Study

Mamoutova et al. [24] present an ontology-based approach to automatic analysis of data storage systems log files extending their work, a knowledge-based approach for enterprise storage system diagnosis using ontology [39]. Their work incorporates expert knowledge stored in a knowledge base as RDF (Resource Description Framework)/XML (Extensible Markup Language) format by converting it to the N-Quads format of the graph database. Mamoutova et al. [24] use an ontology to represent fault symptoms such as damage due to abnormal temperature change, which are then reasoned over using monitored data for diagnostic purposes. SPARQL (https://www.w3.org/TR/rdf-sparql-query/ (accessed on 3 Aug 2021)) and GraphQL+ (https://docs.dgraph.io/query-language (accessed on 3 Aug 2021)) are used to facilitate diagnosis querying. As the authors point out, the limitation is that each fault that needs to be detected must be described by the combination of values and the used monitoring parameters. Furthermore, such an approach is limited in its ability to express abnormal values of a parameter in terms other than a simple threshold or binary value, such as a bounded interval. Mamoutova et al. [24] also use ML-based techniques such as random forest (RF), long-short-term memory (LSTM), gated recurrent unit (GRU), and LSTM with attention in a complex situation where an ontology-based approach fails. This demonstrates the limitations of a semantic-only approach even more.

4.2.2 Machine Learning-Based Study

Su et al. [40] use the RF classification algorithm and SMART attributes to conduct a study on hard drive predictive maintenance. The solution in [40] has the ability to make real-time predictions by utilising technologies such as Apache Hadoop (https://hadoop.apache.org (accessed on 2 June 2021)) and Apache Spark (https://spark.apache.org(accessed on 6 September 2021)). The use of a RF classification algorithm for HD failure prediction can also be seen in [41, 42]. However, in addition to using the same ML algorithm, Shen et al. [41] use a sliding window to reduce the effect of noise and an additional part voting strategy to improve the prediction accuracy. On the other hand, Züfle et al. [42] use additional techniques such as synthetic minority oversampling technique (SMOTE) [43] and enhanced structure-preserving oversampling (ESPO) [44] together with random forest. Similar to Su et al., Züfle et al. and Shen et al., Mashhadi et al. [45] also make use of RF algorithm. Mashhadi et al. conducted a case study of the HD time to failure using SMART attributes in cloud manufacturing settings. The authors perform regression analysis with the RF classification algorithm to predict the time to failure. Further, the authors present findings of specific SMART attributes, their importance and how they correlate with each other across different brands. For example, it has been discovered that higher SMART attribute values, such as SMART 5, SMART 10, and SMART 187, have a strong correlation with failures. The other study, by Li et al. [5], do not use a RF algorithm, but rather a tree-based algorithm based on decision trees (DTs) [8] and gradient boosting regression trees (GBRT) [46]. The DTs was used for failure prediction, while the GBRT was used for health degree evaluation (i.e. a value set for each failed sample between [−1, 0]). Furthermore, a simple voting strategy with DT is used to improve prediction, and the work is evaluated using the simulated scenario.

Han et al. [47] use a streaming approach to predict disc failure with the help of incremental learning algorithms such as DT. The authors follow an ensemble approach combining multiple DTs to overcome limitations such as single DT's diversity and look-ahead. SMART attributes are also used in the work to predict failure. Similar to Han et al., Ganguly et al. [48] also used an ensemble approach for their study. Ganguly et al. conducted a study on hard drive failure prediction with the Azure (https://azure.microsoft.com/en-us/(accessed on 12 September 2021)) cloud platform using a two-step ensemble method, which employ a non-parametric DT at stage 1 and logistic regression (LR) at stage 2. The solution in [48] has been put into production and it has shown to reduce the downtime of virtual machines (VMs) caused by HD.

Studies by Liu et al. [6], Zang et al. [49], and Santo et al. [50], on the other hand, use a deep learning approach for hard drive failure prediction. The work of Liu et al. focuses on cloud storage systems and applied modified recurrent neural networks (RNN). The main difference (in comparison to previous research) is how the current hidden layer is updated, which is by feeding the previous time step hidden layer and output layer. Similarly, the work of Santo et al. used LSTM, RNN based deep learning technique, while the work of Zang et al. make use of adversarial training [51] with SMART attributes. Both the work of Santo et al. and Zang et al. focus on hard drive health prediction. In contrast to previous research, Franklin [52] conducted an empirical study on hard drive failure prediction and observed an increase in the reallocated sector count of one of the SMART attributes prior to a failure.

4.2.3 Summary

In conclusion, the majority of the studies discussed in Sect. 4.2 apply ML techniques or, more recently, a few techniques based on semantic models for HD PdM failure prediction. We present a summary of the existing solutions in Table 4.1. The table presents each study, the main method that has been used (ML-based or semantic-based), and, when available, performance and training time statistics and current limitations. While most of the presented solutions achieve accuracy of failure prediction above 90% and use SMART attributes, context-awareness is rarely addressed. From the presented solutions, only the one by Mamoutova et al. [24] uses semantic technology, namely ontologies, to provide context to the selected ML model.

Table 4.1 Summary of existing HD PdM solutions

Study	Method			Training Time	Were SMART Attributes Used?	Limitations
	ML	Semantics	Performance			
Mamoutova et al. [24]	✔	✔	Precision of 74%.	183 s to ~7 h, depending on the algorithm.	✘	The use of a semantic-only approach is restricted to predefined rules, such as the requirement that each fault be defined by a combination of values and monitoring parameters.
Su et al. [40]	✔	✘	Accuracy of 85.84%.	–	✔	
Shen et al. [41]	✔	✘	Failure detection rates of over 97.67%. False alarm rate of 0.017%.	–	✔	
Mashhadi et al. [45]	✔	✘	R^2 with less than 50%.	–	✔	
Han et al. [47]	✔	✘	Precision, recall, and F1-score are increased by 27.5–71.8%, 15.7–37.4%, and 26.8–53.2% respectively.	Training time is 10.6 s (0.6 s deviation).	✔	

(Continued)

Table 4.1 (Continued)

Study	Method			Training Time	Were SMART Attributes Used?	Limitations
	ML	Semantics	Performance			
Züfle et al. [42]	✔	✖	Accuracy, precision, and recall are 97.642%, 94.913%, and 96.97%, respectively.	The average training time of the multi-class classification approach is 174 s, while for the pre-filtering is 346 s.	✔	As previously stated, studies that rely solely on machine learning lack context awareness. Furthermore, the studies lack benefits such as the ability to incorporate expert knowledge and additional information, such as humidity, which is another reason for the failure associated with the use of KG, aside from the improved results.
Ganguly et al. [48]	✔	✖	Key performance indicators were established and used at different steps, such as design changes in production and pilot in test environment.	–	✔	
Liu et al. [6]	✔	✖	100.0% failure detection rate at a 0.02% false alarm rate.	–	✔	
Zang et al. [49]	✔	✖	Accuracy, precision, and recall are 92.6%, 89%, and 88.7%, respectively.	–	✔	
Santo et al. [50]	✔	✖	Accuracy of 98.45%, precision of 98.33% and recall of 98.34%.	–	✔	

Two of the main limitations of the existing ML solutions as presented in Sect. 4.2 and Table 4.1 is the lack of context awareness (e.g., why and how a failure occurred, how the failure affects the HD overtime) and standardisation when dealing with heterogeneous data types. The numerous ongoing studies demonstrate that the problem of predicting HD failure requires a solution that takes into account the changing technological landscape and advancement.

All these limitations can be resolved with the help of semantic technologies such as ontologies and knowledge graphs, which provide both context and a unified data model in machine-readable format. The use of semantic technology, namely knowledge graphs, enables context-awareness through the relationships that hold between concepts (in a specific domain) as demonstrated in studies such as [24]. As a result, in this study, we present our work on combining KGs and machine learning for HD failure prediction.

4.3 Methodology

Figure 4.1 summarises the methodology that we follow. The first phase is data collection, which included the identification of appropriate data (i.e., the selection of a dataset containing HD failure information from the numerous failure datasets available on the internet) and its download. In our case, the downloaded dataset was tabular in nature and was stored as comma-separated value (CSV) files. Section 4.4.1 contains additional information about the dataset, such as the total number of samples and the location of the collection. The next phase, as shown on Fig. 4.1, is data preprocessing, which consists of the following steps: (i) converting data to KG for RGCN and (ii) splitting data into training and testing sets.

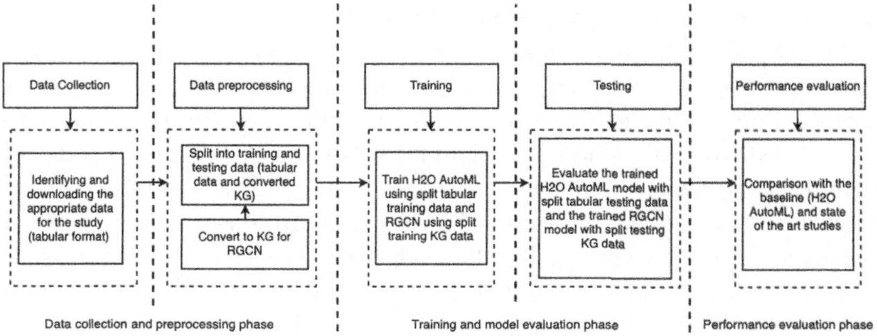

Fig. 4.1 High level overview of followed methodology

Details on how the tabular data is converted into a KG are presented in Sect. 4.4.2. The converted KG serves as an input to RGCN, an ML technique that combines the KG by transforming the KG into low-level representations (details in Sect. 4.4.4) and learning patterns, which is also the proposed approach. For example, let us consider the following KG triples: *("Hard drive", "smart5", "10")*, *("Hard drive", "has humidity", "89")*, *("Hard drive", "storage has average temperature", "65")* and *("Hard drive", "status", "fail")*, which were presented in Sect. 4.1 and contains the information about HD failure. To enhance failure prediction, we train the RGCN model on these KG triples containing information about HD failures. Following training, we pass similar KG triples (i.e., KG triples with missing status information) to generate a prediction, which in this case is the status (i.e., failed or working). This approach to RGCN provides additional benefits, such as eliminating the additional step of performing downstream tasks such as classification, that would otherwise be required if embedding techniques such as Rotate3D [53] and K-BERT [54] were used. RGCN is a generalisation of Graph Convolution Networks (GCNs) that operates on relational graph data (or knowledge graphs) [55]. GCNs are a variant of convolutional neural networks (CNNs) on graphs [56]. Moreover, in addition to the details on KG construction from tabular data presented in Sect. 4.4.2, we refer to the following studies [57, 58] for additional information, as well as study [21] for additional information on KG.

Similarly, during the splitting training and testing data, we split the data into training and testing sets. In this step, we split both the KG and the original tabular data. This is because we also used the H2O (https://www.h2o.ai (accessed on 22 September 2021)) AutoML (https://docs.h2o.ai/h2o/latest-stable/h2o-docs/automl.html (accessed on 22 September 2021)) (Automatic Machine Learning), which provides an automated industrial standard supervised ML algorithm that operates on tabular data [59]. Further, we use it as a baseline for the proposed approach. Section 4.4.3 provides additional information on H2O AutoML. Further details of the data preprocessing are presented in Sect. 4.4.2.

Next, by using the split training data, we perform training in the subsequent step. To train the H2O AutoML, the tabular training data is used, while the KG is used for training the RGCN. Once training is complete, we evaluate the trained H2O AutoML and RGCN models against the split test data. Finally, we perform a performance evaluation by comparing our RGCN results to those of H2O AutoML, which served as a baseline for our RGCN. The model performance is assessed using evaluation metrics (see Sect. 4.5.3), which helped us understand how well the model is likely to perform in an unanticipated scenario. In addition to comparing our results to those of H2O AutoML, we make a comparison with the state of the art studies. The results are presented in Sect. 4.5.4.

Finally, the steps below summarise the step by step application method for the proposed approach. It differs from the approach of the H2O AutoML, which follows the standard ML approach.

1. The first application requirement is for data in the KGs. If only tabular data is available, it must be transformed into the KGs. Section 4.4.2, data preprocessing, goes into greater detail about the data transformation process into KGs and Sect. 4.4.1 discusses the used data. Additionally, we refer to the studies [57, 58] for additional information on converting tabular data to KGs;
2. After obtaining the KGs data, the next step is to divide it into training and testing sets. This step of splitting the data into training and testing set is also common for the H2O AutoML. The task of splitting the data into a training and testing set is performed during the data preprocessing phase;
3. The next step is to train the ML model, which in our case is RGCN, using the split training KG. The details about the training are available in Sects. 4.4.4 and 4.5.2;
4. After training is complete, the model is evaluated using split-testing KGs. Sects 4.5.2 and 4.5.4 contain details about the evaluation and its findings, which are performed and obtained aplying evaluation metrics (see Sect. 4.5.3).

In the case of H2O AutoML (see Sect. 4.4.3), we follow a similar procedure, training, and evaluation, for example, as with RGCN, but with tabular data. Moreover, as an alternative to RGCN, embedding approaches such as Rotate3D [53] and K-BERT [54] can also be used. However, use of such an embedding approaches requires additional ML algorithms to be able to make predictions, as embeddings only transform the KGs into low level representations. This would therefore require more time and effort as one needs to train and optimise multiple algorithms.

4.4 Experiment

In this section, we present details about our experiment. In Sect. 4.4.1, we present details about the used data and data preprocessing in Sect. 4.4.2. Similarly, in Sect. 4.4.3, we present details about H2O AutoML and why we selected it for our study. Finally, in Sect. 4.4.4, we provide details on RGCN, such as the reasons for its selection and use in our study. Additionally, we provide details on the experiment, such as the used hyperparameters and activation functions.

4.4.1 Dataset

Our study focuses on HD failure prediction and also uses the ML technique. In order to successfully apply the ML technique, we needed to train ML models. To train ML models, we needed data, so the first step was to gather the dataset about HD failure. In our study, we use data from Backblaze (https://www.backblaze.com/b2/hard-drive-test-data.html (accessed on 10 June 2021)) as it offers a real-world HD failure dataset. The dataset contains information about HD failures represented by SMART attributes. In our experiment, we used the dataset from the third quarter of 2020. The dataset contains a total of 106 SMART attributes of which 53 are raw values and 53 are normalised values. The values are stored in 92 different files, which after download are combined into one CSV file. Figure 4.2 shows the data distribution after combining the data from all 92 different CSV files. The dataset contains a total of 13,553,809 samples, with only 367 samples representing failed HDs.

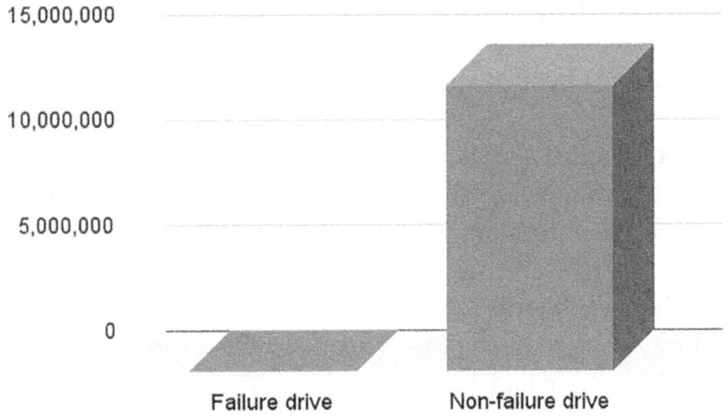

Fig. 4.2 Data distribution

4.4.2 Data Preprocessing

The used data consists of 106 SMART attributes (see Sect. 4.4.1). Each SMART attribute has a different level of importance. It would be beneficial if we use the attributes that are more important in predicting HD failure. For example, SMART 3, which represents spin-up time, is considered less critical. SMART 5, the other SMART attribute, is considered critical (or more important than SMART 3). If we rely on SMART 3 instead of SMART 5, there is a high chance that our prediction result will not be accurate. As a result, the first data preprocessing step in our study was to fine-tune the SMART attributes based on their significance. Table 4.2 shows the selected nine SMART attributes based on their importance for HD failure prediction. The significance of the SMART metrics was determined using information obtained from manufacturers, such as Segate (https://www.seagate.com/gb/en/ (accessed on 23 September 2021)), and a review of the literature. Once we have finalised the SMART attributes that are to be used in our study, the next step is to convert the data into KGs. In case of H2O, we use tabular data with selected SMART attributes (see Table 4.2). Figure 4.3 presents the process of creating the KG.

Table 4.2 List of used SMART attributes and their definitions

SN	SMART Attribute	Definition
1	Smart 5	Reallocated sector count.
2	Smart 10	Spin retry count.
3	Smart 187	Reported uncorrectable errors.
4	Smart 189	High fly writes.
5	Smart 190	Temperature difference or airflow difference.
6	Smart 198	Uncorrectable sector count.
7	Smart 197	Current pending sector count.
8	Smart 199	UltraDMA CRC error count.
9	Smart 188	Connection timeout.

Fig. 4.3 Transforming CSV data into a KG

A Python script is used to transform the combined raw data into a KG, which we implemented. For the transformation of raw data into KGs, we followed the principles of RDF Mapping Language (RML) (https://rml.io (accessed on 24 September 2021)). After the transformation, the raw CSV data is saved in CSV format again, but this time in a triple format (*subject, predicate, object*), denoted by (*s,p,o*) as shown in Fig. 4.4. However, during our experiment, we observed issues such as being out of memory and slow processing when using the KGs stored in CSV. Therefore, to deal with these issues, we transformed the KGs stored in CSV to NetworkX(https://networkx.org (accessed on 24 September 2021)) representation. The NetworkX representation allowed us to represent KGs as a graph, which can be directly fed to RGCN. Similarly, Fig. 4.5 and Fig. 4.6 show the visualisation of

s	p	o
<http://tekrajchhetri.com/failureprediction.owl/HD22896>	<http://tekrajchhetri.com/failureprediction.owl#smart5>	<http://tekrajchhetri.com/failureprediction.owl/100.0>
<http://tekrajchhetri.com/failureprediction.owl/HD22896>	<http://tekrajchhetri.com/failureprediction.owl#smart10>	<http://tekrajchhetri.com/failureprediction.owl/100.0>
<http://tekrajchhetri.com/failureprediction.owl/HD22896>	<http://tekrajchhetri.com/failureprediction.owl#smart187>	<http://tekrajchhetri.com/failureprediction.owl/100.0>
<http://tekrajchhetri.com/failureprediction.owl/HD22896>	<http://tekrajchhetri.com/failureprediction.owl#smart189>	<http://tekrajchhetri.com/failureprediction.owl/100.0>
<http://tekrajchhetri.com/failureprediction.owl/HD22896>	<http://tekrajchhetri.com/failureprediction.owl#smart190>	<http://tekrajchhetri.com/failureprediction.owl/76.0>
<http://tekrajchhetri.com/failureprediction.owl/HD22896>	<http://tekrajchhetri.com/failureprediction.owl#smart198>	<http://tekrajchhetri.com/failureprediction.owl/100.0>
<http://tekrajchhetri.com/failureprediction.owl/HD22896>	<http://tekrajchhetri.com/failureprediction.owl#smart197>	<http://tekrajchhetri.com/failureprediction.owl/100.0>
<http://tekrajchhetri.com/failureprediction.owl/HD22896>	<http://tekrajchhetri.com/failureprediction.owl#smart199>	<http://tekrajchhetri.com/failureprediction.owl/200.0>
<http://tekrajchhetri.com/failureprediction.owl/HD22896>	<http://tekrajchhetri.com/failureprediction.owl#smart188>	<http://tekrajchhetri.com/failureprediction.owl/100.0>
<http://tekrajchhetri.com/failureprediction.owl/HD22896>	<http://tekrajchhetri.com/failureprediction.owl#status>	<http://tekrajchhetri.com/failureprediction.owl/0>

Fig. 4.4 KG stored in CSV

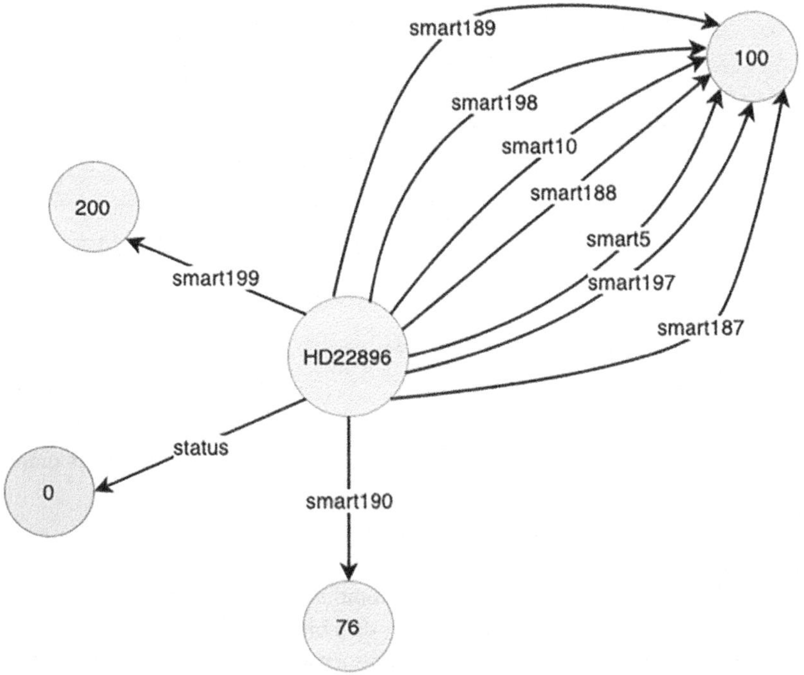

Fig. 4.5 Visualisation of a KG sample—I

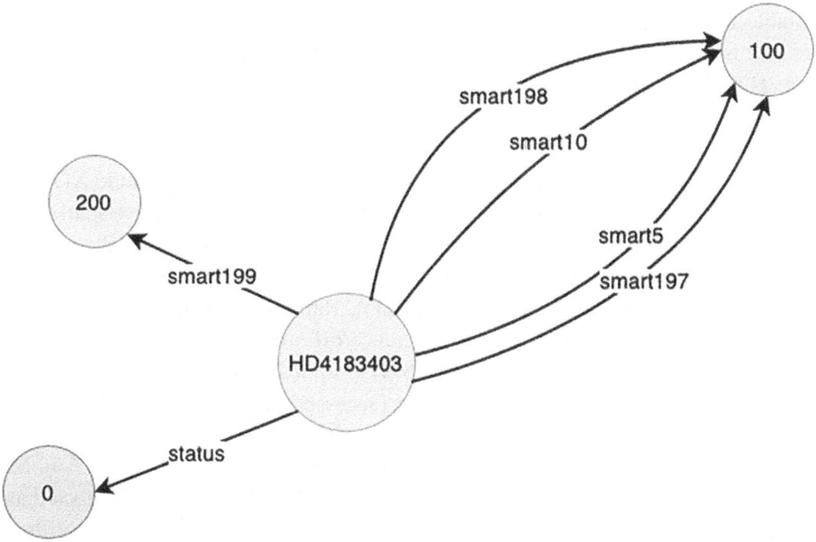

Fig. 4.6 Visualisation of a KG sample—II

an instance of the created KGs. We have removed the Uniform Resource Identifier (URIs) from Figs. 4.5 and 4.6 to simplify the visualisation.

One can observe the difference in the number of relationships and nodes in Figs. 4.5 and 4.6. This is due to missing values in the original data. In the case of the KG instance depicted in Fig. 4.5, there are no missing values, thus all 10 relationships are present. In addition to the nine relationships discussed before, one extra relationship represents the status of the hard drive based on the SMART attributes value. However, in the KG example depicted in Fig. 4.6, there were missing values, resulting in the absence of some relationships and the corresponding nodes (or tail). This is also an advantage in this case as we can ignore the missing values, which would otherwise have to be filled using imputation techniques.

4.4.3 H2O AutoML

H2O AutoML is a fully automated supervised ML algorithm that is part of the H2O framework [59]. H2O is an open-source, distributed ML platform that is designed to scale large datasets and to produce high-quality models, which are suitable for enterprise deployment [59]. Our work uses H2O due to its ability to provide high-quality, enterprise-ready deployment models. Additionally, we consider H2O AutoML because it works with only tabular data (i.e., not KGs) and is the state of the art technique that serves as the baseline for our KGs-based approach.

H2O AutoML provides an implementation for different state of the art algorithms. The implemented base ML algorithms in H2O AutoML include XGBoost Gradient Boosting Machines (XGBoost) (https://docs.h2o.ai/h2o/latest-stable/h2o-docs/data-science/xgboost.html (accessed on 27 September 2021)), Gradient Boosting Machine (GBM) (https://docs.h2o.ai/h2o/latest-stable/h2o-docs/data-science/gbm.html (accessed on 27 September 2021)), Random Forest (RF) (http://docs.h2o.ai/h2o/latest-stable/h2o-docs/data-science/drf.html (accessed on 27 September 2021)), Deep Neural Networks (DNN) (http://docs.h2o.ai/h2o/latest-stable/h2o-docs/data-science/deep-learning.html (accessed on 27 September 2021)) and Generalised Linear Model (GLM) (http://docs.h2o.ai/h2o/latest-stable/h2o-docs/data-science/glm.html (accessed on 27 September 2021)). Further, H2O AutoML provides Stacked Ensembles (http://docs.h2o.ai/h2o/latest-stable/h2o-docs/data-science/stacked-ensembles.html (accessed on 27 September 2021)) algorithms. Stacked ensembles, also known as stacking or super learning, allow us to improve the prediction accuracy by training a *metalearner* on ensemble model predictions, as shown in Fig. 4.7. Stacking ensembles, as opposed to ensemble learning, which takes the weakest learner (such as a decision tree), considers the strongest learned models. H2O uses all models ensemble and best of family models for stacking. The "all models" ensemble contains all the models while the best of the family ensemble only includes the best performing model from each algorithm family [59].

In our experiment with H2O, we used four different algorithms: stacked ensembles, GLM, distributed random forest (DRF), and XGBoost for training and testing. We excluded DNN due to its implementation being unreproducible (https://docs.h2o.ai/h2o/latest-stable/h2o-docs/automl.html(accessed on 22 September 2021)). The data was divided in three sets: for training, testing, and validation. A total of 70% of the data was set aside for the training set, 15% for the validation set, and 15% for the testing set. The training and testing was performed using the system detailed in Sect. 4.5.1. We used a seed value of 123,589,389. The seed value is used to generate pseudo-random numbers, which help achieve reproducibility by producing the same sequence of results as long as we use the same seed value. The algorithms were trained using 6 k-fold cross-validations. The k-fold (i.e., a Monte Carlo [60] method) is a data resampling method used to evaluate the generalisation ability of ML models and to prevent overfitting [61]. It accomplishes this by dividing the data into k subsets of training and validation sets and utilising each fold once for validation and the remaining $k - 1$ subsets for training. Further, we restricted the number

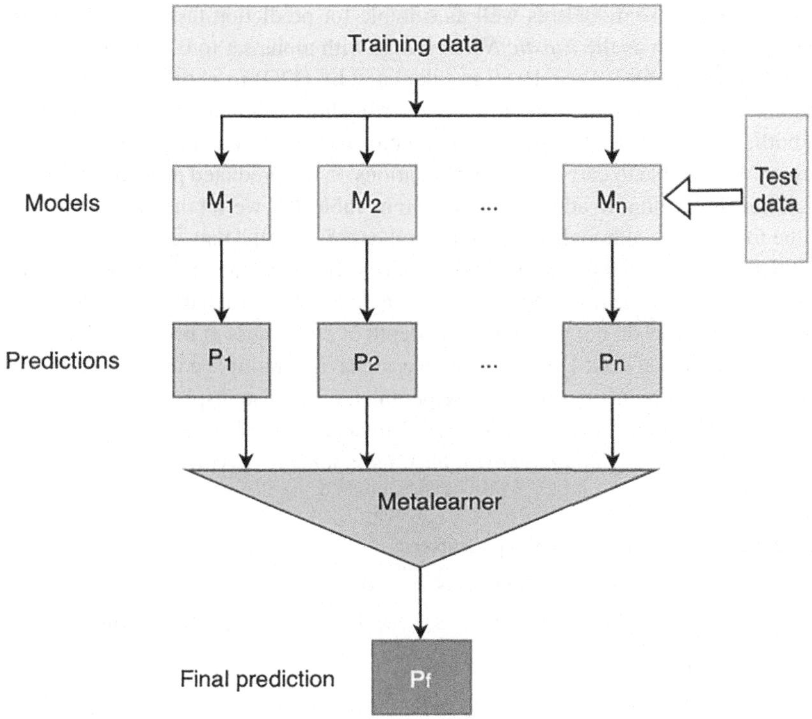

Fig. 4.7 Stacked ensemble

of models to a maximum of 7. H2O also allows us to define a model's time-bound, which specifies the maximum amount of time a model can run during training. In our case, we used the H2O default time limit of one hour. The parameters used, such as the number of folds in k-fold cross validations and the maximum running time of H2O, were determined through experimentation (i.e., by changing parameters). The presented parameters yielded the better performance (see Sect. 4.5.4).

Tables 4.3–4.6 show the tuned hyperparameters of stacked ensemble, GLM, DRF, and XGboost respectively. These hyperparameters were automatically tuned by H2O, which resulted in better performance. As seen in Table 4.3, we ran 99 iterations of the stacked ensemble model, wherein the chosen metalearner was GLM, using its default setting in H2O. Although, H2O provides a number of different metalearners, we have opted for GLM because it is a flexible algorithm for generalisation of L-base models as well as suitable for prediction tasks. We determine the regularisation as the *Elastic Net Penalty* (with alpha set to 0.5 and this causes lambda result to @ 1.21×10^{-7} as calculated by H2O) to regularise the stacked ensemble model since the latter tends to overfit while combining L base algorithms. In both Tables 4.3 and 4.4, the *logit*, link helps the model to gain further predictive power. We are able to carry out transformations on the predicted probabilities using logit transformation. In addition, as shown in Table 4.5, we set the number of trees in the forest as 48, although the default number is 50 and the max depth as 20, which is the default provided by H2O—higher values will make the model more complex and may lead to overfitting. We also set the max leaves on each tree to 82. Note that some of the leaves do not get to the max depth of 20 because at that depth, there are about a million leaf nodes to be split with each having multiple columns resulting in millions of split points per tree. These parameters are also displayed as part of the default DRF output on H2O, thus: *Model summary (number of trees, min. depth, max. depth, mean depth, min. leaves, max. leaves, mean leaves).*

Table 4.3 H2O stacked ensembles parameters

Iterations	Regularisation	Predicators	Metalearner	Link	Lambda
99	Elastic Net (alpha = 0.5, lambda = 1.21×10^{-7})	3	GLM	logit	nlambda = 100, lambda.max = 1.298×10^{-4}, lambda.min = 1.21×10^{-7}, lambda.1se = 4.663×10^{-5}

Table 4.4 GLM parameters

Iterations	Regularisation	Predicators	Link	Lambda
45	Ridge (lambda = 8.302×10^{-8})	465	logit	nlambda = 30, lambda.max = 0.001141, lambda.min = 8.302×10^{-8}, lambda.1se = 2.331×10^{-6}

Table 4.5 DRF parameters

Number of Trees	Min. Depth	Max. Depth	Min. Leaves	Max. Leaves
48	0	20	1	82

Finally, in Table 4.6, we highlight the different hyper parameters for the implemented XGBoost algorithm. Here, we see that although XGBoost has four inbuilt tree types, namely *exact, approx, gpu_hist, and hist*, we have opted for the latter, because it is the fastest tree method. This is as a result of the fact that it runs sketching only once while trying to carry out split finding. Additionally, since the booster is of tree type, the learning rate (eta) is kept at the default 0.3, max depth 10 (4 units greater than the default 6), and sample rate in set at 0.6 which falls within the higher range of the limit 0.0 to 1.0 and can help increase training accuracy. Similar to the other implemented algorithms already mentioned, XGBoost is also a powerful gradient boosting machine (GBM) used to solve many problems today.

Table 4.6 XGBoost parameters

Booster	Number of Trees	Learning Rate	Sample Rate	Max. Depth	Min. Rows	Tree Method
gbtree	99	0.3	0.6	10	5	hist

4.4.4 Relational Graph Convolution Network (RGCN)

RGCN, which was introduced by Schlichtkrull et al. [55] operates on the relational data, taking directed labelled multi-graphs $G = (V, R, E)$ as input. The V in graph G represent nodes (or entities) $v_i \epsilon V$, E represents the edge (or relations) represented by the nodes $(v_i, r, v_k) \epsilon E$ of type relation $r \epsilon R$. Graph Convolution Networks (GCNs), which can be thought of as a subset of differential message passing, provide a more accurate representation of nodes by combining connectivity and neighbourhood features, in contrast to DeepWalk or node2vec (https://snap.stanford.edu/node2vec/(accessed on 12 September 2021)), which rely exclusively on connectivity [62, 63]. RGCN takes GCN a step further by taking relationships into account while retaining GCN's advantages, such as advantages of the neighbourhood node. RGCN evaluates Equation (4.1) while making a neural hidden layer h_i^{l+1} update, wherein N_i^r denotes a set of neighbourhood indices of node i under relation

$r \epsilon R$. The W in the Equation (4.1) represents the weight matrix and $c_{i,r}$ and a problem specific normalisation constant. For details on RGCN, we recommend [55]. Furthermore, unlike GCN, RGCN can deal with heterogeneous relationships [64]. As a result, we consider RGCN in our research.

$$h_i^{l+1} = \sigma \left(\Sigma_{r \epsilon R} \Sigma_{k \epsilon N_i^r} \frac{1}{c_{i,r}} W_r^l h_k^l + W_o^l h_i^l \right) \tag{4.1}$$

The problem of HD failure prediction can be viewed as a node classification task in our study using RGCN, in which we predict the missing node in a KG. In our case, the missing node includes the HD status "fail" or "good". Figure 4.8 shows an example of the node classification. As illustrated in Fig. 4.8, we predict the missing node (denoted by *P*) by feeding the KG with missing nodes to the trained model. Figure 4.9 depicts the detailed approach followed in our study. As illustrated in the Fig. 4.9 method, we begin by training our RGCN model with knowledge graphs and train target labels (or train target). The train target labels contain information about HD failures, which is represented as a node in our KG. Similarly, the test target labels (or test target) include data on HD failures information, which we use to validate our trained model, which we present in Sect. 4.5.4. We used 70% of the data in our RGCN study as a training set and 30% as a testing set.

Our RGCN implementation uses four dense layers and one output layer. The first 2 dense layers are made up of 8 hidden units, while the other 2 are made up of 16 hidden units. Experimentation is used to determine the number of hidden units and the density of the layer. Similarly to the H2O case, the presented parameters produced the better result (see Sect. 4.5.4) in the case of RGCN. This is because making the model more complex with more parameters leads to overfitting, whereas

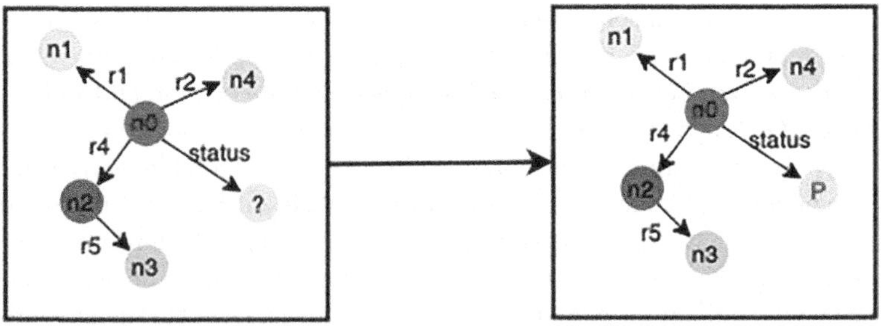

Fig. 4.8 Node classification

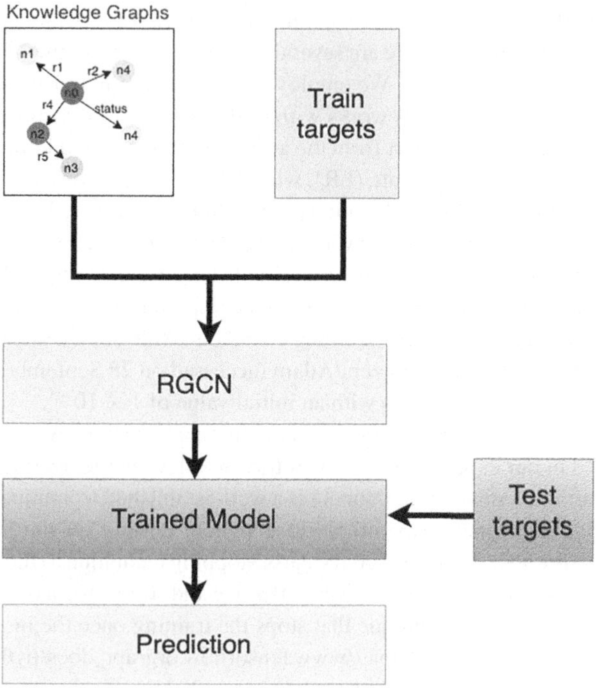

Fig. 4.9 RGCN approach

making the model too simple leads to failure to learn. The activation function is the next most important feature. An activation function distinguishes the neural network from linear models such as linear regression by introducing nonlinearity and assisting the model in learning complex patterns [65]. There are over 20 activation functions available, and choosing the right one is critical [66]. For all of the dense layers in our study, we used the activation function ReLU (https://www.tensorflow.org/api_docs/python/tf/keras/activations/relu (accessed on 27 September 2021)). The reason for this is that ReLU is more resistant to the vanishing gradient problem than other activation functions such as Tanh and Sigmoid [66]. The output layer, however, consists of the sigmoid activation layer. Another critical parameter is the loss function, which quantifies the difference between the prediction and reality. As a result, we always strive to minimise the loss function. Numerous loss functions are available, including mean squared error (MSE) and cross-entropy (CE). The application of loss functions is task-dependent. For instance, the regression problem makes use of the MSE. Due to the classification nature of our task, we chose CE as the loss function. Additionally, there are several variants of CE loss functions, including binary CE and categorical CE. We employ categorical CE in our implementation. This is because categorical CE works with multi-class as well as binary class and therefore is more flexible. Apart from the activation function and loss, another critical parameter is the learning rate (LR), which determines the number of steps the neural network takes during the learning process. If the LR is very large, the chances of divergence are high; if the LR is very small, we may become trapped in the local minima. Both of these situations are undesirable because they impair learning and, ultimately, model performance. Considering the importance of the LR in our implementation, we used an adaptive learning rate Adam (https://www.tensorflow.org/api_docs/python/tf/keras/optimizers/Adam (accessed on 28 September 2021)) that takes into account changing loss with an initial value of 1×10^{-3}.

Overfitting is one of the major problems in deep learning. A similar instance was observed in our experiment, and therefore, to alleviate the overfitting, we used dropout in our implementation. Dropout is a well-established technique for restraining overfitting and functions similarly to a switch, turning off the neurons [67]. In addition to dropout, we also used the early stopping technique to monitor the validation accuracy. Early stopping is a very effective and simple form of regularisation [68]. Early stopping is a technique that stops the training once the monitored metric has stopped improving (https://www.tensorflow.org/api_docs/python/tf/keras/callbacks/EarlyStopping (accessed on 1 October 2021)). Furthermore, due to the sparsity and rapidly growing number of parameters that may be required, learning on a graph can be a difficult task. Therefore to reduce complexity, we enabled parameter sharing in our implementation by setting num_bases to a non-zero value. The training was then carried out for 500 epochs.

4.5 Performance Evaluation

This section contains details about the system and the software used in the experiment. Section 4.5.1 discusses the system setup, providing details about the system's use, such as the number of Graphics Processing Units (GPUs). Section 4.5.2 provides information on training and testing. Section 4.5.3 provides information on the evaluation metrics and the reasons why we considered those evaluation metrics. Finally, in Sect. 4.5.4, we present our experimental results and their comparison to H2O, which we considered as a baseline. We chose H2O as a baseline because H2O is considered the industry-standard ML framework and is widely used in different industrial use cases (https://www.h2o.ai/solutions/#use-cases). In addition to comparison with the H2O, we also compare results with state of the art studies. The selection of the studies to compare were made based on the used similar evaluation metrics and the recency (2018 and later) of the article.

4.5.1 System Setup

We utilised Lambdalabs (https://lambdalabs.com/service/gpu-cloud (accessed on 27 September 2021)) GPU cloud. Our system consists of two NVIDIA RTX A6000 (https://www.nvidia.com/en-us/design-visualization/rtx-a6000/ (accessed on 27 September 2021)) GPUs, each GPU consisting of 48 GB GDDR6 memory, 200 GB Random Access Memory (RAM), and 1 TB secondary storage. Further, it consists of 28 Virtual Central Processing Units (VCPUS). The GPUs are linked together using NVIDIA NVLink (https://www.nvidia.com/en-us/data-center/nvlink/ (accessed on 2 October 2021)), a high-speed direct GPU-to-GPU interconnect, which improves the performance by allowing faster data exchange.

Most of the ML algorithms can be implemented using a variety of programming languages and libraries, such as Python (https://www.python.org (accessed on 2 September 2021)), R (https://www.r-project.org (accessed on 2 September 2021)), and Tensorflow (https://www.tensorflow.org (accessed on 2 September 2021)). Our implementation uses Python version 3 and the StellarGraph [64] Python based ML library for graph-based ML, which is built on Tensorflow version 2. Further, we use the CUDA Compute Unified Device Architecture CUDA) (https://developer.nvidia.com/cuda-zone (accessed on 7 September 2021)) (version 11.2) parallel computing platform and programming model developed by NVIDIA for computation of the GPUs. During our initial experiment phase, we also used the LEO4 (https://www.uibk.ac.at/zid/systeme/hpc-systeme/leo4/ (accessed on 7 September 2021)). LEO4 is a high-performance compute cluster operated by the ZID (IT-Center) at the University of Innsbruck in close collaboration with the Research Area "Scientific Computing".

4.5.2 Training and Testing

The training and testing of RGCN were performed using the Lambdalabs cloud. The details of the used Lambdalabs cloud system are provided in Sect. 4.5.1. The training of the RGCN model was performed for 500 epochs with 70% of the training data. Furthermore, during the training, different strategies such as dropout and early stopping were applied, which are discussed in detail in Sect. 4.4.4. The testing was performed using 30% of the data. Similar to RGCN, we used the Lambdalabs cloud for experiments using H2O. During the initial stage of the experiment, we also used the LEO4 cluster. The H2O training was conducted using 70% of the data similar to RGCN. Various techniques, such as k-fold cross validation, were employed to control overfitting during the training. The rest was used for testing (15% for validation and 15% for testing). Timing-wise, RGCN training took around 2 h , while H2O AutoML training took around 2.5 h. In terms of testing, the amount of time spent on prediction was negligible in comparison to the amount of time spent on training. The details on training, such as the used hyperparameters, their initial values, and the obtained tuned value after training, were presented in Sect. 4.4.3.

4.5.3 Evaluation Metrics

Evaluation metrics in ML help to understand how accurate a model prediction is and indicate how well the model is likely to perform in an unanticipated scenario. In ML, various evaluation metrics such as mean absolute error, mean squared error, accuracy, and recall exist, and thus selecting an appropriate metric is important. This is because other factors, such as data imbalance, must also be considered. Further, studies [69, 70] have shown that relying on a single evaluation metric is not a good idea, especially in the case of highly skewed data. For example, one can achieve high accuracy by simply predicting the dominant-negative class. Despite the model's high accuracy, we are more likely to predict negative for the positive class [70]. Such cases are extremely undesirable and necessitate the use of additional metrics. Therefore, in our study, we have considered four evaluation metrics: (i) accuracy, (ii) precision, (iii) recall, and (iv) Adjusted F-measure (AGF). Accuracy, the first evaluation metric, is the most common and is a widely used metric that measures the overall correctness of the model. Accuracy can be calculated by dividing the total correct predictions by the total predictions, both correct and incorrect using Equation (4.2). The other metric, precision measures the model's exactness, while the recall measures evaluate the model effectiveness on the positive/minority class by measuring the accuracy of positive cases [69]. Equation (4.3) can be used to calculate the precision, and Equation (4.4) for the recall. The F1 score, which is the harmonic mean of precision and recall, explains how well precision and recall are balanced. However, studies have shown that the F1 score (or F1 measure) does not perform well in the case of highly unbalanced data [69]. Therefore, we considered the additional metric—AGF. The AGF metric is an improved version of the F1 score, which can perform well even in case of unbalanced data and thus tell us how well our model performs [69]. AGF can be calculated using Equations (4.5)–(4.7).

$$Accuracy = \frac{TP + TN}{TP + TN + FP + FN} \tag{4.2}$$

$$precision = \frac{TP}{TP + FP} \tag{4.3}$$

$$recall = \frac{TP}{TP + FN} \tag{4.4}$$

$$F_2 = 5 \times \frac{precision \times recall}{(4 \times recall) + precision} \tag{4.5}$$

$$InvF_{0.5} = \frac{5}{4} \times \frac{precision \times recall}{(0.5^2 \times recall) + precision} \tag{4.6}$$

$$AGF = \sqrt{InvF_{0.5} \times F_2} \tag{4.7}$$

4.5.4 Results and Discussion

Figure 4.10 shows the experiment result. This includes our result from the cutting-edge H2O AutoML framework and the proposed method. Further, the evaluation metrics discussed in Section 4.5.3 are included in the experiment result depicted in Fig. 4.10. The Y-axis in Fig. 4.10 represents the percentage, and the X-axis includes the evaluation metrics recall, precision, and accuracy. Overall, we found that both experiments have high accuracy, precision, and recall. On closer inspection, however, we can see a difference in the result. The proposed method outperforms H2O AutoML in terms of performance by 1% improving result from 99% (baseline H2O AutoML) to 100%. In terms of accuracy, the proposed method, KG-based HD failure prediction, outperforms H2O by 1%. The same is true for precision and recall. We can observe from Fig. 4.10 that the proposed KG-based HD failure prediction outperforms state of the art H2O by 1%. Further, in the case of the AGF, we observe a similar pattern to that of accuracy, precision, and recall. The high value of the AFG demonstrates that the result was not affected (or less affected) by the high-class imbalance.

In addition, we also compared our results with similar state of the art studies. Table 4.7 displays the findings from our studies as well as the compared relevant state of the art studies, which were chosen based on their recentness (2018 or later) and use of similar evaluation metrics. The best results were selected from the state of the art studies to compare. As can be seen from Table 4.7, the proposed KGs-based approach performs better despite our high data imbalance (with only 367 fail drives out of 13,553,809) compared to studies such as [49] (758 fail drives and

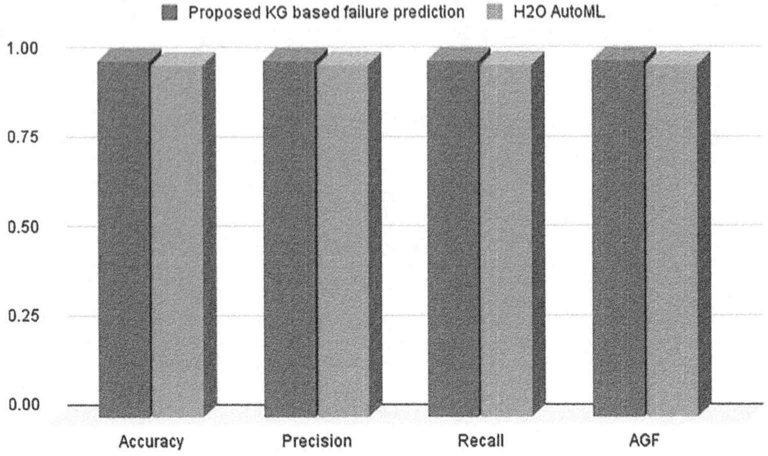

Fig. 4.10 Proposed method versus the state of the art H2O result

Table 4.7 Comparison with state of the art studies

	Accuracy (%)	Precision (%)	Recall (%)	Training Time
Su et al. (2018) [40]	85.84	–	–	–
Zang et al. (2018) [49]	92.6	89	88.7	–
Santo et al. (2020) [50]	98.45	98.33	98.34	–
Han et al. (2020) [47]	–	71.8	37.4	10.6 s (streaming)
Züfle et al. (2020) [42]	97.642	94.913	96.97	174 s, on average
Mamoutova et al. (2021) [24]	–	74	–	183 s–7 h
Our baseline (H2O AutoML)	99	99	99	~2.5 h
Our proposed KG-based approach	100	100	100	~2 h

30,685 healthy drives for the first dataset and 47 fail drives and 7932 healthy drives for the second dataset).

In addition to comparing the accuracy, precision, and recall of our results, we also compared the training time of our solution to that of related work (see Table 4.7). As can be seen in Table 4.7, half of the studies we considered for comparison, with the exception of Züfle et al. [42], Han et al. [47], and Mamoutova et al. [24], did not report training time. Our experiment's training time is significantly longer than Züfle et al. [42] and Han et al.'s [47] work. One of the reasons for the longer time, in our case, is the sample size. We used a sample size of 13,553,809, while Züfle et al. [42] used 68,411. The other reason is that the H2O AutoML approach performs extensive hyperparameter optimisation of multiple algorithms, whereas the KG-based approach requires learning relationships. Similarly, in the case of Mamoutova et al. [24], we observe a significant increase in our training time (compared to Mamoutova et al.'s [24] best of 183 s). However, when we compare our training time to the training time of algorithms such as LSTM, GRU, and LSTM with attention, which is approximately 4–7 h in Mamoutova et al.'s [24], our training time is shorter. Additionally, this demonstrates that training neural networks takes longer.

Finally, the results from our experiment and comparison to state of the art studies and H2O (baseline) substantiate our claim that using a KG can improve failure prediction. This improved failure prediction allows us to detect potential failures prior to their occurrence, allowing us to take proactive action and, as a result, improve the reliability.

4.6 Conclusions and Future Work

In this paper, we described a novel approach for predicting HD failures that combines ML and KGs. According to the evaluation results, combining these two technologies supports context-awareness and helps achieve higher accuracy of failure prediction in comparison to solutions that rely solely on ML. Moreover, the proposed approach can be applied to any other domain that requires prediction tasks, such as disease prediction (or classification). This generality of the presented approach is another benefit of our work. In addition, the use of KGs enables the incorporation of domain knowledge from domain experts and maintains human centricity, a step toward Industry 5.0 [71]. Since different domain experts may hold divergent views, incorporating domain knowledge may introduce bias, which can sometimes result in incorrect decision making. Solving such challenges would entail providing additional domain knowledge. The future work will focus on applying the proposed approach to other domains and industrial settings.

Funding: This research was co-funded by Interreg Österreich-Bayern 2014–2020 programme project KI-Net: Bausteine für KI-basierte Optimierungen in der industriellen Fertigung (grant agreement: AB 292).

Acknowledgements We would like to express our gratitude to the High Performance Computing Center (HPC) at the University of Innsbruck for providing the LEO HPC infrastructure for our experiment. Additionally, we would like to express our profound gratitude to Hermann Schwärzler (HPC staff) for assisting us with HPC-related activities. We would also like to thank Kevin Angele and Elwin Huaman for their assistance and insightful discussions. Finally, we would like to express our gratitude to the anonymous reviewers for providing constructive feedback that aided in the manuscript's improvement.

Bibliography

1. Shun-Feng Su, Imre J Rudas, Jacek M Zurada, Meng Joo Er, Jyh-Horng Chou, and Daeil Kwon. 'Industry 4.0: a special section in IEEE access'. In: *IEEE Access* 5 (2017), pp. 12257–12261.
2. Serge Bonnaud, Christophe Didier, and Arndt Kohler. *Industry 4.0 and Cognitive Manufacturing: Architecture Patterns, Use Cases and IBM Solutions*. Available at: https://www.ibm.com/downloads/cas/M8J5BA6R (accessed on 27 October 2021). 2019.
3. Sule Selcuk. 'Predictive maintenance, its implementation and latest trends'. In: *Proceedings of the Institution of Mechanical Engineers, Part B: Journal of Engineering Manufacture* 231.9 (2017), pp. 1670–1679.
4. Aparna Kumari, Sudeep Tanwar, Sudhanshu Tyagi, and Neeraj Kumar. 'Verification and validation techniques for streaming big data analytics in internet of things environment'. In: *IET Networks* 8.3 (2019), pp. 155–163.
5. Jing Li, Rebecca J. Stones, Gang Wang, Xiaoguang Liu, Zhongwei Li, and Ming Xu. 'Hard drive failure prediction using Decision Trees'. In: *Reliability Engineering & System Safety* 164 (2017), pp. 55–65. https://doi.org/10.1016/j.ress.2017.03.004.
6. Dongshi Liu, Bo Wang, Peng Li, Rebecca J. Stones, Trent G. Marbach, Gang Wang, Xiaoguang Liu, and Zhongwei" Li. 'Predicting Hard Drive Failures for Cloud Storage Systems'. In: *Algorithms and Architectures for Parallel Processing*. Ed. By Sheng Wen, Albert Zomaya, and Laurence T. Yang. Cham: Springer International Publishing, 2020, pp. 373–388.
7. Jing Li, Xinpu Ji, Yuhan Jia, Bingpeng Zhu, Gang Wang, Zhongwei Li, and Xiaoguang Liu. 'Hard Drive Failure Prediction Using Classification and Regression Trees'. In: *Proceedings of the 44th Annual IEEE/IFIP International Conference on Dependable Systems and Networks*. Atlanta, GA, USA, 23–26 June 2014, pp. 383–394. DOI: https://doi.org/10.1109/DSN.2014.44.
8. J. Ross Quinlan. 'Learning decision tree classifiers'. In: *ACM Computing Surveys (CSUR)* 28.1 (1996), pp. 71–72.

9. Oliver Sutton. 'Introduction to k nearest neighbour classification and condensed nearest neighbour data reduction'. In: *University lectures, University of Leicester*. Vol. 1. Leicester, UK, 2012.
10. Raffaella Piccarreta. 'Classification trees for ordinal variables'. In: *Computational Statistics* 23.3 (2008), pp. 407–427.
11. Niko Speybroeck. 'Classification and regression trees'. In: *International journal of public health* 57.1 (2012), pp. 243–246.
12. Jovani Dalzochio, Rafael Kunst, Edison Pignaton, Alécio Pedro Delazari Binotto, Srijnan Sanyal, Jose R. Favilla, and Jorge Luis Victória Barbosa. 'Machine learning and reasoning for predictive maintenance in Industry 4.0: Current status and challenges'. In: *Comput. Ind.* 123 (2020), p. 103298.
13. Thyago Peres Carvalho, Fabrízzio Soares, Roberto Vita, Roberto da Piedade Francisco, João P. Basto, and Symone Gomes Soares Alcalá. 'A systematic literature review of machine learning methods applied to predictive maintenance'. In: *Comput. Ind. Eng.* 137 (2019).
14. Tiago Zonta, Cristiano André da Costa, Rodrigo da Rosa Righi, Miromar José de Lima, Eduardo Silveira da Trindade, and Guann Pyng Li. 'Predictive maintenance in the Industry 4.0: A systematic literature review'. In: *Computers & Industrial Engineering* 150 (2020), p. 106889. https://doi.org/10.1016/j.cie.2020.106889.
15. Wenjun Yang, Dianming Hu, Yuliang Liu, Shuhao Wang, and Tianming Jiang. 'Hard Drive Failure Prediction Using Big Data'. In: *Proceedings of the 2015 IEEE 34th Symposium on Reliable Distributed Systems Workshop (SRDSW)*. Montreal, QC, Canada, 28 September–1 October, 2015, pp. 13–18.
16. Chang Xu, Gang Wang, Xiaoguang Liu, Dongdong Guo, and Tie-Yan Liu. 'Health Status Assessment and Failure Prediction for Hard Drives with Recurrent Neural Networks'. In: *IEEE Transactions on Computers* 65 (2016), pp. 3502–3508.
17. M. Ali, P. Patel, and J. Breslin. 'Middleware for Real-Time Event Detection and Predictive Analytics in Smart Manufacturing'. In: *Proceedings of the 2019 15th International Conference on Distributed Computing in Sensor Systems (DCOSS)*. Santorini Island, Greece, 29-31 May, 2019, pp. 370–376.
18. Christian Krupitzer, Tim Wagenhals,Marwin Züfle, Veronika Lesch, Dominik Schäfer, Amin Mozaffarin, Janick Edinger, Christian Becker, and Samuel Kounev. 'A survey on predictive maintenance for industry 4.0'. In: *arXiv preprint* arXiv:2002.08224 (2020).
19. Anna Johansson. *Machine Learning Is Bad at Context. Here's How We Fix It.* Available online: https://www.computer.org/publications/tech-news/trends/Machine-Learning-Is-Bad-at-Context-Heres-How-We-Fix-It (accessed on 27 September 2021).
20. Anna V Zhdanova, Josip Zoric, Marco Marengo, Herma van Kranenburg, Niels Snoeck, Michael Sutterer, Christian Räck, Olaf Droegehorn, and Stefan Arbanowski. 'Context acquisition, representation and employment in mobile service platforms'. In: *Proceedings of the 15th IST Mobile & Wireless Communications Summit*. Vol. 53. Myconos, Greece, 4–8 June, 2006.
21. Aidan Hogan, Eva Blomqvist, Michael Cochez, Claudia D'amato, Gerard De Melo, Claudio Gutierrez, Sabrina Kirrane, José Emilio Labra Gayo, Roberto Navigli, Sebastian Neumaier, Axel-Cyrille Ngonga Ngomo, Axel Polleres, Sabbir M. Rashid, Anisa Rula, Lukas Schmelzeisen, Juan Sequeda, Steffen Staab, and Antoine Zimmermann. 'Knowl-

edge Graphs'. In: *ACM Comput. Surv.* 54.4 (July 2021), pp. 1–37. https://doi.org/10.1145/3447772.
22. Ioannis Manousakis, Sriram Sankar, Gregg McKnight, Thu D. Nguyen, and Ricardo Bianchini. 'Environmental Conditions and Disk Reliability in Free-cooled Datacenters'. In: *Proceedings of the 14th USENIX Conference on File and Storage Technologies (FAST 16)*. Santa Clara, CA: USENIX Association, 2016, pp. 53–65.
23. Tek Raj Chhetri. 'Improving Decision Making Using Semantic Web Technologies'. In: *The Semantic Web: ESWC 2021 Satellite Events*. Ed. by Ruben Verborgh, Anastasia Dimou, Aidan Hogan, Claudia d'Amato, Ilaria Tiddi, Arne Bröring, Simon Mayer, Femke Ongenae, Riccardo Tommasini, and Mehwish Alam. Cham: Springer International Publishing, 2021, pp. 165–175.
24. Olga Mamoutova, Mikhail Uspenskiy, Sergey Smirnov, and Marina Bolsunovskaya. 'Ontological Approach to Automated Analysis of Enterprise Data Storage Systems Log Files'. In: *Acta Polytechnica Hungarica* 18.9 (2021), pp. 27–47.
25. Dieter Fensel, U Simsek, Kevin Angele, Elwin Huaman, Elias Kärle, Oleksandra Panasiuk, Ioan Toma, Jürgen Umbrich, and Alexander Wahler. Knowledge graphs. Springer, Berlin, Germany, 2020.
26. Hoill Jung, Hyun Yoo, and Kyungyong Chung. 'Associative context mining for ontology-driven hidden knowledge discovery'. In: *Cluster Computing* 19.4 (2016), pp. 2261–2271. https://doi.org/10.1007/s10586-016-0672-8.
27. Nuno Freire and Sjors de Valk. 'Automated interpretability of linked data ontologies: an evaluation within the cultural heritage domain'. In: *Proceedings of the IEEE International Conference on Big Data (Big Data)*. IEEE. Los Angeles, CA, USA, 9–12 December, 2019, pp. 3072–3079. https://doi.org/10.1109/BigData47090.2019.9005491.
28. Shaker El-Sappagh, José M. Alonso, Farman Ali, Amjad Ali, Jun-Hyeog Jang, and Kyung-Sup Kwak. 'An Ontology-Based Interpretable Fuzzy Decision Support System for Diabetes Diagnosis'. In: *IEEE Access* 6 (2018), pp. 37371–37394. https://doi.org/10.1109/ACCESS.2018.2852004.
29. Abderrahim Lakehal, Adel Alti, and Philippe Roose. 'A semantic event based framework for complex situations modeling and identification in smart environments'. In: *International Journal of Advanced Computer Research* 9.43 (2019), pp. 212–221. https://doi.org/10.19101/IJACR.PID33.
30. An Ngoc Lam and Øystein Haugen. 'Applying semantics into Service-oriented IoT Framework'. In: *Proceedings of the IEEE 17th International Conference on Industrial Informatics (INDIN)*. Vol. 1. Espoo, Finland, 23–25 July, 2019, pp. 206–213. https://doi.org/10.1109/INDIN41052.2019.8972295.
31. Qiushi Cao, Ahmed Samet, Cecilia Zanni-Merk, François De Bertrand de Beuvron, and Christoph Reich. 'Combining chronicle mining and semantics for predictive maintenance in manufacturing processes'. In: *Semantic Web* 11 (2020), pp. 927–948. https://doi.org/10.3233/SW-200406.
32. Qiushi Cao, Ahmed Samet, Cecilia Zanni-Merk, François de Bertrand de Beuvron, and Christoph Reich. 'An Ontologybased Approach for Failure Classification in Predictive Maintenance Using Fuzzy C-means and SWRL Rules'. In: *Procedia Computer Science* 159 (2019). Knowledge-Based and Intelligent Information Engineering Systems: Proceedings of the 23rd International Conference KES2019, pp. 630–639. https://doi.org/10.1016/j.procs.2019.09.218.

33. Haithem Mezni, Djamal Benslimane, and Ladjel Bellatreche. 'Context-aware Service Recommendation based on Knowledge Graph Embedding'. In: *IEEE Transactions on Knowledge and Data Engineering* 34.11 (2021), pp. 1–14. https://doi.org/10.1109/TKDE.2021.3059506.
34. Tom Gruber. 'Ontology'. In: *Encyclopedia of Database Systems*. Ed. by LING LIU and M. TAMER ÖZSU. Boston, MA: Springer US, 2009, pp. 1963–1965. https://doi.org/10.1007/978-0-387-39940-9_1318.
35. Marco Kainzner, Christoph Klösch, Dominik Filipiak, Tek Raj Chhetri, Anna Fensel, and Jorge Martinez-Gil. 'Towards reusable ontology alignment for manufacturing maintenance'. In: *CEUR workshop proceedings series (Vol-2941)*. Amsterdam, the Netherlands: SEMANTiCS 2021 EU, 2021.
36. Rajashekarappa and Sunjiv Soyjaudah K.M. 'Self Monitoring Analysis and Reporting Technology (SMART) Copyback'. In: *Computer Networks and Intelligent Computing*. Ed. by K. R. Venugopal and L. M. Patnaik. Berlin, Heidelberg: Springer Berlin Heidelberg, 2011, pp. 463–469.
37. Joerg Schoenfisch, Christian Meilicke, Janno von Stülpnagel, Jens Ortmann, and Heiner Stuckenschmidt. 'Root cause analysis in IT infrastructures using ontologies and abduction in Markov Logic Networks'. In: *Information Systems* 74 (2018). Special Issue on papers presented in the 20th IEEE International Enterprise Distributed Object Computing1 Conference, EDOC 2016, pp. 103–116. https://doi.org/10.1016/j.is.2017.11.003.
38. Matthew Richardson and Pedro Domingos. 'Markov logic networks'. In: *Machine learning* 62.1-2 (2006), pp. 107–136.
39. Olga V. Mamoutova, Mikhail B. Uspenskiy, Anton V. Sochnev, Sergey V. Smirnov, and Marina V. Bolsunovskaya. 'Knowledge Based Diagnostic Approach for Enterprise Storage Systems'. In: *Proceedings of the 2019 IEEE 17th International Symposium on Intelligent Systems and Informatics (SISY)*. Subotica, Serbia, 12–14 September, 2019, pp. 207–212. https://doi.org/10.1109/SISY47553.2019.9111617.
40. Chuan-Jun Su and Shi-Feng Huang. 'Real-time big data analytics for hard disk drive predictive maintenance'. In: *Computers & Electrical Engineering* 71 (2018), pp. 93–101. https://doi.org/10.1016/j.compeleceng.2018.07.025.
41. Jing Shen, Jian Wan, Se-Jung Lim, and Lifeng Yu. 'Randomforest-based failure prediction for hard disk drives'. In: *International Journal of Distributed Sensor Networks* 14.11 (2018), p. 1550147718806480. https://doi.org/10.1177/1550147718806480.
42. Marwin Züfle, Christian Krupitzer, Florian Erhard, Johannes Grohmann, and Samuel Kounev. 'To Fail or Not to Fail: Predicting Hard Disk Drive Failure Time Windows'. In: *Measurement, Modelling and Evaluation of Computing Systems*. Ed. by Holger Hermanns. Cham, Switzerland: Springer International Publishing, 2020, pp. 19–36.
43. Nitesh V Chawla, Kevin W Bowyer, Lawrence O Hall, and W Philip Kegelmeyer. 'SMOTE: synthetic minority over-sampling technique'. In: *Journal of artificial intelligence research* 16 (2002), pp. 321–357.
44. Hong Cao, Xiao-Li Li, David Yew-Kwong Woon, and See-Kiong Ng. 'Integrated Oversampling for Imbalanced Time Series Classification'. In: *IEEE Transactions on Knowledge and Data Engineering* 25.12 (2013), pp. 2809–2822. https://doi.org/10.1109/TKDE.2013.37.
45. Ardeshir Raihanian Mashhadi, Willie Cade, and Sara Behdad. 'Moving towards Real-time Data-driven Quality Monitoring: A Case Study of Hard Disk Drives'. In: *Proce-*

dia Manufacturing 26 (2018), pp. 1107–1115. https://doi.org/10.1016/j.promfg.2018.07.147.
46. Sina Dabiri and Montasir Abbas. 'Evaluation of the gradient boosting of regression trees method on estimating car-following behavior'. In: *Transportation Research Record* 2672.45 (2018), pp. 136–146.
47. Shujie Han, Patrick P. C. Lee, Zhirong Shen, Cheng He, Yi Liu, and Tao Huang. 'Toward Adaptive Disk Failure Prediction via Stream Mining'. In: *Proceedings of the 2020 IEEE 40th International Conference on Distributed Computing Systems (ICDCS)*. Singapore, 29 November 29–1 December, 2020, pp. 628–638. https://doi.org/10.1109/ICDCS47774.2020.00044.
48. Sandipan Ganguly, Ashish Consul, Ali Khan, Brian Bussone, Jacqueline Richards, and Alejandro Miguel. 'A Practical Approach to Hard Disk Failure Prediction in Cloud Platforms: Big Data Model for Failure Management in Datacenters'. In: *Proceedings of the 2016 IEEE Second International Conference on Big Data Computing Service and Applications (BigDataService)*. Oxford, UK, 23–26 August, 2016, pp. 105–116. https://doi.org/10.1109/BigDataService.2016.10.
49. Jianguo Zhang, Ji Wang, Lifang He, Zhao Li, and Philip S. Yu. 'Layerwise Perturbation-Based Adversarial Training for Hard Drive Health Degree Prediction'. In: *Proceedings of the 2018 IEEE International Conference on Data Mining (ICDM)*. Singapore, 17–20 November, 2018, pp. 1428–1433. https://doi.org/10.1109/ICDM.2018.00197.
50. Aniello De santo, Antonio Galli, Michela Gravina, Vincenzo Moscato, and Giancarlo Sperli. 'Deep Learning for HDD health assessment: an application based on LSTM'. In: *IEEE Transactions on Computers* (2020), pp. 1–1. https://doi.org/10.1109/TC.2020.3042053.
51. Alexey Kurakin, Ian Goodfellow, and Samy Bengio. 'Adversarial machine learning at scale'. In: *arXiv preprint* arXiv:1611.01236 (2016).
52. Paul H. Franklin. 'Predicting disk drive failure using condition based monitoring'. In: *Proceedings of the 2017 Annual Reliability and Maintainability Symposium (RAMS)*. Orlando, FL, USA, 23–26 January, 2017, pp. 1–5. https://doi.org/10.1109/RAM.2017.7889647.
53. Chang Gao, Chengjie Sun, Lili Shan, Lei Lin, and Mingjiang Wang. 'Rotate3D: Representing Relations as Rotations in Three-Dimensional Space for Knowledge Graph Embedding'. In: *Proceedings of the 29th ACM International Conference on Information Knowledge Management*. New York, NY, USA: Association for Computing Machinery, 2020, 385–394.
54. Weijie Liu, Peng Zhou, Zhe Zhao, Zhiruo Wang, Qi Ju, Haotang Deng, and Ping Wang. 'K-BERT: Enabling Language Representation with Knowledge Graph'. In: *Proceedings of the AAAI Conference on Artificial Intelligence* 34.03 (7-12 February, 2020), pp. 2901–2908. https://doi.org/10.1609/aaai.v34i03.5681.
55. Michael Schlichtkrull, Thomas N. Kipf, Peter Bloem, Rianne van den Berg, Ivan Titov, and Max Welling. 'Modeling Relational Data with Graph Convolutional Networks'. In: *The Semantic Web*. Ed. by Aldo Gangemi, Roberto Navigli, Maria-Esther Vidal, Pascal Hitzler, Raphaël Troncy, Laura Hollink, Anna Tordai, and Mehwish Alam. Cham, Switzerland: Springer International Publishing, 2018, pp. 593–607.
56. Felix Wu, Amauri Souza, Tianyi Zhang, Christopher Fifty, Tao Yu, and Kilian Weinberger. 'Simplifying graph convolutional networks'. In: *Proceedings of the International*

conference on machine learning. PMLR. Long Beach, CA, USA, 9–15 June, 2019, pp. 6861–6871.

57. Nora Abdelmageed. 'Towards Transforming Tabular Datasets into Knowledge Graphs'. In: *Proceedings of the European Semantic Web Conference*. Springer: Berlin, Germany. 2020, pp. 217–228.
58. Enrique Iglesias, Samaneh Jozashoori, David Chaves-Fraga, Diego Collarana, and Maria-Esther Vidal. 'SDM-RDFizer: An RML Interpreter for the Efficient Creation of RDF Knowledge Graphs'. In: *Proceedings of the 29th ACM International Conference on Information amp; Knowledge Management, Online, 19- 23 October 2020*. New York, NY, USA: Association for Computing Machinery, 2020, 3039–3046.
59. Erin LeDell and Sebastien Poirier. 'H2o automl: Scalable automatic machine learning'. In: *Proceedings of the AutoML Workshop at ICML*. Vol. 2020. Vienna, Austria, 2020.
60. Dirk P. Kroese, Tim Brereton, Thomas Taimre, and Zdravko I. Botev. 'Why the Monte Carlo method is so important today'. In: *WIREs Computational Statistics* 6.6 (2014), pp. 386–392. https://doi.org/10.1002/wics.1314.
61. Daniel Berrar. 'Cross-validation'. In: *Encyclopedia of Bioinformatics and Computational Biology*. Elsevier: Amsterdam, The Netherlands, 2019, pp. 542–545.
62. Justin Gilmer, Samuel S. Schoenholz, Patrick F. Riley, Oriol Vinyals, and George E. Dahl. 'Neural Message Passing for Quantum Chemistry'. In: *Proceedings of the 34th International Conference on Machine Learning*. Ed. by Doina Precup and Yee Whye Teh. Vol. 70. Proceedings of Machine Learning Research. Sydney, Australia: PMLR, 6–11 August, 2017, pp. 1263–1272.
63. Minjie Wang, Da Zheng, Zihao Ye, Quan Gan, Mufei Li, Xiang Song, Jinjing Zhou, Chao Ma, Lingfan Yu, Yu Gai, Tianjun Xiao, Tong He, George Karypis, Jinyang Li, and Zheng Zhang. 'Deep Graph Library: A Graph-Centric, Highly-Performant Package for Graph Neural Networks'. In: *arXiv preprint* arXiv:1909.01315 (2019).
64. CSIRO's Data61. *StellarGraph Machine Learning Library*. Available online: https://github.com/stellargraph/stellargraph (accessed on 15 August 2021). 2018.
65. Sudharsan Ravichandiran. *Hands-On Deep Learning Algorithms with Python*. Packt Publishing: Birmingham, UK, 2019.
66. Chigozie Enyinna Nwankpa, Winifred Ijomah, Anthony Gachagan, and Stephen Marshall. 'Activation functions: comparison of trends in practice and research for deep learning'. English. In: *Proceedings of the 2nd International Conference on Computational Sciences and Technology, (IN-CCST)*. Mohali, India, 17–18 December, 2021, pp. 124–133.
67. Yarin Gal and Zoubin Ghahramani. 'A Theoretically Grounded Application of Dropout in Recurrent Neural Networks'. In: *Advances in Neural Information Processing Systems*. Ed. by D. Lee, M. Sugiyama, U. Luxburg, I. Guyon, and R. Garnett. Vol. 29. Curran Associates, Inc.: Red Hook NY USA, 2016.
68. Kevin P. Murphy. *Probabilistic Machine Learning: An introduction*. MIT Press: Cambridge, MA, USA, 2022.
69. Josephine Akosa. 'Predictive accuracy: a misleading performance measure for highly imbalanced data'. In: *Proceedings of the SAS Global Forum*. Orlando, FL, USA, 2–5 April, 2017, pp. 2–5.

70. Brendan Juba and Hai S Le. 'Precision-recall versus accuracy and the role of large data sets'. In: *Proceedings of the AAAI Conference on Artificial Intelligence*. Vol. 33. 01. Honolulu, HI, USA, 27 January–1 February, 2019, pp. 4039–4048.
71. Saeid Nahavandi. 'Industry 5.0—A Human-Centric Solution'. In: *Sustainability* 11.16 (2019), p. 4371. https://doi.org/10.3390/su11164371.

Optimising Manufacturing Process with Bayesian Structure Learning and Knowledge Graphs

5

Abstract

In manufacturing industry, product failure is costly, as it results in financial and time losses. Understanding the causes of product failure is critical for reducing the occurrence of failure and optimising the manufacturing process. As a result, a number of studies utilising data-driven approaches such as machine learning have been conducted to reduce the occurrence of this failure and to improve the manufacturing process. While these data-driven approaches enable pattern recognition, they lack the advantages associated with knowledge-driven approaches, such as knowledge representation and deductive reasoning. Similarly, knowledge-driven approaches lack the pattern-learning capabilities inherent in data-driven approaches such as machine learning. Therefore, in this paper, leveraging the advantages of both data-driven and knowledge-driven approaches,

This chapter is a copy of the previously published article: **Tek Raj Chhetri**, Sareh Aghaei, Anna Fensel, Ulrich Göhner, Sebnem Gül-Ficici, and Jorge Martinez-Gil. 'Optimising Manufacturing Process with Bayesian Structure Learning and Knowledge Graphs'. In: Proceeding of the 18th International Conference on Computer Aided Systems Theory. Las Palmas de Gran Canaria, Spain, 2023, 1–9. https://doi.org/10.1007/978-3-031-25312-6_70 *Reproduced with permission from Springer Nature.*

Contribution as a first author: The scientific contributions include the following: (i) conceptualisation of the study; (ii) design of the methodology; (iii) implementation of the proposed methodology and execution of experiments; (iv) performing formal analysis and validation of the experiments; (v) data curation and data visualisation; and (vi) writing the manuscript.

T. R. Chhetri, *Improving Decision Making Using Semantic Web Technologies*, https://doi.org/10.1007/978-3-658-45877-5_5

we present a strategy with a prototype implementation to reduce manufacturing product failure. The proposed strategy combines a data-driven technique, Bayesian structural learning, with a knowledge-based technique, knowledge graphs.

5.1 Introduction

Small and medium-sized enterprises (SMEs) as significant contributors in the manufacturing and production industry require ensuring a low failure rate of products to have a healthy production line [1]. Product failure leads to a loss of market share with the increasing competition and customer expectations in the current era of Industry 4.0. Thus, understanding the causes of product failure is essential in order to eliminate the failures or reduce their effects and optimise the manufacturing process.

While manufacturers have made efforts to reduce the occurrence of product failure in SMEs, analysis of the causes by manual inspections is becoming less efficient, expensive, time-consuming and difficult [2]. To address failures occurring at manufacturing with complex processes, diverse techniques can be employed, including data-driven and knowledge-based (or semantic-based) approaches.

In recent years, data-driven approaches have made progress using machine learning (ML) for monitoring, fault diagnosis, optimisation and control. As a data-driven technique, Bayesian networks (BNs) are widely used to access a comprehensive and accurate analysis of complex systems. BNs are probabilistic graphical models to characterise and analyse uncertainty problems through a directed acyclic graph (DAG). The task of learning the dependency graph from data is called structure learning [3]. Although the state-of-the-art solutions (e.g., using continuous optimisation) have achieved learning the structure of a BN with many variables, they are not easily interpretable and informative about dependencies between the variables. In contrast, semantic-based techniques (e.g., using knowledge graphs (KGs)) allow to define the basic concepts and primary semantic relationships in a domain and provide deductive reasoning.

In this paper, we propose and develop a hybrid model for evaluating and predicting product quality in SMEs' production lines and consequently reducing the failure rates. We utilise structure learning to find and represent probabilistic dependency relationships among the variables and then use KGs to enrich semantic interoperability and exchange information between humans or machines. The main contributions of our paper are summarised as follows: (i) we take advantage of structure learning in BNs to reflect the dependencies among variables in SMEs' manufacturing processes through identifying DAGs; (ii) to overcome the lack of semantic interoperability in the extracted DAGs, we employ the idea of KGs; (iii) we generate and annotate an OWL ontology based on the DAG obtained through the Bayesian structure learning process to create a KG.

The paper is organised as follows. Sect. 5.2 provides an overview on the related works. The methodology is discussed in Sect. 5.3, and Sect. 5.4 provides a detailed explanation about the implementation. The evaluation is discussed in Sect. 5.5. Sect. 5.6 concludes the paper and gives directions for future research.

5.2 Related works

A number of studies, such as [4], [5] and [6], have been conducted on the use of semantic technologies and BNs, demonstrating the advantages of combining the two. Existing research focuses on either integrating BNs into existing ontologies or using ontologies to model BNs. For example, Riali et al. [6] extended the ontology (i.e., fuzzy ontology) with BNs to incorporate probabilistic knowledge present in real-world applications. On the other hand, Chen et al. [5] use ontology to model BNs to represent causal relationships between additive manufacturing. Cao et al. [5], similarly, use ontology and BN to investigate dynamic risk propagation on supply chains. A risk propagation ontology is created (or customised) according to the domain and then it is transformed into a BN.

In summary, the work described above presumes ontology to be existing, which can be viewed as a limitation given the dynamic nature of the settings. In an ontology, for instance, all concepts are predefined, and if there is a change in manufacturing steps, such as the addition or subtraction of certain steps, the ontology must be modified accordingly. Our proposed work can account for these dynamic circumstances, automatically generating the ontology and KG, thus helping industry, especially SMEs that are often limited in resources.

5.3 Methodology

In this paper, we describe our approach to manufacturing process optimisation in detail. Fig. 5.1 summarises the approach taken in our study, with details provided in the following subsections.

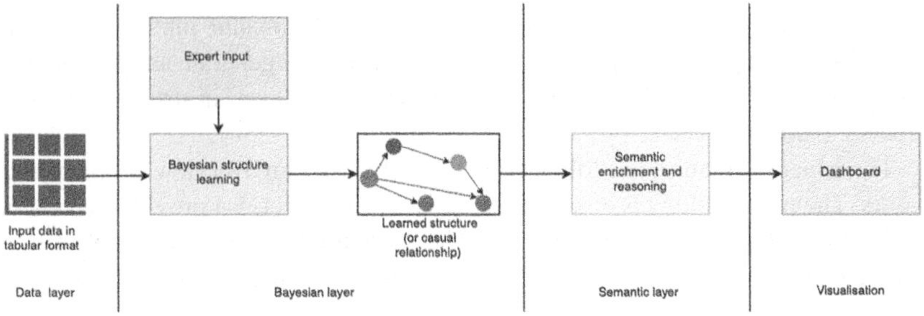

Fig. 5.1 Proposed Methodology

5.3.1 Data layer

The data layer is the first component to interact with the data. The data layer reads and preprocesses the input data. Preprocessing is used to ensure the data quality. For example, the input data for some features may be incomplete (i.e., it may contain missing values). Additionally, the data may include values on various scales. This is because missing values and inputs with varying scales result in suboptimal performance. The data layer's preprocessing performs imputation to fill in missing input and scaling values in different ranges to a common range.

5.3.2 Bayesian layer

The Bayesian layer provides two major functionalities: learning the dependency graph of a BN from data, which is referred to as structure learning; and integrating expert inputs (or domain knowledge), a feature of BN [7]. The Bayesian layer yields the DAG as shown in Fig. 5.1 after performing the structure learning, which represents the learned relationships between the features. The Bayesian structure learning is based on [8] and [9], which perform structure learning by formulating combinatorial structure learning problem as continuous optimisation problems, thereby eliminating the combinatorial overhead.

5.3.3 Semantic layer

The semantic layer enables capabilities such as reasoning and data enrichment inherent in semantic technology. Reasoning makes use of relationships and the deductive power of logic to generate new inferences (i.e., meaningfulness from the data).

Additionally, the use of KG also enables interoperability, which is important when integrating with other external systems. To leverage semantic technology, the semantic layer converts the learned DAG to the corresponding semantic representation, specifically an ontology and a KG. Furthermore, the semantic layer provides reasoning via SPARQL queries.

Algorithm 1: OWL Ontology generator from DAG

Input: DAG graph G as an adjacency list
Result: OWL ontology O, ontology class mapper C_m, ontology object property mapper O_m, ontology data property mapper D_m

```
OWL Ontology ← initialise namespace;
for each unique nodes in G do
  | create an OWL class as subclass of owl:Thing
end
for each subgraph g in G do
  | if g has child nodes then
  |   | create an OWL ObjectProperty class with relation R ;
  |   | assign parent node as domain;
  |   | assign child node(s) as range;
  | end
  | for each node n in child nodes do
  |   | create OWL DataProperty class;
  |   | assign n as domain ;
  |   | assign data type as range ;
  | end
end
Return O, C_m, O_m, D_m;
```

Algorithm 1 (and Algorithm 2) generates (and annotates) an OWL ontology based on the DAG obtained through Bayesian structure learning, in contrast to studies such as [10], which merge the BN into the existing ontology. This is especially advantageous when there is no ontology, which is frequently the case with SMEs. Additionally, this provides benefits, as one can take advantage of semantic technology's benefits without having any prior knowledge of it. Algorithm 1 takes the learned DAG graph G in an adjacency list format as an input. After creating the OWL class as a subclass of the *owl:Thing*, the object property is created, taking into account the connectivity of the nodes in G. In our study, the object property is defined as *isInfluencedByNode*. The *Node* in the object property *isInfluencedByNode* represents the name of the influencing node (or parent node). Our study consists of the two data properties, namely, *isOriginatedFromNode* and *hasInfluenceFactorOfNode*. *isOriginatedFromNode* is a data property of type xsd:string that contains information about how the relationship was discovered (i.e., based on expert input or learned via structure learning). The *hasInfluenceFactorOfNode* property specifies the degree to which the child node is influenced and is of type xsd:decimal. When the relationship is defined by a domain expert, the *hasInfluenceFactorOfNode* has a weight of 1. Algorithm 2 uses ontology information such as class, object properties and data properties, as well as the ontology itself and the graph G, to annotate the ontology and create the KG.

Algorithm 2: Ontology Annotation

Input: DAG graph G as an adjacency list, OWL ontology O, ontology class mapper C_m, ontology object property mapper O_m, ontology data property mapper D_m
Result: Annotated OWL ontology

```
for each subgraph g in G do
    if g has child nodes then
        for each nodes n in child nodes do
            create an instance i for node n;
            create ObjectProperty restriction mapping O_m to C_m in O for instance i;
            insert value to D_m for instance i;
        end
    end
end
Return Annotated OWL ontology;
```

Figure 5.2 shows the ontology generated using Algorithm 1. Fig. 5.2 shows the ontology generated using Algorithm 1. Each of the algorithms for annotation and ontology generation has a time complexity of $O(n^2)$. The ontology and KG instances that were generated are based on the power transformer dataset [11]. We can see in Fig. 5.2 (i.e., ontology) that some classes are not connected. The reason for this is, that structured learning was unable to establish a connection between those disjointed classes. This also demonstrates the inherent uncertainty of structure learning.

5.3.4 Visualisation

The visualisation component provides the user interface for interaction. For example, the visualisation component interactively displays the results of the semantic reasoning, assisting both experts and non-experts in comprehending the variables' relationships. Fig. 5.3 shows the visualisation of the results of the semantic reasoning performed via SPARQL. The semantic reasoning in Fig. 5.3a shows all the KG instances having an influence factor (or weight) greater than or equal to 0.37 and Fig. 5.3b shows the nodes that are being influenced by *Co2* nodes. Moreover, the visualisation also provides an interface that allows one to set the hyperparameters, such as DAG filter threshold, L1 and L2 regularisation, for the structure learning.

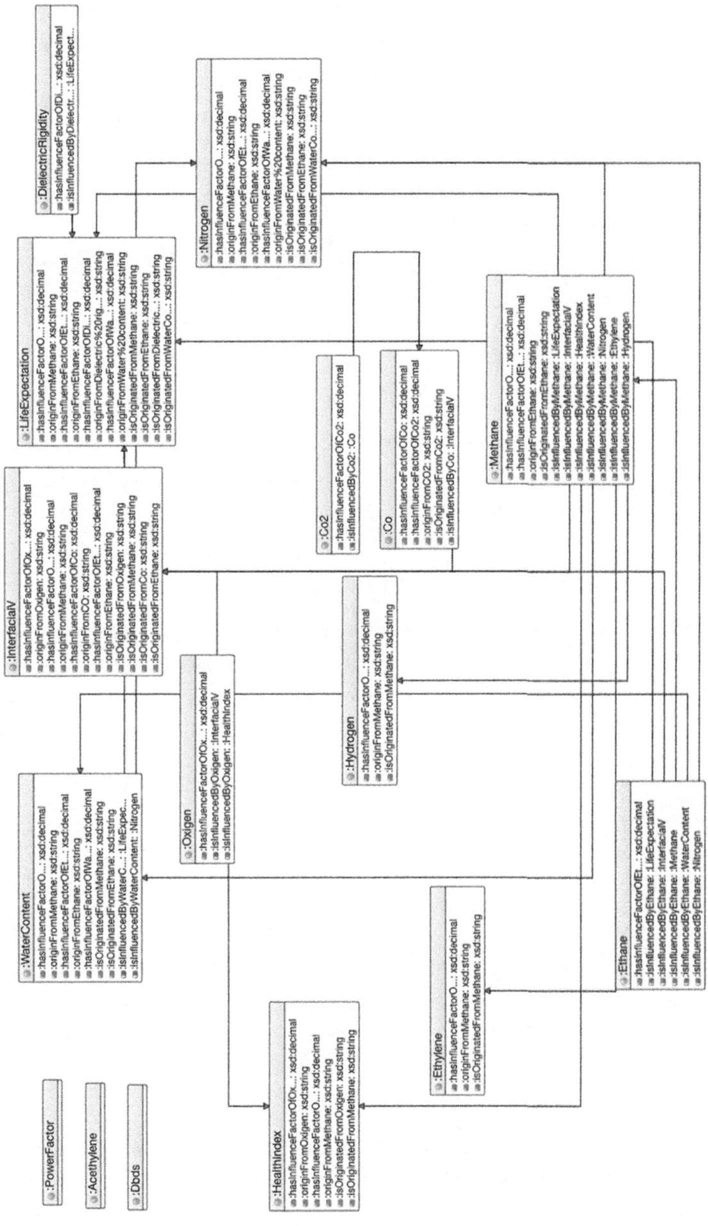

Fig. 5.2 Automatically generated OWL ontology based on DAG learned from Bayesian structure learning

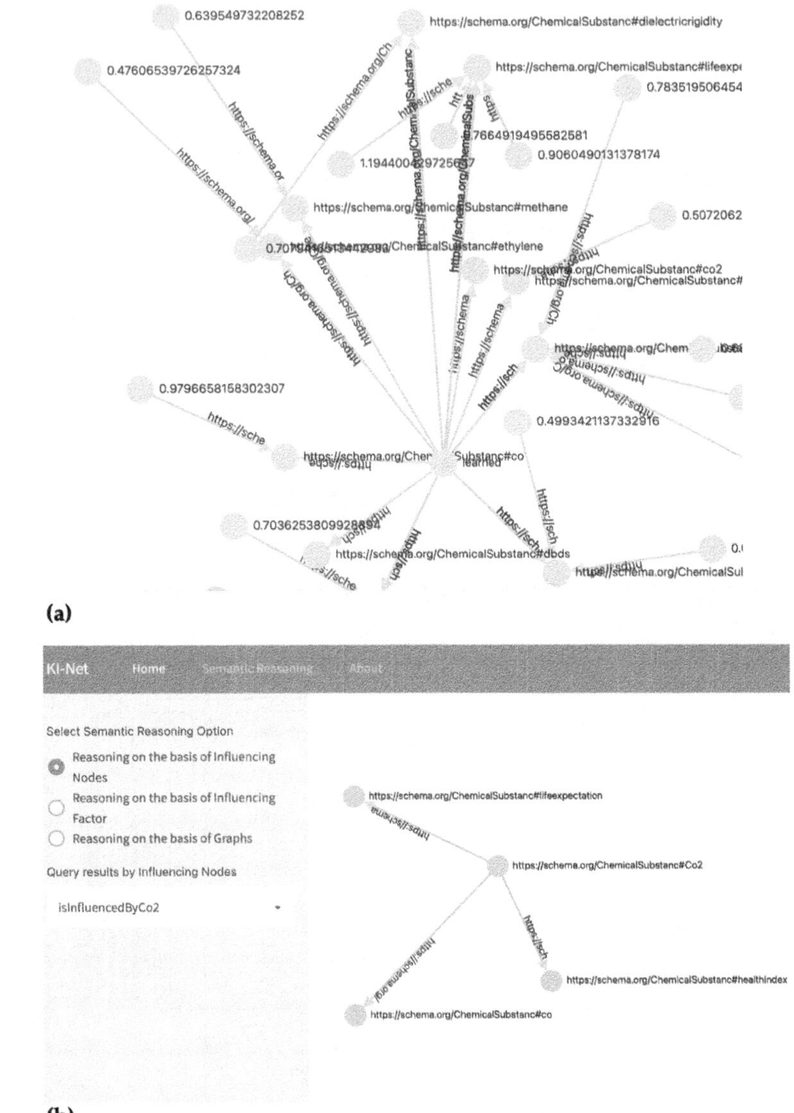

Fig. 5.3 (**a**) Visualisation of semantic reasoning results according to influencing factor (or weights). (**b**) Visualisation of the outcomes of semantic reasoning according to their influencing nodes (or class)

5.4 Implementation

Python version 3.7 and Streamlit version 1.7.0 were used for the implementation of the proposed work. For the implementation of the Bayesian structure learning algorithms discussed in Sect. 5.3.2, we use CausalNex [12] version 0.11.0. CausalNex is a Python library for Bayesian Networks and causal reasoning. Owlready2 version 0.37 [13] was used for ontology generation and annotation as discussed in Sect. 5.3.3. Similarly, RDFLib version 6.1.1 was used for SPARQL queries in order to interact with the KG, and Streamlit agraph was used for the visualisation if the KG and the DAG. The other libraries scikit-learn version 1.1.1, NetworkX version 2.7.1 and pandas version 1.4.1 were used for handling data such as data preprocessing. The source code is available openly on GitHub[1]

5.5 Evaluation

When investigating a product failure, investigators would typically want to know the interdependence of the various manufacturing steps, as well as their relationships and effects on other steps. And since our work is focused on minimising product failure, we evaluated our work by evaluating if the generated KG would answer the question that would arise during the failure analysis. Tab. 5.1 presents the questions of interest for product failure analysis and their respective answers (i.e., how KG answers the raised questions).

Tab. 5.1 Competency questions pertaining to product failure analysis and the corresponding answers

Questions	Answer
What are the interdependencies between the various manufacturing steps (or what are the interdependencies with step X)?	Interdependencies between various manufacturing steps are answered by the object property *isInfluencedByNode*.
How does manufacturing step X influence manufacturing step Y, or what is the effect of manufacturing step X on step Y?	The effect of manufacturing step X on step Y data property *isInfluencedByNode*.
How are the interdependencies between the various stages of production determined? Is it based on expert knowledge or independent data-driven learning?	The data property *isOriginatedFromNode* provides an answer to how the interdependencies were deduced.

[1] Code: https://github.com/tekrajchhetri/ki-net.

In addition, it is essential that the generated ontology is consistent and error-free. This is due to the fact that inconsistent ontology can lead to problems, such as erroneous inferences. We ran the Hermit[2] reasoner to evaluate the consistency of the generated ontology, which confirmed that the generated ontology had no consistency. The duration of the reasoner was roughly 60 milliseconds.

5.6 Conclusions and Future Work

In this paper, we presented our work on manufacturing process optimisation using KG and BN, which, to the best of our knowledge, is among the first attempt to bridge the gap in the industrial sector's usage of KGs in manufacturing. The use of the KG provides the interoperability, semantics (or meaning) of data and further allows for reasoning, which can be extremely beneficial when analysing failures in sectors such as manufacturing. In addition, the application of KG permits interpretability, a benefit that techniques such as deep learning lack.

Future work would consist of applying the proposed method to other domains or deploying it in industrial environments. In addition, one could extend the work by incorporating additional domain knowledge and applying machine learning to KG for improved results, as we demonstrated in our previous study [14].

Acknowledgements The research reported in this paper has been funded by European Interreg Austria-Bavaria project KI-Net (grant number: AB292). We would also like to thank Oleksandra Roche-Newton for her assistance in the manuscript preparation and Simon Außerlechner, system engineer at STI Innsbruck, for facilitating servers for experimentation.

Bibliography

1. Ziqiu Kang, Cagatay Catal, and Bedir Tekinerdogan. 'Product failure detection for production lines using a data-driven model'. In: *Expert Systems with Applications* 202 (2022), p. 117398. https://doi.org/10.1016/j.eswa.2022.117398.
2. Seokho Kang, Eunji Kim, Jaewoong Shim, Wonsang Chang, and Sungzoon Cho. 'Product failure prediction with missing data'. In: *International Journal of Production Research* 56.14 (2018), pp. 4849–4859.
3. Mauro Scanagatta, Antonio Salmerón, and Fabio Stella. 'A survey on Bayesian network structure learning from data'. In: *Progress in Artificial Intelligence* 8.4 (2019), pp. 425–439.

[2] http://www.hermit-reasoner.com

4. Shoufeng Cao, Kim Bryceson, and Damian Hine. 'An Ontology-based Bayesian network modelling for supply chain risk propagation'. In: *Industrial Management & Data Systems* 119.8 (2019), pp. 1691–1711. https://doi.org/10.1108/IMDS-01-2019-0032.
5. Ruimin Chen, Yan Lu, Paul Witherell, Timothy W. Simpson, Soundar Kumara, and Hui Yang. 'Ontology-Driven Learning of Bayesian Network for Causal Inference and Quality Assurance in Additive Manufacturing'. In: *IEEE Robotics and Automation Letters* 6.3 (2021), pp. 6032–6038. https://doi.org/10.1109/LRA.2021.3090020.
6. Ishak Riali, Messaouda Fareh, and Hafida Bouarfa. 'A Semantic Approach for Handling Probabilistic Knowledge of Fuzzy Ontologies.' In: *ICEIS (1)*. 2019, pp. 407–414.
7. David Heckerman. 'A Tutorial on Learning With Bayesian Networks'. In: (2020). https://doi.org/10.48550/ARXIV.2002.00269.
8. Xun Zheng, Bryon Aragam, Pradeep Ravikumar, and Eric P. Xing. 'DAGs with NO TEARS: Continuous Optimization for Structure Learning'. In: *Advances in Neural Information Processing Systems*. 2018.
9. Xun Zheng, Chen Dan, Bryon Aragam, Pradeep Ravikumar, and Eric P. Xing. 'Learning sparse nonparametric DAGs'. In: *International Conference on Artificial Intelligence and Statistics*. 2020.
10. Foni A. Setiawan, Eko K. Budiardjo, and Wahyu C.Wibowo. 'ByNowLife: A Novel Framework for OWL and Bayesian Network Integration'. In: *Information* 10.3 (2019). https://doi.org/10.3390/info10030095.
11. Ricardo Arias. *Data for: Root cause analysis improved with machine learning for failure analysis in power transformers*. 2020. https://doi.org/10.17632/RZ75W3FKXY.1.
12. Paul Beaumont, Ben Horsburgh, Philip Pilgerstorfer, Angel Droth, Richard Oentaryo, Steven Ler, Hiep Nguyen, Gabriel Azevedo Ferreira, Zain Patel, and Wesley Leong. *CausalNex*. https://github.com/quantumblacklabs/causalnex Last Accessed 25 April 2022. Oct. 2021.
13. Jean-Baptiste Lamy. 'Owlready: Ontology-oriented programming in Python with automatic classification and high level constructs for biomedical ontologies'. In: *Artificial Intelligence in Medicine* 80 (2017), pp. 11–28. https://doi.org/10.1016/j.artmed.2017.07.002.
14. Tek Raj Chhetri, Anelia Kurteva, Jubril Gbolahan Adigun, and Anna Fensel. 'Knowledge Graph Based Hard Drive Failure Prediction'. In: *Sensors* 22.3 (2022). https://doi.org/10.3390/s22030985.

Towards Improving Prediction Accuracy and User-Level Explainability using Deep Learning and Knowledge Graphs: A Study on Cassava Disease

6

Abstract

Food security is currently a major concern due to the growing global population, the exponential increase in food demand, the deterioration of soil quality, the occurrence of numerous diseases, and the effects of climate change on crop yield. Sustainable agriculture is necessary to solve this food security challenge. Disruptive technologies, such as of artificial intelligence, especially, deep learning techniques can contribute to agricultural sustainability. For example, applying deep learning techniques for early disease classification allows us to take timely action, thereby helping to increase the yield without inflicting unnecessary environmental damage, such as excessive use of fertilisers or pesticides. Several studies have been conducted on agricultural sustainability using deep learning techniques and also semantic web technologies such as ontologies and knowledge graphs. However, the three major challenges remain: (i) the lack of

This chapter is a copy of the previously published article: **Tek Raj Chhetri**, Armin Hohenegger, Anna Fensel, Mariam Aramide Kasali and Asiru Afeez Adekunle. 'Towards improving prediction accuracy and user-level explainability using deep learning and knowledge graphs: A study on cassava disease'. In: Expert Systems with Applications (2023). https://doi.org/10.1016/j.eswa.2023.120955

Contribution as a first author: The scientific contributions include the following: (i) conceptualisation of the study; (ii) design and implementation of a methodology; (iii) performing formal analysis and validation; (iv) data curation and data visualisation; and (v) writing the manuscript.

T. R. Chhetri, *Improving Decision Making Using Semantic Web Technologies*,
https://doi.org/10.1007/978-3-658-45877-5_6

explainability of deep learning-based systems (e.g. disease information), especially to non-experts like farmers; (ii) a lack of contextual information (e.g. soil or plant information) and domain-expert knowledge in deep learning-based systems; and (iii) the lack of pattern learning ability of systems based on the semantic web, despite their ability to incorporate domain knowledge. Therefore, this paper presents the work on disease classification, addressing the challenges as mentioned earlier by combining deep learning and semantic web technologies, namely ontologies and knowledge graphs. The findings are: (i) 0.905 (90.5%) prediction accuracy on large noisy dataset; (ii) ability to generate user-level explanations about disease and incorporate contextual and domain knowledge; (iii) the average prediction latency of 3.8514 seconds on 5268 samples; (iv) 95% of users finding the explanation of the proposed method useful; and (v) 85% of users being able to understand generated explanations easily–show that the proposed method is superior to the state-of-the-art in terms of performance and explainability and is also suitable for real-world scenarios.

6.1 Introduction

With one-third of the global population (2.37 billion) already experiencing moderate or severe food insecurity [1] and a rapidly expanding global population, which is expected to reach 9–10 billion by 2050 [2], the agriculture sector is under immense pressure to increase food production. This pressure is further exacerbated by climate change, which has led to a decline in soil quality and the occurrence of numerous diseases such as paddy stackburn [3, 4], which have a significant effect on the economy. According to the United Nations Food and Agriculture Organisation, plant diseases cost the global economy over $220 billion annually [5].

Today, modern technologies, specifically artificial intelligence (AI), are used to combat the issue of plant disease. This is due to the predictive capacity of AI technologies, which enables early identification of potential diseases and prompt preventative measures, thereby reducing loss. As a result, a large number of studies (see Sect. 6.2) have been conducted on plant disease detection and classification using AI technologies, particularly deep learning (DL), a sub-field of machine learning (ML). There has been a substantial improvement in the prediction performance of DL, with an increased prediction accuracy of 90 percent (or even higher in some cases) for disease detection and classification [6]. However, DL-based techniques suffer from the explainability issue [7, 8].

To combat the issue of explainability in DL, the AI academic community has been actively investigating mathematical approaches, such as LIME (local interpretable model-agnostic explanations) [9] and SHAP (SHapley Additive exPlanations) [10], to improve the DL model explainability [11]. However, explainability techniques based on SHAP and LIME are not suitable for non-experts (or end users). Additionally, Yang et al.'s [11] study confirms the same: the explainability techniques based on SHAP and LIME provide an explanation from the computer scientists' perspective, not the user's, thereby widening the gap in user-centred explainability techniques.

Agriculture is one of the sectors dominated by non technological experts (or non-experts), such as farmers. Therefore, any technological solution aimed at the agricultural sector, e.g. for disease detection and classification, must be centred on farmers, as they are the end users, in order to be effective. The use of SHAP and LIME based explanations is therefore ineffective. For example, say there are the three input features (or independent variables) A, B, and C and the dependent variable (or target label) Y. Using SHAP, information about, for example, the impact of A, B, and C on predicting Y but not the explanation of Y can be obtained. These SHAP-derived explanations are helpful for understanding model choices, but they are not very useful for farmers (or non-experts), for whom knowing about the disease would be most helpful. Figure 6.1 shows the explainability using SHAP for cassava (Fig. 6.1a). Figure 6.1b (leftmost image) displays the explanations generated by the SHAP that illustrate the importance of the features upon which the predictions were based. As can be observed from Fig. 6.1b, SHAP-based explanations are not useful for users, i.e. farmers. Existing studies, particularly those based on DL in agriculture (see Sect. 6.2), are mostly concentrated on performance improvement and therefore lack user-level explainability. This therefore constitutes the first motivation for this work. However, the importance of the performance improvement made by existing works (Sect. 6.2) cannot be understated. This is because having just explainability would not solve the problem, as the identification of a potential disease must also be correct, which is the other focus of this work. Therefore, both explainability and prediction accuracy are equally important.

The second motivation is the limited contextual information in existing studies and the exclusion of the domain knowledge, such as in DL (or DL-based studies) [12, 13]. Domain knowledge is knowledge acquired by domain experts over time and is a valuable source of information unavailable in datasets like images. Moreover, images have limited contextual information [14]. For example, images lack information about the relationship between plant types, the area they are grown in, and the environmental conditions, such as soil moisture, of that region and their impact on plant health. Both domain knowledge and contextual information help in

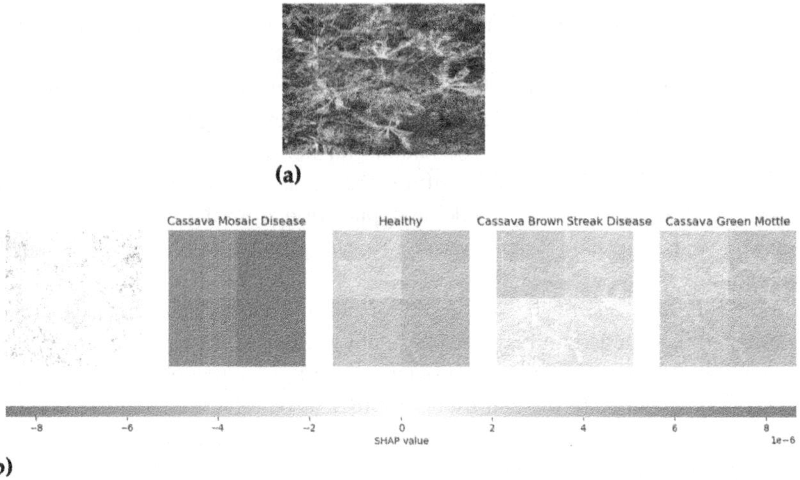

Fig. 6.1 Explainability using SHAP. (**a**) Input image with disease label "Cassava Mosaic Disease" (**b**) The leftmost image with different colours highlights the features that had an impact on the prediction. The four images on the right, labelled "Cassava Mosaic Disease", "Healthy", "Cassava Brown Streak Disease," and "Cassava Green Mottle," are the top 4 predictions

the improvement of performance, support explainability, and ensure the safety of AI by preventing, for example, hallucinations [14]. Semantic technologies, namely ontologies and knowledge graphs (KGs), on the other hand, can incorporate domain expert knowledge, provide reasoning capability, and also enables context awareness to support explainability [13, 15]. Studies have also been conducted using semantic technology for disease classification such as by Lacasta et al. [16] and Jearanaiwongkul et al. [17]. However, such approaches based on semantic technology are limited in terms of their capabilities, such as their ability to learn complex patterns like statistical approaches like DL. Therefore, there is a need to synergize DL-based approaches with semantic technology-based approaches, particularly in the domain of agriculture, so that the benefits of both worlds can be obtained, which are lacking in current work. In the Dagstuhl Seminars report [18], Claudia d'Amato made a similar point about combining symbol-based methods, e.g. methods based on KGs, and numerical methods like ML.

Therefore, to address the limitations discussed above, this paper presents the research to improve the classification of plant diseases by combining semantic technologies and DL. The main objectives of this research are as follows: (i) to generate user-level (or user-comprehensible natural language) explanations about diseases; and (ii) to improve the prediction accuracy of disease classification by incorporating domain knowledge and contextual information, such as effects of soil moisture and relative humidity on plant health, using semantic technology and combining it with DL. This study on plant disease classification focuses on cassava plants. This is because of the importance of cassava plants. Cassava, which is mostly grown in Africa, is the fourth most important staple crop and plays a significant role in the diets of over a billion people around the world [19]. The following contributions are made in response to this study's objectives:

1. A generic approach is proposed to combine semantic technology and DL in order to improve prediction accuracy and generate user-comprehensible natural language explanations using cassava disease classification as a case study.
2. The reusable cassava disease ontology is developed to enable the incorporation of domain-specific cassava disease knowledge.
3. The proposed approach is designed and implemented as deployable software to facilitate reusability and evaluated the proposed method for both performance and explainability.

The remainder of the paper is organised as follows. Section 6.2 presents the related works. Section 6.3 details the proposed approach and Sect. 6.4 provides details about the experiment, including the dataset, system information, evaluation metrics used, and the implementation. Section 6.5 discusses the results and finally, Sect. 6.6 provides the conclusion.

6.2 Related Works

This section provides an overview of the related work. Section 6.2.1 provides a brief overview of the explainable AI techniques. Section 6.2.2 provides an overview of the ML-based studies, whereas Sect. 6.2.3 provides an overview of the semantic technology-based studies. In the review, the studies [20, 21] that focus on the explainability of DL, for example, using SHAP have been excluded as this study is focused on user-level explanations for non-experts.

Additionally, because the focus of this work is on plant diseases, the review of the work only examines related works in this area with particular focus on cassava plant.

6.2.1 Explainable AI Techniques

The majority of the work on explainability focuses on using techniques like SHAP and LIME [22]. Mitrentsis & Lens [23] and Kuzlu et al. [24] use the techniques SHAP and LIME in their work for explainability. Unlike the cases of SHAP and LIME, Toubeau et al.'s [25] explainibility is based on the attention mechanism. However, similar to the case of the SHAP and LIME-based explanations, the explanations of Toubeau et al.'s [25] work are also focused on understanding the impact of input variables on the prediction outcome. Unique to previous works, Bahani et al.'s [26] work uses the knowledge base, which contains the explanations of the target labels, to provide explainability for the predictions made, a work inline to the proposed approach of this study. The mapping is done via fuzzy logic. In addition, new model-agnostic approaches similar to SHAP and LIME have evolved recently for graph neural networks (GNNs) [27] and their variants. Examples of such explainability techniques include GNNExplainer [28] and CF-GNNExplainer [29], where CF represents the counterfactual. Recently, Sammani et al. [30] introduced a GPT (Generative Pre-Trained Transformer)-based language model that can simultaneously make predictions and generate natural language explanations, similar to the research in this study. Two limitations exist: the first is the requirement for large training data, and the second is that the accuracy of the generated explanations may not be accurate due to the hallucinations [14]. Further, Sammani et al.'s [30] approach lacks the benefit that comes with the use of the KGs, which is the ability ot incorporate additional contextual information. Yang et al.'s [31] work focuses on generating knowledge aware explanations for natural language inference using KGs, for which they propose a generative model that makes use of the KGs. In particular, the KGs are used to address the following problems: (i) lack of conformance to the common sense of existing models; and (ii) their lack of informativeness. However, the focus of this work is on language tasks, and their application to a multimodal scenario such as in this study remains unexplored. Moreover, Yang et al.'s [31] work demonstrates the additional benefits that can be realised by utilising KGs (or semantic technology). Similarly, other works, such as the one by Amador-Domínguez [32] focus on explainability to understand the predictions made by ML models. Their work focuses on generating explanations of KG embedding predictions.

In conclusion, the majority of works on explainability are not geared towards non-experts and are primarily concerned with comprehending predictions and the implications of input variables on final predictions. Some works, such as the one by Sammani et al. [30], focus on generating natural language explanations. However, their work lacks the benefits that can be obtained through the use of KGs, and there are limitations such as the need for a large amount of training data. Therefore, there is still a need for further research on explainability approaches that can be both reliable and useful to non-experts, the issue that the proposed work addresses.

6.2.2 ML-based Studies

Emmanuel et al. [6] conducted research on the classification of cassava diseases utilising the pretrained models VGG16 and MobileNet V2. Emmanuel et al. demonstrated the utility of their proposed hybrid kernel methods by attaining a 90.1% accuracy rate. The hybrid kernel methods combine the quadratic kernel with the squared exponential kernel. Similarly, Kumar et al. [33] conducted a study on cassava disease detection. Their work focuses on improving accuracy by ensembling different computer vision models: EfficientNet, SEResNeXt, ViT, DeIT and MobileNetV3. With their result of 90.75% accuracy, Kumar et al. [33] have demonstrated the effectiveness of their proposed approach. Ravi et al. [34] conducted a study using attention-based models on cassava disease classification. Similar to the case of Kumar et al. [33], Ravi et al. [34] demonstrated the advantages of ensembling by achieving the best accuracy of 87.08%, where they combined the penultimate layer features of A_EfficientNetB4, A_EfficientNetB5, and A_EfficientNetB6. The combined final model is called A_L_EfficientNet. In a similar effort to improve the prediction accuracy of cassava plant disease, Ahishakiye et al. [35], proposed ensemble model combining Generalized Learning Vector Quantization (GLVQ), Generalized Matrix LVQ (GMLVQ), and Local Generalized Matrix LVQ (LGMLVQ). Their work achieves an accuracy of 82% (100% with overfitting) using the ensemble model. This work also builds on these findings about the advantage of ensemble models, which in the case of this study combine semantic technology with DL, and addresses the limitations of explainability that have not been addressed by these studies. Paiva-Peredo [36] similarly conducted a study on the classification of cassava disease using pretrained models such as VGG16, RASNET50, and MobileNetV2. A total of 12 different models were examined for cassava disease classification. Paiva-Peredo achieved the best accuracy of 74.77% with DenseNet169.

Similar to other studies, Chen et al. [37] conducted studies on cassava disease classification using pretrained models like EfficientNet. However, unlike other works, Chen et al. [37] proposed a cross-entropy loss and demonstrated the robustness of cross-entropy loss in noisy datasets, achieving an accuracy of 89.3%. This work, particularly the DL, makes use of the cross-entropy loss, takes advantage of the findings of Chen et al. [37], and makes further improvements both in terms of accuracy and explainability. Unlike previous studies, Anitha & Saranya [38] demonstrated the benefits of the data augmentation for cassava disease achieving an accuracy 90%. Their work makes use of convolutional neural network (CNN). A similar benefit of data augmentation has been demonstrated byRiaz et al. [39] for cassava disease classification. Their work uses the pretrained DL model EfficiennetB3 and achieves an accuracy of 83.03%. As with the case of Chen et al. [37], this work also takes advantage of these findings about the data augmentation.

Too et al. [40] conduct a comparative study of the fine-tuning of DL models: VGG 16, Inception V4, ResNet with 50, 101, and 152 layers, and DenseNets with 121 layers, for identifying plant diseases based on images of leaves. According to their analysis of the plantVillage dataset, the DenseNets model outperforms other models, achieving an accuracy of up to 99.75%. Alita et al. [41] also conducted a comparative study and discovered that EfficientNet B5 and B4 were the most effective models on the plantVillage dataset, even outperforming Too et al.'s [40] discovery of DenseNets.

Chen et al. [3] and Ferentinos [42] investigated the plant disease. Similar to Too et al. [40], their research focuses on using plant leaf images for disease detection (or classification) and employs computer vision based on DL. The Ferentinos [42] study uses an open database containing images of 25 different plants, and Chen et al. [3] use the dataset from the Fujian Institute of Subtropical Botany in Xiamen, China. Chen et al. [3] introduced location-wise soft attention to pre-trained MobileNet-V2, improving disease identification. On the other hand, Ferentinos [42] evaluated the specific convolutional neural network (CNN) models, such as AlexNetOWTBn, GoogLeNet and VGG. Ferentinos [42] made an important discovery that CNN models trained on images of laboratory conditions perform significantly worse in the real-world, dropping a success rate (i.e. accuracy of detection) as low as 33%.

Similarly, Nagasubramanian et al. [43], Roy & Bhaduri [44], Abbas et al. [45], Bedi & Gole [46], Ashwinkumar et al. [47], Shah et al. [48] and Sahu & Sinha [49] conducted studies on plant disease detection and classification using images (of plant leaves) and CNN models such as VGG-FCN-VD16, VGG-FCN-S, DenseNet121, and ResNet50. The study of Shah et al. [48], similarly to Too et al. [40], uses the plantVillage dataset. However, unlike Too et al. [40], which focuses on comparative studies, the work of Shah et al. [48] concentrates on interpretability via visualisation. The study of Ashwinkumar et al. [47], on the other hand, proposed an automated model for detecting and classifying plant leaf diseases and used MobileNet and emperor penguin optimiser algorithm. The proposed model was evaluated by conducting a simulated experiment. The study of Abbas et al. [45] focuses on tomato disease classification and uses DenseNet121 and plantVillage datasets. However, unlike other studies using the plantVillage dataset, the study of Abbas et al. [45], in addition to DenseNet121, also employs conditional generative adversarial networks to generate synthetic images to complement the lack of data. Roy & Bhaduri [44] conducted a multi-class plant disease classification using an improved version of the YOLOV4 [50] algorithm, while Sahu & Sinha [49] showed an improvement in disease classification using transfer learning with models such as VGG-16, Inception V3, and ResNet50. Bedi & Gole [46], however, proposed a hybrid approach based on CNN and a convolutional autoencoder (CAE) network, where CAE is used to reduce the dimensionality of the input leaf images and CNN to classify the disease based on the image.

This study addresses the three major limitations of previously discussed studies. They are: (i) not including domain knowledge; (ii) only using the limited contextual information of images; and (iii) the lack of user-level explainability along with the performance improvement.

6.2.3 Semantic-based Studies

Jearanaiwongkul et al. [17] propose a semantics-based system (i.e. system architecture) for identifying rice diseases. In addition, a rice disease ontology [51] was developed by reusing the rice ontology, plant protection ontology [52], and plant disease ontology [53]. The authors further show how the developed ontology can be used given a farmer's observation. However, the presented system architecture is yet to be implemented. Similarly, Lacasta et al. [16] present their work on an agricultural recommendation system based on SPARQL (SPARQL Protocol and Resource Description Framework Query Language) queries for crop protection to help with the identification of pests and selection of suitable treatments. To facilitate the recommendation system, the authors developed the "Pests in Crops and their Treatments" ontology. Rodríguez-García et al. [54] present their research on integrated pest management (IPM), a decision support system for crop pest identification and disease recognition. The purpose of their work is to reduce the virulence of the pests and also to manage the disease. Their work incorporates the CropPestO ontology [55] and natural language processing (NLP) into a symptom analyzer to provide a diagnosis and treatment based on the symptoms provided. Due to the fact that the ontology is populated with information from the official Spanish guide, it is only helpful for Spanish-speaking users. Lagos-Ortiz et al. [56], similar to Rodríguez-García et al. [54], present a decision support system to assist farmers in making effective decisions regarding the diagnosis of plant disease. Similar to other semantics-based studies, their work is dependent on ontology, specifically the phytopathology ontology. The phytopathology ontology is developed by reusing the plant disease ontology [53].

Similar to the case of ML-based studies discussed in Sect. 6.2.2, this work also takes advantage of existing semantic-based studies, such as Jearanaiwongkul et al. [17]. In particular, this study addresses the following major limitations of semantic-based approaches: (i) their inability to learn complex patterns like DL; and (ii) improving prediction accuracy.

6.3 Materials and Methods

This section describes the proposed approach. However, prior to discussing the proposed approach, the ontology modelling will be discussed in Sect. 6.3.1. This is because ontology is one of the core components of the proposed approach and ontology also supports the generation of user-comprehensible natural language explanations about disease. Section 6.3.2 provides details about the proposed approach that combines the semantic technology and DL.

6.3.1 Ontology Modelling

This section describes the ontology utilised in this research. Section 6.3.1.1 describes the ontology requirements (i.e. the ontology's scope). Section 6.3.1.2 describes the ontology's development, which follows the ontology development guidelines from [57].

6.3.1.1 Ontology Requirements

The first step to developing any ontology is to define the scope of the ontology, such as what it covers (or should model). The scope of the ontology in this research is as follows:

- The ontology should cover three different categories (or domains), namely, sensor observations, cassava plant disease, and cassava plant environments.
- The ontology should be able to classify the cassava disease based on the sensor observations information in an understandable manner.

Following the scope, the ontology should be able to answer the competency questions (CQs), which were derived based on the research question. The CQs are as follows:

1. What are all the possible diseases that cassava plants could have?
2. What is the possible disease that cassava plants can have the following symptoms of A, B,...?
3. How is the cassava plant's environment and the sensor observation related to the cassava plant?
4. What are the symptoms of a cassava plant with disease X?
5. What diseases are caused by viruses (or bacteria, or fungi)?

6.3.1.2 Ontology Development

Figure 6.2 shows the ontology, which was developed based on the CQs outlined in Sect. 6.3.1.1. The ontology makes use of the SOSA (Sensor, Observation, Sample, and Actuator) ontology [58], whose concepts are denoted by the prefix $sosa$ in Fig.6.2. Numerous ontologies exist for plant diseases, such as the plant stress ontology[1]. In addition, there is a cassava ontology[2] that models information such as cassava characteristics. The existing ontologies are modelled as exhaustive knowledge sources, which differs from the use case of this study and necessitates the creation of a new ontology for cassava disease. In order to develop the ontology, the disease hierarchy from Jearanaiwongkul et al. [17] study is adopted, in which they modelled the rice disease. The ontology used in this study can be easily expanded to include information from other ontologies, including the cassava ontology and the plant stress ontology. The modelled cassava disease in the ontology of this study is marked by the prefix $cassava - disease$, as can be seen in Fig.6.2.

The $cassava - disease : PlantDisease$ models the information about the cassava disease with its subclass $cassava - disease : BacterialPlantDisease$, $cassava - disease : ViralPlantDisease$ and $cassava - disease : Fungal PlantDisease$ in a similar fashion as [17]. The cassava disease symptoms are modelled using class $cassava - disease : DiseaseSymptom$. To model the information about the field, the classes $cassava - disease : Soil$ and $cassava - disease : Field$ were used. The classes $cassava - disease : Soil$ and $cassava - disease : Field$ are also connected to the sensor ontology for observing specific properties such as humidity. Moreover, the classes $cassava - disease : Soil$ and $cassava - disease : Field$ are also connected to the class $cassava - disease : Plant$. This is because the conditions of the field will have an impact on the plant's disease and are

[1] https://wiki.plantontology.org/index.php/Plant_Stress_Ontology

[2] https://cropontology.org/ontology/CO_334

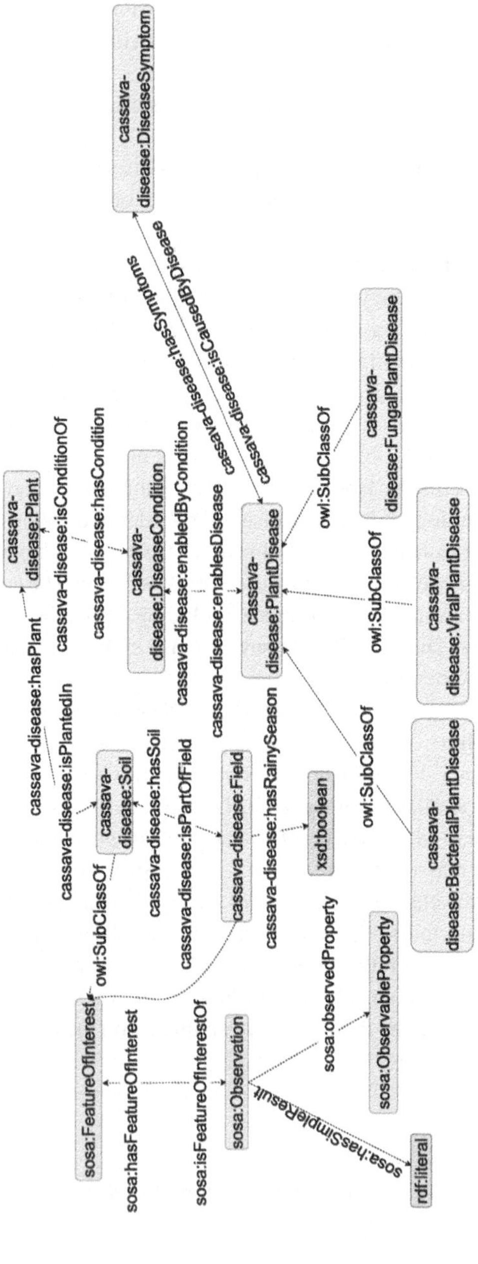

Fig. 6.2 Domain ontology

connected via object properties $cassava-disease : isPlantedIn$ and $cassava-disease : hasPlant$. The concept $cassava - disease : DiseaseCondition$ is introduced to have more fine-grained information about the cassava disease and represents the conditions that are favourable for the occurrence of the disease. The $cassava-disease : DiseaseCondition$ class is linked to a disease with the property *enablesDisease*, and its inverse *enabledByCondition*, which allows to infer the disease given certain disease conditions.

6.3.2 Proposed Approach

This section describes the proposed approach in detail. Figure 6.3 illustrates the proposed method, which combines DL and semantic technology to improve cassava disease prediction and enable explainability. As shown in Fig.6.3, the proposed method consists of three major elements: the vision model, the semantic model, and the decision engine. This is based on a microservices strategy where each component of the software is built separately based on its functionality. Moreover, the proposed approach is also implemented as deployable software following the microservices strategy (see Sect. 6.4.3). The high-level overview of the proposed approach, which is discussed in detail in the subsequent sections, is summarised as follows:

- First, the cassava image is taken and passed through the vision model, which performs the image classification using the vision transformer, from which the prediction result is obtained in terms of the prediction probability.
- Second, the sensor information, such as temperature and soil moisture, is passed through the semantic model, which also performs the classification but using semantic technology, i.e. domain ontology and reasoning using Semantic Web Rule Language (SWRL) rules. Similar to the case of the vision model, the output is obtained in terms of prediction probability. In addition to the prediction probability, the symptoms information and explanations are also obtained as outputs.
- Finally, the prediction results from the vision model and semantic model are combined (or ensembled) using weighted majority voting. In the proposed approach, the component that performs this task is referred to as the decision engine. After combining the predictions, the explanations are generated by fetching the information from the domain ontology.

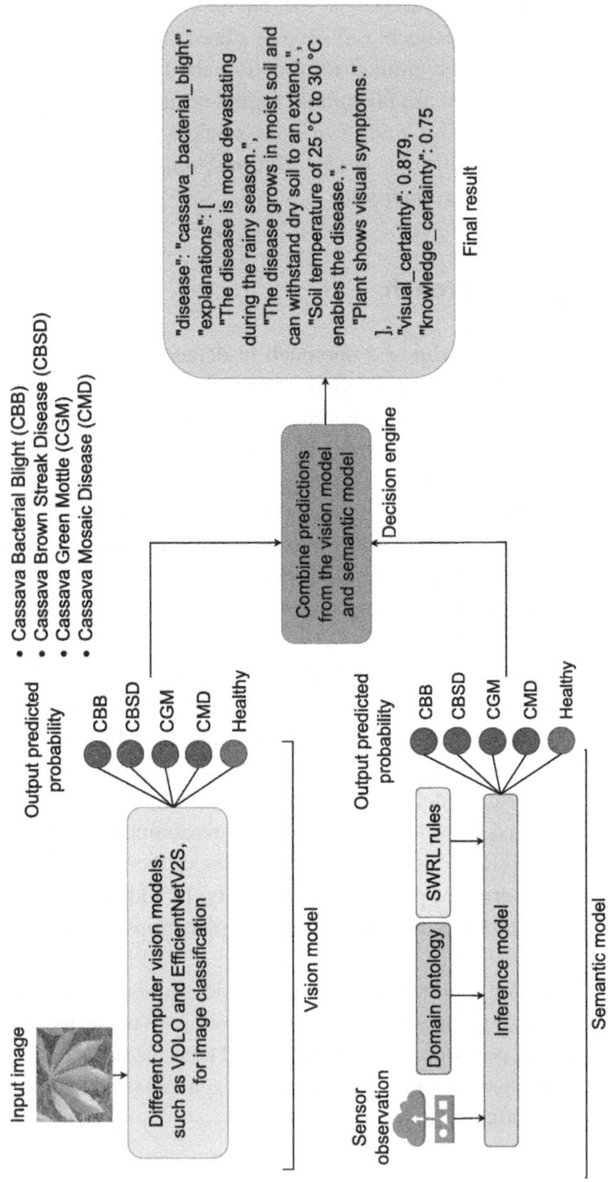

Fig. 6.3 Proposed approach

6.3.2.1 Vision Model

The vision model performs the image classification task, making disease predictions based on cassava image data. This research utilises the vision transformer within the vision model. However, the experiment with other pre-trained models such as RESNEXT50_32X4[3] and EfficientNetV2S [59] were also performed. In contrast to CNN, the vision transformer is the most recent advancement in computer vision and is utilised by the vision model. The vision transformer, via the attention mechanism, enables the modelling of long-range dependencies and provides greater flexibility for modelling visual content [60]. The vision model in this study employs the state-of-the-art vision transformer, vision outlooker (VOLO), from Yuan et al. [60], the first model of its kind to achieve an accuracy of greater than 87% on the ImageNet[4]-1K benchmark dataset without additional training data. VOLO improves by introducing a lightweight attention mechanism that can represent fine-level information based on aggregation and extrapolation and reduces the complexity of expensive dot products (i.e. $Softmax(Q^T K/\sqrt{d})$, where d is a dimension) by linear projection.

The vision model receives the image as input and generates a prediction regarding the plant's health, whether it is healthy or infected with a particular disease. The output of the prediction is the predicted probability, which indicates the likelihood that a particular disease will occur.

6.3.2.2 Semantic Model

The semantic model, as its name suggests, is based on semantic technology and is the second component of the proposed methodology. The semantic model performs SWRL (Semantic Web Rule Language) [61] reasoning over the input sensor observation, such as soil temperature, soil moisture, and relative humidity, using the domain ontology (see Sect. 6.3.1). The SWRL reasoning can be defined as a reasoning that corresponds to finding new assertions $\hat{A} \ni A \in H$ based on the set of SWRL rules R of the form $R = B \rightarrow H$ applied on the domain ontology O of the form $O = (T, A)$, where T refers to the terms (also called the vocabulary) that capture the particular domain and is the union of the classes (C) and properties (P). The $A \ni A_C \cup A_P$ in ontology denotes assertions made regarding classes and properties. The B in the SWRL rules represent the body axioms, also called as antecedent and H, which is also referred to as consequent, is the head axiom. Figure 6.4 shows the snippet of the SWRL rule used in this study, where $hasCondition(?plant, CBBSoilTemperature) \in H$ and the remaining belongs to B. The SWRL rule in Fig.6.4 is use for predicting CBB (cassava bacterial blight)

[3] https://pytorch.org/vision/main/models/generated/torchvision.models.resnext50_32x4d.html

[4] https://www.image-net.org

disease based on the soil temperature (or sensor observation). The inference model component of the semantic model performs the reasoning. Like the vision model, the semantic model yields the final output in terms of probability. In contrast to the vision model, the semantic model also generates disease explanations based on the reasoning result (or prediction) using the domain ontology. Since no sensor dataset is available, the simulated sensor data (see Sect. 6.4.1) are used for the semantic model. Figure 6.5 shows semantic model prediction.

```
Plant(?plant),
isPlantedIn(?plant, ?soil),
isFeatureOfInterestOf(?soil, ?obs),
observedProperty(?obs, SoilTemperature),
hasSimpleResult(?obs, ?result),
greaterThanOrEqual(?result, 25),
lessThanOrEqual(?result, 30),
-> hasCondition(?plant, CBBSoilTemperature)
```

Fig. 6.4 A snippet of the CBB disease SWRL rule based on observations of soil temperature that is utilised by the semantic model for disease classification


```
{
  "cassava_mosaic_disease": {
    "probability": 0.6666666666666666,
    "symptoms": "The disease usually causes the following visual symptoms:
        mosaic, mottling, twisted leaflet, reduction in size of leaves and
        plants.",
    "explanations": [
      "The disease able to adapt to different soil moisture levels.",
      "Soil temperature of 20 °C to 32 °C enables the disease."
    ]
  }
}
```


Fig. 6.5 A snippet of prediction from the semantic model after performing SWRL reasoning over the sensor observation

Following is a summary of the overall steps involved in the semantic model:

- First, inference model component of the semantic model obtains the sensor observation, such as temperature and soil moisture.
- The inference model then populates (or annotates) the domain ontology with the received sensor observation (i.e. creates KG instance).
- Lastly, the corresponding SWRL based on sensor observations is retrieved, and reasoning is performed for disease prediction.

6.3.2.3 Decision Engine

The decision engine combines (or ensembles) the predictions from the vision model and the semantic model to produce the final prediction. The steps involved in combining the results of the semantic model and vision model are depicted in Algorithm 3. As shown in Algorithm 3, the predictions represented by the probabilities from the vision model $(predictionVisionmodel)$ and semantic model $(predictionSemanticmodel)$ are obtained. The predictions from the vision model and the semantic model are then ensembled $(finalPrediction)$. The weighted majority voting [62], as indicated by Equation 6.1, is used for ensembling the prediction results. The reason for considering weighted majority voting is that it allows for fine-grained control over the prediction results, as a greater weight can be assigned to the classifier on which one wishes to rely. This is beneficial in certain situations, like those with poor visibility. For instance, during periods of poor visibility, such as the winter or rainy season, it may be desirable to rely on sensor observations that are not affected by inclement weather, which in the case of this study is the semantic model. This can be accomplished by assigning a greater weight to the semantic model's predictions. i represents the classifier and p_{ci} represents the predicted probability. w_i in Equation 6.1 is the weight of the classifier. In this study, there are two different classifiers: the semantic model and the vision model, and therefore, the value of i in Equation 6.1 is 2. The CBSD (cassava brown streak disease), CMD (cassava mosaic disease), CBB (cassava bacterial blight), CGM (cassava green mite) and Healthy in Equation 6.1 represent different classes (or target variable).

For example, let $p_{vision\_model} = [0.21, 0.05, 0.05, 0.19, 0.5]$[5] be the prediction (i.e. as predicted probability) from the vision model and $p_{semantic\_model} = [0.49, 0.3, 0.4, 0.5, 0.19]$ be the prediction from the semantic model. With only a vision model, the prediction would be $healthy$ and the prediction only based on a semantic model would be the CMD. Now, if the weight $w_{vision\_model} = 0.3$ is assigned to the vision model and $w_{semantic\_model} = 0.8$ to the semantic model, the

[5] The probabilities of occurrence are as follows: CBB, CBSD, CGM, CMD, and Healthy.

resulting prediction would be $Prediction_{decision\_engine}$ = [0.414, 0.232, 0.305, 0.415, 0.275] and the disease (or resulting target label) would be CMD. However, if the weight is changed as $w_{semantic\_model} = w_{vision\_model} = 0.5$, the final prediction would be $Prediction_{decision\_engine}$ = [0.35, 0.175, 0.225, 0.345, 0.345] and the disease would be disease CBB. This weighted majority voting approach used by the decision engine, therefore, allows fine-grained control over the predictions. At the same time, if the weights differ by a large margin, say 0.8 (or 80%), that can have a negative impact on the prediction. Therefore, it is recommended not to have a large weight difference unless one wishes to rely more on one model (or classifier). Moreover it is recommended to utilise the suitable weights and finding the suitable weights necessitates experimentation as the weights differs from use case to use case similar to other ML hyperparameters.

Following the combination of the predictions from the vision model and the semantic model, the final prediction is obtained. The final prediction about the disease is then used for generating the user-comprehensible natural language explanations. The explanations are generated by retrieving disease information from the domain ontology based on the final results of the prediction. The final prediction results, along with the user-comprehensible explanations and the confidence score from the individual vision and semantic models, are returned in a JSON (JavaScript Object Notation) format as shown in Fig. 6.6.

Algorithm 3: Algorithm to combine the prediction results from the vision model and semantic model

Input: Disease predictions from the semantic model and vision model
Output: Disease prediction with user-level explanation about disease

```
predictionVisionmodel ← Vision model predicted probability score;
predictionSemanticmodel ← Semantic model predicted probability score;
finalPrediction ← combine_predictions(predictionVisionmodel, predictionSemanticmodel);
explanation ← get_explanation_about_disease(finalPrediction);
finalResult← combine_results_for_user(finalPrediction, explanation, predictionVisionmodel,
    predictionSemanticmodel);
return finalResult;
```

$$\begin{aligned} & Prediction_{decision\_engine} = argmax_c \sum_{i=1}^{n} w_i p_{ci} \\ & c \epsilon \{CBB, CBSD, CGM, CMD, Healthy\} \\ & i = \{Vision \quad model, Semantic \quad model\} \end{aligned} \tag{6.1}$$

```
{
  "disease": "cassava_bacterial_blight",
  "explanations": [
    "The disease is more devastating during the rainy season.",
    "The disease grows in moist soil and can withstand dry soil
    to an extend.",
    "Soil temperature of 25 °C to 30 °C enables the disease.",
    "Plant shows visual symptoms."
  ],
  "visual_certainty": 0.879,
  "knowledge_certainty": 0.75
}
```


Fig. 6.6 The final prediction result after combining the predictions from the vision model and semantic model along with the user-level explanations about the disease and the prediction confidence of the vision model (visual_certainty) and semantic model (knowledge_certainty)

6.4 Experiment

This section provides details about the experiment. Section 6.4.1 provides information about the datasets and Sect. 6.4.2 provides information about the libraries and system used for the implementation and to conduct experiment. Section 6.4.3 details the implementation of the proposed approach as deployable software. In a similar fashion, Sect. 6.4.4 describes the evaluation metrics, and Sect. 6.4.5 describes training and testing.

6.4.1 Datasets

This research utilises the cassava image dataset made available by the Makerere University AI Lab[6] for training the convolutional neural networks (or image classification). The Makerere University AI Lab provided two distinct datasets for a Kaggle competition, one in 2019[7] and one in 2020[8] [63]. In this study the combined dataset from (2019 and 2020), which is available at [64] is utilised. The combined

[6] https://air.ug/

[7] https://www.kaggle.com/c/cassava-disease

[8] https://www.kaggle.com/c/cassava-leaf-disease-classification

dataset consists of 27053 image samples in total. The dataset, along with the healthy images, contains the four most common cassava diseases: CBSD, CMD, CBB and CGM. The details about these diseases are available in the study by Mwebaze et al. [63]. Figure 6.7 shows the distribution of four prevalent cassava diseases and the healthy images in this study's dataset. From Fig.6.7, it can observed that the dataset contains only a small number of healthy samples, which is 2893, out of the total dataset. Moreover, it can also be observed that the occurrence of the CMD disease is more prevalent, which is why CMD occupies a large number of samples in the dataset, followed by CBSD, CGM, and CBB.

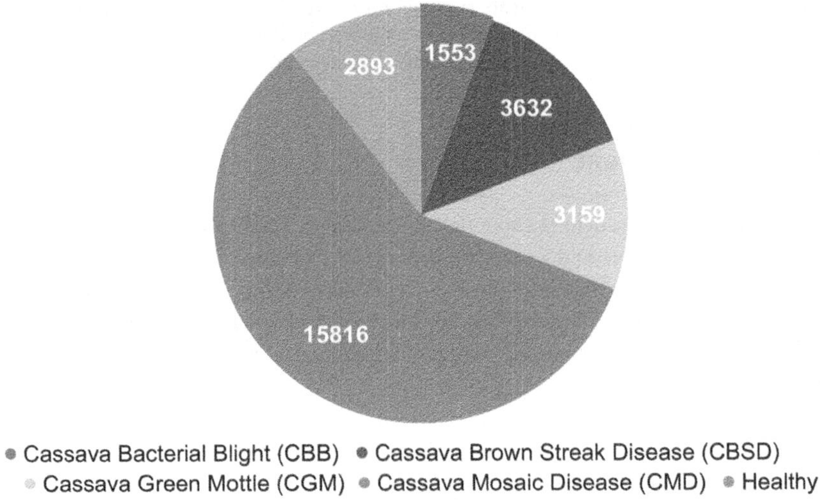

Fig. 6.7 Distribution of cassava image data based on target class labels

The dataset was collected via crowd sourcing from approximately 200 farmers whose farms were located in various regions of Uganda [63]; as a result, their quality varies, making it challenging to perform computer vision tasks. Figure 6.8 depicts the visualisation of the images extracted from the dataset for each disease and the healthy sample. The 2020 dataset contains additional complexities, such as multiple diseases associated with each plant, in comparison to the 2019 dataset [63]. Therefore, the complexity of the combined dataset is anticipated to be greater.

Fig. 6.8 Images of cassava corresponding to the five classes in the dataset, including healthy cassava leaves and four prevalent diseases

The semantic model (or for semantics-based disease classification) requires sensor data, such as soil information for cassava plants, but no such dataset exists. Because of this, the simulated data were generated. This approach to the generation and use of simulated data is inspired by other areas of computer science like cloud computing, ML, and predictive maintenance research, where, in the absence of real-world data, simulated data is generated and used [65–69]. For example, in a study by Chhetri et al., in the absence of target labels in the dataset, the target labels were generated manually following the failure characteristics of the cloud computing environment [70], which is a situation analogous to the generation of cassava disease sensor data in this study. The dataset was created using information obtained from experts about the cassava plant. The simulated sensor data was generated with a uniform distribution range for each of the five classes, simulating the favourable disease condition. On the basis of available expert knowledge about cassava plants, the distribution's limits were chosen manually so that the probability p of a certain condition occurring is $50 < p <= 65$. Moreover, Table 6.1 shows the simulated sensor data for each of the cassava diseases. The minimum and maximum values (i.e. indicated by Min and Max) in Table 6.1 indicate the limits of the uniform distribution, while the $probability$ indicates the likelihood that the input will fall within the specified disease. The lower and upper boundaries (i.e. $Lower$ and $Upper$ in Table 6.1) indicate the rule boundaries used in the SWRL reasoning for semantics-based classification. In the case of "healthy", however, there is no probability value. This is because, for other diseases, the same value of sensor observation can cause different diseases. For example, if the soil moisture value is 0.5, then it could lead to both CBB and CBSD. This is not the case in the case of "healthy" and is the reason for not having the probability value. The effects of moisture, humidity, PH (Potential of Hydrogen), and temperature on crops (i.e. including cassava) have been extensively studied, therefore, the readers are recommended to studies [71, 72] for additional information on their implications.

Table 6.1 The rules that are used for generating sensor data. Moisture and relative humidity are measured in percentage, indicated by the range 0–1, and temperature in degrees Celsius (0–100). The PH is measured in units between 0–14

Disease	Sensor	Lower	Upper	Min	Max	Probability
CBB	Soil moisture	0.3	1	0.1	1	77.78%
	Soil PH	6.5	7.2	6.3	7.5	58.33%
	Soil temperature	25	30	23	31	62.50%
CBSD	Relative humidity	0.7	0.85	0.65	0.88	65.22%
	Soil moisture	0.1	1	0	1	90.00%
	Soil temperature	10	32	5	33	78.57%
CGM	Soil moisture	0.7	1	0.55	1	66.67%
	Relative humidity	0.7	1	0.6	1	75.00%
	Soil temperature	27	40	24	40	81.25%
CMD	Temperature	30	50	24	50	76.92%
	Soil moisture	0.3	1	0.1	1	77.78%
	Soil temperature	20	32	18	34	75.00%
	Relative humidity	0.8	1	0.7	1	66.67%
Healthy	Soil moisture	–	–	0.2	0.8	–
	Soil moisture	–	–	0.2	0.8	–
	Soil temperature	–	–	5	40	–
	Relative humidity	–	–	0.2	0.8	–
	temperature	–	–	10	50	–
	Soil PH	–	–	3	10	–

6.4.2 System Setup

This section describes the software and libraries utilised in the implementation of the proposed system. In addition, this section includes details about the systems used to conduct the experiment.

Table 6.2 Overall configuration of the LEO4

Node type	Nodes	Cores/Nodes	Memory/Nodes	GPUs
Standard	44	28 × Broadwell	64 GB	–
Big memory	4	28 × Broadwell	512 GB	–
Fat memory	1	80 × Skylake	3000 GB	–
GPU	1	28 × Skylake	384 GB	4 × Nvidia Tesla V100

Table 6.3 Specification of Nvidia Tesla V100 GPU used in LEO4

Performance	Double precision	7.8 TFlop/s (Teraflops per second)
	Single precision	15.7 TFlop/s
	Tensor	31.3 TFlop/s
		125 TFlop/s
Interconnect	NVLINK	300GB/s
Memory	Capacity	32GB
	Bandwidth	900GB/s

Table 6.4 shows the list of the libraries and software that were utilised to implement the proposed work. The implementation is performed in the Python[9] programming language. Docker[10], FastAPI[11], and Requests[12] are used to modularise the implementation. Owlready2[13] is used to deal with the semantic model, namely, ontologies and KGs, and to perform reasoning. PyTorch[14] is used for the implementation of the vision model and BentoML[15] is used for model serving purposes. The library timm [16] is used for model implementations and ImageNet weights.

[9] https://www.python.org/

[10] https://www.docker.com/

[11] https://fastapi.tiangolo.com/

[12] https://requests.readthedocs.io/en/latest/

[13] https://owlready2.readthedocs.io/en/v0.37/

[14] https://pytorch.org/

[15] https://docs.bentoml.org/en/latest/

[16] https://timm.fast.ai/

Table 6.4 A list of the libraries and software used to implement the proposed method

Libraries/Software	Version
Python	3.10
Docker	20.10
Owlready2	0.37
FastAPI	0.75.1
Requests	2.27.1
BentoML	1.0.0a7
PyTorch	1.12.0
timm	0.6.5

The supercomputer LEO4[17] is used to perform the experiment. LEO4 is a high performance compute cluster at the University of Innsbruck. Table 6.2 shows the overall configuration of the LEO4. LEO4 consists of a total of 50 nodes totalling 1452 cores and a total memory of 8.4 terabytes. LEO4 is powered by either Broadwell or Skylake Intel Xeon processors. Similarly, the LEO4 GPU (graphics processing unit) node utilised in the experiment consists of 4 Nvidia Tesla V100[18] GPUs with a total memory of 384 GB (gigabytes) per node. Table 6.3 shows the detail specification of the LEO4 GPU, Nvidia Tesla V100[19] providing details on performance, memory and interconnectivity. In particular, GPU used in LEO4 has NVLink[20] connectivity for high-speed data transfer. Moreover, the LEO4 uses a high-performance, low latency 100 Gb/s (gigabits per second) infiniband interconnect for MPI (Message Passing Interface) communications in order to communicate between nodes and GPFS (General Parallel File System) file system.

6.4.3 Implementation

This section describes the implementation details of the proposed approach as deployable software to facilitate the reusability and accessibility of the proposed work in real-world deployment scenarios. The implementation follows the

17 https://www.uibk.ac.at/zid/systeme/hpc-systeme/leo4/

18 https://www.nvidia.com/en-us/data-center/v100/

19 https://www.uibk.ac.at/zid/systeme/hpc-systeme/common/software/leo-gpu.html

20 https://www.nvidia.com/en-us/data-center/nvlink/

microservices strategy (or architecture). This is because of the scalability that microservices offer. The microservices allow scaling of the individual components independently. With the microservices architecture, for instance, compute-intensive system components can be deployed on high-performance servers or cloud systems. The source code for the implementation and other resources, such as ontology, are available at [73].

For the implementation of the vision model service, BentoML is used, which is an open-source model serving framework at a production scale and provides easy deployment of the ML models[21] [§§§]. The implementation of BentoML for model serving includes the following steps: (i) saving the trained model weight with BentoML; (ii) defining the service configuration, such as defining the API (Application Programming Interface) service for prediction using the @svc.api decorator; and (ii) performing input image preprocessing, such as resizing. The runner is then invoked, which translates the API definition into an HTTP (Hypertext Transfer Protocol) endpoint `/predict` for making a prediction.

The semantic model (or semantic classifier) REST (Representational State Transfer) Service implementation makes use of libraries such as FastAPI and Owlready2 and the domain ontology. The semantic model consists of the three endpoints. `/soils/{soil_id}/observations` is used for sensor observations of soil data, such as soil temperature. The second endpoint, `/fields/{field_id}/observations`, is used for observations in the field, such as whether it rained. The endpoint `/plants/{plant_id}/disease-vector` is used to retrieve the specific disease information about the particular plant based on its unique identifier (ID). The ID in this study is initialised as a number between 1–6. Using the domain ontology and SWRL reasoning, the disease information is retrieved. Pellet Reasoner available in Owlready2 is used to perform the reasoning. In addition, in order to prevent any unnecessary inconsistencies in predictions, the previous observations are deleted. The domain ontology, which is saved as OWL file, is loaded at service startup and stored in an internal triple store.

The decision engine, which is implemented as another service component, consists of the realisation of the decision engine steps outlined in Sect. 6.3.2. The decision engine takes the image and plant information as an input and calls REST endpoints `/predict` and `/plants/{plant_id}/disease-vector` from the image classifier service component and semantic models service component to obtain the predictions. The obtained predictions are then combined to produce the final prediction along with their explanations. The relevant information is retrieved from the domain ontology and the explanations are generated based on the obtained predictions.

6.4.4 Evaluation Metrics

In ML, the evaluation metrics help to understand the performance of the model (or how well the model is likely to perform) in an untested scenario. In this study, the evaluation of the proposed approach is made in terms of accuracy and prediction latency to make the inference.

6.4.4.1 Accuracy, Precision, Recall and F1 Score:

The accuracy measures the overall correct predictions made by the model. Precision, also known as the positive predicted value, measures the model's exactness, i.e. the proportion of positives correctly identified, whereas recall measures the actual positives correctly identified. Recall is also known as sensitivity or the rate of true positives. The F1 score represents the harmonic mean of the precision and recall.

Accuracy, precision, recall and F1 score can be calculated using Equations 6.2, 6.3, 6.4 and 6.5 respectively. In Equations 6.2, 6.3, and 6.4, the TP stands for the true positive value and the TN for the true negative. In the same way, FP in represents a false positive, and FN is a false negative. True positives and true negatives are values that the model accurately predicts for both the positive and negative class labels, in this case, cassava disease and healthy. The false positive, on the other hand, is the prediction that is identified by the model as positive while in reality, it is not. The false negative, however, is similar to the false positive but for the negative class.

$$Accuracy = \frac{TP + TN}{TP + TN + FP + FN} \tag{6.2}$$

$$Precision = \frac{TP}{TP + FP} \tag{6.3}$$

$$Recall = \frac{TP}{TP + FN} \tag{6.4}$$

$$F1 \quad Score = 2 \times \frac{Precision \times Recall}{Precision + Recall} \tag{6.5}$$

6.4.4.2 Prediction Latency:

The prediction latency quantifies the time required to make a prediction. The prediction latency is measured by calculating the difference between the invocation and response time using Equation 6.6. The t_i in Equation 6.6 represents the prediction invocation time and t_r is the response time.

$$Latency_{prediction} = t_i - t_r \tag{6.6}$$

6.4.5 Training and Testing

This section describes the training and testing of the different pre-trained models, RESNEXT50 [74], EfficientNetV2S [75] and VOLO, that were experimented with. These models, RESNEXT50, EfficientNetV2S, and VOLO, were chosen based on their superior performance, which has been shown in earlier studies such as Chen et al. [37] and Ravi et al. [34]. In addition, this section describes the testing of the proposed method that combines the predictions from the vision model and the semantic model.

The training and testing of the different pre-trained models, VOLO, EfficientNetV2S and RESNEXT50 was performed using the cassava image dataset (see Sect. 6.4.1). 80% of the dataset was used for training, and the remaining 20% was used for testing. Figure 6.9 illustrates the distribution of the test data, which demonstrates that, similar to the original dataset, the test data is unbalanced. Transfer learning was utilised for the model's training using Pytorch. Similarly, the library timm was used to load the model and pretrained ImageNet weights. The hyperparameters used for different pre-trained models for training are specified in Table 6.5. The values of the hyperparameters in this study were determined based on experimentation and the authors' prior experience with ML research [13, 70]. The training was performed over 10 epochs with a batch size of 32 for RESNEXT50_32X4D and

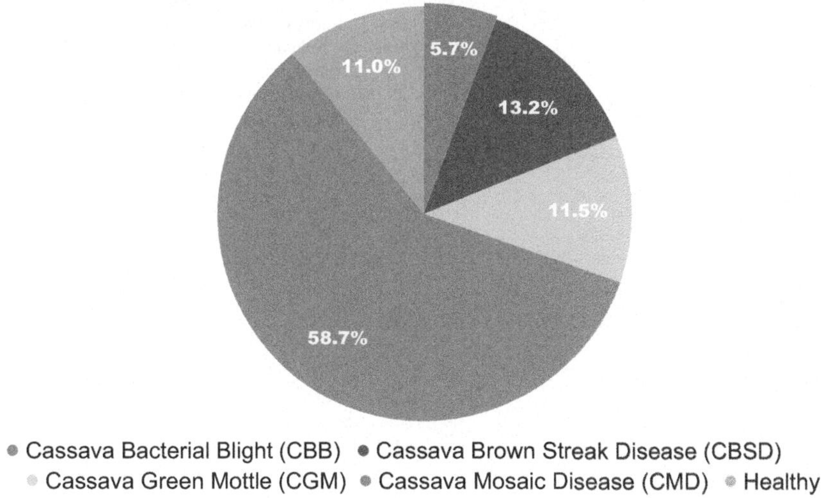

Fig. 6.9 Class-based distribution of test cassava image data

16 for EfficientNetV2S and VOLO. The other significant criterion is the learning rate, which determines the success of the learning process (how well the algorithm learns). The Adam optimiser[21] with a learning rate of 10^{-4} and weight decay of 10^{-6} is employed. The Adam optimiser is an adaptive learning rate optimiser capable of handling dynamic situations, such as a loss that is either increasing or decreasing. Moreover, the learning rate scheduler is also used with a cosine annealing schedule with warm restarts [76]. As a loss function, the Taylor Cross Entropy Loss [77] with label smoothing [78] is used, which has been demonstrated to be robust against the noisy dataset [37]. A value of 0.05 is used for label smoothing. Additionally, following the findings of the previous works, the different data augmentation techniques are used, details of which are available in Table 6.5. In the case of the semantic models, however, no training is required as the semantic models are based on SWRL rules and the rules are defined manually.

Table 6.5 Hyperparameters of various CNN-based vision models and a vision transformer, where LR is the learning rate, p is the probability, std is the standard deviation, T_0 represents the number of iterations for the first restart, T_mult is a factor increase for T_i after restart, and eta_min is the minimum LR

Model	Batch size	Hyperparameters			
		LR	Loss	LR scheduling	Data augmentation
RESNEXT50_-32X4D	32	1.00E-04	Taylor cross entropy loss with label smoothing	Cosine annealing warm restarts scheduling with T_0=10, T_mult=1, and eta_min=1e-6	RandomResizedCrop HorizontalFlip(p = 0.5) Transpose(p = 0.5) VerticalFlip(p = 0.5) ShiftScaleRotate(p = 0.5) Normalize(mean = [0.485, 0.456, 0.406], std = [0.229, 0.224, 0.225])
EfficientNetV2S (256x256)	16				
EfficientNetV2S (384x384)	16				
VOLO-D1 (224x224)	16				
VOLO-D2 (224x224)	16				
VOLO-D1 (384x384)	16				
VOLO-D2 (384x384)	16				

[21] https://pytorch.org/docs/stable/generated/torch.optim.Adam.html

In the case of the testing, however, different levels of testing were performed. The different tests that were performed are presented below.

1. The first test are conducted on the various pre-trained computer vision models that are being examined. 20% of the test cassava dataset was used for this purpose.
2. The second evaluation concerned the proposed method, which combines a semantic model and a vision model to improve the accuracy of disease predictions and provide user-level disease explanations. As different computer vision models are experimented with, the one with the highest performance is selected (evaluated in Step 1) to combine with the semantic model. The explainability was evaluated qualitatively using three identified dimensions: (i) correctness, i.e. if the generated explanations are correct; (ii) usefulness, i.e. whether the generated explanations are helpful to the users; and (iii) comprehension, i.e. whether the generated explanations are understandable to the users. The accuracy of the explanations was manually examined by inspecting the explanations that were generated. Regarding the remaining two dimensions, comprehension and usefulness, an online survey[22] was conducted. The survey asked participants if they were able to understand the SHAP-based explanations as well as the explanations provided by the proposed approach. The survey also asked about the usefulness of these explanations, both based on SHAP and the proposed method in terms of understanding the disease. In addition to questions about explanability, the survey also asked questions related to demographics, age groups, and education. The details of how the survey is conducted and the evaluations will be presented in Sect. 6.5
3. The third test is about latency. As this study implements the proposed approach into a fully deployable system (see Sect. 6.4.3), the prediction latency is also evaluated.

The results of the tests conducted will be discussed in Sect. 6.5.

6.5 Results and Discussion

This section provides the experimental results from the experiment in this study. Moreover, this study also provides a comparison of the experimental results with the state-of-the-art study.

---

[22] The survey questions are available in GitHub where the code is stored.

As discussed in Sect. 6.4.5, the first evaluation is about pre-trained models. Table 6.6 shows the accuracy of the vision transformer, VOLO, and also other CNN models, such as EfficientNetV2S and RESNEXT50, that were experimented with. In the result of the vision model, only the accuracy score of the models experimented with except for the best model, for which the precision, recall, and f1 score were also recorded. The reason for only recording accuracy, despite the fact that sometimes accuracy can be deceptive, is because of the test data distribution (see Sect. 6.4.5), which is unbalanced but not in such a manner that it can lead to deceptive results. This is also consistent with other studies [36, 37] that are used for comparison with the work of this study, which also only records accuracy. From Table 6.6, it can be observed that the VOLO (or vision transformer) clearly outperforms the corresponding CNN models. The other interesting observation that can be made is that the VOLO is also the model with the lowest performance. The VOLO-D1 with an image size of 224 is the model with the lowest performance, while the VOLO-D2 with an image size of 384 is the model with the highest performance. Moreover, the precision, recall, and F1 scores for the best performing model, VOLO-D2, are 0.828, 0.807, and 0.818, respectively, indicating the robustness of the model. However, the accuracy of the VOLO in this study is consistent with the original study, in which VOLO-D1 was the lowest performing model. The second best-performing model is EfficientNetV2S, with an image size of 384. This is similar to the VOLO where both VOLO-D1 and VOLO-D2 with an image size of 384 are performing better. This is because as the size gets smaller, the features get lost and have an impact on the performance as observed. The EfficientNetV2S and RESNEXT50, with an image size of 256, have a comparable performance with a small variation of 0.0063%. The best performing VOLO model makes an improvement of 0.012% compared to the best performing EfficientNetV2S model and an improvement of 0.024% compared to that of RESNEXT50.

Table 6.6 A performance comparison of various CNN-based vision models and a vision transformer

Model	Image size	Accuracy (%)
RESNEXT50_32X4D	256x256	0.8721
EfficientNetV2S	256x256	0.8785
EfficientNetV2S	384x384	0.8840
VOLO-D1	224x224	0.8256
VOLO-D2	224x224	0.8764
VOLO-D1	384x384	0.8914
VOLO-D2	**384x384**	**0.8964**

Figure 6.10 likewise shows the confusion matrix of the VOLO (best performing) model and Table 6.7 shows the individual class-level performance evaluation of VOLO. As can be observed from the confusion matrix and also from the precision and recall, there is still high misclassification. For example, the higher accuracy can be seen in the case of CBB but a huge drop in precision and recall. This is because of the class imbalance. A similar observation has been made by Paiva-Peredo [36] and Chen et al. [37] in their study, observing misclassification due to a large class imbalance. In the case of CMD, however, no such drop is observed, all precision, recall, and accuracy are higher, greater than or equal to 94%. However, upon close observation of the precision and recall, there is no significant difference between them, indicating no case of overfitting or underfitting. Moreover, similar conclusions can be drawn from the F1 score. The reason for this is that the dataset that is used in this study contains noisy data. The images were taken by farmers and have different lighting conditions, for example, and therefore, have an impact on the performance. Moreover, studies such as [42] have demonstrated that the accuracy of computer vision models in real-world datasets can drop as low as 33 percent.

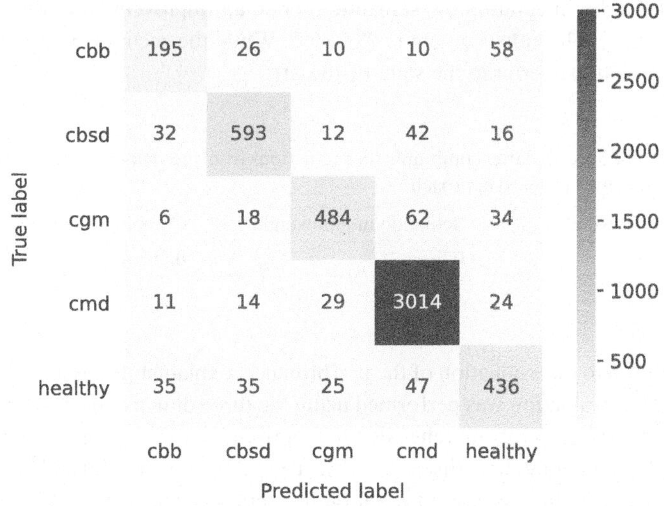

Fig. 6.10 Confusion matrix of the VOLO-D2 model with an image size of 384x384, i.e., the best performing vision model

Table 6.7 Individual class-level performance evaluation of the VOLO-D2 model with an image size of 384x384, i.e., the best performing vision model

Class name	Precision	Recall	Accuracy	F1-score
CBB	0.699	0.652	0.964	0.675
CBSD	0.864	0.853	0.963	0.859
CGM	0.864	0.801	0.963	0.831
CMD	0.949	0.975	0.955	0.962
Healthy	0.768	0.754	0.948	0.761

As discussed in Sect. 6.4.5, the second evaluation focuses on the proposed method, which is to combine the vision model with the semantic model. For this, the best performing vision model is taken, which in the case of this study is VOLO-D2 with an image size of 384x384 (or VOLO-D2@384x384). Table 6.8 shows the accuracy after combining the vision model with the semantic model. Moreover, Table 6.8 also shows the weight that is used for weighted majority voting. As can be clearly observed that by integrating the semantic model, an improvement in the accuracy has been made. The enhancement is 0.0086%. While the accuracy improvement is modest, it is still superior to the state-of-the-art.

Table 6.8 The accuracy after combining the predictions from the vision model and the semantic model, i.e., the proposed approach

Vision model weight	Semantic model weight	Combined accuracy
0.5	0.5	**0.905**

In addition to the evaluation of the performance, explainability is also evaluated. A qualitative evaluation was performed using the three dimensions: (i) correctness; (ii) usefulness; and (iii) comprehension to determine whether the generated natural language explanations about disease (see Sect. 6.3.2.3) were helpful and informative enough to convey the disease information to users. For correctness, the generated explanations were checked by manually inspecting the explanations by the authors and comparing the explanations against the information present in the ontology, as the explanations were based on the information present in the ontology. The generated explanations were found to be correct (100%) and aligned with the predictions. The second dimension is usefulness, where the generated explanations were evaluated to see whether they were informative enough. The comprehension dimension is the third. This evaluation examines the generated natural language explanations to determine if they are sufficiently comprehensive and written in a natural language that avoids technical jargon that is incomprehensible to non-expert users. Regarding the evaluation of the second and third dimensions, i.e. usefulness and comprehension, an online survey was conducted following the study by Ball [79]. Figure 6.11 depicts the steps taken to assess the second and third dimensions.

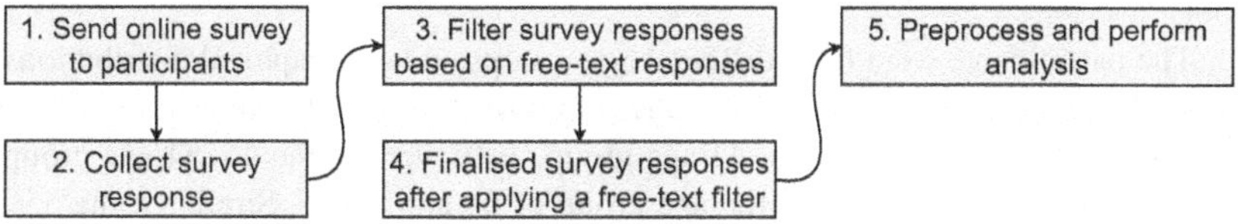

Fig. 6.11 The evaluation process for an online survey

First, the designed survey was shared among the participants to gather their opinions. The participants were invited via private channels and their peer group. The following criteria were used for inviting the participants: (i) they had to be over 18 years old; and (ii) they had to have a valid email address and access to a computer or mobile phone in order to be able to take the survey. In addition, the farming experience, which is a major focus, is also considered but not a hard requirement. This is to evaluate the benefits of the explanations of the proposed approach in other domains, as the proposed approach is generalisable. While inviting participants from other domains, the education level was taken into account. The final invited participants had backgrounds in computer science, healthcare, social science, agriculture, finance, education, and engineering. A total of 22 responses were collected. Since the survey was conducted online, random responses are possible. To avoid random responses, the collected survey data was subsequently filtered based on the free-text responses provided in the survey. Following data filtering, two responses were eliminated from the survey. The responses were removed when they were highly inconsistent, no corresponding explanations were provided, or random answers were given in the free-text option. After preprocessing, the remaining 20 responses were used for additional analysis and to draw conclusions. The responses were anonymised, cleaned[23], i.e. removing free-text responses as they were not consistent and organised as part of the preprocessing. Furthermore, as a part of

[23] The cleaned version of the survey data is available in the GitHub repository where the code is present.

the preprocessing, adjustments to the responses[24] were also made for the question that asked the participants to rate the usefulness of the explanations (measured on a scale between 1 and 5). This is because of the observed anomaly. For example, the participants responded that they did not find the explanations useful and also did not understand the explanations, but despite this, some participants rated the explanations as useful (measured on a scale between 1 and 5). Corrections to such responses were made by adjusting the given rating to 1, which means "not at all useful". The analysis is performed using Tableau[25], a data visualisation and analysis tool.

The participants were from different age groups and geographical distributions. 50% of the participants were in the age group of 25–34, 25% were in the 18–14 age group, 10% were in the 35–44 age group, 10% were in the 45–54 age group, and the remaining 5% were in the age group of 65 and above. Similarly, the 55% of the participants were from Nigeria, 15% were from Ghana, and the remaining 10% each came from Austria, the Netherlands, and the United States of America. In terms of educational qualifications, a majority of the participants (50%) have either a bachelor's degree completed or are pursuing one. Similarly, 30% of respondents are either studying for or have completed a PhD, followed by those with a master's degree (completed or studying for), who constitute 15% of the participants. 5 percent of the participants are at the diploma level. The occupational backgrounds, which are shown in Fig. 6.12, of the participants vary widely. However, despite the varying occupational backgrounds, the majority of the respondents are either still involved in or were involved in farming in the past. Sixty-five percent of respondents indicated that they are currently engaged in farming or have been in the past.

In terms of AI familiarity, the majority of survey respondents, 90%, were familiar with AI. However, as can be observed in Fig. 6.13, the majority of them were not experts, only around 5% had a good understanding of AI. The remainder had either heard of AI or had a moderate understanding of it. Following the occupational data, a conclusion can be made that the majority of respondents are non-expert AI users, which makes the survey results more useful for the evaluation, as the explainability is geared towards regular users and not AI specialists.

The original input image, the corresponding prediction (top 1), and the SHAP explanation values were displayed in order to assess the explainability of the SHAP. The SHAP explainability image from Sect. 6.1 is used. Then, a yes-or-no question is asked to determine whether the survey participants found the explanation helpful

[24] Only the responses related to SHAP explanations (or the breakdown of SHAP explanations' usefulness) were modified. Adjustments were made to four responses.

[25] https://www.tableau.com/

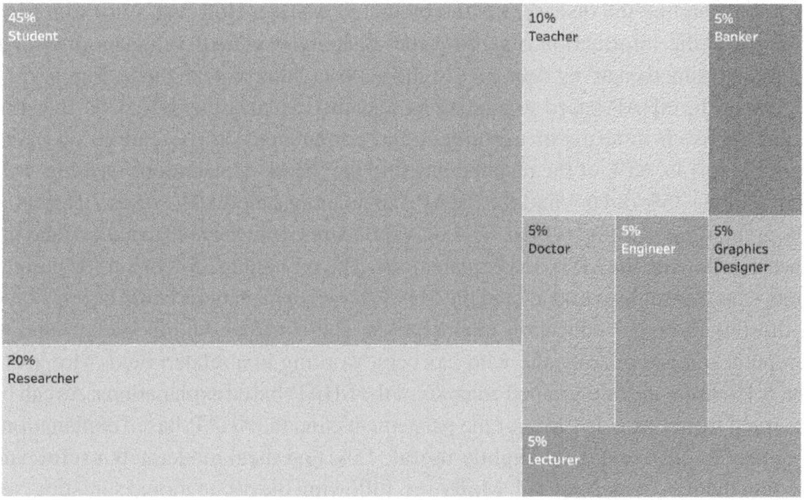

Fig. 6.12 Occupation-based distribution of survey respondents

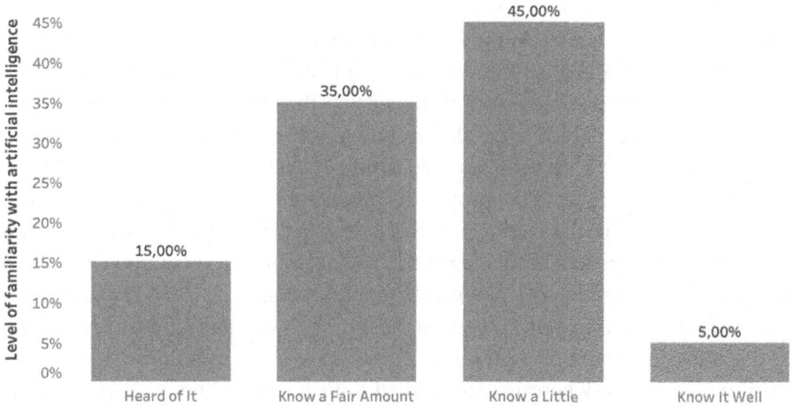

Fig. 6.13 The familiarity of the participants with AI, which is measured on a scale of 1–5. The respective options are: (1) never heard of it, (2) heard of it, (3) know a little, (4) know a fair amount, and (5) know it well

for understanding the disease, i.e. the predicted disease. However, prior to posing a question, the information regarding the meaning of SHAP values is provided. After analysing the survey data, an insightful observation can be made. Figure 6.14 compares the SHAP-based explanations and the explanations based on the proposed approach in terms of usefulness and comprehension. As can be observed from Fig. 6.14a, 65% of the respondents find the SHAP explanations (see Fig. 6.1) useful, while 35% did not find the SHAP explanations helpful. However, in terms of comprehension (see Fig. 6.14b), 65% of respondents were not able to understand the disease following SHAP-based explanations. The remaining 35% of survey participants who were able to understand the SHAP-based explanations could be attributed to those with higher education qualifications and someone with a background in computer science or someone who has been working in a related field. Moreover, Fig. 6.15 shows the fine-grained analysis of the SHAP-based explanations. As can be observed from Fig. 6.15, 25% of the participants find the SHAP-based explanations very useful, 20% find them slightly useful, 15% find them moderately useful, and 5% find them extremely useful. Moreover, following the occupational statistics (see Fig. 6.12), it can said that the SHAP-based explanations are not very useful, even for highly qualified people such as researchers. Overall, a significant proportion of participants find the SHAP-based explanations to be little to moderately useful (Tabelle 6.9).

Similarly, when it comes to the explainability of the proposed method for this study, as shown in Fig. 6.14c, 95% of participants find the explanations helpful (or useful), with 5% being the exception. Regarding the comprehension, 85% of the participants (see Fig. 6.14d) were able to understand the explanations of the proposed approach, while 15% were not able to understand. This indicates that there is still room for improvement in the proposed approach, which can be one of the future research directions. Similar feedback was received in the open-text response, where participants mentioned that there is a need to add examples of symptoms in explanations, suggested adding images along with textual explanations, and also suggested providing explanations on how to prevent the illness. A similar response to not being able to see the images is also provided in the case of the usefulness of proposed method explainability where it was marked with response "no", i.e. participants did not find useful. Table 6.10 in Appendix, Sect. **G**, provides the free-text survey responses from the participants for both SHAP and the proposed approach. Additionally, in comparison with the comprehension of SHAP-based explainability, the proposed approach's comprehension is 50% higher, demonstrating the advantages of this study's explainability approach.

Furthermore, Fig. 6.16 further depicts a fine-grained evaluation of the usefulness (or helpfulness) of the explanations generated by the proposed method. As can be

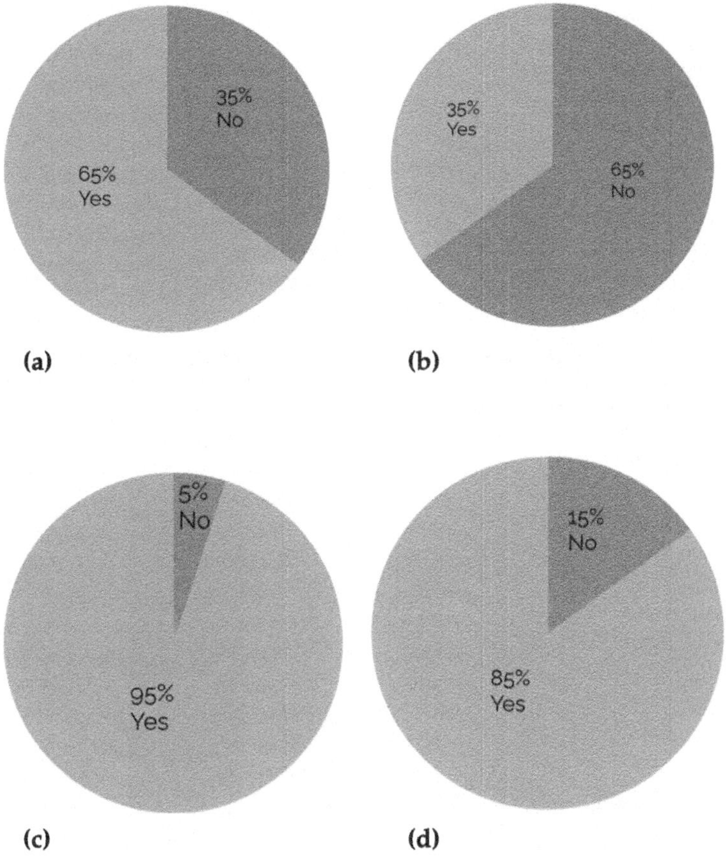

Fig. 6.14 Comparison of the usefulness and comprehension of the SHAP-based explanations (top) and the proposed approach (bottom). (**a**) Distributions of the participants responses according to the usefulness of the explanations generated using SHAP. (**b**) Participant distributions based on their comprehension of SHAP-based explanations. (**c**) Distributions of the participants responses based on the usefulness of the explanations generated using the proposed approach. (**d**) Participant distributions based on their comprehension of the proposed approach explanations

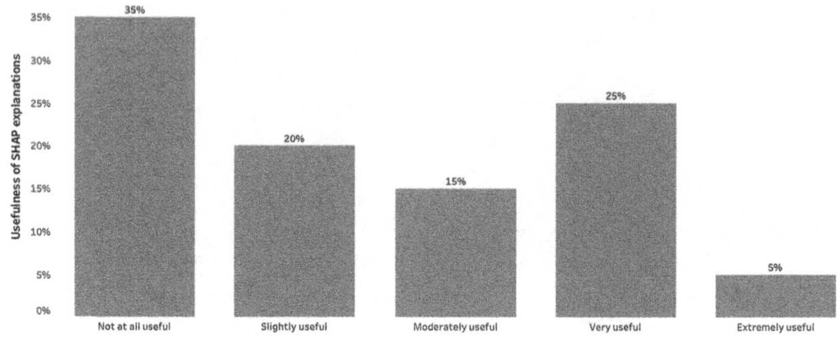

Fig. 6.15 The level of usefulness of the SHAP explanations that are measured on a scale of 1–5. The respective options are: (1) not at all useful, (2) slightly useful, (3) moderately useful, (4) very useful, and (5) extremely useful

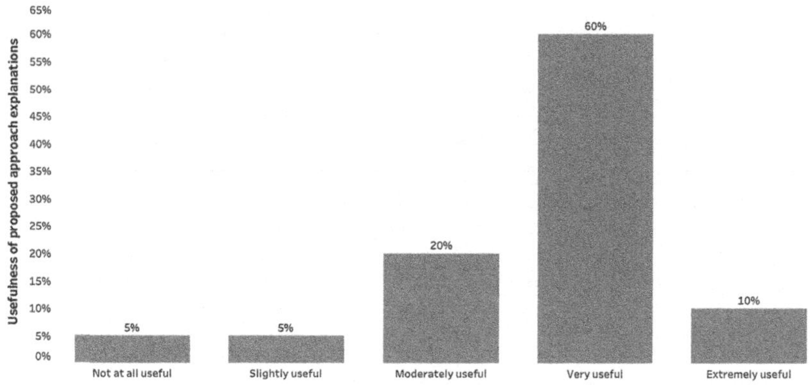

Fig. 6.16 The level of usefulness of the explanations that are measured on a scale of 1–5 and that are based on the proposed approach of this study. The respective options are: (1) not at all useful, (2) slightly useful, (3) moderately useful, (4) very useful, and (5) extremely useful

observed from Fig. 6.16, with the exception of 5% of participants, all of them find the explanations generated by the proposed approach useful. Overall, 10% find the explanations of the proposed approach extremely useful, 60% find them very useful, 20% find them moderately useful, and 5% find them slightly useful. Upon comparing the usefulness of the proposed approach with the SHAP-based explanations, it clearly shows the benefit of the explainability based on the proposed approach and validates the claim about the benefits of the proposed explainability approach.

In summary, the following conclusions can be drawn from the evaluation of the survey response: (i) the visualisation of SHAP-based explanations is still useful even if they are not comprehensible, (ii) the proposed approach's explainability is very effective both in terms of usefulness and comprehension compared to explanations based on SHAP (or LIME), which are the popular and becoming a de-facto standard in ML explainability [80], (iii) the fact that participants from diverse fields were able to understand and find the explanations useful demonstrates the very high value of the proposed explainability approach, even in other domains, and (iv) despite being highly effective, there is still room for improvement in the explainability of the proposed approach, which is to show where in the plant the diseases are and add more explanations to the cause and remedy of the diseases.

Table 6.9 shows the comparison of the proposed approach results with the state-of-the-art studies in terms of the accuracy. The study's relevance (i.e. the study utilises the same dataset as in this study) is the primary criterion for its selection. The second criterion is based on its recency (2022 and 2023). In addition, the best performance is selected from state-of-the-art studies when selecting performance for

Table 6.9 A comparison of our proposed method to the state-of-the-art studies in terms of accuracy and user-level explainability

Study	Model/Methods	Accuracy	User-level explanation
Emmanuel et al. [6]	MobileNet V2	0.901	No
Ahishakiye et al. [35]	Ensemble of GLVQ, GMLVQ and LGMLVQ	0.82	No
Kumar et al. [33]	Ensemble of EfficientNet, SEResNeXt, ViT, DeIT and MobileNetV3	0.9075	No
Paiva-Peredo [36]	DenseNet169	0.7477	No
Chen et al. [37]	Smooth-Taylor CE	0.893	No
Ravi et al. [34]	A_L_EfficientNet	0.8708	No
Riaz et al. [39]	EfficiennetB3	0.8303	No
Anitha & Saranya [38]	CNN with data augmentation	0.90	No
Our proposed approach	**Fusion of DL and semantic technology**	**0.905**	**Yes**

comparison. Table 6.9 clearly demonstrates that the proposed method outperforms state-of-the-art methods, with the exception of Kumar et al.'s [33] work, which outperforms the result of this study by 0.0025. However, there are two important differences to take into account: (i) Kumar et al.'s [33] work does not provide explainability, and (ii) this study uses a large, noisy cassava image dataset. This is because this study uses the combined datasets released by the Makerere University AI Lab in 2019 and 2020 (see Sect. 6.4.1), while Kumar et al.'s [33] work only uses the dataset from 2019. A similar situation is present in other studies. Therefore, conclusion can be made that the proposed method is robust.

The third evaluation is on latency, as discussed in Sect. 6.4.5. Figure 6.17 illustrates the average inference time for of the proposed approach. The semantic model requires an average of 2.91 seconds, while the vision model requires only 0.91 seconds. The vision model utilises GPUs, whereas the semantic model does not. This is one reason for the significant difference in inference time between the vision model and semantic model. In addition, the combined average inference time is 3.85 seconds, which is acceptable given the nature of the task (i.e. no hard real-time requirements). Therefore, with this, a conclusion can be drawn that the proposed approach is also suitable for real-world deployment.

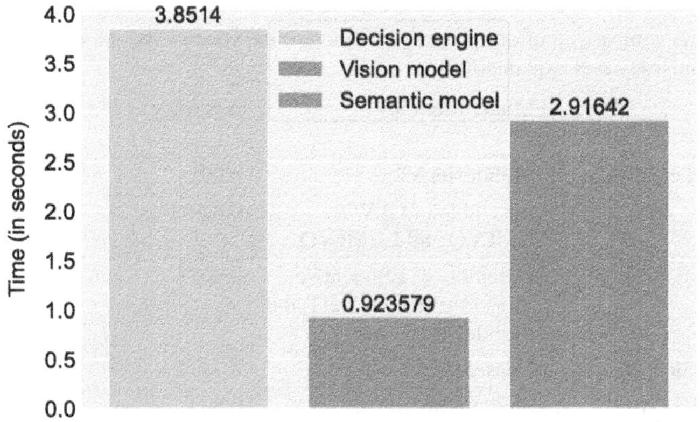

Fig. 6.17 The average prediction time (or prediction latency) measured for 5268 samples for vision models, semantic models, and the combination of predictions from vision and semantic models (i.e. decision engine)—a proposed approach

6.6 Conclusion

This study presents novel work on combining semantic technology and DL with a focus on cassava disease. This research demonstrated how semantic technology and DL can be combined to address the following limitations: (i) the lack of domain knowledge and contextual information in DL (see Sect. 6.3), and (ii) the lack of user-level explainability of DL (see Sect. 6.3.2.3). Moreover, by combining semantic technology and DL, as demonstrated by the results and comparison with the state-of-the-art works (see Sect. 6.5), this study also addressed the limitations of semantic technology, which are their limited abilities to learn complex patterns like DL. Furthermore, through the latency evaluation, this study demonstrated the suitability of the proposed approach for real-world scenarios.

From the performance evaluation and comparison with state-of-the-art studies, this study demonstrated the benefits of the proposed method and its robustness. However, the true benefit lies in the generalisability of the proposed approach, which can be used to solve other problems in the agricultural (and also other) domain, its ability to incorporate domain knowledge and generate, generate user-level explainability (see Sect. 6.3.2.3) and combine the symbolic approach based on semantic technology with a non-symbolic approach, also referred to as a numeric approach (or neuro-symbolic approach). This is particularly important when building AI (or AI systems) in a societal context, as the majority of the users are non-experts, and it is essential that they do not blindly trust predictions from the AI system. Moreover, this work enables the ability to include knowledge and rich contextual information that is not available in data, e.g. images, that helps in improving prediction, as demonstrated by the result (see Table 6.8), and build trustworthy AI systems.

However, if the domain knowledge is inaccurate or highly biased, it can act as a bottleneck, decreasing rather than increasing the accuracy of the prediction. Therefore, the information (or domain knowledge) should be incorporated with extreme caution, and multiple domain experts should be involved to eliminate (or reduce) bias. In the case of strict real-time requirements, the semantic model's performance can be a bottleneck, and this is therefore regarded as a limitation of this study that requires future improvement.

As potential future work, three directions are identified. The first is to make additional performance enhancements and incorporate more domain knowledge. The second objective is to apply the proposed work to domains, such as healthcare, that require AI systems that are explainable, have good performance, and can also make use of domain knowledge. The third research direction is to improve the explainability further following the user response, as discussed in Sect. 6.5.

Acknowledgements This research is partially supported by Interreg Österreich-Bayern 2014–2020 programme project KI-Net: Bausteine für KI-basierte Optimierungen in der industriellen Fertigung (grant agreement: AB 292). We would like thank to the High-Performance Computing Centre (HPC) at the University of Innsbruck for providing the LEO HPC infrastructure for our experiment. We also want to express our gratitude to Michael Fink, a member of the HPC staff, for his assistance with HPC administrative tasks and for accelerating the procedure to reduce delay.

Appendix

Table 6.10 The responses from the participants that provides reasons why they selected a particular option. The responses presented in this table remove responses that include text such as "I don't understand" or incomplete answer

SHAP-based explanations	Explanations based on proposed approach
Free-text response providing the reasons why participants selected the option "yes" for usability and comprehension for the yes-or-no question.	
1. The color in the prediction and explanation is same. 2. The spots show the affected area. 3. It affects chlorophyll production and leads to the reduction in crop yield.	1. It gave a written explanation of the disease. 2. It's clear what the disease is, the explanation is given and the percentage certainty are given as well. 3. The written text helps. 4. Learnt that the disease occurs mostly in moist soil. 5. Because the text tell the exact thing and it can be understood. 6. The generated explanation gave a view of how the disease thrives and this will aid in how to combat it. 7. Form the generated explanation, I could decipher that cassava mosaic is a high casualty disease that affects cassava plants. 8. There's a proper breakdown on the casual environment for this particular disease. 9. It explains the predisposing factors that could promote the disease growth. 10. I learnt that the disease could be devastating during the rainy season.

(Continued)

Table 6.10 (Continued)

SHAP-based explanations	Explanations based on proposed approach
Free-text response providing the reasons why participants selected the option "no" for usability and comprehension for the yes-or-no question.	
1. Prediction is not clear to me. 2. The explanation is just a series of dots on a canvas. However, from the text above the prediction image, I am able to tell what the disease is. 3. Not clear how the cassava disease affects plants and where it shows up on the plant.	The explanation is not visible.
Free-text response providing the reasons why participants gave particular scores for usefulness ratings that are measured on a scale between 1 and 5.	
1. I did not understand How the prediction model is made and how the explanation helps or adds to diagnose and explain additional information about the disease. 2. Not clear if the photo shows a distribution of the disease on the plant as in location (leaves or roots). 3. Because the colour is based on the observations. Some people may perceive the colour in different way.s 4. I responded NO because I am not an avid user of AI and the generated images could not be easily understood. 5. It requires a high level of knowledge to understand. 6. It will help farmers to identify the disease faster. 7. It explains how wide the disease has spread.	1. Since the prediction and explanation are correct, it is helpful to know when the disease is worse, what soil condition and temperature. 2. It's straight forward. 3. The explanation could be improved in terms of for instance cause, how it can be fixed and perhaps, other diseases that may look the same even to a human observer 4. Should add examples of the symptoms in the text. 5. Having more explanation with some graphics as well would be helpful. 6. I gave the above rating because seeing the explanation above is an Avenue to know how to move with the precautions necessary to combat the disease 7. Easily understood. 8. It gave detailed information about the disease 9. I often see the plabts on the field 10. Not technical to understand.

Bibliography

1. United Nations. *The Sustainable Development Goals Report 2021.* https://unstats.un.org/sdgs/report/2021/The-Sustainable-Development-Goals-Report-2021.pdf, note = Last accessed on 10 October 2022, year=2021.
2. Rohit Sharma, Sachin S Kamble, Angappa Gunasekaran, Vikas Kumar, and Anil Kumar. 'A systematic literature review on machine learning applications for sustainable agriculture supply chain performance'. In: *Computers & Operations Research* 119 (2020), p. 104926.
3. Junde Chen, Defu Zhang, Md Suzauddola, and Adnan Zeb. 'Identifying crop diseases using attention embedded MobileNet-V2 model'. In: *Applied Soft Computing* 113 (2021), p. 107901. https://doi.org/10.1016/j.asoc.2021.107901.
4. Tawseef Ayoub Shaikh, Tabasum Rasool, and Faisal Rasheed Lone. 'Towards leveraging the role of machine learning and artificial intelligence in precision agriculture and smart farming'. In: *Computers and Electronics in Agriculture* 198 (2022), p. 107119. https://doi.org/10.1016/j.compag.2022.107119.
5. Food and Agriculture Organization of the United Nations. *Climate change fans spread of pests and threatens plants and crops, new FAO study).* (Last accessed on 31.03. 2023). 2021. URL: https://www.fao.org/news/story/en/item/1402920/icode/.
6. Ahishakiye Emmanuel, Ronald Waweru Mwangi, Petronilla Murithi, Kanobe Fredrick, and Taremwa Danison. 'Classification of cassava leaf diseases using deep Gaussian transfer learning model'. In: *Engineering Reports* (2023), e12651. https://doi.org/10.1002/eng2.12651.
7. Ahmad Chaddad, Jihao Peng, Jian Xu, and Ahmed Bouridane. 'Survey of Explainable AI Techniques in Healthcare'. In: *Sensors* 23.2 (2023), p. 634. https://doi.org/10.3390/s23020634.
8. Manas Gaur, Keyur Faldu, and Amit Sheth. 'Semantics of the Black-Box: Can Knowledge Graphs Help Make Deep Learning Systems More Interpretable and Explainable?' In: *IEEE Internet Computing* 25.1 (2021), pp. 51–59. https://doi.org/10.1109/MIC.2020.3031769.
9. Marco Tulio Ribeiro, Sameer Singh, and Carlos Guestrin. "'Why Should I Trust You?": Explaining the Predictions of Any Classifier'. In: *Proceedings of the 22nd ACM SIGKDD International Conference on Knowledge Discovery and Data Mining.* KDD '16. San Francisco, California, USA: Association for Computing Machinery, 2016, 1135–1144. https://doi.org/10.1145/2939672.2939778.
10. Scott M Lundberg and Su-In Lee. 'A Unified Approach to Interpreting Model Predictions'. In: *Advances in Neural Information Processing Systems.* Ed. by I. Guyon, U. Von Luxburg, S. Bengio, H. Wallach, R. Fergus, S. Vishwanathan, and R. Garnett. Vol. 30. Curran Associates, Inc., 2017.
11. Lingxue Yang, Hongrun Wang, and Léa A. Deleris. 'What Does It Mean to Explain? A User-Centered Study on AI Explainability'. In: *Artificial Intelligence in HCI.* Ed. by Helmut Degen and Stavroula Ntoa. Cham: Springer International Publishing, 2021, pp. 107–121.
12. Andreas Holzinger and Heimo Müller. 'Toward Human–AI Interfaces to Support Explainability and Causability in Medical AI'. In: *Computer* 54.10 (2021), pp. 78–86. https://doi.org/10.1109/MC.2021.3092610.

13. Tek Raj Chhetri, Anelia Kurteva, Jubril Gbolahan Adigun, and Anna Fensel. 'Knowledge Graph Based Hard Drive Failure Prediction'. In: *Sensors* 22.3 (2022), p. 985. https://doi.org/10.3390/s22030985.
14. Manas Gaur, Kalpa Gunaratna, Shreyansh Bhatt, and Amit Sheth. 'Knowledge-Infused Learning: A Sweet Spot in Neuro-Symbolic AI'. In: *IEEE Internet Computing* 26.4 (2022), pp. 5–11. https://doi.org/10.1109/MIC.2022.3179759.
15. Soumya Sharma, Bishal Santra, Abhik Jana, Santosh Tokala, Niloy Ganguly, and Pawan Goyal. 'Incorporating Domain Knowledge into Medical NLI using Knowledge Graphs'. In: *Proceedings of the 2019 Conference on Empirical Methods in Natural Language Processing and the 9th International Joint Conference on Natural Language Processing (EMNLP-IJCNLP)*. Hong Kong, China: Association for Computational Linguistics, Nov. 2019, pp. 6092–6097. https://doi.org/10.18653/v1/D19-1631.
16. Javier Lacasta, F. Javier Lopez-Pellicer, Borja Espejo-García, Javier Nogueras-Iso, and F. Javier Zarazaga-Soria. In: *Computers and Electronics in Agriculture* 152 (2018), pp. 82–89. https://doi.org/10.1016/j.compag.2018.06.049.
17. Watanee Jearanaiwongkul, Chutiporn Anutariya, and Frederic Andres. 'An Ontology-Based Approach to Plant Disease Identification System'. In: *Proceedings of the 10th International Conference on Advances in Information Technology*. IAIT 2018. Bangkok, Thailand: Association for Computing Machinery, 2018. https://doi.org/10.1145/3291280.3291786.
18. Michael Benedikt, Kristian Kersting, Phokion G. Kolaitis, and Daniel Neider. 'Logic and Learning (Dagstuhl Seminar 19361)'. In: *Dagstuhl Reports* 9.9 (2020). Ed. by Michael Benedikt, Kristian Kersting, Phokion G. Kolaitis, and Daniel Neider, pp. 1–22. https://doi.org/10.4230/DagRep.9.9.1.
19. Clementina Oluwafunke Ajayi and Adewale Isaac Olutumise. 'Determinants of food security and technical efficiency of cassava farmers in Ondo State, Nigeria'. In: *International Food and Agribusiness Management Review* 21.7 (Sept. 2018), pp. 915–928. https://doi.org/10.22434/ifamr2016.0151.
20. Ming-Cheng Chan, Kai-Chih Pai, Shao-An Su, Min-Shian Wang, Chieh-Liang Wu, and Wen-Cheng Chao. 'Explainable machine learning to predict long-term mortality in critically ill ventilated patients: a retrospective study in central Taiwan'. In: *BMC Medical Informatics and Decision Making* 22.1 (2022), p. 75. https://doi.org/10.1186/s12911-022-01817-6.
21. Ke Zhang, Peidong Xu, and Jun Zhang. 'Explainable AI in Deep Reinforcement Learning Models: A SHAP Method Applied in Power System Emergency Control'. In: *2020 IEEE 4th Conference on Energy Internet and Energy System Integration (EI2)*. 2020, pp. 711–716. https://doi.org/10.1109/EI250167.2020.9347147.
22. R. Machlev, L. Heistrene, M. Perl, K.Y. Levy, J. Belikov, S. Mannor, and Y. Levron. 'Explainable Artificial Intelligence (XAI) techniques for energy and power systems: Review, challenges and opportunities'. In: *Energy and AI* 9 (2022), p. 100169. https://doi.org/10.1016/j.egyai.2022.100169.
23. Georgios Mitrentsis and Hendrik Lens. 'An interpretable probabilistic model for short-term solar power forecasting using natural gradient boosting'. In: *Applied Energy* 309 (2022), p. 118473. https://doi.org/10.1016/j.apenergy.2021.118473.
24. Murat Kuzlu, Umit Cali, Vinayak Sharma, and Özgür Güler. 'Gaining Insight Into Solar Photovoltaic Power Generation Forecasting Utilizing Explainable Artificial Intelligence

Tools'. In: *IEEE Access* 8 (2020), pp. 187814–187823. https://doi.org/10.1109/ACCESS.2020.3031477.
25. Jean-François Toubeau, Jérémie Bottieau, Yi Wang, and François Vallée. 'Interpretable Probabilistic Forecasting of Imbalances in Renewable-Dominated Electricity Systems'. In: *IEEE Transactions on Sustainable Energy* 13.2 (2022), pp. 1267–1277. https://doi.org/10.1109/TSTE.2021.3092137.
26. Khalid Bahani, Hamza Ali-Ou-Salah, Mohammed Moujabbir, Benyounes Oukarfi, and Mohammed Ramdani. 'A Novel Interpretable Model for Solar Radiation Prediction Based on Adaptive Fuzzy Clustering and Linguistic Hedges'. In: *Proceedings of the 13th International Conference on Intelligent Systems: Theories and Applications*. SITA'20. Rabat, Morocco: Association for Computing Machinery, 2020. https://doi.org/10.1145/3419604.3419807.
27. José Jiménez-Luna, Francesca Grisoni, and Gisbert Schneider. 'Drug discovery with explainable artificial intelligence'. In: *Nature Machine Intelligence* 2.10 (2020), pp. 573–584. https://doi.org/10.1038/s42256-020-00236-4.
28. Zhitao Ying, Dylan Bourgeois, Jiaxuan You, Marinka Zitnik, and Jure Leskovec. 'GNNExplainer: Generating Explanations for Graph Neural Networks'. In: *Advances in Neural Information Processing Systems*. Ed. by H. Wallach, H. Larochelle, A. Beygelzimer, F. d'Alché-Buc, E. Fox, and R. Garnett. Vol. 32. Curran Associates, Inc., 2019.
29. Ana Lucic, Maartje A. Ter Hoeve, Gabriele Tolomei, Maarten De Rijke, and Fabrizio Silvestri. 'CF-GNNExplainer: Counterfactual Explanations for Graph Neural Networks'. In: *Proceedings of The 25th International Conference on Artificial Intelligence and Statistics*. Ed. by Gustau Camps-Valls, Francisco J. R. Ruiz, and Isabel Valera. Vol. 151. Proceedings of Machine Learning Research. PMLR, 2022, pp. 4499–4511.
30. Fawaz Sammani, Tanmoy Mukherjee, and Nikos Deligiannis. 'NLX-GPT: A Model for Natural Language Explanations in Vision and Vision-Language Tasks'. In: *Proceedings of the IEEE/CVF Conference on Computer Vision and Pattern Recognition (CVPR)*. 2022, pp. 8322–8332.
31. Zongbao Yang, Yinxin Xu, Jinlong Hu, and Shoubin Dong. 'Generating knowledge aware explanation for natural language inference'. In: *Information Processing Management* 60.2 (2023), p. 103245. https://doi.org/10.1016/j.ipm.2022.103245.
32. Elvira Amador-Domínguez, Emilio Serrano, and Daniel Manrique. 'GEnI: A framework for the generation of explanations and insights of knowledge graph embedding predictions'. In: *Neurocomputing* 521 (2023), pp. 199–212. https://doi.org/10.1016/j.neucom.2022.12.010.
33. Hrishikesh Kumar, Sanjay Velu, Are Lokesh, Kuruguntla Suman, and Srilatha Chebrolu. 'Cassava Leaf Disease Detection Using Ensembling of EfficientNet, SEResNeXt, ViT, DeIT and MobileNetV3 Models'. In: *Proceedings of the International Conference on Paradigms of Computing, Communication and Data Sciences*. Ed. by Rajendra Prasad Yadav, Satyasai Jagannath Nanda, Prashant Singh Rana, and Meng-Hiot Lim. Singapore: Springer Nature Singapore, 2023, pp. 183–193.
34. Vinayakumar Ravi, Vasundhara Acharya, and Tuan D. Pham. 'Attention deep learning-based large-scale learning classifier for Cassava leaf disease classification'. In: *Expert Systems* 39.2 (2022), e12862. https://doi.org/10.1111/exsy.12862.
35. Emmanuel Ahishakiye, Waweru Mwangi, Petronilla Murithi, Ruth Wario, Fredrick Kanobe, and Taremwa Danison. 'An Ensemble Model Based on Learning Vector Quan-

tization Algorithms for Early Detection of Cassava Diseases Using Spectral Data'. In: *Digital-for-Development: Enabling Transformation, Inclusion and Sustainability Through ICTs*. Ed. by Patrick Ndayizigamiye, Hossana Twinomurinzi, Billy Kalema, Kelvin Bwalya, and Mncedisi Bembe. Cham: Springer Nature Switzerland, 2023, pp. 320–328.

36. Ernesto Paiva-Peredo. 'Deep Learning for the Classification of Cassava Leaf Diseases in Unbalanced Field Data Set'. In: *Advanced Network Technologies and Intelligent Computing*. Ed. by Isaac Woungang, Sanjay Kumar Dhurandher, Kiran Kumar Pattanaik, Anshul Verma, and Pradeepika Verma. Cham: Springer Nature Switzerland, 2023, pp. 101–114.
37. Yipeng Chen, Ke Xu, Peng Zhou, Xiaojuan Ban, and Di He. 'Improved cross entropy loss for noisy labels in vision leaf disease classification'. In: *IET Image Processing* 16.6 (2022), pp. 1511–1519. https://doi.org/10.1049/ipr2.12402.
38. J Anitha and N Saranya. 'Cassava leaf disease identification and detection using deep learning approach'. In: *International Journal of Computers Communications & Control* 17.2 (2022). https://doi.org/10.15837/ijccc.2022.2.4356.
39. Syed Mursleen Riaz, Muhammad Ahsan, and Muhammad Usman Akram. 'Diagnosis Of Cassava Leaf Diseases and Classification Using Deep Learning Techniques'. In: *2022 16th International Conference on Open Source Systems and Technologies (ICOSST)*. 2022, pp. 1–8. https://doi.org/10.1109/ICOSST57195.2022.10016854.
40. Edna Chebet Too, Li Yujian, Sam Njuki, and Liu Yingchun. 'A comparative study of fine-tuning deep learning models for plant disease identification'. In: *Computers and Electronics in Agriculture* 161 (2019). BigData and DSS in Agriculture, pp. 272–279. https://doi.org/10.1016/j.compag.2018.03.032.
41. Ümit Atila, Murat Uçar, Kemal Akyol, and Emine Uçar. 'Plant leaf disease classification using EfficientNet deep learning model'. In: *Ecological Informatics* 61 (2021), p. 101182. https://doi.org/10.1016/j.ecoinf.2020.101182.
42. Konstantinos P. Ferentinos. 'Deep learning models for plant disease detection and diagnosis'. In: *Computers and Electronics in Agriculture* 145 (2018), pp. 311–318. https://doi.org/10.1016/j.compag.2018.01.009.
43. Koushik Nagasubramanian, Sarah Jones, Asheesh K. Singh, Soumik Sarkar, Arti Singh, and Baskar Ganapathysubramanian. 'Plant disease identification using explainable 3D deep learning on hyperspectral images'. In: *Plant Methods* 15.1 (2019), p. 98. https://doi.org/10.1186/s13007-019-0479-8.
44. Arunabha M. Roy and Jayabrata Bhaduri. 'A Deep Learning Enabled Multi-Class Plant Disease Detection Model Based on Computer Vision'. In: *AI* 2.3 (2021), pp. 413–428. https://doi.org/10.3390/ai2030026.
45. Amreen Abbas, Sweta Jain, Mahesh Gour, and Swetha Vankudothu. 'Tomato plant disease detection using transfer learning with C-GAN synthetic images'. In: *Computers and Electronics in Agriculture* 187 (2021), p. 106279. https://doi.org/10.1016/j.compag.2021.106279.
46. Punam Bedi and Pushkar Gole. 'Plant disease detection using hybrid model based on convolutional autoencoder and convolutional neural network'. In: *Artificial Intelligence in Agriculture* 5 (2021), pp. 90–101. https://doi.org/10.1016/j.aiia.2021.05.002.
47. S. Ashwinkumar, S. Rajagopal, V. Manimaran, and B. Jegajothi. 'Automated plant leaf disease detection and classification using optimal MobileNet based convolutional neural

networks'. In: *Materials Today: Proceedings* 51 (2022). CMAE'21, pp. 480–487. https://doi.org/10.1016/j.matpr.2021.05.584.
48. Dhruvil Shah, Vishvesh Trivedi, Vinay Sheth, Aakash Shah, and Uttam Chauhan. 'ResTS: Residual Deep interpretable architecture for plant disease detection'. In: *Information Processing in Agriculture* 9.2 (2022), pp. 212–223. https://doi.org/10.1016/j.inpa.2021.06.001.
49. Prakash Sahu and Vivek Kumar Sinha. 'Plant Disease Detection Using Transfer Learning with DL Model'. In: *Mobile Computing and Sustainable Informatics*. Ed. by Subarna Shakya, Klimis Ntalianis, and Khaled A. Kamel. Singapore: Springer Nature Singapore, 2022, pp. 169–180.
50. Alexey Bochkovskiy, Chien-Yao Wang, and Hong-Yuan Mark Liao. 'Yolov4: Optimal speed and accuracy of object detection'. In: *arXiv preprint* arXiv:2004.10934 (2020).
51. Jeffrey Detras, Frances Nikki Borja, Kenneth McNally, Ramil Mauleon, Julie Mae Pasuquin William, Eusebio Ruaraidh, Sackville Hamilton, and Cécile Grenier. *Rice Ontology*. https://cropontology.org/term/CO_320:ROOT. (Online; accessed 19-July-2022). 2016.
52. Ammar Halabi. *Plant Protection Ontology*. https://sites.google.com/site/ppontology/home (Online; accessed 19-July-2022). 2009.
53. American Phytopathological Society. *Plant Disease Ontology*. https://github.com/Planteome/plant-diseaseontology (Online; accessed 18-July-2022). 2016.
54. Miguel Ángel Rodríguez-García, Francisco García-Sánchez, and Rafael Valencia-García. 'Knowledge-Based System for Crop Pests and Diseases Recognition'. In: *Electronics* 10.8 (2021). https://doi.org/10.3390/electronics10080905.
55. Miguel Ángel Rodríguez-García and Francisco García-Sánchez. 'CropPestO: An Ontology Model for Identifying and Managing Plant Pests and Diseases'. In: *Technologies and Innovation*. Ed. by Rafael Valencia-García, Gema Alcaraz-Marmol, Javier Del Cioppo-Morstadt, Néstor Vera-Lucio, and Martha Bucaram-Leverone. Cham: Springer International Publishing, 2020, pp. 18–29.
56. Katty Lagos-Ortiz, José Medina-Moreira, Mario Andrés Paredes-Valverde, Winston Espinoza-Morán, and Rafael Valencia-García. 'An Ontology-Based Decision Support System for the Diagnosis of Plant Diseases'. In: *Journal of Information Technology Research (JITR)* 10.4 (2017), pp. 42–55. https://doi.org/10.4018/JITR.2017100103.
57. Natalya F Noy and Deborah L McGuinness. *Ontology development 101: A guide to creating your first ontology*. 2001.
58. Krzysztof Janowicz, Armin Haller, Simon J.D. Cox, Danh Le Phuoc, and Maxime Lefrançois. 'SOSA: A lightweight ontology for sensors, observations, samples, and actuators'. In: *Journal of Web Semantics* 56 (2019), pp. 1–10. https://doi.org/10.1016/j.websem.2018.06.003.
59. Mingxing Tan and Quoc V. Le. *EfficientNetV2: Smaller Models and Faster Training*. 2021.
60. Li Yuan, Qibin Hou, Zihang Jiang, Jiashi Feng, and Shuicheng Yan. 'Volo: Vision outlooker for visual recognition'. In: *arXiv preprint* arXiv:2106.13112 (2021).
61. Ian Horrocks, Peter F Patel-Schneider, Harold Boley, Said Tabet, Benjamin Grosof, and Mike Dean. 'SWRL: A semantic web rule language combining OWL and RuleML'. In: *W3C Member submission* 21.79 (2004), pp. 1–31.

62. Sebastian Raschka and Vahid Mirjalili. *Python machine learning*. Packt Publishing Ltd, 2017.
63. Ernest Mwebaze, Timnit Gebru, Andrea Frome, Solomon Nsumba, and Jeremy Tusubira. *iCassava 2019 Fine-Grained Visual Categorization Challenge*. 2019. https://doi.org/10.48550/ARXIV.1908.02900.
64. Sajan Gohil. *Dataset: Cassava plant disease Merged 2019–2020*. https://www.kaggle.com/datasets/srg9000/cassava-plant-disease-merged-20192020 (Last accessed 27.07.2022). 2021.
65. Alessandra Anzolin, Jlenia Toppi, Manuela Petti, Febo Cincotti, and Laura Astolfi. 'SEED-G: Simulated EEG Data Generator for Testing Connectivity Algorithms'. In: *Sensors* 21.11 (2021), p. 3632. https://doi.org/10.3390/s21113632.
66. Fairouz Fakhfakh, Hatem Hadj Kacem, and Ahmed Hadj Kacem. 'Simulation tools for cloud computing: A survey and comparative study'. In: *2017 IEEE/ACIS 16th International Conference on Computer and Information Science (ICIS)*. 2017, pp. 221–226. https://doi.org/10.1109/ICIS.2017.7959997.
67. Ajay Rawat, Rama Sushil, Amit Agarwal, and Afzal Sikander. 'A New Approach for VM Failure Prediction using Stochastic Model in Cloud'. In: *IETE Journal of Research* 67.2 (2021), pp. 165–172. https://doi.org/10.1080/03772063.2018.1537814.
68. A. Kannammal, M. Guhanesvar, and R. R. Venketesz. 'Predictive Maintenance for Remote Field IoT Devices—A Deep Learning and Cloud-Based Approach'. In: *Mobile Computing and Sustainable Informatics*. Ed. by Subarna Shakya, George Papakostas, and Khaled A. Kamel. Singapore: Springer Nature Singapore, 2023, pp. 567–585.
69. Klaus Greff, Francois Belletti, Lucas Beyer, Carl Doersch, Yilun Du, Daniel Duckworth, David J. Fleet, Dan Gnanapragasam, Florian Golemo, Charles Herrmann, Thomas Kipf, Abhijit Kundu, Dmitry Lagun, Issam Laradji, Hsueh-Ti (Derek) Liu, HenningMeyer, YishuMiao, Derek Nowrouzezahrai, Cengiz Oztireli, Etienne Pot, Noha Radwan, Daniel Rebain, Sara Sabour, Mehdi S. M. Sajjadi, Matan Sela, Vincent Sitzmann, Austin Stone, Deqing Sun, Suhani Vora, Ziyu Wang, Tianhao Wu, Kwang Moo Yi, Fangcheng Zhong, and Andrea Tagliasacchi. 'Kubric: A Scalable Dataset Generator'. In: *Proceedings of the IEEE/CVF Conference on Computer Vision and Pattern Recognition (CVPR)*. 2022, pp. 3749–3761.
70. Tek Raj Chhetri, Chinmaya Kumar Dehury, Artjom Lind, Satish Narayana Srirama, and Anna Fensel. 'A Combined System Metrics Approach to Cloud Service Reliability Using Artificial Intelligence'. In: *Big Data and Cognitive Computing* 6.1 (2022), p. 26. https://doi.org/10.3390/bdcc6010026.
71. A.R. Seena Radhakrishnan, G. Suja, and J. Sreekumar. 'How sustainable is organic management in cassava? Evidences from yield, soil quality, energetics and economics in the humid tropics of South India'. In: *Scientia Horticulturae* 293 (2022), p. 110723. https://doi.org/10.1016/j.scienta.2021.110723.
72. Ratinun Luampon and Suparerk Charmongkolpradit. 'Temperature and relative humidity effect on equilibrium moisture content of cassava pulp'. In: *Research in Agricultural Engineering* 65.1 (2019), pp. 13–19.
73. Tek Raj Chhetri, Armin Hohenegger, Anna Fensel, Kasali Mariam Aramide, and Asiru Afeez Adekunle. *Code: Towards an Explainable Artificial Intelligence Using Deep Learning and Knowledge Graphs: A Study on Cassava Disease*. https://github.com/Research-Tek/xai-cassava-agriculture (Last accessed 28.03.2023). 2022.

74. Saining Xie, Ross Girshick, Piotr Dollar, Zhuowen Tu, and Kaiming He. 'Aggregated Residual Transformations for Deep Neural Networks'. In: *Proceedings of the IEEE Conference on Computer Vision and Pattern Recognition (CVPR)*. 2017.
75. Mingxing Tan and Quoc Le. 'EfficientNetV2: Smaller Models and Faster Training'. In: *Proceedings of the 38th International Conference on Machine Learning*. Ed. by Marina Meila and Tong Zhang. Vol. 139. Proceedings of Machine Learning Research. PMLR, 2021, pp. 10096–10106.
76. Ilya Loshchilov and Frank Hutter. 'Sgdr: Stochastic gradient descent with warm restarts'. In: *arXiv preprint* arXiv:1608.03983 (2016).
77. Lei Feng, Senlin Shu, Zhuoyi Lin, Fengmao Lv, Li Li, and Bo An. 'Can cross entropy loss be robust to label noise?' In: *Proceedings of the Twenty-Ninth International Conference on International Joint Conferences on Artificial Intelligence*. 2021, pp. 2206–2212.
78. Rafael Müller, Simon Kornblith, and Geoffrey E Hinton. 'When does label smoothing help?' In: *Advances in Neural Information Processing Systems*. Ed. by H. Wallach, H. Larochelle, A. Beygelzimer, F. d'Alche-Buc, E. Fox, and R. Garnett. Vol. 32. Curran Associates, Inc., 2019.
79. Helen L. Ball. 'Conducting Online Surveys'. In: *Journal of Human Lactation* 35.3 (2019). PMID: 31084575, pp. 413–417. https://doi.org/10.1177/0890334419848734.
80. Daniele Scapin, Giulia Cisotto, Elvina Gindullina, and Leonardo Badia. 'Shapley Value as an Aid to Biomedical Machine Learning: a Heart Disease Dataset Analysis'. In: *2022 22nd IEEE International Symposium on Cluster, Cloud and Internet Computing (CCGrid)*. 2022, pp. 933–939. https://doi.org/10.1109/CCGrid54584.2022.00113.

7 Data Protection by Design Tool for Automated GDPR Compliance Verification Based on Semantically Modeled Informed Consent

Abstract

The enforcement of the GDPR in May 2018 has led to a paradigm shift in data protection. Organizations face significant challenges, such as demonstrating compliance (or auditability) and automated compliance verification due to the complex and dynamic nature of consent, as well as the scale at which compliance verification must be performed. Furthermore, the GDPR's promotion of data protection by design and industrial interoperability requirements has created new technical challenges, as they require significant changes in the design and implementation of systems that handle personal data. We present a scalable data protection by design tool for automated compliance verification and auditability based on informed consent that is modeled with a knowledge graph. Automated compliance verification is made possible by implementing a regulation-to-code process that translates GDPR regulations into well-defined technical and organizational measures and, ultimately, software code. We demonstrate the effectiveness of the tool in the insurance and smart cities domains. We highlight ways in which our tool can be adapted to other domains.

This chapter is a copy of the previously published article: **Tek Raj Chhetri**, Anelia Kurteva, Rance J. DeLong, Rainer Hilscher, Kai Korte, and Anna Fensel. 'Data Protection by Design Tool for Automated GDPR Compliance Verification Based on Semantically Modeled Informed Consent'. In: Sensors 22.7 (2022). https://doi.org/10.3390/s22072763

Contribution as a first author: The scientific contributions include the following: (i) conceptualisation of the study; (ii) design of the methodology; (iii) implementation and deployment of the proposed methodology and execution of experiments; (iv) performing formal analysis and validation of the experiments; (v) data curation and data visualisation; and (vi) writing the manuscript.

T. R. Chhetri, *Improving Decision Making Using Semantic Web Technologies*,
https://doi.org/10.1007/978-3-658-45877-5_7

7.1 Introduction

The enforcement of the General Data Protection Regulation (GDPR) [1] has transformed the landscape of personally identifiable information (PII) sharing (or processing). Any company (or individual) dealing with the PII of EU citizens must first obtain informed consent (Art. 6) from the data subject (i.e., an identifiable natural person according to Art. 4 (1)) if none of the other options of Art. 6 apply, regardless of their location [2]. Further, specific requirements for informed consent need to be met as well. Consent should be specific, unambiguous, freely given, and one should be able to withdraw it with the same ease as when it was given (Art. 6). However, these requirements have also posed significant challenges to companies regarding the automation of compliance verification. Several software tools for GDPR compliance have already been developed that cover some steps required for automated compliance verification (e.g., [3–7]). In most cases, these tools address only a specific subset of the GDPR regulations, such as audit (or auditability) [8] or only consent management. None of the surveyed tools implement a comprehensive process that translates technical and organizational measures (TOMs) into code that are required by the GDPR but are insufficiently defined.

According to the International Association of Privacy Professionals (IAPP) [9] annual privacy governance report (2020) [10], only 47% of the European companies are "fully" or "very" compliant (up from 39% in 2019). There is a need for solutions that can help companies automate GDPR compliance verification, as noncompliance with the GDPR can result in severe fines (Art. 83).

Having reviewed the existing GDPR compliance verification tools and their limitations, we have identified several issues (see Sect. 7.3) that many companies still face. A major challenge for companies, when complying with the GDPR, is to adhere to the *"principles of data protection by design"* and *"data protection by default"* (Rec. 78). Examples of such principles include the implementation of technical and organizational measures that ensure data integrity and confidentiality (Art. 32 (1) and Rec. 46) and the prevention of unauthorized disclosure or access to personal data (Art. 32 (2)), which all add another layer of complexity. A further challenge is the representation of consent in a consistent and uniform manner, which is required for interoperability and is currently lacking in existing GDPR solutions [4]. Companies also need to deal with dynamic consent (i.e., data subjects have the right to withdraw their consent at any time according to Art. 7 (3)), while remaining compliant with the regulation (or meeting compliance obligations). An example of the dynamic nature of consent is a broken consent chain due to a property ownership transfer, as described in [11], that is often encountered in the insurance domain. A system that can handle dynamic consent should be able to not only successfully detect broken consent chains but also support the re-establishment of valid consent. Finally, the scalability of processes such as automated compliance and audit is still a significant challenge, particularly in industries such as insurance and smart cities where time is critical and delays can result in additional monetary charges for businesses [8].

In light of current challenges and industrial requirements, and building on our initial idea [12], we present a scalable tool for automated GDPR compliance based on semantically modeled informed consent (part of the the smashHit [13] project). Compliance refers to the verification that a person's data are used according to that person's informed consent. Our work adheres to data protection by design principles by implementing a novel regulation-to-code process that translates GDPR regulations first into protection goals defined by the Standard Data Protection Model (SDM) and then into well-defined technical and organizational measures (TOMs; details in Sect. 7.4.1). Both the SDM and TOM steps of this process are executed by the legal team associated with the smashHit project. The same legal team is also supervising the implementation of TOMs into code. Our tool makes extensive use of semantic technologies, specifically a knowledge graph (KG) and an ontology (both developed in collaboration with legal experts), for representing informed consent as defined by the GDPR. Semantic technology is also regarded as one of the best practices in RegTech [14] and Ryan et al. [6]. Knowledge graphs, for example, provide a consistent consent representation in a machine-readable format, support data interoperability, and faster and easier knowledge discovery [15]. Numerous semantic models for consent exist as shown in the survey by Kurteva et al. [16] and their use for cases such as GDPR compliance verification is evident, as shown in, e.g., [17].

7.1.1 Goal

The primary objective of our work is to automate GDPR compliance verification with the help of semantics and a regulation-to-code process. To achieve this, we present a scalable, ready-to-be-deployed data protection by design tool, which utilizes a legal KG. Automated compliance verification and the handling of broken consent chains are the two main functionalities supported by our tool. The second objective is to show that GDPR regulations can be translated into code via several intermediate steps. All system requirements have been derived from our two business use cases related to data sharing (see Appendix B).

7.1.2 Contributions

With our work, we make the following contributions:

- We present a scalable tool for automated GDPR compliance verification based on informed consent, with a use case in smart cities and insurance (see Appendix B) that can be generalized to other domains. By "scalable", we mean a system design (i.e., architecture) that adapts to incoming requests, such as scaling up as the number of requests increases.
- We present a process with a sequence of intermediate steps (regulation -> SDM—TOM -> code) that translates legal regulations into code. We show that implemented TOMs can be systematically evaluated and automatically tested (in Sect. 7.7.2).
- Our tool supports data interoperability through the use of semantic technology (ontology and a KG).
- Our tool implements a solution for broken consent chains based on two industrial use cases.

The rest of the paper is structured as follows. Section 7.2 provides background information on the challenges of data sharing as a result of the GDPR. Section 7.3 provides an overview of the related works. Section 7.4 summarizes the GDPR TOMs and the KG upon which our work is based on. Section 7.5 discusses the architecture of compliance verification tool and Sect. 7.6 provides details on its implementation. Section 7.7 presents the evaluation, which is followed by conclusions in Sect. 7.8.

7.2 Background

This section provides a high-level overview of the GDPR's impact on the data sharing landscape (or data processing landscape), highlighting the importance of our work. As shown in Fig. 7.1, we observe two distinct data sharing scenarios: (i) situation prior to GDPR implementation with no consent requirement, and (ii) situation with GDPR. Prior to the GDPR, there was no requirement for consent, and thus the data sharing (or processing) process was simple and straightforward, as the data controllers (DC) (Art. 4(7)) and data processors (DP) (Art. 4(8)) were not required to deal with consent or any regulatory laws such as the GDPR. However, with the implementation of the GDPR, the data sharing and data processing landscape has shifted and has become more complicated. This shift is illustrated in Fig. 7.1. DP and DC are not only required to obtain consent, but they must also comply with other GDPR requirements (see Table 7.1) and be able to demonstrate compliance (i.e., show that they are doing only what was consented to by the data subject) to regulatory bodies upon request.

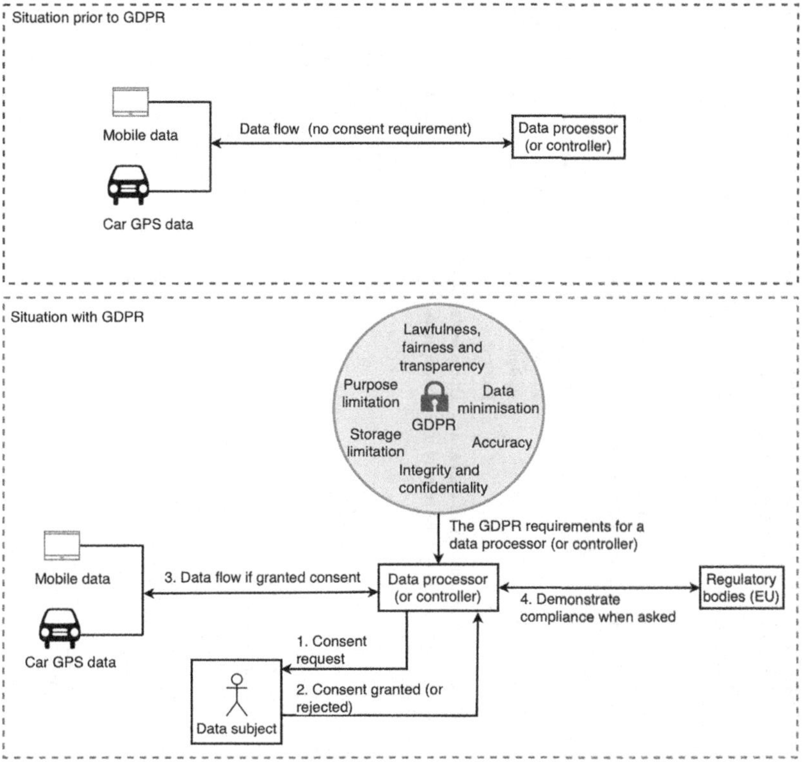

Fig. 7.1 The areas of concern that need to be focused on in light of the changing data sharing/processing landscape as a result of GDPR implementation

Table 7.1 GDPR principles and associated SDM protection objectives, their scope and purpose, as well as the associated technical–organizational measures (TOMs) and their implementations in our compliance verification tool

GDPR Principles	SDM Protection Goal	Scope and Purpose	TOM	Our TOM Implementation	Our Tool's Component
Purpose limitation (Art. 5(1)(b))	Unlinkability	Takes the principle of purpose limitation into account; defines the permissible purpose changes.	Role concepts with graduated access rights on the basis of identity management and secure authentication process.	JavaScript Object Notation (JSON) [18] Web Tokens (JWT) [19]-based access control is implemented. Further, customization of standard JWT token-based access is implemented, enabling role-based endpoint access.	API layer
Storage limitation (Art. 5(1)(e))	Availability	Ensuring the availability of data at a certain time for those who require it at that time.	Documentation of data syntax.	PEP-8 [20] coding convention is followed throughout the entire code base; code is commented for better understandability. Swagger (an interface description language for describing RESTful APIs) is used to document the RESTful APIs.	All components
Lawfulness, fairness and transparency (Art. 5(1)(a))	Transparency	The extent and the form in which data processing should be kept transparent towards data subjects and supervisory authorities; information and disclosure obligations pursuant to Art. 12 et seq. GDPR, the notification obligation pursuant to Art. 34 GDPR, the documentation of the processing pursuant to Art. 30 GDPR.	Documentation of consents, their revocations and objections.	Consent and their states, such as revocations, are stored in the GraphDB [21] database, as well as logged in the MongoDB [22] database.	Compliance, Consent, Audit

(Continued)

Table 7.1 (Continued)

GDPR Principles	SDM Protection Goal	Scope and Purpose	TOM	Our TOM Implementation	Our Tool's Component
Accuracy (5(1)(d)), Integrity and confidentiality (Art. 5(1)(f))	Intervenability	The extent to which data subject rights are to be granted; how data subjects can exercise their rights, how to ensure that requests are made in a legitimate manner, what corrections can be taken in the processing of personal data (e.g., by rectification, erasure, or limitation of the processing of personal data) and in what form data can be transferred by or to other controllers.	Operational possibility of compiling, consistently rectifying, blocking and erasure of all stored personal data.	All data are stored in the KG with a unique ID and these data are processed via REST API endpoints; by providing personal information that resolves to a unique ID, users can access their data via a user interface.	Compliance, Consent
Integrity and confidentiality (Art. 5(1)(f))	Confidentiality	Takes care that the disclosure of certain data is denied to those who are not authorized to have access to it; takes into account the processes, systems, and services potentially vulnerable to unauthorized access.	Encryption of data.	Deterministic searchable encryption technique is used to encrypt the data. The Rivest-Shamir-Adleman (RSA) [23] with Public Key Cryptography (PKCS) Standards) #1 Optimal Asymmetric Encryption Padding (OAEP) is used for asymmetric Advanced Encryption Standard (AES) [24] session key encryption and chained three layers AES for data encryption. Further, implementation of authentication procedure. & Identity management is used to ensure that only registered components have access to endpoints.	Security

(Continued)

Table 7.1 (Continued)

GDPR Principles	SDM Protection Goal	Scope and Purpose	TOM	Our TOM Implementation	Our Tool's Component
Integrity and confidentiality (Art. 5(1)(f)), Accountability (Art. 5(2))	Integrity	Ensuring that data related to an identified or identifiable person are kept intact and up-to-date; ensuring that the processes, systems, and services are correctly planned, operated, and controlled according to the intended purpose.	Protection against external influences.	Security measures such as encryption, role-based access controls to prevent unauthorized data access. Audits and tests to document functionality, risks, security gaps.	Security, Audit
Data minimization (Art. 5(1)(c))	Data minimization	Implementation of the data minimization requirement of the GDPR; establishment of retention periods for personal data and processes to ensure compliance.	Reduction of non-required attributes of data subjects.	Consent creation REST API endpoint defines minimal set of variables for processing.	Consent

For example, it is necessary to maintain a log of data processing operations in order to demonstrate compliance by a DC (or a DP). This is to demonstrate to the appropriate authority that only consent-based processing is being carried out. Additionally, it is necessary to perform compliance checks on data sharing (or data processing) activities on a regular basis to ensure that everything is performed in accordance with consent. For example, regular checks need to verify that consents are actually still active and have not been revoked or have expired. Moreover, performing these tasks manually becomes impossible in cases such as smart cities and car insurance because of the scale at which they must be performed. As a result, automated solutions that can handle these tasks on a large scale are required.

7.3 Related Work

This section provides an overview of existing state-of-the-art solutions for GDPR compliance verification. A summary of the existing solutions and their limitations is presented in Sect. 7.3.2 and Table 7.3.

7.3.1 Compliance Verification

Ranise and Siswantoro [25] present a scalable approach for automated legal compliance checking based on security policies, which were translated into formal rules, in the context of the European Data Protection Directive (EU DPD) [26]. However, the work was completed before the acceptance of GDPR, which can be seen as a limitation. Further, formal rules are restrictive, and legal input is hard to implement. TOMs and semantics have not been considered.

Robol et al. [27] propose a privacy-by-design framework, which supports the development of GDPR compliant systems. The authors focus on the STS-ml extension of the Socio-Technical Security (STS) [28] method, which can be used to express and verify privacy policy rules. The implementation of a tool that enables automatic compliance based on the STS-ml is planned as future work, which can be seen as a limitation. TOMs have not been considered.

The use of semantics, specifically an ontology, for GDPR compliance is explored by Westphal et al. [29], who propose a framework that consumes and transforms privacy policies into rules. In addition to compliance based on one's informed consent, the framework is also able to perform compliance based on relevant GDPR obligations. Evaluation details have not been presented. The limitations of the framework with regards to performance and scalability are unknown. TOMs have not been considered.

By deriving the main obligations of actors such as data protection officer (DPO), data subject (DS), and requirements for compliance that need to be met, Rhahla et al. [3] propose guidelines for implementing a GDPR compliance verification framework for Big Data systems (i.e., systems that can handle high volumes of unstructured data [30]). However, there is a lack of implementation details and information if the solution was developed with input from and validated by legal experts, which can be seen as a limitation. Further, the study did not take into account any TOMs or the use of semantic technology to solve issues such as information interoperability.

Brodin [31] present a framework for GDPR compliance to assist small and medium-sized enterprises (SMEs) in adapting to GDPR. Compliance is achieved by adopting an employee's work style to the designed work routines, policies, and templates. The framework involves practitioners and has been empirically and theoretically evaluated. However, little to no details about the actual implementation and the used technologies are presented in [31]. Further, the framework does not provide process automation, and scalability issues are present.

Camilo [32] proposes a blockchain-based tool for GDPR consent management, which allows individuals to exercise their rights (e.g., give, revoke consent), and supports auditing of consent transactions and processing activities. Although several GDPR Articles have been followed for compliance and a proof-of-concept prototype has been implemented, specific implementation details have not been provided. The evaluation has shown that blockchain supports transparency and traceability when it comes to data processing and consent. However, blockchain's immutability clashes with GDPR's "rights to erasure" [33]. It is not clear if scalability and performance evaluations have been conducted and if TOMs were considered.

Arfelt et al. [8] present a tool for automated GDPR compliance monitoring, which focuses on auditing at scale. The authors use metric first-order temporal logic (MFOTL) [34] to formalize GDPR requirements and the MonPoly [35] monitoring tool to determine whether the logs confirm the given MFOTL formula and to check for violations. The work is validated by using industry data logs. However, it focuses on compliance monitoring and only implements a few of the GDPR clauses. Semantics were not utilized and TOMs were not considered.

Piras et al. [36] present an architecture for a privacy-by-design platform for GDPR compliance as part of the Data govErnance For supportiNg gDpr (DEFeND) [37] project. The platform is capable of organizing and analyzing individual's data privacy preferences and the consent itself. Further, it is able to monitor run-time execution of functionalities and to detect and respond to security breaches. However, there is a lack of implementation details and the scalability is unknown.

Similarly to [32], Truong et al. [38] propose a blockchain-based platform for data management in compliance with GDPR, which grants and validates permissions regarding data usage by utilizing smart contracts. The performance evaluation of the implemented tool has shown that with high workload, the latency rises and bottleneck issues are present. Issues such as data interoperability have not been addressed.

Barati et al. [39], built upon their previous work in [5, 40], and propose a GDPR compliance verification method in the Internet of Things (IoT) based on multiple smart contracts using blockchain (Etherium [41]). The evaluation shows that the execution time of operations such as compliance verification is highly dependent on the interest of the blockchain miners. Further, the authors acknowledge that focusing mainly on data privacy (e.g., visibility of how data is used by smart devices) and less on the security of the operations can be seen as a limitation in their work [39].

Kirrane et al. [17] present the SPECIAL-K platform for personal data processing transparency and GDPR compliance, which makes use of semantic technology, namely vocabularies. Compliance is achieved by using the HermiT [42] reasoner over semantically modeled privacy policies and event logs. In addition, Kirrane et al. propose several *"choke points"* such as increased number of users and different privacy policy complexity, which can be used for the evaluation of similar compliance frameworks. Although using semantic technology, TOMs have not been considered and latency issues are present when dealing with different complexities of privacy policies.

Bonatti et al. [43] present the SPECIAL policy language that can be used to model consent, obligations, and policies in a machine-understandable way with OWL [44] and an approaches for automated GDPR compliance verification. Compliance is performed based on ad hoc reasoning algorithms (see [45] for details). Based on the evaluation results, further process optimizations are needed. TOMs were not considered.

Mahindrakar and Joshi [46] also focus on utilizing semantics and blockchain for GDPR compliance. Legal knowledge from privacy policies is transformed into a KG, which is later integrated with blockchain to support auditing. Compliance is performed with the help of reasoning over rules related to specific data operations. Although the proposed decentralized solution eases compliance [46] and uses semantics, it also uses blockchain, which is a limitation, as discussed in [16, 33]. Addressing privacy-by-design issues has been set as future work.

Barati and Rana [47] encode GDPR rules as opcodes in smart contracts in a cloud-based environment to automatically verify data operations. The evaluation of the prototype showed that as the number of operation increases, the consumed gas increases as well. The authors found a correlation between the fee paid by a data subject and the rate of violation detection—the violation detection increases when the number of operations decreases [47]. A current limitation of the study is that it has not yet investigated how the "right to be forgotten" can be implemented, having in mind the use of blockchain.

Ryan et al. [6] present a set of requirements for GDPR compliance based on RegTech [14] and a prototype implementation of a GDPR compliance verification tool that can assist DPOs in maintaining GDPR accountability. The authors utilize semantics (the Data Privacy Vocabulary (DPV) [48] and PROV-O [49] ontologies). The evaluation showed that the tool helps achieve 100% compliance for accuracy, retention, and security, only 50% compliance for data breaches, and 40% regarding data subject rights. However, TOMs were not considered and the scope of the work is limited to providing information needed for compliance verification to DPOs.

Semantics and blockchain are also used by Merlec et al. [7], who present a dynamic consent management system for personal data usage in compliance with GDPR. The system supports functionalities such as data provisioning, user management, and authentication. Some of the known limitations, as mentioned by the authors in [7], include the complexity of the presented solution, immutability of blockchain, and the automation of security and privacy policies verification and GDPR compliance checking, which is planned as future work.

Hamdani et al. [50] combine machine learning (ML) with rule-based reasoning and propose a framework for automated GDPR compliance checking. Compliance is based on Article 13 and 14 and uses the OPP-115 [51] taxonomy to capture 10 rules from these articles. The combination of rules and ML has shown to accurately predict both coarse-grained and fine-grained data processing. However, the framework is limited with regards to the types of documents it covers. The use of multiple compliance documents, such as data protection impact assessments (DPIAs) [52], is set as future work, and TOMs were not considered.

Similarly to our work, Daoudagh et al. [53] also focus on data sharing in smart cities and propose a privacy-by-design platform for compliance. The implemented solution preserves individuals' privacy by utilizing various authentication mechanisms, such as zero-knowledge proofs, it can support data management and traceability, and it is compliant with GDPR principles such as data minimization and purpose limitation. Although the system has been implemented and utilizes the DPV [48] ontology, details about how exactly compliance verification is performed have not been provided, and only two TOMs have been considered.

Finally, Tokas et al. [54] propose a policy language that models different GDPR principles, purposes, access rights, and a static rule-based approach for compliance based on specific privacy policies. Although the work is based on several GDPR articles, including data protection by design, improvements are needed regarding the language's expressivity (e.g., to model DC (or DP), data retention periods). Further, the proposed static mechanism does not fully automate GDPR compliance, and TOMs have not been considered.

7.3.2 Summary

This section presents a comparison of our solution to the reviewed state-of-the-art projects. Table 7.3 (see Appendix C) highlights several characteristics that we have derived from our two use cases and the need for a scalable GDPR compliance solution that supports data interoperability and compliance verification automation. Given the volume of processing required for use cases such as smart cities, we considered scalability as a critical factor. When comparing the solutions, we also considered the implementation of GDPR-required TOMs. Details on TOMs are presented in Sects. 7.4.1 and 7.7.2. The industrial use case provides information on whether the work was conducted based on real industrial use cases. Finally, we considered the implementation level of the solutions as it helps distinguish between ready-to-be-deployed and proof-of-concept solutions. In Table 7.3, a check mark indicates that a feature has been addressed, while a cross mark indicates that a feature is either not implemented, there is a limitation, or it is unknown (i.e., no information was provided in the study).

The details on the implementation notation used in Table 7.3 are presented below.

- **P** indicates that GDPR compliance has only been proposed or guidelines provided without actually implementing a proof of concept or implementation.
- **PoC** indicates the completion of a proof of concept (or experimental implementation that is not at the prototype level).
- **PT** indicates that a prototype implementation has been completed.
- **FM** indicates ready-to-deploy work that can be integrated via Representational State Transfer (REST) Application Programming Interface (API). With ready-to-deploy code, we refer to an implementation that can be deployed and integrated with minimal configuration.

As shown in Table 7.3, the solutions which utilize semantics and allow consent creation/revocation do not fully automate GDPR compliance and do not consider TOMs. The studies which automate compliance have experimental PoC implementation; thus cannot be directly deployed and used. Although all these solutions have undergone performance evaluation, a scalability evaluation was performed only for [46, 50]. Apart from [25], none of the studies discussed the ease of adapting their respective approaches to other regulatory frameworks. Most importantly, a review of related works reveals that the majority of current studies lack consent creation and revocation features. In comparison to all of the studies in Table 7.3, our solution is not only capable of performing automated GDPR compliance verification but it also implements a robust regulation-to-code process that translates GDPR regulations into well-defined TOMs via the SDM. It also supports interoperability by using a KG. Further, it has undergone extensive performance and scalability evaluation based on real-world industrial usecases and has a PT implementation, which allows it to be deployed and used straight away. The following sections present the details about its design, implementation, and evaluation.

7.4 KG Overview and Legal Background

This section presents details about the two main tasks that allow us to implement a scalable automated GDPR compliance verification tool based on semantically modeled informed consent. A tool that implements a set of legal regulations (such as the GDPR) requires a way of translating these regulations into a unified machine-readable format. Modeling and verifying consent across a variety of domains (e.g., our two uses cases discussed in Sect. 7.1 and Appendix B) can be achieved with the help of a semantic data model (e.g., the KGs). Our approach to address the regulations-to-code task adds a software implementation step to the previously established methodology that translates vaguely-defined GDPR TOM requirements to so-called protection goals defined by SDM [55], and finally, well-defined TOMs are important as they enable data protection by design, that can be implemented in code. All legal entities that filter into the compliance verification process (including protection goals) need to be semantically represented and readily accessible to other integrating components. A particularly flexible and extendable way of doing so is a legal KG.

7.4.1 GDPR and Relevant TOMs

Our GDPR compliance verification tool follows the *"data protection by design and by default"* principle to ensure GDPR compliance (Table 7.1). A key instrument here is the implementation of *"appropriate technical and organizational measures which are designed to implement data protection principles [...] in an effective manner and to integrate the necessary safeguards into the processing in order to [...] protect the rights of data subjects"* (Art. 25 (1)). This includes the adoption of internal policies (Rec. 78). It is the responsibility of the DC (or DP) to implement TOMs to ensure and to be able to demonstrate that processing is performed in accordance with the GDPR (Art. 4 (7), Art. 24). The implementation of TOMs also mitigates the risk to the rights and freedoms of natural persons posed by the processing of their personal data (Art. 32 (1)).

Legal requirements are not easily translated into technical implementations. The SDM [55] was developed to serve this exact translation function. The SDM translates legal requirements into corresponding protection goals that can be directly implemented as TOMs. GDPR requirements and their mapped protection goals are summarized in [55] (Table in Sect. C2, p. 28). The SDM:

- Systematizes data protection requirements in form of protection goals.
- Systematically derives generic measures from the protection goals, supplemented by a catalog of reference measures.
- Systematizes the identification of risks in order to determine protection requirements of the data subjects resulting from the processing.
- Offers a procedure model for modeling, implementation, and continuous control and testing of processing activities.

Table 7.1 lists each SDM protection goal and its relation to the respective GDPR principle(s). Further, Table 7.1 associates protection goals with specific TOMs and their current implementation in the automated GDPR compliance verification tool.

7.4.2 Legal KG

The main data source for performing compliance verification is a KG, which is based on the smashHitCore [56] ontology and is stored in the GraphDB graph database (see Fig. 7.2). The KG models informed consent as defined by GDPR Art. 7 and Rec. 32. Concepts such as contracts, sensor data, data processing, and the involved entities are represented as well. When it comes to the consent itself, the KG represents its (1) state (e.g., granted/not granted, revoked, withdrawn), (2) purpose, (3) duration, (4) the requested data and its type (e.g., sensor data), (5) types of data processing (e.g., analysis, retrieval, adaptation, collection) associated with consent, (6) entities related to consent (e.g., DC (or DP), data subject, etc.), and (7) the time and date of a consent state change.

Consent is collected via consent forms, which have been evaluated against GDPR's requirements for informed consent (Art.7, 12, 13, and Rec. 32) by the legal experts (i.e., manual evaluation) participating in the smashHit project. With the help of APIs, the data from the consent forms are sent to predefined Simple Protocol and Resource Description Framework Query Language (SPARQL) [57] queries, which annotate and create unique consent instances in the KG. The KG can be accessed directly via the SPARQL API [58] provided by GraphDB. The advantages of using semantic models such as KGs for consent are also discussed in [59, 60].

7.5 System Architecture

In this section, we present the details of our architecture for an automated GDPR compliance verification tool, which addresses current data sharing and processing challenges (see Sect. 7.3). The main goal of our work is to simplify and automate GDPR compliance verification with the help of semantics and a regulation-to-code process, as shown in Fig. 7.1 (see Sect. 7.2).

Figure 7.2 presents the architecture of the automated GDPR compliance verification tool, which follows a microservices architecture pattern. A microservices architecture pattern is one in which all modules are cohesive, independent processes that interact through messages [61]. This specific architectural pattern provides a solution to problems such as technology lock-in for developers and dependency

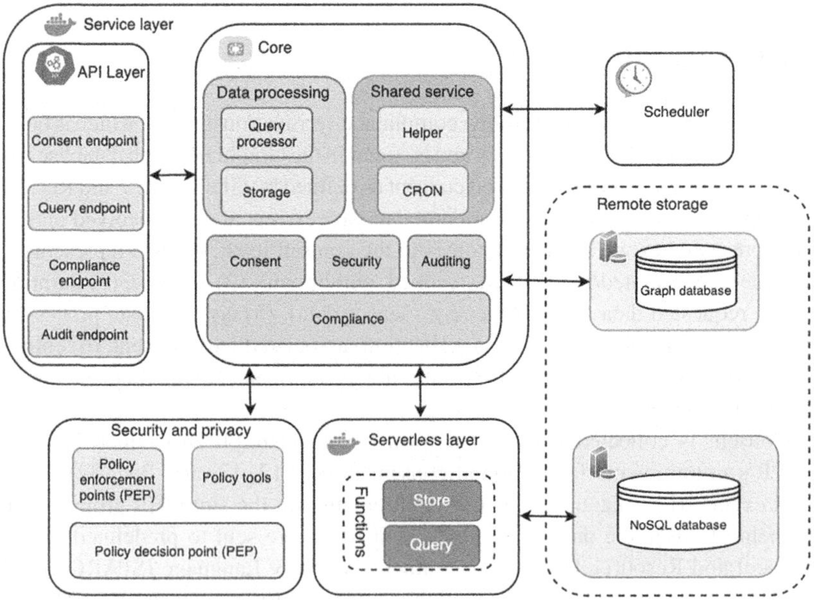

Fig. 7.2 Architecture of the automated GDPR compliance verification tool

problems that monolithic patterns suffer from [61, 62]. Moreover, the microservices pattern supports scalability (one of the challenges and industrial requirements in Sect. 7.1) by allowing for scaling of individual small components [63, 64]. Additionally, the flexibility and maintainability of microservices architectures are reasons to consider them.

7.5.1 Service Layer

The service layer implements core functionality required for automated compliance verification and related supporting operations such as consent creation. It is divided into two parts: (i) the *API layer* and (ii) the *core*. The *API layer* and *core* components are discussed in detail in the subsections below.

7.5.1.1 API Layer

The API layer serves as the primary entry point for the tool and exposes REST endpoints. The API layer provides access to the compliance verification tool's functionalities via REST endpoints. In addition to exposing the tool's access, one of the major features of the API layer is the ability to enable role-based access, which prevents unauthorized access and is one of the GDPR TOMs (see Sect. 7.4.1). Algorithm 4 (more details in implementation Sect. 7.6.2.1) shows the steps for enabling role-based access. The organizational code in Algorithm 4 is a unique identifier assigned manually (i.e., by an administrator) and is provided to othecon tool.

Algorithm 4: Role-based API endpoint access

Input: JWT token
Result: Returns grant access or HTTP 403 forbidden response

verify_jwt_in_request();
claims ← extract_hashed_claims_value_from_jwt_token();
hasValidClaim ← verify_hashed_claims_value_from_database(claims);
if *hasValidClaimsl is True and hasValidOrganisationCode* **then**
  return grant access;
else
  return HTTP 403 Forbidden response;
end

7.5.1.2 Data Processing

The data processing module is responsible for data management in order to support required operations, such as compliance checking, consent creation, and auditing. The data processing module is further subdivided into two components, the query processor and storage, according to the type of data processing operations it supports. The query processor module contains the SPARQL queries required to deal with consent (i.e., consent data in KG), while the storage module handles the query processor's execution.

7.5.1.3 Shared Service

The shared services include modules that assist other modules in their operations, such as compliance, consent, and security. This shared service module's purpose is to increase reusability by abstracting away common functionality from other modules. As with data processing, the shared services module is composed of two subcomponents: helper and CRON. The CRON is a unique shared service shared by the scheduler and compliance that initiates an automated compliance check in response to the scheduler's trigger. The helper, however, is shared across multiple modules, such as consent and security.

7.5.1.4 Security

The security module incorporates safeguards such as encryption to ensure confidentiality, which is also one of the TOMs (see Sect. 7.4.1). Furthermore, the security module supports the GDPR's *"data protection by design"* and *"data protection by default"* principles. To support *"data protection by design"*, the security module includes two critical features: deterministic layered encryption and a decryption scheme, the architecture of which are illustrated in Figs. 7.3 and 7.4, respectively.

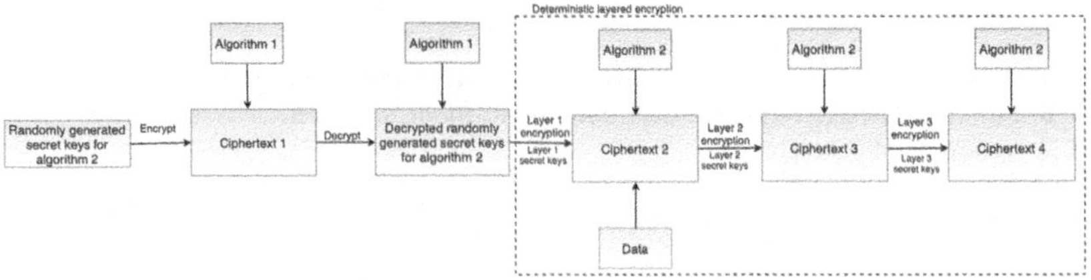

Fig. 7.3 Architecture of encryption scheme

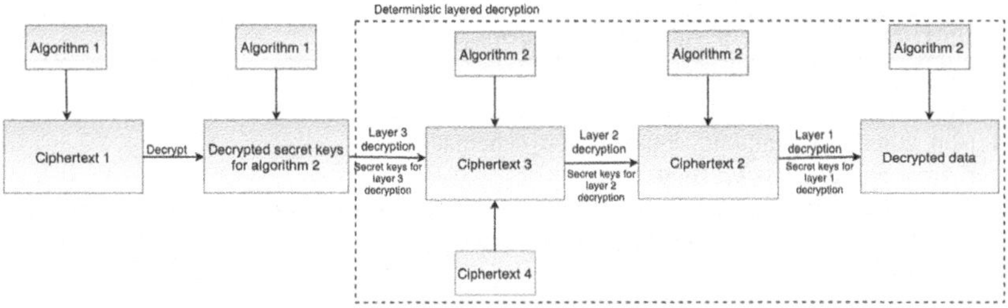

Fig. 7.4 Architecture of decryption scheme

Both the encryption and decryption schemes employ a hybrid algorithm (implementation details in Sect. 7.6.2.4). This is motivated by the established benefits of hybrid (i.e., using symmetric and asymmetric encryption techniques) approaches, as demonstrated by Zou et al. [65]. Furthermore, deterministic encryption enables secure querying of data over the database, and layered encryption strengthens the security, which can be increased or decreased as required.

7.5.1.5 Consent

The consent module assists in ensuring that only necessary and required consent information is used, thereby minimizing data usage, which is one of the GDPR's TOMs (see Sect. 7.4.1). Figure 7.5 shows the consent JSON schema used by the consent module and its representation in the legal KG. In particular, the consent module carried out this task of ensuring that only required information is used by performing JSON schema (see Fig. 7.5a) validation. The JSON schema was created according to legal KG and, therefore, validation of the JSON schema ensures that consent (i.e., input consent in JSON format) is in accordance with legal KG. The steps for performing the consent validation are depicted in Algorithm 5 (implementation details in Sect. 7.6.2.5). The consent module also performs the task of transforming consent information in JSON format into the KG. The reason for this approach (i.e., not taking KG directly as opposed to JSON) is that not all businesses, particularly small and medium-sized enterprises (SMEs), have expertise in semantic technology. Thus, using the JSON format for interaction reduces the complexity and overhead associated with dealing with semantics, while allowing SMEs to take advantage of its benefits.

Algorithm 5: Consent validation for consent creation

```
Input: Consent in JSON format
Result: Returns success or error response
json_consent ← validate_consent_json_schema();
if json_consent is valid then
    map_consent ← transform_and_map_to_legal_kg(json_consent);
    response ← create_consent(map_consent);
    return response;
else
    return Error response;
end
```

The consent validation (i.e., *validate_consent_json_schema*), for example, validates that all the required fields, such as purpose information, are present. Further, the consent validation validates that the consent input has the valid required data types. For instance, the consent granted and the expiration date must be in a valid date and time format and *DataProcessing* should be a list of string. Similarly, the transformation to legal KG step (i.e., *transform_and_map_to_legal_kg*) transforms the JSON input to the KG representation by adding appropriate details. For example, converting date and time format JSON input (e.g., consent granted time) to SPARQL date format [66] and adding an appropriate relationship, such as *hasPurpose* (see Fig. 7.5b) for the purpose of consent input. Moreover, the transformation step also performs additional validation, such as checking if the consent granted time is in a specific date format (e.g., universal time format).

The *Agent* in the consent JSON schema represents the DC (or DP)'s information. The *Resource* contains information about the actual data collected from the data subject that the data processor or controller desires for data processing purposes, such as GPS data. The *DataProcessing* signifies the purpose for which the data will be used, for example, marketing.

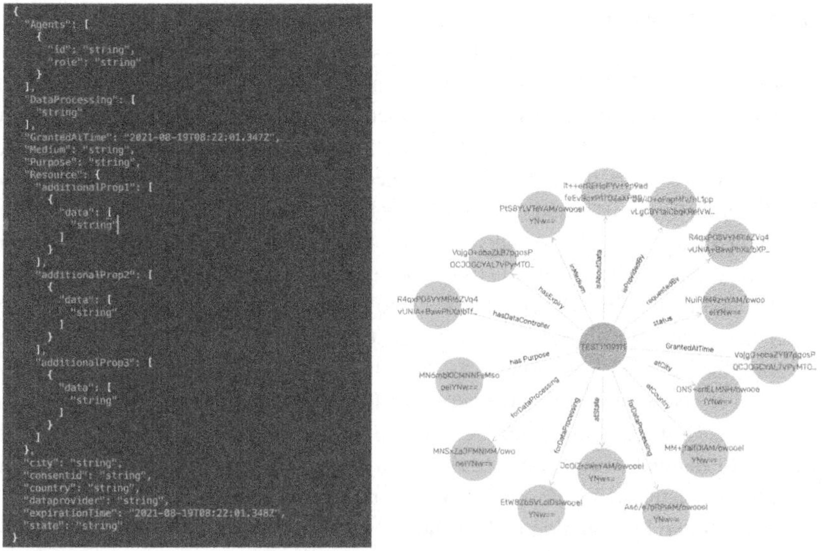

(a) **(b)**

Fig. 7.5 A snapshot of the JSON schema used for consent and the consent module's creation (or representation) of consent in the legal KG. (**a**) Consent JSON schema. (**b**) KG representation of consent in GraphDB after successful validation

7.5.1.6 Auditing

One of the core principles of the GDPR is transparency (see Sect. 7.4.1), which requires that information about the processing of personal data be readily available. Furthermore, transparency aids accountability, which is defined as demonstrating compliance with GDPR obligations in a measurable manner [67]. The auditing module promotes accountability by enabling access to data processing details such as whether valid consent was obtained, whether data processing was carried out in accordance with the consent, and whether no data processing occurred in the event of consent expiration or revocation. Additionally, this information assists a DC (or DP) in demonstrating compliance, as it is the information required to be presented to authorities (implementation and auditing examples in Sect. 7.6.2.6). The auditing module, which makes the personal data processing information available to both the DC (or DP) and the data subject, is critical to transparency and is the module's major functionality.

7.5.1.7 Compliance

The compliance module is the heart of the system; it conducts compliance checks to ensure that DC (or DP)) have obtained informed consent from data subjects for both accessing the data and the processing applied to it (i.e., no consent is violated). A consent violation occurs when the DC (or DP) acts in a manner inconsistent with the consent. For instance, if a user (or data subject) has provided informed consent for the DC (or DP) to collect and use mobile Global Positioning System (GPS) data for research purposes, the DC (or DP) should collect and use GPS data exclusively for research purposes. The use of data for purposes other than research and the collection of data other than GPS would constitute a violation of consent, a punishable offense under the GDPR. Furthermore, in the case of automated compliance check (i.e., the compliance check instantiated by the scheduler based on scheduled time), the detection of a consent violation triggers a notification alert (details in implementation Sect. 7.6.2.7), thereby allowing DC (or DP) to take appropriate actions. While in the case of manual compliance checks, such as the one instantiated by the DC (or DP) for a particular data subject or consent, no alert is triggered.

As illustrated by Equation (7.1), cand the security and privacy compliance decision. The compliance module is responsible for the core compliance decisions, and the security and privacy module for security and privacy compliance decisions (details in Sect. 7.5.2). The core compliance decision is the combination of consent validity, data processing purpose, data processing rights, and data processing operations. Simultaneously, security and privacy compliance decisions are made in conjunction with the data subject's privacy preferences and the DC (or DP) privacy policy.

$$\begin{aligned} compliance = (&core\_compliance\_decision \\ &\wedge security\_and\_privacy\_compliance\_decision) \end{aligned} \tag{7.1}$$

Let ds represent the data subject and dc_dp the DC (or DP). Similarly, let $consent_{ds} = \{C_{ds}, P_{ds}, R_{ds}, D_{ds}\}$ represent the consent information from data subject and $processing_{dc\_dp} = \{P_{dc\_dp}, R_{dc\_dp}, D_{dc\_dp}\}$ the data processing information obtained from the DC (or DP), where P denote the purpose, R the resources from which the data is collected (e.g., GPS), and D the information about the actual data processing to be carried out (e.g., data analysis). The C, on the other hand, contains information about the expiration of the granted consent. The core compliance decision then can be represented as shown by Equation (7.2). The consent validity check verifies that the consent is still valid and has not expired, while the purpose validity, processing rights validity, and data processing validity checks compare the consent to information obtained from the data processor (or controller).

$$\begin{aligned} core\_compliance\_decision = \ & hasValidConsent(C_{ds}) \\ & \wedge\ hasValidPurpose(P_{ds}, P_{dc\_dp}) \\ & \wedge\ hasValidProcessingRights(R_{ds}, R_{dc\_dp}) \\ & \wedge\ isDoingValidDataProcessing(D_{ds}, D_{dc\_dp}) \end{aligned} \tag{7.2}$$

Compliant behavior necessitates satisfying Equation (7.1), which begins with evaluating the core compliance decision (i.e., Equation (7.2)). The process of determining compliance is immediately halted if any of the conditions are determined to be false, as compliance requires satisfying all of the conditions. The notification alert is then passed, providing the detailed information, such as where the compliance check failed or everything is fine in the case of success.

Consider the following consent information: (i) purpose = safety research on driving, (ii) granted time = 2018-08-22:18T08:22:01.3474Z, (iii) resources = GPS, and (iv) data processing activity = data analysis. Consider the following information as information about processing obtained from a DC (or DP): (i) resources = GPS, VSS (vehicle speed sensor), (ii) purpose = safety research on driving, and (iii) data processing activity = data analysis.

Example 1. *Assume for the moment that the scheduler is set to run the compliance check daily at time 21:01.3474Z. The current time is 2019-05-22:18T08:21:01.3474Z and the expiry time for the consent is* C_{ds} *= 2019-05-22:18T08:20:01.3474Z. When the compliance check operation is performed (i.e., when Equation (1) is evaluated), the compliance module determines that the consent has expired (i.e., at* $hasValidConsent(C_{ds})$*) and that no data processing should be permitted. The compliance module begins by updating the consent status to invalid and notifying the DC (or DP).*

Example 2. *In this example, assume that consent is valid (i.e., it has not expired or has not been revoked). The DS has granted consent for only GPS data (i.e.,* R_{ds} *= GPS) to be collected (i.e., the DC (or DP) has only GPS data processing rights). The DC (or DP) does, however, collect data from both GPS and VSS (i.e.,* $R_{dc\_dp} = \{GPS, VSS\}$*). The compliance status will then be invalid during the compliance check (i.e., at* $hasValidProcessingRights(R_{ds}, R_{dc\_dp})$*). A similar situation can also exist if all core compliance decisions were to pass but security and privacy decisions were to fail.*

In the case of the broken consent chain, a similar compliance check step is performed, thereby invalidating the existing consent. For example, DS A, who has given consent to share car data, sells the car (which is the source of the data) to a new DS B. Here, the existing consent chain should be invalidated as it is no longer valid. Upon receiving this update via an API, the compliance tool invalidates the existing consent. However, in the case of revocation, the DS must initiate the compliance request by providing specific consent information such as a consent ID. Our tool will invalidate the consent after performing the necessary checks.

7.5.2 Security and Privacy

Security typically concerns itself with the objectives of *confidentiality*, *integrity*, and *availability* of *data*. Privacy adds to these objectives a concern for the right of a person (*DS*) to authorize and restrict the use of data that are *about*, or describe, that person to some extent (*personal data*). The common aspects of security and privacy induce us to establish a common framework within which to conceptualize and implement their related objectives. When implementing security and privacy, we exploit the distinction between *mechanism* and *policy*. Security and privacy policies are expressions of specific rules governing permissions and restrictions to the access and use of data. Security and privacy mechanisms implement data controls that may be applied in practice to enforce a policy. Ideally, mechanisms are built to not embody a particular policy but rather a policy framework, and thus to be able to interpret and enforce any policy expressed within that framework. The benefit of this approach is that it provides the flexibility to make a broad range of modifications to policy without the need to revisit the implementation of the mechanism.

7.5.2.1 Policy Tools

The policy tools provide a policy specification language for expressing security and privacy policies for representing *privacy preference* and *privacy policy* within a framework based on the Next Generation Access Control (NGAC) standard [68]. A preference on the part of a data subject represents rules that constrain the handling of its data that the data subject has expressed through a process of informed consent. A privacy policy on the part of a data processor represents claims concerning what processing will be performed on the data subject's personal information, the purpose for which it is performed, and commitments about the handling of personal data by the data processor and sharing with third parties.

7.5.2.2 Policy Enforcement Points (PEP)

When a data processor seeks to perform a data processing operation on an item of personal data associated with a data subject, the processor calls a policy enforcement point to access the data. Although the PEP operates with the privilege to access the data of the data subject, it is *trusted* to make that data available to its caller only if a query to the policy decision point, citing the processor, the processing to be performed, and the purpose of the processing, returns with a "grant" response. There may be multiple PEPs in a system, or a PEP may even be within a remote data processing system.

7.5.2.3 Policy Decision Points (PDP)

Policies, including data processor privacy policies and data subject privacy preferences, are stored within the PDP mechanism for use to compute response to queries from PEPs. A query asks whether a specific operation on a particular data subject's personal data by a particular data processor is permissible under the policy, and if so, what the obligations are that the data processor must fulfill after it uses the data.

7.5.2.4 Compliance-Related Policy Decisions

The PDP provides several policy query interfaces based on privacy preferences and privacy policies. The queries carry out computations over policy representations that are constructed from information gathered from the smashHitCore ontology [56] and from the KGs. The first of these queries may come from the component tasked with obtaining consent. It utilizes the combination of a data subject's current privacy preference (as resulting from a consent) and a DC (or DP)'s privacy policy. The returned information may be used by the consent-gathering user interface to confirm that the privacy policy of a data processor complies with the data subject's current preference, or to highlight the areas of noncompliance. This information may be provided to the data subject for consideration in modifying the subject's consent/preference or in denying consent.

The second of the queries may come from any component tasked with responding to a request from a data processor for permission to perform a particular data processing operation on the personal data of a particular data subject. The computation of this query uses the processor's prior declared privacy policy and the data subject's current preference (corresponding to a valid consent) to determine whether the data processing operation, and its purpose, conform to the parameters granted in the data subject's consent. The returned value is a "grant" or "deny". In the case of "grant", the return includes any obligations that the processor must fulfill following the data access/use. A "grant" response may also include a *warrant*, which is a unique token that may be presented to the PEP that is enforcing access to the requested data item.

7.5.3 Scheduler

The scheduler supports time-based event scheduling. The scheduler is pivotal in our work because it enables the automated compliance check to be performed on a regular basis, based on the scheduled time using the shared service CRON.

7.5.4 Remote Storage

The remote storage facilitates storing of the consent and the compliance verification tool decision for purposes such as auditing. The graph database and the NoSQL database [69] are the two types of databases that make up the remote storage. The graph database is because of the involvement of semantic technology (i.e., KG). Furthermore, the reason for using an NoSQL database is because of the scalability it offers and the schema-less data storage feature that is suitable for storing the information logs.

7.5.5 Serverless Layer

The serverless layer provides the serverless function for logging and querying compliance verification tool decisions, such as consent revocation, that are necessary for auditing. The reason for the use of serverless is the features serverless offers, such as scalability and ease of deployment [70].

7.6 Implementation

This section provides detailed information on the implementation of the automated GDPR compliance verification tool. Section 7.6.1 details the libraries used, and Sect. 7.6.2 provides details on the implementation of individual components of the tool.

7.6.1 Experimental Setup

Table 7.2 summarizes the libraries that were used in our implementation. The selection of these libraries was made based on the requirements of our tool. For example, GraphDB was selected for its ontological reasoning capabilities required for a KG and SQLite for providing a lightweight relational database setup. Similarly, MongoDB was chosen due to its support for horizontal scalability and its suitability for storing logs. In our implementation, MongoDB Atlas [71] was used to run three replicas hosted on Amazon Web Services (AWS) [72].

Table 7.2 Information about the software (or libraries) that were used in the implementation

Software (or Libraries)	Version
Python [73]	3.8
SWI-Prolog [74]	7.6.4
Flask [74]	1.1.2
Flask-RESTful [76]	0.3.8
Flask-SQLAlchemy [77]	2.5.1
Requests [78]	2.25.1
Flask Apispec [79]	0.11.0
Pycryptodome [80]	3.10.1
Flask-JWT-Extended [81]	4.2.1
FuzzyWuzzy [82]	0.18.0
NLTK [83]	3.6.2
Spacy [84]	3.0.6
SPARQLWrapper [85]	1.8.5
PyMongo [86]	3.11.4
Docker ([87] Community Edition)	20.X
SQLite [88]	2.6
GraphDB free edition	9.4.1
MongoDB [22]	5.0.6

The service layer is deployed using a Docker container in a system with 16 GB (gigabyte) random-access memory (RAM), a 2.3 gigahertz (GHz) Quad-Core Intel Core i7 processor, and 500 GB storage. However, for scalability testing, the service layer was deployed in a Kubernetes [89] cluster with a total of 12 CPU (central processing unit) cores, 24 GB RAM, and 480 GB storage. The cluster was divided into three nodes, each with four CPU cores, 8 GB of RAM, and 160 GB of storage. For the Kubernetes cluster, we used Linode [90], which provides infrastructure as a service. The security and privacy component is deployed on a virtual machine with two virtual CPUs, 4 GB of RAM, and 40 GB storage. Similar to the service layer, the OpenFaaS layer is deployed on a virtual machine using a Docker container. The virtual machine has four virtual CPUs, 8 GB of RAM, and a storage capacity of 12 GB. GraphDB is installed on a server powered by an Intel Core i9-9900K processor, 64 GB of RAM, and a 1 TB NVMe storage. All of the deployment setups use Linux [91] with variant distributions such as Ubuntu [92] and Debian [93].

7.6.2 Automated GDPR Compliance Verification Tool Implementation

This section provides detailed information about the implementation of the components that make up our tool, such as the API and compliance layers.

7.6.2.1 API Layer

The API layer implements the REST endpoints. Furthermore, the API layer provides a custom JWT implementation (see Algorithm 4) to enable role-based access as demanded by GDPR's integrity and confidentiality principle (Art. 5(1)(f)) by extending Flask-JWT-Extended. JWT is an Request for Comments (RDF) 7519 [94] open industry-standard method for securely representing claims between two parties. As demonstrated in Algorithm 4, the hashed claim value is extracted first from the JWT token after verifying JWT in the request (i.e., a valid JWT token exists in the request header). The extracted claim value is then compared to the database containing the user's information. Additionally, a check is made against the organization's unique identifier. After passing both checks on hashed claims and organizational identifiers, the valid token is returned, enabling grant access. If the request fails, an HTTP 403 Forbidden response is returned, effectively blocking access to the compliance verification tool (or REST endpoints). This customized implementation of JWT to enable role-based access is designed with a focus on user-friendliness and thus follows a similar approach to enabling JWT via decorators. As a result, enabling role-based access is as simple as including the appropriate decorator, which is accomplished by using the syntax *@decorator_name()*. Furthermore, our API layer implementation uses standard REST practices such as the OpenAPI [95] Specification (OAS) version 2.0 and Swagger to describe the REST endpoints (see Fig. 7.6).

Fig. 7.6 A snapshot of the REST API's endpoints in Swagger

Figure 7.7 summarizes our role-based endpoint access implementation. As shown in Fig. 7.7b, valid JWT credentials must be transmitted in order to obtain a JWT token; thus, a registration (with user credentials such as username and password and an unique organizational identifier) is needed. Figure 7.7a shows the sequence diagram for JWT user (human or software agent) registration. The organization's identifier is assigned manually (i.e., by an administrator) and is provided to other parties accessing the compliance verification tool. Using the organizational identifier, a unique hash token (or role or role token) generated based on timestamp is assigned. This hash token, together with the organizational identifier, is used to verify the role and access authorization to the appropriate REST endpoint(s).

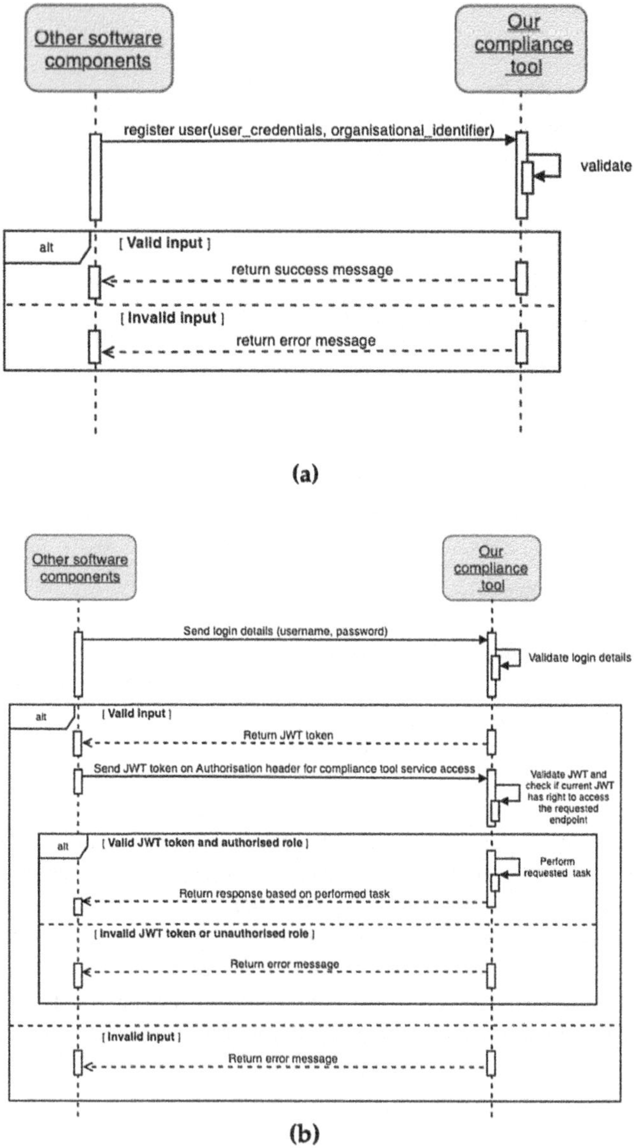

Fig. 7.7 Sequence diagram for JWT user registration and role-based endpoint access by other software components. Any third-party application that interacts with our tool is represented by the other software components. (**a**) Sequence diagram JWT user registration. (**b**) Sequence diagram for role-based service access

7.6.2.2 Data Processing

The implementation of the data processing module consists of predefined SPARQL queries with the necessary consent information to be filled in during run-time. The queries are organized according to the various operations supported by the tool, such as auditing and compliance checking. Figure 7.8 illustrates a snapshot of the SPARQL query used to obtain consent ID information as part of the data processing module's query processor component.

```
def prefix(self):
    prefix = textwrap.dedent("""
        PREFIX : <http://ontologies.atb-bremen.de/smashHitCore#>
        PREFIX gconsent: <https://w3id.org/GConsent#>
        PREFIX rdf: <http://www.w3.org/1999/02/22-rdf-syntax-ns#>
        PREFIX dc: <http://purl.org/dc/elements/1.1/>
        PREFIX dpv: <http://www.w3.org/ns/dpv#>
    """)
    return prefix

def consentID_by_consentprovider_ID(self, consentprovider_ID):
    """
    Get consent ID by consent provider ID(
    or data provider or data subject)
    :param consentprovider_ID: Unique ID mapped to data subject
    :return: consentID
    """
    query = textwrap.dedent("""{0}
            SELECT ?ConsentID
             WHERE {{
             ?ConsentID a
             <http://ontologies.atb-bremen.de/smashHitCore#ConsentID>.
              ?ConsentID :isProvidedBy :{1}.
               FILTER NOT EXISTS
               {{ ?ConsentID :RevokedAtTime ?RevokedAtTime.}}
            }}""").format(self.prefix(),
                          self.encobj.encrypt_aes(consentprovider_ID)
                          )

    return query
```

Fig. 7.8 A snippet of code from the query processor module

7.6.2.3 Shared Service

The shared service module implements functions, such as *function_map* and *list_to_query* (see Fig. 7.9), that are used by other modules, such as data processing, thereby improving code reusability and abstracting complexity. The *function_map* performs the mapping to the actual function, while the *list_to_query* function converts the array of JSON inputs into the SPARQL query format for supporting consent creation activities by the consent module.

```
def function_map(self, name):
    """ Map to actual function
    :param name: input key based on which function is mapped
    :return: mapped function name
    """
    mapfunc = {
                "bulk_consentid": self.bulk_consentID,
                "consentID_by_consentprovider_ID": self.consentID_by_consentprovider_ID,
                 "granted_consent_by_consentID": self.granted_consent_by_consentID,
                 "consent_by_consentID": self.consent_by_consentID,
                 "all_details_by_dataprovider":self.all_details_by_dataprovider,
                 "audit_by_consentid":self.audit_by_consentid,
                 "all_consent_for_compliance":self.all_consent_for_compliance,
                 "all_consent_for_compliance_cid":self.all_consent_for_compliance_cid,
                   "all_consent_for_compliance_dataprovider":
                     self.all_consent_for_compliance_dataprovider,
                }
    return mapfunc[name]

def list_to_query(self, data, whatfor, EncryptObj):
    """ Convert list of data processing information to SPARQL query strings
    :input: data<list>
    :input: whatfor<string> - SPARQL property
    :returns: SPARQL query string
    """
    querydata = ""
    for vlaue in data:
        strs = ":"+whatfor+" :" + EncryptObj.encrypt_aes(vlaue) + ";\n"
        querydata = strs + querydata
    return querydata
```

Fig. 7.9 Sample code snapshot of the helper component of shared service module

7.6.2.4 Security

The security module implements encryption and decryption following the encryption and decryption architectures presented in Sect. 7.5.1.4 by using Pycryptodome. Asymmetric encryption, RSA [23], is used as Algorithm 1 (see Fig. 7.3) and a symmetric encryption, AES [24], as Algorithm 2 (see Fig. 7.4). The reason for the selection of RSA is because of its proven capability and security robustness over the last nearly 30 years. The reason for considering AES, an encryption technique standardized by National Institute of Standards and Technology (NIST) [96], is that AES is considered the de facto standard for symmetric encryption and it is fast and secure [97]. When asymmetric encryption is used, storing encrypted data in a database presents a challenge when it comes to querying the data. The encryption must be deterministic, which is why symmetric encryption was chosen to encrypt the actual data as in Algorithm 2. Our AES implementation allows for searchable encryption while preserving the required confidentiality.

The RSA implementation uses the PKCS #1 OEAP [98] padding scheme, which is defined by RFC 8017 [99]. RSA is used in our implementation to encrypt and decrypt the keys of the symmetric encryption algorithm. The RSA key is generated dynamically at run-time, the first time the application is deployed, if the key does not already exist. A key with a length of 1024 bits is generated and exported. The exported key is password protected using PKCS#8, an RFC 5208 [100] standard for storing and transferring keys. To protect the generated RSA keys, we used the PKCS#8 protection scheme *scryptAndAES128-CBC* in our implementation. Similarly, the AES (or Algorithm 2) implementation, as shown in Figs. 7.3 and 7.4, is multilayered, three in our case. For example, when our layered AES implementation generates the ciphertext ***C***, the plain text ***P*** is passed through multiple encryptions (E) as $E(E(E(P, k1, iv1), k2, iv2), k3, iv3)$ using unique secret keys $K = \{k1, k2, k3\}$ and IV keys $IV = \{iv1, iv2, iv3\}$ at each step. This multilayered AES encryption enhances security and makes it more difficult for attackers to decrypt the encrypted ciphertext. In the case of decryption (D), similar steps as in encryption are performed, but in the reverse order, as $D(D(D(C, k3, iv3), k2, iv2), k1, iv1)$, to obtain the plain text P. By changing the layers in the security module, the AES layers can be adjusted (increased or decreased) as needed. A 32-bit secret key and a 16-bit IV key are used in our AES implementation. The implementation also employs Bellare et al. [101] encrypt-then-authenticate-then-translate (EAX) mode, which enables both authentication and privacy of the encrypted message. Moreover, when the application is deployed, all of the keys for each AES layer are generated dynamically during runtime, just like RSA if the key does not exist.

7.6.2.5 Consent

The implementation of consent module comprises the realization of Algorithm 5, which performs the consent validation, taking consent in a consent JSON format following consent JSON schema (see Fig. 7.5a) and transforming it into KG for consent creation. The marshmallow [102] is used to validate consent (i.e., the consent JSON schema validation). Marshmallow is a framework-agnostic object serialization library for converting complex data types, such as objects, to and from native Python data types [102].

Figure 7.5b shows the KG representation (or creation) of informed consent, while Fig. 7.10 depicts the response that is sent following a successful creation of a consent instance. Additionally, as illustrated in Fig. 7.5b, the consent information is encrypted. This is to prevent gaining insights about the data subject.

```
{
    "act_status_code": 7100,
    "decision": "CONSENT_CREATION_SUCCESS",
    "decision_token": "ad2730ddc474705eefbf71f317f4302991759905ac2a5b1
136ad0e051d067c9fdd801d09d81ccb3bb46e8d399b4737fb0f5d5a9527e484da9
334f414baa902d3",
    "timestamp": "1629356568.026326"
}
```


Fig. 7.10 A snapshot of the consent creation response

7.6.2.6 Auditing

The auditing module implements two categories of auditing, namely, partial auditing and full auditing. Both the partial and full audits can be conducted with consent or by the data provider using a unique consent (or data provider) identifier. The partial auditing provides only high-level information, such as consent decision and its status (e.g., revoked). Full auditing provides complete information including the consent itself, consent status, and compliance check decisions. Figures 7.11 and 7.12 show the partial auditing and full auditing response, respectively. Moreover, auditing based on a single consent only provides information about that individual consent, whereas auditing based on the data provider provides information on all consents provided by that data provider.


```
{
    "act_status_code": 7200,
    "decision": "AUDIT_SUCCESS",
    "decision_token": "22c7cb94b1bd1e75c956d1b186856f00d950b54405500e7e74d6adb34447ee2a9465588f1285f02f5c1f7489525e868ea
b8461516 79bb26eac3dc6fbe3bd1a22",
    "message": "{'consent_id': 'TEST01PR', 'consent_decision': [{'_id': {'$oid': '6124926f97c0380213ce3c25'},
      'act_status_code': 7100, 'decision': 'CONSENT_CREATION_SUCCESS', 'decision_token': '69ff736efc1134d5e7c20071215bf4
97f1dc2bd411fc84f2a1cd6e90ab9ce5c0bc4af1ffdbfcfcab53e9a83d74a6db1f7c99ca362f3471c5b0f73027b83ab08c', 'timestamp':
      1629779534.584106, 'consent_id': 'TEST01PR'}]}",
    "timestamp": "1629779711.554654"
}
```


Fig. 7.11 Sample response to a request for partial auditing based on consent


```
{
    "act_status_code": 7200,
    "decision": "AUDIT_SUCCESS",
    "decision_token": "694532b9606ed719ce9f347626ee1226db6fd7fdbcde28840e5d02c0c1c855c50596d10147882ba09dd94e31175c3c50c947b
cd903c09984c5ba31f33e39a6e5",
    "message": "{'consent_id': 'CS30311', 'consent_decision': [{'_id': {'$oid': '615185440df2a2a477ffc053'},
      'act_status_code': 7100, 'decision': 'CONSENT_CREATION_SUCCESS', 'decision_token': '0546f43e98bdc3fd1cf635f7e30d0278d
32a3755555bb33c2781ae9224ec10647436 4a442ff0443b874f3645c60a6f211af46c6712af819b6116b20269d440a4', 'timestamp':
      1632725283.782546, 'consent_id': 'CS30311'}, {'_id': {'$oid': '6151855ff448f6f44431ed86'}, 'act_status_code': 8000,
      'decision': 'BROKEN_CONSENT_CHECK_SUCCESS', 'decision_token': '93047165f10250fa706b5c11a76951128d32bdc3c072e6d80e8b85
5f2c5f041873c7fcc2850d5955d4a0f41b5dca1f1f99b9a9c080e725a317d61ed26d2f9838', 'timestamp': 1632725310.948141, 'reason':
      'ownership changed', 'consent_id': 'CS30311'}], 'consent_data': {'CS30311': [{'DataController':
      '60a55c9dd79dbc757698041ea'}, {'Purpose': 'marketing'}, {'Data': {'SensorDataCategory': {'data': ['gps', 'speed']}}},
      {'Duration': '"2021-11-18 16:47:44.950000+00:00"^^xsd:dateTime'}, {'City': 'Innsbruck'}, {'DataProcessing':
      ['marketing', 'analysis']}, {'DataProvider': 'DP12117120112'}, {'DataRequester': 'None'}, {'Medium': 'mobile'},
      {'State': 'Tyrol'}, {'RevokedAtTime': '"1632725309.197789"^^xsd:dateTime'}, {'Country': 'Austria'},
      {'GrantedAtTime': '"2021-09-18 16:47:44.950000+00:00"^^xsd:dateTime'}]}}",
    "timestamp": "1632725324.601058"
}
```


Fig. 7.12 Sample response to a request for full auditing based on consent

7.6.2.7 Compliance

The compliance module implements three different levels of compliance checking, namely, consent-based, data provider-based, and automated compliance checking by executing Equation (7.1). Similar to consent-based auditing, consent-based compliance checking performs a compliance check of the single consent. In contrast, data provider-based compliance checking performs a compliance check on all the consents associated with the particular data provider whose compliance is being checked. In the case of automated compliance checking, however, the compliance check is performed for all active consents. The sample responses to compliance checks based on data provider, individual consent, and automated compliance checks are shown in Figs. 7.13a,b and 7.14. Additionally, as discussed in Sect. 7.5.1.7, when an automated compliance check is performed, a notification alert is created. This requires configuring an external notification URL to receive notifications about the result of the compliance check. The external notification URL is a URL that the DC (or DP) must provide in order for the alert to be received. No notification is sent in the case of consent-based and data provider-based compliance checks. This


```
{
  "act_status_code": 9000,
  "decision": "COMPLIANCE_STATUS",
  "decision_token": "c6ad48bf3c8f554dee20c82c708e3fd39bd5ce394918a2eb6e709fd8ecb
  8cd0dc270f55b504888556cc1dbda860ff98d9ce4c554892774234a30457b99890a8",
  "message": "{'compliance_check': [{'consent_info': {'ConsentID':
    'TEST110911134541145455', 'data_requester_id': '60a55c9dd79bc757698041ea',
    'data_controller_id': 'None', 'data_provider_id': 'TESTCOMPLIANCEDP002'},
    'compliance_status': 'Everything is good and compliant'}, {'consent_info':
    {'ConsentID': 'TEST110911134541145455512', 'data_requester_id':
    '60a55c9dd79bc757698041ea', 'data_controller_id': 'None',
    'data_provider_id': 'TESTCOMPLIANCEDP002'}, 'compliance_status':
    {'dataprocessing': 'Dataprocessing is different than what was consented'}}]}
    ",
  "timestamp": "1630599061.149812"
}
```


(a)


```
{
  "act_status_code": 9000,
  "decision": "COMPLIANCE_STATUS",
  "decision_token": "f813f8ac0f857e854a274c5306a69458bd1509f3ac4475e41ee083312c5
  c617da1e98c20c376707dd1d2f5b5258eec864db0445aeff859c9dfa94fef10484093",
  "message": "{'compliance_check': [{'consent_info': {'ConsentID':
    'TEST110911134541145455578932', 'data_requester_id':
    '60a55c9dd79bc757698041ea', 'data_controller_id': 'None',
    'data_provider_id': 'TESTCOMPLIANCEDP001'}, 'compliance_status':
    'Everything is good and compliant'}]}",
  "timestamp": "1630594826.415491"
}
```


(b)

Fig. 7.13 Compliance check response. (**a**) Compliance check based on data provider. (**b**) Compliance check based on a single consent

```
{
  "compliance_check": [
    {
      "consent_info": {
        "ConsentID": "TEST110911134541145455",
        "data_requester_id": "60a55c9dd79bc757698041ea",
        "data_controller_id": "None",
        "data_provider_id": "TESTCOMPLIANCEDP002"
      },
      "compliance_status": "Everything is good and compliant"
    },
    {
      "consent_info": {
        "ConsentID": "TEST1109111345411454557893",
        "data_requester_id": "60a55c9dd79bc757698041ea",
        "data_controller_id": "None",
        "data_provider_id": "TESTCOMPLIANCEDP001"
      },
      "compliance_status": {
        "consent_expired": "Consent has expired so consent has been automatically revoked"
      }
    },
    {
      "consent_info": {
        "ConsentID": "TEST11091113454114545578932",
        "data_requester_id": "60a55c9dd79bc757698041ea",
        "data_controller_id": "None",
        "data_provider_id": "TESTCOMPLIANCEDP001"
      },
      "compliance_status": "Everything is good and compliant"
    }
  ]
}
```


Fig. 7.14 Sample response for an automated compliance check

is because consent-based and data provider-based compliance checks are initiated manually via REST endpoints and the result of the compliance check is returned as a response to the same REST endpoint that initiated the check.

The implementation employs a fuzzy string matching technique based on the Levenshtein distance (i.e., edit distance) and computes the token set ratio, which is used to determine the match's similarity. FuzzyWuzzy [82], a fuzzy string matching Python library, was used to implement a fuzzy string matching technique. Additionally, natural language processing techniques such as tokenization and stemming were used to address grammar and spelling errors.

7.6.2.8 Security and Privacy

The security and privacy implementation extends the NGAC languages and tools for privacy policy specification and enforcement, by the inclusion of *purposes* for processing of personal data, *retention* periods for data, fine-grained data processing operations, and other concepts common in extant privacy policy frameworks. In addition to the extension to the NGAC declarative policy language, the implementation of the security and privacy modules also includes an experimental implementation of the SecPAL for Privacy (S4P) language [103] that provides more explicit representation of delegation and distinction of roles in the handling of personal information.

7.6.2.9 Serverless Layer

The serverless layer implements the *store* and *query* serverless functions as shown in Fig. 7.15 to support logging and querying operations of decisions made by the compliance verification tool using OpenFaaS [104]. OpenFaaS (or the Functions as a Service) is an open-source framework which allows building serverless functions on top of the containers.

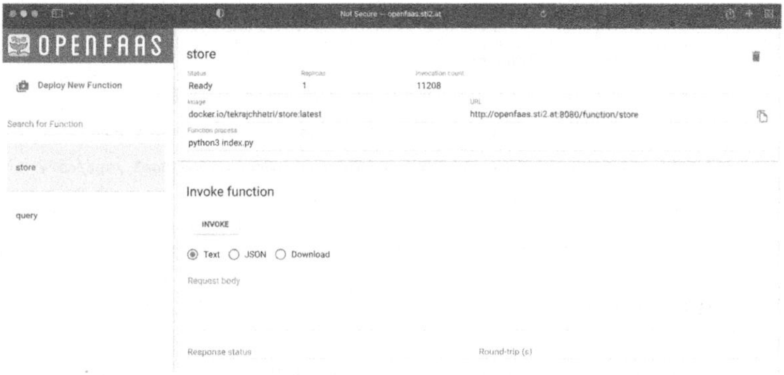

Fig. 7.15 Deployed OpenFaas functions

7.6.2.10 Scheduler

The scheduler makes use of Ofelia, a docker-based job scheduler [105], to handle time-based job scheduling tasks. Listing 4 shows the script used in our implementation to schedule the job. The time interval for the automated compliance checking can be adjusted by updating time in Listing 4. Further, in the script we can see *tekactool* and *parser*. *tekactool* is the docker deployment of our compliance verification tool that Ofelia scheduler depends on to run (or trigger) automated compliance check via shared service component CRON, while *parser* is the other docker image that the Ofelia scheduler requires.

Listing 4: Ofelia scheduler docker script

```
ofelia:
    image: mcuadros/ofelia:latest
    depends_on:
      - tekactool
      - parser
    command: daemon --docker
    restart: always
    volumes:
      - ./:/app
      - /var/run/docker.sock:/var/run/docker.sock:ro
    labels:
      ofelia.job-run.datecron.image: "parser"
      ofelia.job-run.datecron.schedule: "@every 86400s"
      ofelia.job-run.datecron.command: "python3 /app/core/cron/Cron.py"
```

7.7 Evaluation

This section presents the evaluation of our tool with regards to performance and scalability. We have evaluated the execution overhead of our tool's key functionalities (consent creation, auditing, and compliance verification). Scalability testing was completed as well. This is due to the fact that our tool is a part of smashHit, and smashHit is driven by two business use cases in industries such as automobile insurance and smart cities [11]. Both use cases require a scalable solution to handle a large number of users. Our tool was also evaluated in terms of GDPR compliance to ensure that it, itself, is GDPR-compliant. Section 7.6.1 provides details about the testing system setup. Section 7.7.1 describes the performance evaluation, while Sect. 7.7.2 presents the evaluation based on GDPR.

7.7.1 Performance and Scalability

As presented in Sect. 7.7, our performance evaluation focuses on auditing, compliance verification, and consent creation. We measured the time it takes to create ten different consent instances. The required consent information was provided manually. The X-axis in Fig. 7.16 represents the consent creation indicated by CS. The

Y-axis represents the time taken in seconds. Figure 7.16 shows a steady curve with few rises and falls in time. The decrease in time, particularly for CS4, and the increase for CS9 and CS10, are due to the amount of payload sent while requesting to create consent. The size of the payload depends on the amount of the information present in the consent (or JSON input). For CS4, 856 bytes were sent, while for CS9 and CS10, it was around 1023 bytes, and the rest of the payload was around 950 bytes. With the increasing payload, more consent information, such as processing details, was passed. According to our observations, the average time required to create consent is approximately 7.3 s. This time period for consent creation also includes the time required for intermediate steps such as consent validation and conversion to legal KG, and also the time required for consent information encryption, as consent information is stored encrypted.

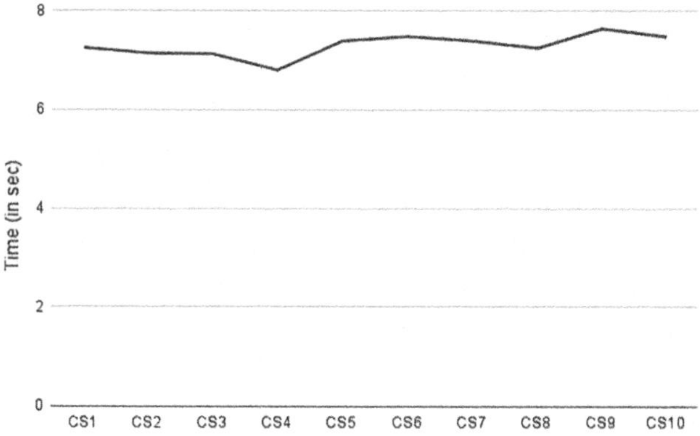

Fig. 7.16 Time spent on consent creation

Figure 7.17a depicts the compliance evaluation based on consent, while Fig. 7.17b depicts the compliance checking evaluation time based on the data provider. The data provider is a data subject who owns the data and retains the right to decide whether or not to share it with the DC (or DP) for processing. Similar to consent creation, Y-axis of both Fig. 7.17a,b represents the execution time in seconds. The X-axis, on the other hand, represents compliance based on consent, indicated by CC in Fig. 7.17a, and compliance based on data provider, indicated by DPC in Figs. 7.17b. The term DPC stands for data provider compliance (or also compliance based on data provider). The observed variation in compliance checking in Fig. 7.17a, similar to consent creation, is due to the amount of information present in the consent that must be assessed.

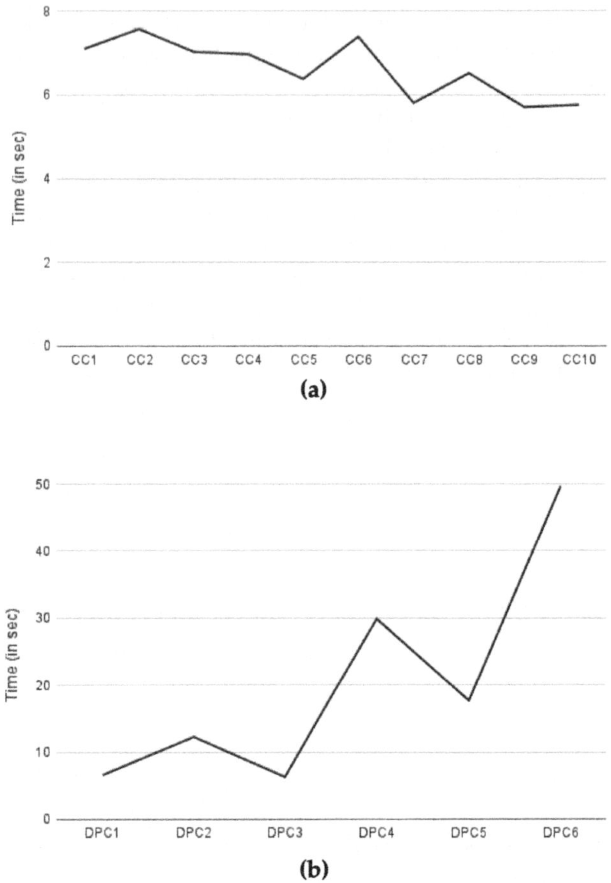

Fig. 7.17 Time spent on compliance checks. (**a**) Execution time for compliance check based on consent. (**b**) Execution time for compliance check based on data provider

Overall, compliance checking (i.e., core compliance) based on consent took an average of 6.6 s. However, the time required for compliance checking varies greatly depending on the data provider, as a data provider may have multiple consents. Data providers 1 and 3 each have only one consent; thus, we observed a similar time in compliance checking as indicated by DPC1 and DPC2 in Fig. 7.17b.

Similarly, data provider 2 had two consents, so the time required for compliance checking is nearly twice (see DPC2 in Fig. 7.17b) that of data provider 1. Other data providers such as 4, 5, and 6, exhibited a similar pattern as can be observed in Fig. 7.17b from the graph indicated by DPC4, DPC5, and DPC6, respectively. Regardless of the number of consents, we observed a similar time to a compliance check based on consent on average, which is 6.12 s. This compliance check evaluation, however, excluded the privacy and security component as it is only called when all of the core compliance decisions are evaluated as true. As a result, we assessed privacy and security separately. In the case of granted case, the privacy and security component takes an average of 0.12392 milliseconds and 0.1234 milliseconds in a denied decision case. If security and privacy are also utilized, a compliance check takes an additional 0.12392 and 0.1234 milliseconds to that of core compliance checking time.

The evaluation for auditing based on consent and data provider, such as compliance checking, is shown in Fig. 7.18a,b. The Y-axis represents time in seconds. The X-axis represents auditing based on consent, as indicated by FCA in Fig. 7.18a, and auditing based on data provider, as indicated by FDPA in Fig. 7.18b. The letter F in both figures denotes full auditing (discussed in Sect. 7.6.2.6). The full auditing is expected to take more time because it considers all information. Auditing exhibits a similar pattern to compliance checking, as shown in Figs. 7.18a,b. Auditing based on consent took about 7 s on average, and auditing based on data provider took about 22 s. The delay in auditing based on data provider is due to checking all consents and decision logs specific to the data provider. In comparison to compliance checking based on data providers, which only checks active consent, auditing provides an audit for all consent, even if it is not active (e.g., revoked consent). Similar to the consent creation, both the compliance checking and the auditing time also involve the time for activities such as performing decryption, which is a time-consuming activity [106].

To summarize, we can observe a higher time in the performance evaluation. This is because of the associated additional time-consuming activities such as layered encryption and decryption (see Figs. 7.3 and 7.4). This is also a known trade-off that comes with increased security [107].

From the loosely coupled architecture of the tool and the use of scalable technologies, such as Docker and serverless, we can observe the scalability features, as this allows scaling of the individual components. Numerous studies, such as [108–110], have demonstrated the scalability of the loosely coupled architecture and the support provided by technologies such as Docker and serverless. Moreover, to the observed scalability of the tool from the loosely coupled architecture, we also performed a scalability testing with the Kubernetes platform, as discussed in Sect. 7.6.1. When evaluating the scalability, we only looked at resource consumption and the number of scaled pods [111] (i.e., the smallest deployable computing units that

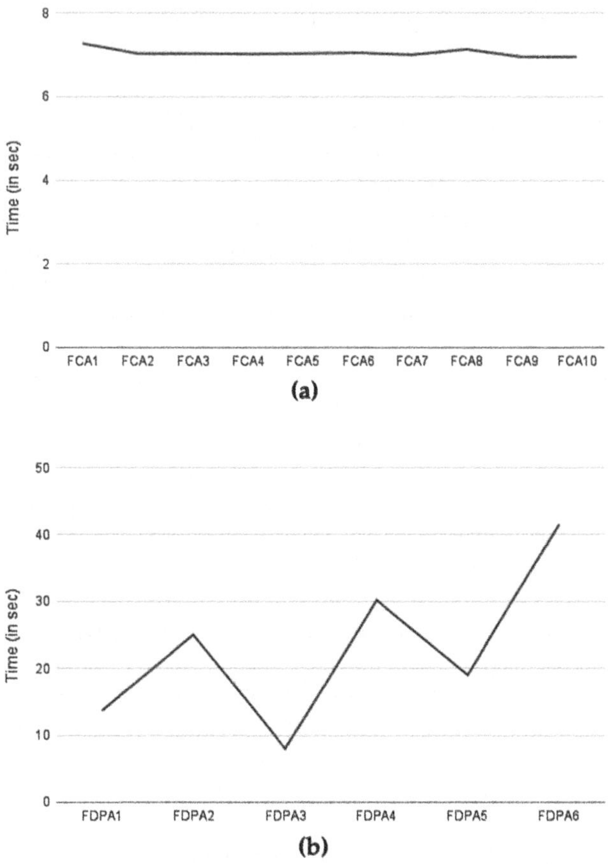

Fig. 7.18 Time spent on auditing. (**a**) Execution time for full audit based on consent. (**b**) Execution time for full audit based on data provider

Kubernetes [89] allows you to create and manage). The horizontal pod autoscaler, which we used in our scalability testing deployment, automatically scales the number of pods into the number of replicas based on the set observed metrics such as average CPU utilization and average memory utilization [112]. Three replicas and a load balancer are used in the initial deployment. The load was generated using a load generation script. The autoscale replicas of pods were limited to 40, and the observed metrics for the scale used in our testing were average CPU utilization. The CPU utilization scalability threshold was set to 95%. We were able to successfully autoscale the application to the defined number of pods as the load generation script increased the load. The time it took to create new replicas was approximately 5–6 s. On Linode cluster 1, which also includes the load balancer, we observed nearly the maximum 324.58% CPU utilization. Similarly, on Linode clusters 2 and 3, we observed maximum CPU utilization of 96.91% and 119.16%, respectively, and I/O rates of 81.97, 28.74, and 12.60 blocks/s. However, network utilization was around 4.77 Mb/s for cluster 1 and 1.05 Mb/s and 132.36 Kb/s for clusters 2 and 3. Finally, to simulate virtual users, we used the open-source load-testing tool locust [113]. We observed a similar result for scalability with a locust, an automated load generator, simulating 52,200 users, making a maximum of 241 requests per second (minimum 100 requests per second). With the scalability testing, we observed that the tool is able to scale with the growing load (i.e., requests), proving that the application supports scalability provided that the necessary setup (i.e., configuration of appropriate scaling such as autoscaling) is made.

7.7.2 TOMs

The goal of our tool is to enable transparency in data sharing (and processing) by automatically performing tasks such as compliance verification based on informed consent granted by data subjects. In this section, we present the evaluation of the implemented TOMs (see Table 7.1), which is also one of our work's contributions (see Sect. 7.1). The qualitative evaluation was conducted in accordance with the TOMs. This is also a common method of privacy evaluation used by researchers such as Ryan et al. [6] to assess their work using the Irish Data Protection Commission's self-assessment checklist [114].

We have considered seven protection goals identified in relation to GDPR principles, as shown in Table 7.1. The SDMs' protection goals are implemented in our compliance verification tool as TOMs. Table 7.1 contains information about the SDMs' protection goals as well as the relevant TOMs. Both automated and manual evaluations were performed. For the automated method, the test cases were written and executed using Python's unittest [115] test framework. The unit test was written with various conditions, with some expected to fail and others expected to pass. For example, we ran three different tests for role-based access, which is also one of the TOMs. We tested endpoint access without a valid JWT in the first test case. In the second test case, we tested endpoint access using a valid JWT token but an unauthorized role, and in the third test case, we tested endpoint access using a valid JWT token and an authorized role. We expected the test to fail in the first two cases. The failure here indicates that the application is inaccessible and returns an invalid

HTTP status code as defined in the application, such as 403, indicating forbidden access, which is then asserted to be true in order to pass the unit test. When we pass everything valid in the third case, we expect the application to be accessible with the valid response and HTTP status code. To pass the test, the response is asserted to evaluate to true. Additionally, for tasks such as auditing, a manual evaluation was conducted. For example, in the case of auditing, when the audit responses were manually retrieved, a manual verification that everything was as expected was performed. Based on the testing, we were able to meet all of the SDMs protection objectives. The scope of our study's SDM protection goals was constrained by the identified TOMs, which are listed in Table 7.1.

7.8 Conclusions

In this paper, we present a data protection By design tool for automated GDPR compliance verification based on semantically modeled informed consent. We also present a novel systematic approach for translating the GDPR legislation into code while considering industrial requirements such as interoperability and scalability (see Table 7.3). This includes the systematization of the steps that are required for automating compliance checks and implementing necessary security measures (i.e., such as TOMs). Further, we present the technical factors that must be considered in order to satisfy industrial requirements. Our tool follows a microservices architecture, which supports scalability and flexibility and utilizes semantic technology (e.g., KG) to facilitate data interoperability. By conducting scalability testing (i.e., testing with simulated users and checking if the tool scales with the growing number of users) (see Sect. 7.7.1), we have validated our tool's scalability. The performance evaluation (see Sect. 7.7.1) provides information on the associated overhead for tasks such as compliance checking and consent creation, which is useful for the future improvements of the tool. The conducted GDPR TOMs evaluation (see Sect. 7.7.2) has confirmed that GDPR requirements, such as confidentiality and the adoption of data protection by design principles, have been satisfied and utilized. Finally, the comparative analysis with existing work, presented in Table 7.3, indicates that our work advances the field by addressing the limitations of current studies (see Sect. 7.3) and industrial needs. As a result of the collaboration with legal experts and industrial partners, our work can support SMEs, which usually lack the necessary resources to implement their own GDPR compliance tools. The source code of our tool is publicly available on GitHub [116].

While our work can be generalized to other domains, it was driven by specific use cases (see Appendix B) and thus may fall short of requirements from other domains.

We consider this as one of its limitations. Another limitation is the compliance performance bottleneck in the long run due to the growing number of compliance checks that must be performed.

In addition to addressing the existing challenges (see Sect. 7.3), we have also learned some valuable lessons. These lessons include the following:

- Translating regulations into a machine-readable format requires a considerable effort with regard to the collaboration between legal and technology experts. Both the law and computer science fields necessitate the precise definition of concepts. The translation of these concepts to a machine-readable format needs to be precise as well.
- A well-designed core semantic model is key to achieving a common understanding of specific information across different systems. However, the integration of existing ontologies is challenging, as each ontology presents concepts from a different perspective.
- The early and consistent collaboration with business (or industry) use case partners and legal experts helps understand the requirements and implications from both perspectives. This helps the system design and implementation adapt to business needs, while fulfilling legal requirements.
- The use of semantic technology has shown to have various benefits for our work. However, existing and well-established industry systems do not always utilize semantics. This required us to to adapt our implementation to the industry requirements. To ease the process, we have selected a JSON format to communicate the consent information and compliance check results.
- Scalability, interoperability, and the simplification of the integration processes are critical for use case partners, as is the tool's consent creation functionality. Any tool's design and implementation must be tailored to such requirements.

In conclusion, the main benefits of our work are (i) systematization of the translation of legal requirements into code following specific industrial needs (i.e., such as the problem of broken consent chains), (ii) generalizability into other data sharing domains and regulatory frameworks, and (iii) lessons learned, which would benefit anyone working in this domain, particularly new researchers and developers. We have also addressed existing limitations such as interoperability and scalability. Future work will include the following: (i) extending the work to other data-sharing domains and regulatory frameworks; (ii) improving performance of the tool by parallelizing core processes. A possible direction in relation to our future work could be to incorporate additional functionalities, such as audit search, and to incorporate other GDPR legal bases, such as contracts.

Abbreviations

The following abbreviations are used in this manuscript:

AES	Advanced Encryption Standard
API	Application Programming Interface
CPU	Central Processing Unit
DC	Data Controller
DP	Data Processor
DPO	Data Protection Officer
DPV	Data Privacy Vocabulary
DS	Data Subject
DEFeND	Data Privacy Governance for Supporting GDPR
EAX	Encrypt-Then-Authenticate-Then-Translate
EU DPD	European Data Protection Directive
GDPR	General Data Protection Regulation
GHz	Gigahertz
GPS	Global Positioning System
HTTP	Hypertext Transfer Protocol
JSON	JavaScript Object Notation
JWT	JSON Web Token
KG	Knowledge Graph
MFOTL	Metric First-order Temporal Logic
ML	Machine Learning
NGAC	Next Generation Access Control
NIST	National Institute of Standards and Technology
OAEP	Optimal Asymmetric Encryption Padding
OAS	OpenAPI Specification
OWL	Web Ontology Language
PEPs	Policy Enforcement Points
PII	Personally Identifiable Information
PKCS	Public Key Cryptography Standards
RAM	Random Access Memory
REST	Representational State Transfer
RSA	Rivest-Shamir-Adleman
S4P	SecPAL for Privacy
SDM	Standard Data Protection Model
SMEs	Small and Medium-sized Enterprises
SMT	Satisfiability Modulo Theories
SPARQL	Simple Protocol and Resource Description Framework Query Language
STS	Socio-Technical Security
TOMs	Technical and Organisational Measures
URL	Uniform Resource Locator

Chapter Appendix

A Maths Symbols

$\wedge$ Logical conjunction operator.

B Use Case Overview

Figure 7.19 provides a high-level overview of the insurance use case where data subject (or customer) vehicle data are shared with the insurer after receiving consent from the data subject. The automated compliance verification tool performs necessary tasks such as consent creation and validation to allow for data sharing. Similarly, Fig. 7.20 provides an overview of the smart city use case. As shown in Fig. 7.20, the data from the data subject are shared with the company providing (or handling) data services to the city maintenance department. The shared data consist of feedback about the city, such as potholes in the road and the data subject information.

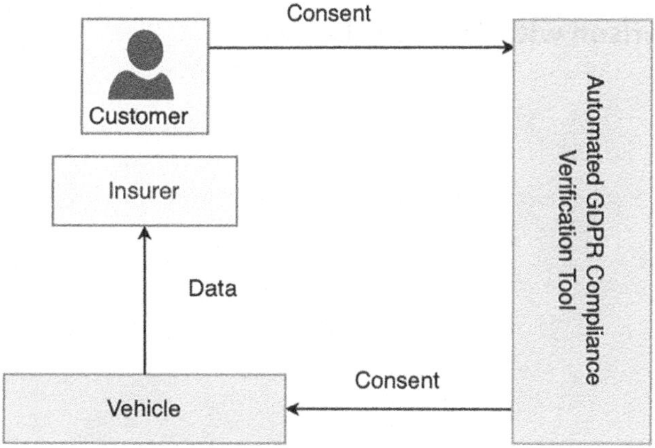

Fig. 7.19 High-level overview of the insurance use case

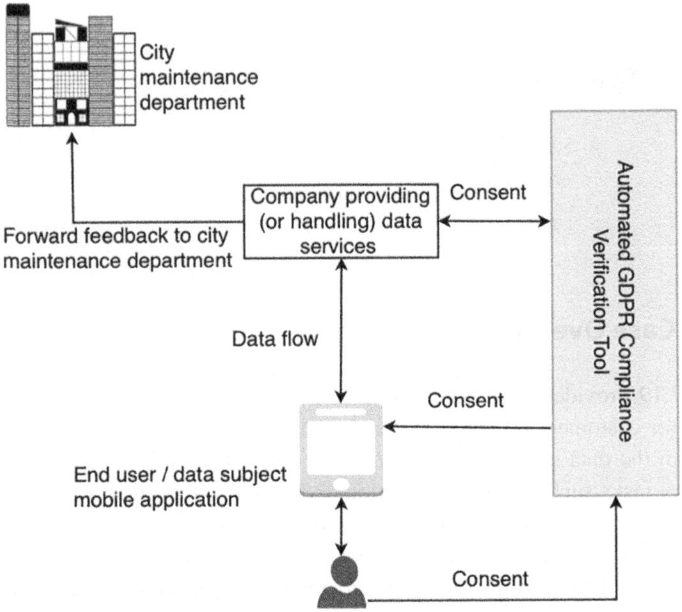

Fig. 7.20 High-level overview of the smart city use case

C Comparison with State-of-the-Art

Table 7.3 Comparison of our automated GDPR compliance verification tool with reviewed state-of-the-art.

Study	Consent Create/Revoke	Automated Compliance Checking	Interoperability	Scalability	TOMs Implemented	Implementation	Ease of Incorporation into Other Laws	Performance Evaluation	Industrial Use Case
Ranise and Siswantoro [25]	✘/✘	✔	✘	✘	✘	PoC	✔	✔	✔
Robol et al. [27]	✘/✘	✘	✔	✔	✘	PoC	✘	✘	✘
Westphal et al. [29]	✘/✘	✘	✘	✘	✘	P	✘	✘	✔
Brodin [31]	✘/✘	✘	✘	✘	✘	P	✘	✘	✔
Camilo [32]	✔/✔	✘	✘	✘	✘	PoC	✘	✘	✘
Alfred et al. [8]	✘/✘	✘	✘	✘	✘	PoC	✘	✘	✔
Piras et al. [36]	✘/✘	✘	✘	✘	✘	P	✘	✘	✔
Truong et al. [38]	✔/✔	✘	✘	✔	✘	PT	✘	✔	✘
Barati et al. [39]	✔/✘	✘	✘	✔	✘	PoC	✘	✔	✘
Kirrane et al. [17]	✔/✔	✘	✔	✔	✘	PT	✘	✔	✘
Bonati et al. [43]	✔/✔	✔	✔	✘	✘	PoC	✘	✔	✘
Mahindrakar and Joshi [46]	✔/✘	✔	✘	✔	✘	PoC	✘	✔	✘
Barati and Rana [47]	✔/✔	✘	✔	✔	✘	PoC	✘	✔	✔
Alfred et al. [8]	✘/✘	✘	✘	✘	✘	PoC	✘	✘	✔
Piras et al. [36]	✘/✘	✘	✘	✘	✘	P	✘	✘	✔
Truong et al. [38]	✔/✔	✘	✘	✔	✘	PT	✘	✔	✘
Barati et al. [39]	✔/✘	✘	✘	✔	✘	PoC	✘	✔	✘
Kirrane et al. [17]	✔/✔	✘	✔	✔	✘	PT	✘	✔	✘
Bonati et al. [43]	✔/✔	✔	✔	✘	✘	PoC	✘	✔	✘

(Continued)

Table 7.3 (Continued)

Study	Consent Create/Revoke	Automated Compliance Checking	Interoperability	Scalability	TOMs Implemented	Implementation	Ease of Incorporation into Other Laws	Performance Evaluation	Industrial Use Case
Mahindrakar and Joshi [46]	✔/✖	✔	✖	✔	✖	PoC	✖	✔	✖
Barati and Rana [47]	✔/✔	✖	✔	✔	✖	PoC	✖	✔	✔
Ryan et al. [6]	✖/✖	✖	✖	✖	✖	PoC	✖	✖	✔
Merlec et al. [7]	✔/✖	✖	✖	✔	✖	PT	✖	✔	✖
Hamdani et al. [50]	✔/✖	✔	✔	✔	✖	PoC	✖	✔	✔
Daoudagh et al. [53]	✔/✔	✖	✔	✔	✖	FM	✖	✔	✔
Tokas et al. [54]	✔/✔	✖	✖	✖	✖	PoC	✖	✔	✖
Our work	✔/✔	✔	✔	✔	✔	FM	✔	✔	✔

Bibliography

1. European Parliament and Council. 'Regulation (EU) 2016/679 of the European Parliament and of the Council of 27 April 2016 on the protection of natural persons with regard to the processing of personal data and on the free movement of such data, and repealing Directive 95/46/EC (General Data Protection Regulation)'. In: *Official Journal of the European Union, L119* (May 2016). Available online: https://eurlex.europa.eu/eli/reg/2016/679/oj (accessed on 3 December 2021) .
2. Vincenzo Mangini, Irina Tal, and Arghir-Nicolae Moldovan. 'An Empirical Study on the Impact of GDPR and Right to Be Forgotten—Organisations and Users Perspective'. In: *Proceedings of the 15th International Conference on Availability, Reliability and Security*. ARES '20. Virtual Event, Ireland: Association for Computing Machinery, 2020, pp. 1–9. https://doi.org/10.1145/3407023.3407080.
3. Mouna Rhahla, Sahar Allegue, and Takoua Abdellatif. 'A framework for GDPR compliance in big data systems'. In: *International Conference on Risks and Security of Internet and Systems, Hammamet, Tunisia, 29–31 October 2019*. Springer: Berlin/Heidelberg, Germany. 2019, pp. 211–226. https://doi.org/10.1007/978-3-030-41568-6_14.
4. Paul Ryan, Martin Crane, and Rob Brennan. 'Design Challenges for GDPR RegTech'. In: *Proceedings of the 22nd International Conference on Enterprise Information Systems—Volume 2: ICEIS, Prague, Czech Republic, 5–7 May 2020*. INSTICC: Milan, Italy. SciTePress: Setubal, Portugal, 2020, 2020, pp. 787–795. https://doi.org/10.5220/0009464507870795.
5. Masoud Barati and Omer Rana. 'Enhancing User Privacy in IoT: Integration of GDPR and Blockchain'. In: *Blockchain and Trustworthy Systems*. Ed. by Zibin Zheng, Hong-Ning Dai, Mingdong Tang, and Xiangping Chen. Singapore: Springer Singapore, 2020, pp. 322–335. https://doi.org/10.1007/978-981-15-2777-7_26.
6. Paul Ryan, Martin Crane, and Rob Brennan. 'GDPR Compliance tools: best practice from RegTech'. In: *International Conference on Enterprise Information Systems, Online, 26–28 April 2021*. Springer: Cham, Switzerland, 2021.
7. Mpyana Mwamba Merlec, Youn Kyu Lee, Seng-Phil Hong, and Hoh Peter In. 'A Smart Contract-Based Dynamic Consent Management System for Personal Data Usage under GDPR'. In: *Sensors* 21.23 (2021). https://doi.org/10.3390/s21237994.
8. Emma Arfelt, David Basin, and Søren Debois. 'Monitoring the GDPR'. In: *European Symposium on Research in Computer Security*. Ed. by Kazue Sako, Steve Schneider, and Peter Y. A. Ryan. Springer International Publishing: Cham, Switzerland, 2019, pp. 681–699.
9. *International Association of Privacy Professionals (IAPP)*. Available online: https://iapp.org. (accessed on 12 December 2021).
10. IAPP. *IAPP-FTI Consulting Privacy Governance Report 2020*. Technical Report. Available online: https://iapp.org/media/pdf/resource_center/IAPP_FTIConsulting_2020PrivacyGovernanceReport.pdf (accessed on 8 December 2021).
11. The smashHit project. *Public Report D1.3 Public Innovation Concept*. Available online: https://www.smashhit.eu/wpcontent/uploads/2021/03/smashHit_D1.3_Public_Innovation_Concept_v100.pdf (accessed on 19 December 2021).
12. Tek Raj Chhetri. 'Improving Decision Making Using Semantic Web Technologies'. In: *The Semantic Web: ESWC 2021 Satellite Events*. Ed. by Ruben Verborgh, Anasta-

sia Dimou, Aidan Hogan, Claudia d'Amato, Ilaria Tiddi, Arne Bröring, Simon Mayer, Femke Ongenae, Riccardo Tommasini, and Mehwish Alam. Cham: Springer International Publishing, 2021, pp. 165–175.

13. *The smashHit EU H2020 project*. Available online: https://smashhit.eu (accessed on 5 January 2022).
14. *RegTech*. Available online: https://www.regnology.net/en/ (accessed on 23 December 2021).
15. Dieter Fensel, Umutcan Simsek, Kevin Angele, Elwin Huaman, Elias Kärle, Oleksandra Panasiuk, Ioan Toma, Jürgen Umbrich, and Alexander Wahler. *Knowledge Graphs: Methodology, Tools and Selected Use Cases*. Springer: Cham, Switzerland, 2020.
16. Anelia Kurteva, Tek Raj Chhetri, Harshvardhan J Pandit, and Anna Fensel. 'Consent through the lens of semantics: State of the art survey and best practices'. In: *Semantic Web* (2021), pp. 1–27. https://doi.org/10.3233/SW-210438.
17. Sabrina Kirrane, Javier D. Fern'andez, Piero Bonatti, Uros Milosevic, Axel Polleres, and Rigo Wenning. 'The SPECIAL-K Personal Data Processing Transparency and Compliance Platform'. In: *ArXiv* abs/2001.09461 (2020).
18. *Introducing* JSON. Available online: https://www.json.org/json-en.html (accessed on 2 January 2022).
19. *JSON Web* Tokens (JWT. Available online: https://jwt.io (accessed on 27 December 2021).
20. Nick Coghlan Guido van Rossum Barry Warsaw. PEP 8—Style Guide for Python Code. Available online: https://www.python.org/dev/peps/pep-0008/ (accessed on 2022).
21. *GraphDB*. Available online: https://graphdb.ontotext.com (accessed on 7 January 2022).
22. *MongoDB*. Available online: https://www.mongodb.com (accessed on 10 December 2021).
23. Çetin Kaya Koç, Funda Özdemir, and Zeynep Ödemiş Özger. 'Rivest-Shamir-Adleman Algorithm'. In: *Partially Homomorphic Encryption*. Springer: Berlin/Heidelberg, Germany, 2021, pp. 37–41.
24. Douglas Selent. 'Advanced encryption standard'. In: *Rivier Academic Journal* 6.2 (2010), pp. 1–14.
25. Silvio Ranise and Hari Siswantoro. 'Automated Legal Compliance Checking by Security Policy Analysis'. In: *Computer Safety, Reliability, and Security*. Ed. by Stefano Tonetta, Erwin Schoitsch, and Friedemann Bitsch. Springer International Publishing: Cham, Switzerland, 2017, pp. 361–372. https://doi.org/10.1007/978-3-319-66284-8_30.
26. European Parliament. *European Data Protection Directive (EU DPD)*. Available online: https://eur-lex.europa.eu/legal-content/EN/TXT/?uri=celex%3A31995L0046 (accessed on 2 January 2022).
27. Marco Robol, Mattia Salnitri, and Paolo Giorgini. 'Toward GDPR-Compliant Socio-Technical Systems: Modeling Language and Reasoning Framework'. In: *The Practice of Enterprise Modeling*. Ed. by Geert Poels, Frederik Gailly, Estefania Serral Asensio, and Monique Snoeck. Springer International Publishing: Cham, Switzerland, 2017, pp. 236–250. https://doi.org/10.1007/978-3-319-70241-4_16.
28. Fabiano Dalpiaz, Elda Paja, and Paolo Giorgini. *Security requirements engineering: designing secure socio-technical systems*. MIT Press: Cambridge, MA, USA, 2016.

29. Patrick Westphal, Javier David Fernandez Garcia, Sabrina Kirrane, and Jens Lehmann. 'SPIRIT: a semantic transparency and compliance stack'. In: Proceedings of the 14th International Conference on Semantic Systems Vienna Austria, 10–13 September. 2018.
30. T. Ramalingeswara Rao, Pabitra Mitra, Ravindara Bhatt, and Adrijit Goswami. 'The big data system, components, tools, and technologies: a survey'. In: *Knowledge and Information Systems* (2018), pp. 1–81. https://doi.org/10.1007/s10115-018-1248-0.
31. Martin Brodin. 'A framework for GDPR compliance for small-and medium-sized enterprises'. In: *European Journal for Security Research* 4.2 (2019), pp. 243–264. https://doi.org/10.1007/s41125-019-00042-z.
32. Juan Camilo et al. 'Blockchain-based consent manager for GDPR compliance'. In: *Open Identity Summit 2019* (2019) .
33. Maryam Davari and Elisa Bertino. 'Access Control Model Extensions to Support Data Privacy Protection based on GDPR'. In: *2019 IEEE International Conference on Big Data (Big Data), Los Angeles, CA, USA, 9–12 December*. 2019, pp. 4017–4024. https://doi.org/10.1109/BigData47090.2019.9006455.
34. David A. Basin, Felix Klaedtke, Samuel Müller, and Eugen Zalinescu. 'Monitoring Metric First-Order Temporal Properties'. In: *Journal of the ACM (JACM)* 62 (2015), pp. 1–45. https://doi.org/10.1145/2699444.
35. David Basin, Matúš Harvan, Felix Klaedtke, and Eugen Zălinescu. 'MONPOLY: Monitoring usage-control policies'. In: *International conference on runtime verification*. Springer. 2011, pp. 360–364.
36. Luca Piras, Mohammed Ghazi Al-Obeidallah, Andrea Praitano, Aggeliki Tsohou, Haralambos Mouratidis, Beatriz Gallego-Nicasio Crespo, Jean Baptiste Bernard, Marco Fiorani, Emmanouil Magkos, Andres Castillo Sanz, et al. 'DEFeND architecture: a privacy by design platform for GDPR compliance'. In: *International Conference on Trust and Privacy in Digital Business, Linz, Austria, 26–29 August*. Springer: Berlin/Heidelberg, Germany. 2019, pp. 78–93. https://doi.org/10.1007/978-3-030-27813-7_6.
37. *The DEFeND project*.Available online: https://www.defendproject.eu (accessed on 27 December 2021).
38. Nguyen Binh Truong, Kai Sun, Gyu Myoung Lee, and Yike Guo. 'GDPR-Compliant Personal Data Management: A Blockchain-Based Solution'. In: *Trans. Info. For. Sec.* 15 (2020), 1746–1761. https://doi.org/10.1109/TIFS.2019.2948287.
39. Masoud Barati, Omer Rana, Ioan Petri, and George Theodorakopoulos. 'GDPR Compliance Verification in Internet of Things'. In: *IEEE Access* 8 (2020), pp. 119697–119709. https://doi.org/10.1109/ACCESS.2020.3005ss509.
40. David Basin, Søren Debois, and Thomas Hildebrandt. 'On Purpose and by Necessity: Compliance Under the GDPR'. In: *Financial Cryptography*. Springer: Berlin/Heidelberg, Germany, 2018. https://doi.org/10.1007/978-3-662-58387-6_2.
41. *Ethereum*. Available online: https://ethereum.org/en/ (accessed on 7 October 2021).
42. Data and Knowledge Group, University of Oxford. *HermiT OWL Reasoner*. Available online: http://www.hermit-reasoner.com (accessed on 20 October 2021).
43. Piero A. Bonatti, Sabrina Kirrane, Iliana M. Petrova, and Luigi Sauro. 'Machine Understandable Policies and GDPR Compliance Checking'. In: *KI—Künstliche Intelligenz* 34.3 (2020), pp. 303–315. https://doi.org/10.1007/s13218-020-00677-4.

44. Sean Bechhofer, Frank van Harmelen, Jim Hendler, Ian Horrocks, Deborah L. McGuinness, Peter F. Patel-Schneider, and Lynn Andrea Stein. *OWL Web Ontology Language*. Available online: https://www.w3.org/TR/owl-ref/ (accessed on 20 December 2021).
45. Piero A. Bonatti. 'Fast Compliance Checking in an OWL2 Fragment'. In: *Proceedings of the Twenty-Seventh International Joint Conference on Artificial Intelligence, IJCAI-18*. International Joint Conferences on Artificial Intelligence Organization Stockholm Sweden, 13–19 July, 2018, pp. 1746–1752. https://doi.org/10.24963/ijcai.2018/241.
46. Abhishek Mahindrakar and Karuna Pande Joshi. 'Automating GDPR Compliance using Policy Integrated Blockchain'. In: *2020 IEEE 6th Intl Conference on Big Data Security on Cloud (BigDataSecurity), IEEE Intl Conference on High Performance and Smart Computing, (HPSC) and IEEE Intl Conference on Intelligent Data and Security (IDS)*. 2020, pp. 86–93. https://doi.org/10.1109/BigDataSecurity-HPSC-IDS49724.2020.00026.
47. Masoud Barati and Omer Rana. 'Tracking GDPR Compliance in Cloud-based Service Delivery'. In: *IEEE Transactions on Services Computing* 15.3 (2020), pp. 1498–1511. https://doi.org/10.1109/TSC.2020.2999559.
48. Data Protection Vocabularies and Controls W3C Community Group. *Data Privacy Vocabulary (DPV)*. Available online: https://github.com/dpvcg/dpv (accessed on 4 January 2022).
49. Timothy Lebo, Satya Sahoo, Deborah McGuinness, Khalid Belhajjame, James Cheney, David Corsar, Daniel Garijo, Stian Soiland-Reyes, Stephan Zednik, and Jun Zhao. *PROVO: The PROV Ontology*. English. W3C Recommendation. World Wide Web Consortium: Boston, MA, USA, 2013.
50. Rajaa El Hamdani, Majd Mustapha, David Restrepo Amariles, Aurore Troussel, Sébastien Meeùs, and Katsiaryna Krasnashchok. 'A Combined Rule-Based and Machine Learning Approach for Automated GDPR Compliance Checking'. In: *Proceedings of the Eighteenth International Conference on Artificial Intelligence and Law, São Paulo, Brazil, 21–25 June*. Association for Computing Machinery: NewYork, NY, USA, 2021, 40–49.
51. Shomir Wilson, Florian Schaub, Aswarth Dara, Frederick Liu, Sushain Cherivirala, Pedro Leon, Mads Andersen, Sebastian Zimmeck, Kanthashree Sathyendra, N. Russell, Thomas Norton, Eduard Hovy, Joel Reidenberg, and Norman Sadeh. 'The Creation and Analysis of a Website Privacy Policy Corpus'. In: *In Proceedings of the 54th Annual Meeting of the Association for Computational Linguistics, Berlin, Germany, 7–12 August*. Aug. 2016, pp. 1330–1340. https://doi.org/10.18653/v1/P16-1126.
52. GDPR. *Available online: Data Protection Impact Assessments, Article 35 of GDPR (accessed on 20 December 2021)*.
53. Said Daoudagh, Eda Marchetti, Vincenzo Savarino, Jorge Bernal Bernabe, Jesús García-Rodríguez, Rafael Torres Moreno, Juan Antonio Martinez, and Antonio F. Skarmeta. 'Data Protection by Design in the Context of Smart Cities: A Consent and Access Control Proposal'. In: *Sensors* 21.21 (2021). https://doi.org/10.3390/s21217154.
54. Shukun Tokas, Olaf Owe, and Toktam Ramezanifarkhani. 'Static checking of GDPR-related privacy compliance for object-oriented distributed systems'. In: *Journal of Logical and Algebraic Methods in Programming* 125 (2022), p. 100733. https://doi.org/10.1016/j.jlamp.2021.100733.

55. Conference of the Independent Data Protection Supervisory Authorities of the Federation and the Länder. *The Standard Data Protection Model—A method for Data Protection advising and controlling on the basis of uniform protection goals, Version 2.0b*. Available online: https://www.datenschutzzentrum.de/uploads/sdm/SDM-Methodology_V2.0b.pdf (accessed on 15 December 2021). 2020.
56. *smashHitCore ontology*. Available online: https://smashhiteu.github.io/smashHitCore/ (accessed on 9 January 2022).
57. *SPARQL Query Language for RDF*. Available online: https://www.w3.org/TR/rdf-sparql-query/ (accessed on 5 November 2021).
58. *smashHitCore GraphnDB SPARQL Endpoint*. Available online: https://smashhitactool.sti2.at/sparql (accessed on 5 January 2022).
59. Anelia Kurteva. 'Implementing Informed Consent with Knowledge Graphs'. In: *The Semantic Web: ESWC 2021 Satellite Events*. Ed. by Ruben Verborgh, Anastasia Dimou, Aidan Hogan, Claudia d'Amato, Ilaria Tiddi, Arne Bröring, Simon Mayer, Femke Ongenae, Riccardo Tommasini, and Mehwish Alam. Springer International Publishing: Cham, Switzerland, 2021, pp. 155–164. https://doi.org/10.1007/978-3-030-80418-3_28.
60. Christof Bless, Lukas Dötlinger, Michael Kaltschmid, Markus Reiter, Anelia Kurteva, Antonio J Roa-Valverde, and Anna Fensel. 'Raising Awareness of Data Sharing Consent Through Knowledge Graph Visualisation'. In: *Further with Knowledge Graphs*. IOS Press: Amsterdam, The Netherlands, 2021, pp. 44–57. https://doi.org/10.3233/SSW210034.
61. Nicola Dragoni, Saverio Giallorenzo, Alberto Lluch Lafuente, Manuel Mazzara, Fabrizio Montesi, Ruslan Mustafin, and Larisa Safina. 'Microservices: Yesterday, Today, and Tomorrow'. In: *Present and Ulterior Software Engineering*. Ed. by Manuel Mazzara and Bertrand Meyer. Springer International Publishing: Cham, Switzerland, 2017, pp. 195–216. https://doi.org/10.1007/978-3-319-67425-4_12.
62. Harihara Subramanian and Pethuru Raj. *Hands-On RESTful API Design Patterns and Best Practices: Design, develop, and deploy highly adaptable, scalable, and secure RESTful web APIs*. Packt Publishing Ltd.: Birmingham, UK, 2019.
63. Lorenzo De Lauretis. 'From Monolithic Architecture to Microservices Architecture'. In: *2019 IEEE International Symposium on Software Reliability Engineering Workshops (ISSREW), Berlin, Germany, 28–31 October*. 2019, pp. 93–96. https://doi.org/10.1109/ISSREW.2019.00050.
64. Wilhelm Hasselbring and Guido Steinacker. 'Microservice Architectures for Scalability, Agility and Reliability in E-Commerce'. In: *2017IEEE International Conference on Software Architecture Workshops (ICSAW), Gothenburg, Sweden, 5-7 April*. 2017, pp. 243–246. https://doi.org/10.1109/ICSAW.2017.11.
65. Lin Zou, Ming Ni, Yiting Huang, Wenfeng Shi, and Xiaoxia Li. 'Hybrid Encryption Algorithm Based on AES and RSA in File Encryption'. In: *Frontier Computing*. Ed. by Jason C. Hung, Neil Y. Yen, and Jia-Wei Chang. Springer: Singapore, 2020, pp. 541–551.
66. *SPARQL 1.1 Query Language*. Available online: https://www.w3.org/TR/sparql11-query/ (accessed on 15 December 2021).
67. Jenna Lindqvist. 'New challenges to personal data processing agreements: is the GDPR fit to deal with contract, accountability and liability in a world of the Internet of Things?'

In: *International Journal of Law and Information Technology* 26.1 (Dec. 2017), pp. 45–63. https://doi.org/10.1093/ijlit/eax024.

68. INCITS 565-2020. *Information Technology—Next Generation Access Control (NGAC). ANSI: Washington, DC, USA, 2020*. Available online: https://standards.incits.org/apps/group_public/project/details.php?project_id=2328 (accessed on 29 December 2021).
69. *NoSQL Database*. Available online: https://hostingdata.co.uk/nosql-database/ (accessed on 9 December 2021).
70. Simon Eismann, Joel Scheuner, Erwin van Eyk, Maximilian Schwinger, Johannes Grohmann, Nikolas Herbst, Cristina L. Abad, and Alexandru Iosup. 'Serverless Applications: Why, When, and How?' In: *IEEE Software* 38.1 (2021), pp. 32–39. https://doi.org/10.1109/MS.2020.3023302.
71. *Atlas Database. Deploy a multi-cloud database*. Available online: https://www.mongodb.com/atlas/database (accessed on 10 December 2021).
72. *Amazon Web Services (AWS)*. Available online: https://aws.amazon.com (accessed on 6 December 2021).
73. *Python*. Available online: https://www.python.org (accessed on 1 December 2021).
74. *SWI Prolog*. Available online: https://www.swi-prolog.org (accessed 10 January 2022).
75. *Flask*. Available online: https://flask.palletsprojects.com/en/2.0.x/ (accessed on 19 December 2021).
76. *Flask-RESTful*. Available online: https://flask-restful.readthedocs.io/en/latest/ (accessed on 17 December 2021).
77. *Flask-SQLAlchemy*. Available online: https://flask-sqlalchemy.palletsprojects.com/en/2.x/ (accessed on 28 December 2021).
78. *Requests: HTTP for Humans*. Available online: https://docs.python-requests.org/en/latest/ (accessed on 10 December 2021).
79. *flask-apispec: Auto-documenting REST APIs for Flask*. Available online: https://flask-apispec.readthedocs.io/en/latest/ (accessed on 15 December 2021).
80. *PyCryptodome*. Available online: https://www.pycryptodome.org/en/latest/src/introduction.html (accessed on 9 January 2022).
81. *Flask-JWT-Extended's documentation*. Available online: https://flask-jwt-extended.readthedocs.io/en/stable/ (accessed on 14 December 2021).
82. *FuzzyWuzzy*. Available online: https://github.com/seatgeek/fuzzywuzzy (accessed on 29 November 2021).
83. *NLTK*. Available online: https://www.nltk.org (accessed on 18 December 2021).
84. *spaCy: Industrial-Strength Natural Language Processing*. Available online: https://spacy.io (accessed on 15 December 2021).
85. *SPARQL Endpoint interface to Python*. Available online: https://sparqlwrapper.readthedocs.io/en/latest/ (accessed on 4 January 2022).
86. *PyMongo*. Available online: https://pymongo.readthedocs.io/en/stable/ (accessed on 7 December 2021).
87. *Docker*. Available online: https://www.docker.com (accessed on 4 January 2022).
88. *SQLite*. Available online: https://sqlite.org/index.html (accessed on 14 December 2021).
89. *Kubernetes*. Available online: https://kubernetes.io (accessed on 6 December 2021).
90. *Linode*. Available online: https://www.linode.com (accessed on 6 December 2021).
91. *Linux*. Available online: https://www.linux.org (accessed on 22 December 2021).
92. *Ubuntu*. Available online: https://ubuntu.com (accessed on 4 December 2021).

93. *Debian*. Available online: https://www.debian.org (accessed on 14 December 2021).
94. *Data tracker*. Available online: https://datatracker.ietf.org/doc/html/rfc7519 (accessed on 29 December 2021).
95. *OpenAPI Initiative*. Available online: https://www.openapis.org (accessed on 19 December 2021).
96. *National Institute of Standards and Technology (NIST)*. Available online: https://www.nist.gov (accessed on 11 December 2021).
97. FIPS 197; Advanced Encryption Standard (AES). *National Institute of Standards and Technology: Gaithersburg, MD, USA*. 2001.
98. Neha Garg and Partibha Yadav. 'Comparison of asymmetric algorithms in cryptography'. In: *Journal of Computer Science and Mobile Computing (IJCSMC)* 3.4 (2014), pp. 1190–1196.
99. *RFC 8017*. Available online: https://www.rfc-editor.org/info/rfc8017 (accessed on 11 January 2022).
100. *RFC 5208*. Available online: https://www.ietf.org/rfc/rfc5208.txt (accessed on 11 January 2022).
101. Mihir Bellare, Phillip Rogaway, and D. Wagner. *EAX: A Conventional Authenticated-Encryption Mode*. IACR Eprint Archive. Available online: http://eprint.iacr.org/2003/069 (accessed on 05 January 2022). 2003.
102. *marshmallow: simplified object serialization*. Available online: https://marshmallow.readthedocs.io/en/stable/index.html (accessed on 19 October 2021).
103. Mo Becker, Alexander Malkis, and Laurent Bussard. *S4P: A Generic Language for Specifying Privacy Preferences and Policies*. Technical Report MSR-TR-2010-32. 2010.
104. Alex Ellis. *OpenFaas*. Available online: https://www.openfaas.com (accessed on 5 December 2021).
105. *Ofelia scheduler*. Available online: https://github.com/mcuadros/ofelia (accessed 10 November 2021).
106. B. Padmavathi and S. Ranjitha Kumari. 'A Survey on Performance Analysis of DES; AES and RSA Algorithm along with LSB Substitution Technique'. In: *International Journal of Science and Research (IJSR)* 2 (2013), pp. 170–174.
107. A. Nadeem and Muhammad Younus Javed. 'A Performance Comparison of Data Encryption Algorithms'. In: *2005 International Conference on Information and Communication Technologies, Karachi, Pakistan, 27-28 August*. 2005, pp. 84–89. https://doi.org/10.1109/ICICT.2005.1598556.
108. Chinmaya Kumar Dehury, Satish Narayana Srirama, and Tek Raj Chhetri. 'CCoDaMiC: A framework for Coherent Coordination of Data Migration and Computation platforms'. In: *Future Generation Computer Systems* 109 (2020), pp. 1–16. https://doi.org/10.1016/j.future.2020.03.029.
109. Alpana Kakkar and Armaan Farshori. 'Server-Less Cloud Computing—An Economical Solution for Business Operations'. In: *Innovations in Computer Science and Engineering*. Springer: Berlin/Heidelberg, Germany, 2020, pp. 145–154.
110. Minh Thanh Chung, Nguyen Quang-Hung, Manh-Thin Nguyen, and Nam Thoai. 'Using Docker in high performance computing applications'. In: *2016 IEEE Sixth International Conference on Communications and Electronics (ICCE), Ha-Long, Vietnam, 27–29 July*. 2016, pp. 52–57. https://doi.org/10.1109/CCE.2016.7562612.

111. *Kubernetespods*. Available online: https://kubernetes.io/docs/concepts/workloads/pods/ (accessed on 1 November 2021).
112. *Horizontal Pod Autoscaling*. Available online: https://kubernetes.io/docs/tasks/run-application/horizontalpod-autoscale/ (accessed on 2 January 2022).
113. *Locust*. Available online: https://locust.io (accessed on 11 December 2021).
114. Data Protection Commissioner. *Self-Assessment Checklist GDPR Readiness Checklist Tools*. Available online: https://www.dataprotection.ie/en/organisations/resourcesorganisations/self-assessment-checklist (accessed on 6 October 2021).
115. *Uniitest*. Available online: https://docs.python.org/3/library/unittest.html (accessed on 5 December 2021).
116. *GDPR compliance tool*. Available online: https://github.com/tekrajchhetri/GDPR_compliance_tool (accessed on 12 January 2022).

Enabling Privacy-Aware Interoperable and Quality IoT Data Sharing with Context

8

Abstract

Sharing Internet of Things (IoT) data across different sectors, such as in smart cities, becomes complex due to heterogeneity. This poses challenges related to a lack of interoperability, data quality issues and lack of context information, and a lack of data veracity (or accuracy). In addition, there are privacy concerns as IoT data may contain personally identifiable information. To address the above challenges, this paper presents a novel semantic technology-based framework that enables data sharing in a GDPR-compliant manner while ensuring that the data shared is interoperable, contains required context information, is of acceptable quality, and is accurate and trustworthy. The proposed framework also accounts

---

This chapter is a copy of the article that has been submitted for publication: **Tek Raj Chhetri**, Chinmaya Kumar Dehury, Blesson Varghese, Anna Fensel, Satish Narayana Srirama and Rance J. DeLong. 'Enabling privacy-aware interoperable and quality IoT data sharing with context'. In: Future Generation Computer Systems (2024). https://doi.org/10.1016/j.future.2024.03.039.

Contribution as a first author: The scientific contributions include the following: (i) conceptualisation of the study; (ii) design of the methodology; (iii) implementation and deployment of the proposed methodology and execution of experiments; (iv) performing formal analysis and validation of the experiments; (v) data curation and data visualisation; and (vi) writing the manuscript.

Supplementary Information The online version contains supplementary material available at https://doi.org/10.1007/978-3-658-45877-5_8.

T. R. Chhetri, *Improving Decision Making Using Semantic Web Technologies*,
https://doi.org/10.1007/978-3-658-45877-5_8

for the edge/fog, an upcoming computing paradigm for the IoT to support real-time decisions. We evaluate the performance of the proposed framework with two different edge and fog-edge scenarios using resource-constrained IoT devices, such as the Raspberry Pi. In addition, we also evaluate shared data quality, interoperability and veracity. Our key finding is that the proposed framework can be employed on IoT devices with limited resources due to its low CPU and memory utilization for analytics operations and data transformation and migration operations. The low overhead of the framework supports real-time decision making. In addition, the 100% accuracy of our evaluation of the data quality and veracity based on 180 different observations demonstrates that the proposed framework can guarantee both data quality and veracity.

8.1 Introduction

The Internet of Things (IoT) ecosystem continues to expand alongside other newer computing paradigms, such as edge/fog computing, leading to exponential growth in data. With the IoT ecosystem, we refer to the integrated layer of IoT hardware, software, and connectivity [1]. The term "big data" is used to refer to these massive amounts of data generated by the IoT [2]. For example, IoT connections are expected to reach 83 billion by 2024, rising from 35 billion in 2020 [3]. As the IoT ecosystem expands, so do the associated complexities and challenges arising from heterogeneity, such as data interoperability, accuracy, and quality. These issues must be addressed as the IoT is implemented in crucial sectors, such as healthcare for remote robot surgery [4].

Figure 8.1 provides a high-level overview of the use of IoT in different environments by integrating recent edge/fog computing paradigms and highlights the corresponding challenges. The first challenge is associated with data quality and accuracy. The term "accuracy" is also referred to as "data veracity". Data quality issues occur due to reasons, such as sensor calibration inaccuracies and environmental effects that cause erroneous observations [5–7]. With data quality, we refer to the suitability of data (or fitness to use) for a specific application or task [8]. More than 50 studies have been conducted using advanced statistical and machine learning techniques to ensure that the observation values are not erroneous [7]. This is because poor-quality data can lead to poor or flawed decisions. However, such post-hoc approaches as anomaly and outlier detection are expensive and not suitable for real-time. Data integrity is also important and is a key challenge [6, 9].

Therefore, there is a need for a scalable solution that intrinsically addresses the data quality challenge and also addresses the data veracity problem. Furthermore, there is a need for understanding data veracity in the context of edge/fog that will enable decision making in smart cities and autonomous driving.

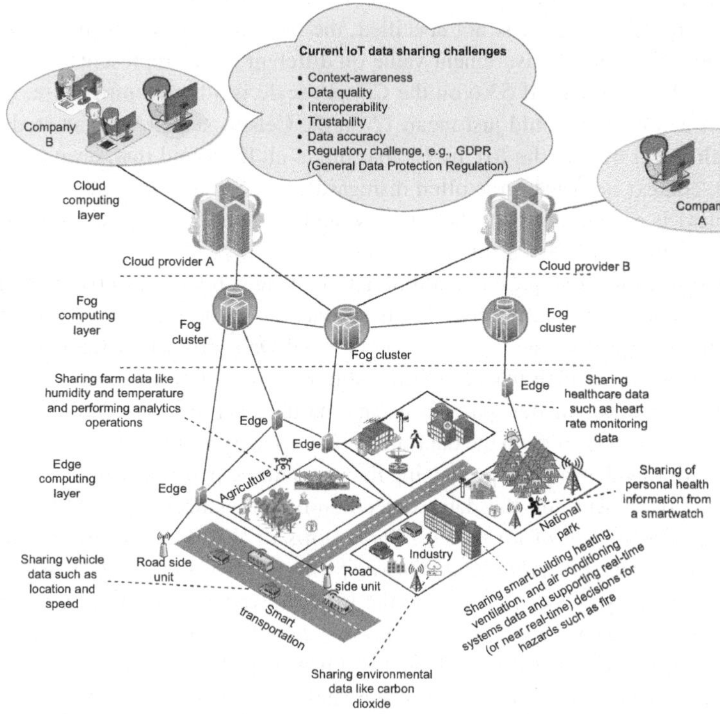

Fig. 8.1 IoT data sharing environment with an edge/fog scenario and the associated challenges

Interoperability and the lack of context are other challen-ges [2, 5, 6, 9]. Interoperability is the ability of heterogeneous systems to exchange and consume data [10]. Interoperability, for example, accounts for 40% of the potential benefits of the IoT, which is anticipated to have a yearly economic impact of $11.1 trillion by 2025 [11]. Interoperability is essential to enable the exchange and use of information across heterogeneous systems. Context (or contextual information) in the case of data sharing is the set of interrelated conditions describing the data, such as sensor information, units of measurement, and the observed property. This is extremely crucial as the heterogeneity of the IoT grows and its use in automated decision making increases. In addition, the availability of context facilitates accurate decision making. Temperature, for instance, can be measured on a variety of scales; if the unit of measurement, for example, is not specified, the likelihood of errors increases. This is because the same measurement value on different scales represents different meanings. For example, if 53.6 on the Celsius scale is a high temperature, in Fahrenheit it is not, as it would just mean 12 on the Celsius scale. A recent study on data quality and trust in the IoT by Byabazaire et al. [5] found that, despite its importance, context information is often disregarded. According to Byabazaire et al. [5], context is a component of data quality, and no solutions have considered context information while assessing data quality.

Data sharing in the IoT presents additional challenges related to privacy and trust [12, 13]. For example, the privacy concern has led to the implementation of legislation to safeguard privacy, such as the General Data Protection Regulation (GDPR) in 2018 [14], which has added an additional layer of complexity. GDPR aims to improve privacy and transparency in data sharing and processing through the notion of informed consent from the data subject (i.e., a natural person) which must be obtained prior to sharing and processing data containing personally identifiable information (PII) concerning the data subject. Non-compliance with GDPR can result in a *maximum fine of up to 20 million euros or 4% of the firm's global annual revenue for the preceding financial year, whichever is greater (Article 83)*. Consequently, privacy is also a concern in the IoT [15] where applications such as smart cities, vehicle data sharing, and healthcare generally involve PII data.

Trust has been extensively studied [5, 12]. Over fifty studies have been done on IoT trust management using methods like statistical approaches and also the blockchain, similar to works on data quality [12]. However, they are primarily concerned with the composition and management of IoT services and have not addressed issues such as heterogeneity [12]. Studies on trust focusing on IoT data, such as those by Byabazaire et al. [16], have also been conducted, proposing a framework to derive the trust metric from the shared IoT data. However, Byabazaire et al.'s [16] framework focuses on deriving trust from shared data, as opposed to trust as an intrinsic metric of real-time data sharing. In addition, as pointed out by Byabazaire et al. [16], their work does not address memory or computational costs, which are essential in the case of the IoT due to its resource-constrained nature. Fortineo et al. [13], in their survey on trust and reputation in the IoT, further highlights the need to consider the resource constrained nature of IoT and the newer edge/fog computing paradigms. There is a need for a privacy-aware solution for data sharing that incorporates an intrinsic trust metric.

Therefore, the proposed framework introduces a trust metric intrinsic to the shared. In addition, the proposed framework includes consent checking to ensure privacy and compliance with GDPR. This is because the integration of the trust metric (or score) helps determine the extent to which one should rely on shared data. The same, i.e., the significance and necessity of the trust metric (or score), is emphasized by Byabazaire et al. [5] in their survey on data quality and trust in IoT for secure end-to-end data sharing, along with the difficulties such as how to securely propagate the trust metric. Additionally, trust metrics have been implemented in other contexts, such as Google search [17], where trustable sources are ranked highly. This further emphasizes the significance of the trust metric.

The proposed framework, which addresses the aforementioned challenges (or problems), such as interoperability, quality, privacy, and trust issues in IoT data sharing in a heterogeneous environment, uses semantic technology. Semantic technology, specifically ontologies and knowledge graphs (KGs), which are based on the linked-data concept, can represent real-world relationships, be used to build knowledge, and can also provide reasoning, interoperability, data enrichment, and data variety handling capabilities [18]. In addition, the proposed approach makes use of the blockchain, which provides properties such as tamperproofness [19] and makes the proposed solution suitable even for an untrustworthy environment.

The proposed framework supports real-time (or near real-time) decision making and utilizes low resources, as evidenced by the following findings: (i) an average CPU utilization at the edge and fog, respectively, of 33.61% and 15.62% for analytics operations and 12.35% and 1.24% for data transformation and migration operations; (ii) an average time to perform analytics operations at the fog layer of 1.1 seconds and the edge of 7.2 seconds; and (iii) 51 megabytes of memory utilization.

The paper is organized as follows. Section 8.2 provides background information, the motivation for our work, and the contributions. Section 8.3 provides an overview of the related work. Section 8.4 provides an overview of methodology used in our study for ontology modeling as well as for weighted trust metric. Section 8.5 details the proposed system (or framework). Section 8.6 provides information on the experimental setup and implementation. Section 8.7 provides details on the experiment and evaluation of our work. Finally, Sect. 8.8 provides the conclusion.

8.2 Background, Motivation & Contribution

Data sharing and integration are vast and extremely important in today's connected world. However, despite the importance of data sharing, the number of works in this area is limited [20]. Additionally, with the rise of new technology and industrial and legal requirements, the data sharing and integration landscape continuously evolves, introducing new opportunities and obstacles. One such instance is the implementation of the GDPR, which has altered the data sharing paradigm. For example, our previous work [21] that the proposed framework in this paper extends established a data pipeline framework for secure and accurate data migration and does not cover GDPR. Moreover, Yang et al. [20] recently proposed an edge data sharing framework named EdgeShare for industrial IoT data sharing using blockchain. However, as with other works, the other important aspects, such as data quality and legal regulations, still need to be covered to provide a holistic data sharing solution.

8.2.1 Motivation

The major motivation for this work is the existing challenges, such as data quality and their impact in supporting decision making tasks in domains like healthcare and smart cities. For example, three-quarters of IoT projects fail solely because of the data quality issue [6, 7]. In a manner analogous to data quality, the other motivations include challenges, lack of context awareness, trust, accuracy, and interoperability, all of which affect decision making. For example, one can only imagine the repercussions of having data, even a simple temperature measurement, without appropriate context or an interoperability issue in patient monitoring systems. In addition, the limited work in data sharing [20] and the need for a comprehensive solution that addresses the previously-mentioned challenges, a lesson learned from our previous work [22] and the smashHit[1] project, serve as additional motivation.

Moreover, it is just as essential to understand the implications of the new technological solutions, particularly with regard to supporting real-time (or near real-time) decision making in edge/fog scenarios, as it is to address the previously mentioned challenges. The reason is the growing use of IoT in industries such as healthcare and manufacturing, which require real-time (or near real-time) decision making. It is the same reason, i.e., the need to support the real-time requirements and to reduce the latency caused by cloud-IoT communication, the edge/fog paradigms

[1] https://smashhit.eu

were introduced [23]. Understanding the suitability of the proposed solution to support real-time decision making constitutes the another motivation for our work.

In line with the motivations, this research seeks to answer the following research questions:

1. How can we assure accurate and trustworthy data sharing in an interoperable manner in a complex, heterogeneous environment such as a smart city to support data-driven decision making?
2. Can we assure the need for real-time (or near real-time) decision making, i.e., support analytics operation in a constrained environment while addressing other challenges such as interoperability and data veracity?

8.2.2 Contribution

Based on the motivation of our work, we make the following contributions.

1. The design and implementation of a privacy-aware interoperable IoT data sharing framework based on semantic technology and blockchain that intrinsically guarantees data quality based on predefined criteria and also ensures data veracity.
2. An introduction of the weighted trust metric (see Sect. 8.4.2) that is intrinsic to shared data and considered within an edge/fog scenario.
3. Assessing context information as a component of data quality, for which, according to [5], there are currently no solutions.
4. The design and implementation of the framework to provide data analytics capability to support real-time decision making requirements at edge/fog, along with interoperable and quality data sharing.
5. Finally, the performance evaluation of the proposed framework in terms of memory and CPU (Central processing unit) overhead and execution time with two different edge and fog-edge scenarios utilizing resource-constrained IoT devices such as the Raspberry Pi.

8.3 Related Work

In this section, we provide an overview of related works focusing on IoT data sharing. The summary of related works includes studies that address issues such as interoperability, data quality, and accuracy. Additionally, our review includes studies that examine GDPR-compliant IoT data sharing and excludes studies that do not focus on privacy from a GDPR perspective. Similarly, studies that do not directly address the sharing and processing of IoT are excluded from the review of related works. The related works are grouped into two categories: (i) semantic-based studies, which utilize semantic technology (Sect. 8.3.1), and (ii) non-semantic technological studies (Sect. 8.3.2), which do not utilize semantic technology in their work. The other section, Sect. 8.3.3, provides a summary of the related works.

8.3.1 Semantic Technology-based Study

Rubí et al. [24] focuses on environmental data sharing in smart cities. The work uses the semantic technology, as in our study, to enable interoperability and also takes into account the changing computing landscape, such as fog computing. The work of Rubí et al. [24], however, does not focus on other aspects, such as ensuring data veracity and GDPR. Loukil et al. [25] present a privacy-preserving blockchain-based platform, PATRIoT, for IoT data sharing. The work is GDPR-focused and makes use of semantic technology, specifically the LIoPY ontology [26], which models the privacy requirements. Moreover, the work takes into consideration the limited computing capability of IoT devices. The work, however, does not consider other aspects such as interoperability and accuracy (or veracity) of shared data, which are very important in sectors such as healthcare. Strassner et al. [27] proposed a semantic technology based architecture for interoperable IoT data sharing and also considered fog computing. However, as highlighted by Strassner et al. [27], the implementation and performance evaluation are left for future work. Reda et al. [28], likewise, conducted research on the integration and sharing of heterogeneous healthcare wearable data using semantic technology. Reda et al. [28] developed a web portal for integrating, sharing and analyzing IoT data. The proposed approach has been verified using IoT data collected in RDF (Resource Description Framework)[2] format. Reda et al. [28], similar to our study, also applied the SWRL (Semantic Web Rule Language) rule to detect the vital signs of health conditions like a cardiac event. The other aspects of the data, such as veracity, were not the focus of the work. Zappatore et al. [29] conducted a study using semantic technology for IoT in healthcare (or wellness). In their work, Zappatore et al. [29] proposed a new ontology, the FitBit API ontology, for interoperability. Moreover, it also proposed an architecture platform named App4Health and considered the edge/fog tier. How-

[2] https://www.w3.org/RDF/

ever, the interoperability layer only exists at the cloud tier (or in the cloud), and further implementation is planned as a future work.

8.3.2 Non-semantic Technological Study

Makhdoom et al. [30] present a privacy-preserving and blockchain-based framework for IoT data sharing. The work by the use of the blockchain addresses the security issue and also covers GDPR requirements such as data sharing based on consent. This study, like ours, only stores the transaction hash in the blockchain. However, the study does not address the interoperability challenge and also does not provide analytics capability as in our work. Moreover, integration of fog (or fog nodes) is left as a future work.

Abdullah et al. [31] propose a privacy-aware framework, the PRISED tangle, for IoT data sharing in healthcare. The work of Abdullah et al. [31] uses IOTA Tangle, which is a zero-fee, zero-miner, zero-block distributed ledger technology (DLT) for the IoT [32]. The IOTA Tangle uses a new data structure based on directed acyclic graphs. Moreover, the authors have also considered GDPR in their framework, enabling GDPR-compliant health data sharing. With the use of the DLT, the authors have addressed privacy issues. However, issues such as interoperability and data quality remain unresolved. Bai et al. [33], similar to the previous studies, proposed a framework for the sharing and storage of healthcare data using blockchain. However, unlike previous work, the framework of Bai et al. [33] supports the GDPR's "right to be forgotten" rule and uses IPFS[3] (the InterPlanetary File System) for data storage. The framework, as the authors point out, is computationally intensive, necessitating the use of systems with greater computational capacity, and thus is unsuitable for the edge/fog scenario. Additionally, other aspects of data, such as quality, have not been considered.

Similar to Makhdoom et al. [30], Alamri et al. [34] present a framework to enable interoperable and GDPR-compliant IoT-based personal health record data sharing using blockchain. The work considers the privacy aspect, as in our study from the GDPR perspective, and also interoperability following HL7 FHIR[4]. However, the work does not ensure data veracity, and also, implementation is left as future work. Tsiouris et al. [35] propose an interoperable telehealth platform that enables the sharing of IoT data with a remote cloud for data storage and analytics. As

[3] https://ipfs.tech/

[4] http://hl7.org/fhir/

with Alamri et al. [34], Tsiouris et al. [35] also relies on HL7 FHIR[5] standards for interoperability. The edge unit, which constitutes one of the key component of Tsiouris et al.'s [35] work, is responsible for managing IoT devices and tasks and enabling data exchange with the cloud. However, the work does not deal with issues such as data veracity (or accuracy) and privacy, which are even more critical in the health sector. Additionally, interoperability can be achieved only after data is processed in the remote cloud, as the cloud is the repository for the core interoperable technologies. Halim et al. [36] proposed a general framework for interoperable IoT data sharing. The proposed framework stores the metadata information, such as ownership, in a SQL (Structured Query Language) database and the IoT data in a NoSQL database. The framework consists of three key components: a device management layer for the abstraction of IoT devices, a data management layer for handling data, and a service layer that provides services to applications such as access to data. However, as with other studies, data veracity and quality aspects are not the focus.

Poojara et al. [37] propose a serverless data pipeline for IoT data sharing in the fog and cloud computing. The work of Poojara et al. [37] also evaluates the trade-offs of the proposed serverless data pipeline for different types of fog computing workloads, such as Anenas [38] and custom video processing. However, the work does not consider the interoperability and legal regulations such as GDPR.

8.3.3 Summary

In short, the review highlights that related works are devoted to specific aspects of IoT data sharing requirements such as interoperability but lack coverage of all the critical aspects: privacy, accuracy (or data veracity), and data quality, which are required for end-to-end IoT data sharing. Table 8.1 shows a comparison of our work to the state-of-the-art works, highlighting the current research gaps. For the comparison, we have considered the following criteria: (i) privacy from a GDPR perspective; (ii) interoperability; (ii) data quality; (iv) data veracity; (v) trust metric (or score); (vi) analytics operation indicated by analytics; (vii) considerations for the edge/fog scenario; and (viii) finally, the performance evaluation. The data quality in Table 8.1 reflects both the evaluation of the context information and the data themselves. In the case where a study covers either one of these data quality aspects, they are indicated with a check mark. Similarly, the analytics in Table 8.1 represent if the study has implemented any kinds of analytics (or reasoning) operations to

[5] http://hl7.org/fhir/

Table 8.1 Comparison with state-of-the-art

Study	Privacy	Interoperability	Dataquality	Dataveracity	Trust metric	Analytics	Edge/Fog	Performance evaluation
Rubí et al. (2021) [24]	×	✓	×	×	×	✓	×/✓	✓
Loukil et al. (2020) [25]	✓	×	×	×	×	×	×/×	✓
Strassner et al. (2016) [27]	×	✓	×	×	×	×	×/✓	×
Reda et al. (2022) [28]	×	✓	✓	×	×	×	×/×	×
Zappatore et al. (2023) [29]	×	✓	×	×	×	✓	✓/✓	×
Makhdoom et al. (2020) [30]	✓	×	×	×	×	×	×/×	✓
Abdullah et al. (2022) [31]	✓	×	×	×	×	✓	×/×	✓
Bai et al. (2022) [33]	✓	×	×	×	×	×	×/×	✓
Alamri et al. (2021) [34]	✓	✓	×	×	×	×	×/×	×
Tsiouris et al. (2020) [35]	×	✓	×	×	×	×	✓/×	✓
Halim et al. (2022) [36]	×	✓	✓	×	×	×	✓/×	✓
Poojara et al. (2022) [37]	×	×	×	×	×	✓	✓/✓	✓
Our study	✓	✓	✓	✓	✓	✓	✓/✓	✓

support real-time decision making with an edge-and-fog scenario. The check mark (✓) indicates that the compared criteria were incorporated into the study's design, implementation, or both. The cross (×), on the other hand, indicates that either the compared criteria were not considered or there was no information in the study. As can be observed from Table 8.1, our study covers the needed aspects of data, such as quality, veracity, and privacy, that are required in an end-to-end data sharing scenario, thereby demonstrating the benefits of our work. Furthermore, several works on IoT privacy have been conducted, such as the one by Liu et al. [39], which do not address GDPR and have not been considered in our related works. However, such works can be regarded as relevant for future work as they can be integrated into our framework, which already enables GDPR-compliant data sharing and processing.

In light of the existing research challenges, we present our work which enables privacy-aware IoT data sharing and processing while simultaneously providing interoperability and assures both quality and accuracy (or veracity). In addition to privacy, interoperability, accuracy, and quality aspects, our work also considers the intelligence at the edge or fog levels to support real-time (or near real-time) decision making. For example, the increasing use of IoT for monitoring, such as in power plants, necessitates real-time decision making. This can be accomplished by the use of edge or fog computing. However, the reviewed studies fail to take into account this essential factor that our work does.

8.4 Methodology

This section provides details about the methodology that is adopted for ontology modeling and the trust metric (also referred to as the trust score or trustworthiness score). The methodology that is employed in our work is applicable in other contexts.

Furthermore, the ontology enables the integration of heterogeneous data sources, such as in the case of smart cities [40].

Moreover, this section also provides an overview of the functional and non-functional requirements. The preliminaries of the concepts are available as supplementary material (see Appendix A).

8.4.1 Ontology Modeling

The ontology is the core of our systems, as it facilitates interoperability and further enables reasoning capabilities. We followed the standard ontology modeling practice [41], wherein the first step is to define the scope of the ontology (or ontology requirements), such as what the ontology should model (or cover). Since this research is concerned with the sharing of IoT data, the ontology's scope should be established in a similar manner. The scope of our ontology is outlined below. The ontology as well as the source code can be accessed at [42].

1. The ontology should be able to represent sensor information and observation results, as well as context such as units of measurement describing observation results.
2. Based on what the sensors see, the ontology should be able to support reasoning (or analytics) operations, like creating an alert in our case.

According to our scope (i.e., ontology requirements), the ontology must be able to answer the competency questions (CQs) listed below. These CQs are derived from our proposed framework, which is aimed at addressing the challenges of IoT data sharing, such as data quality issues.

CQ 1. What is making an observation?
CQ 2. What is the sensor observing, such as temperature (i.e., observed property), and in what units?
CQ 3. When was the observation made?
CQ 4. How can we ensure the reliability and accuracy (i.e., data veracity) of data?
CQ 5. What type of edge reasoning is carried out?

Figure 8.2 shows the ontology used in our study that was developed following our CQs. The ontology used in our study is small, i.e., it only includes a limited number of concepts pertaining to sensors and their observation. Our study's small ontology is due to the different focus of our work, which is to demonstrate the use of ontology to address challenges such as interoperability, as opposed to ontology engineering that focuses on creating large ontologies. However, the methodology adopted for our ontology modeling can be used to model larger ontologies in a collaborative setting or extend the scope of the ontology used in our study. The ontology used in this study reuses the concepts from the two different ontologies, namely SOSA [43] and the OM (Ontology of units of Measure) [44]. We consider SOSA [43] ontology compared to other ontologies like DogOnt [45] due to its wide adoption. In Fig. 8.2, the reused classes and properties from the OM and SOSA ontologies are denoted by the prefixes *om* and *sosa*, respectively. The prefix *sricats* shows that the concepts are unique to this study.

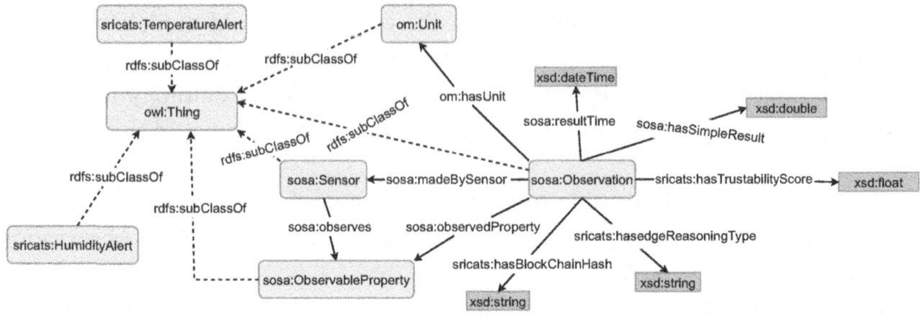

Fig. 8.2 Ontology used in our study

With CQ 1, CQ 2, and CQ 3, the ontology captures information about the sensor observation result and also context information describing the observation, such as units in which observation was made and the time when observation was made. The *sosa:Sensor* class and property *sosa:madeBySensor* provides an answer to CQ1, while *sosa:Observation* class and *sosa:-resultTime* property provides an answer to CQ3. In a similar manner, classes *sosa:Observation*, *sosa:ObservableProperty* and *om:Unit*, as well as their respective properties *om:hasUnit*, *sosa:-hasSimpleResult*, and *sosa:-observedProperty* provides an answer to our CQ 2. Moreover, the ontology can be easily expanded to include additional context information, such as location, based on the requirements. In addition, this incorporation of context information into the ontology enables us to validate using SHACL (Shapes constraint language) as part of the data quality, which is one of the limitations highlighted by [5] and one of our contributions.

The properties *sricats:hasTrustabilityScore* and *sricats: hasBlockchainHash* provides an answer to our CQ 4 and the property *sricats:hasEdgeReasoningType* as well as the classes *sricats:TemperatureAlert* and *sricats:HumidityAlert* answers CQ 5. The *sricats:TemperatureAlert* and *sricats:HumidityAlert* are clas-ses representing alert operations specific to the humidity and temperature observations, respectively. The reason for this separation is to make concepts explicit and follows the ontology definition. These concepts, namely *sricats:TemperatureAlert* and *sricats:HumidityAlert*, can be thought of as target labels in the case of machine learning and are used in SWRL reasoning to perform the classification task. For instance, we wish to predict, based on the temperature observation value, whether or not the temperature alert should be triggered. The *sricats:-hasEdgeReasoningType* provides information on the types of reasoning to perform, such as temperature or humidity in our case.

The prefix *rdfs* in Fig. 8.2 represents the RDF schema[6], which provides a vocabulary for RDF. *sricats:hasBlockchainHash*, on the other hand, contains the blockchain transaction hash value, which is subsequently used to verify data veracity (or accuracy), and *sricats:hasTrustabilityScore* stores the trustworthiness score.

8.4.2 Trust Metric

Equation 8.1 illustrates the weighted trust metric (or score) that we employ in our research. The trust score (or metric) is a function of the trust factor F and its weight W. The trust score ranges from 0 to 1, with higher numbers indicating greater trustworthiness. The trust factor F defines the criteria for trust. It can be either 0 or 1, indicating whether the trust criteria have been met. W, which sums to 1, represents the weight that has been assigned to each of the established trust criteria. This weighted approach accounts for the subjectivity of trust by permitting individuals to assign weights to each of the defined trust criteria based on their level of trust.

$$trust\_score\,(t_s) = \sum_{i=1}^{n} F_i \times W_i,\ where\ F_i \in \{0, 1\},\ 0 \leq W_i \leq 1\ and \sum W_i = 1 \tag{8.1}$$

In our study, we considered three social trust criteria (or factors): manufacturer, location where IoT is deployed, and deployment by, i.e., who deployed the IoT. The weights assigned were 0.5, 0.3, and 0.2 for manufacturer, location, and deployment, respectively. The considerations for these trust factors derive from [46, 47]. For instance, if an IoT device manufactured by Texas Instruments is deployed, the level of trust would be high. This is because of their reputation, and studies [46, 47] have already demonstrated the relation between social factors such as reputation and trust in the case of the IoT. However, these criteria can be easily expanded to incorporate additional criteria; doing so is a trivial task.

8.4.3 Functional and Non-functional Requirements

In this section, we describe the system's functional and non-functional requirements. These requirements are derived from our research questions and are consistent with other research. For instance, Gupta [48] has also highlighted the non-functional

---

[6] https://www.w3.org/TR/rdf-schema/

requirement of performance efficiency, one of the key challenges in edge (or edge computing) due to its resource-constrained nature. The below-described functional and non-functional requirements serve as the premise for designing the proposed system.

Functional requirements:

1. Upon receiving (or reading) the sensor data, the system must check for consent before further processing.
2. Given the successful consent check, the system should compute the trust score, generate the hash of the data for the data veracity check, and store the generated hash in the blockchain.
3. After successfully calculating the trust score and storing the hash in the blockchain (or blockchain hash) the system should convert the sensor data, the trust score, and the blockchain hash into the KG representation according to the ontology.
4. Upon data migration to a new location, the system should be able to reconstruct the hash from the KG and conduct a data veracity check. In addition, the system should be able to perform data quality tests using SHACL after data veracity checks have been completed successfully.

Non-functional requirements:

1. The proposed system should be resource-efficient, i.e., suitable for deployment on resource-constrained IoT devices, with minimal CPU and memory usage.
2. To support scalability, the system should permit the disintegration of its components similar to microservices architecture.
3. The system should be lawfully compliant; for instance, data processing should only occur with explicit consent, and the use of blockchain should not violate GDPR.
4. The system should support real-time (or near real-time) decision making.
5. The system should support interoperability and ensure the data's accuracy and trustworthiness.

8.5 Proposed System

This section provides a conceptual high-level architecture description designed after reviewing the existing works. Figure 8.3 shows the architecture of the proposed system (or framework). Additionally, the design of the proposed system is governed by the functional and non-functional requirements outlined in Sect. 8.4.3. The following subsections provide detailed information about the proposed system's components, consistent with other studies [21, 22, 24, 25, 36].

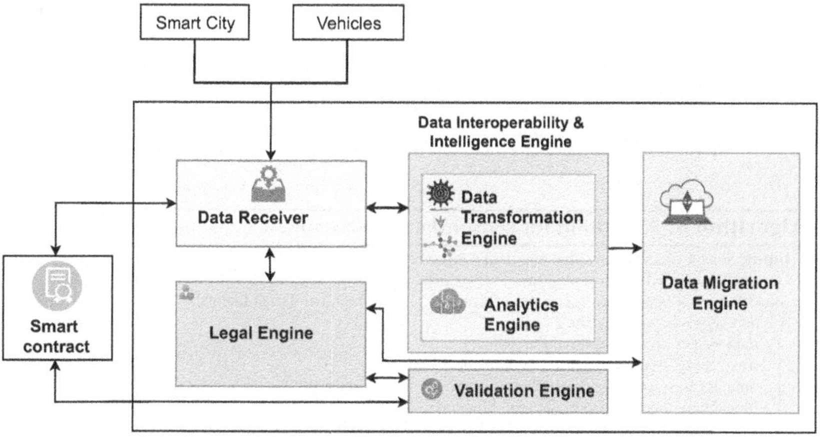

Fig. 8.3 Proposed framework architecture

8.5.1 Data Source

The data source comprises various sources that generate data through IoT devices. These sources include smart cities, smart vehicles, smart homes, wearable health devices, and hospitals, such as using environmental sensors in smart cities to monitor noise levels, air quality, and pollution and smart inhalers in hospitals to monitor patients.

8.5.2 Smart Contract

The smart contract in the framework represents a blockchain smart contract. In our case, it represents the Ethereum blockchain smart contract. The smart contract in our study contains the smart contract definitions (i.e., code), such as to store the hash. The reason for using the blockchain to store hashes is because generated hashes can be compromised by exploiting flaws [49]. The storage of hashes in the blockchain ensures that the hashes are tamper-proof and can be relied upon while performing a data veracity check.

8.5.3 Data Receiver

The data receiver is the first component to interact with the data from the sensor and is the one upon which the other components of the proposed systems depend, such as the analytics engine, to perform tasks such as data analytics in order to enable intelligence. The received sensor data is processed, such as by enriching it with additional context information like observation units, prior to being transformed into the KG representation for interoperability. Algorithm 6 shows the steps for data processing by the data receiver component.

Algorithm 6: Algorithm for sensor data processing

```
Input: Sensor observation value and data subject consent
Output: Data in KG representation
sensorSetup ← Sensor configuration information such as name and trust factors;
if check_consent = True then
    data ← get_sensor_observation_value();
    trust_score ← compute_trust_score(sensorSetup);
    data_hash ← generate_hash(data, trust_score, timestamp);
    blockchain_hash ← store_data_in_blockchain(data_hash);
    data_in_kg_format ← transform_to_kg(data, blockchain_hash, trust_score, sensorSetup);
    return data_in_kg_format;
else
    No processing;
```

As the aim is also to enable GDPR-compliant data sharing, first the consent is checked to ensure that there is appropriate consent from data subject (or natural person) to process sensor data. For this data receiver component interacts with the legal engine of the framework. After that, the sensor data is read, and the trust score is computed (see Sect. 8.4.2). The trust score calculation in Algorithm 6 is indicated by the function $compute\_trust\_score(sensorSetup)$. The $sensorSetup$ contains information about the sensors and the trust factors (or criteria). Following the computation of the trust score, a hash is generated, which is later used for data veracity purposes. The hash is generated using a timestamp (date and time) value together with the trust score and the actual data. The computation of the hash is indicated by indicated by $generate\_hash(data, trust\_score, timestamp)$. sha256 is used for hash generation. The generated hash, represented by $data\_hash$ variable in Algorithm 6, is then stored in a blockchain smart contract, ensuring the integrity of the hash because of the immutability of the blockchain. The blockchain hash (i.e., $blockchain\_hash$ in Algorithm 6) is a hash of a blockchain transaction that was generated while storing the data hash in blockchain, which in our case is the Ethereum. This is especially important because it enables data sharing in untrusted environments with the assurance that data veracity can be verified. The reason for only storing hashes instead of complete data in the blockchain is because of the contradiction of the blockchain with the GDPR's right to erasure (Article 17), as data stored in the blockchain cannot be deleted. Finally, the data is transformed into a KG representation, using the data, blockchain hash, trust score, and sensor configuration information, and by interacting with the transformation engine. $transform\_to\_kg(data, blockchain\_hash, trust\_score, sensor-Setup)$ in Algorithm 6 represents this transformation stage. In the absence of consent, no processing, not even reading the sensor data, is performed.

8.5.4 Data Transformation Engine

The data transformation engine is one of the core components, its tasks include the conversion of raw data to their respective semantic representations, namely, KG, thereby enabling interoperability. The interoperability occurs through the use of the ontology that defines concepts with a shared meaning (see evaluation Sect. 8.7.2.4) [50, 51]. The following steps summarize the data transformation process.

1. The first step is to define the namespaces[7] by reusing the existing ontology where possible.
2. The subsequent step involves extracting the relevant information from the input data.
3. The third (or final) step is to perform a mapping of the extracted information from the input data as per the concepts (i.e., class, object properties, and data properties) defined in an ontology. The descriptions of the ontology used in our study are presented in Sect. 8.4.1.

Additionally, the data transformation engine converts the generated KG into a format compliant with SPARQL[8] for data migration. SPARQL is a query language for KG (or RDF graphs).

[7] https://www.w3.org/TR/2004/REC-owl-guide-20040210/#Namespaces

[8] https://www.w3.org/TR/sparql11-overview/

8.5.5 Legal Engine

The legal engine is responsible for checking if there is valid consent for the requested data processing activity, thereby ensuring that the processing is GDPR-compliant. The steps involved in checking the consent are shown in Algorithm 7. First, consent is obtained from the data subject (or natural person) and is checked against the data processing operations that is intended to be carried out. This is to ensure that the data processing activities adhere to the consent provided. The data processing information is obtained from other components of the framework at different stages, such as during initial sensor data processing and during validation and analytics operations. For example, one can deploy multiple sensors at home but may consent to share or process certain sensor data, and that too for a specific purpose. Following the check, the final status represented by true or false is returned. The status indicates that everything is fine and data processing activities can be carried out, while the false status indicates that there's no consent. "No consent" here could mean either no consent at all or not for the requested processing activity or sensor. In Algorithm 7 $processing\_information()$ and $obtain\_consent\_from - \_data\_subject()$ are used to obtain the data processing and consent information, respectively.

Algorithm 7: Algorithm for checking consent

Input: Data and consent from data subject
Output: Status indicating whether or not to continue data processing activities

consent ← obtain_consent_from_data_subject();
dataProcessing ← processing_information();
if $check(consent, dataProcessing) = True$ **then**
    return status True;
else
    return status False;

8.5.6 Validation Engine

The validation engine performs the data validation tasks to ensure the following: (i) data accuracy (or veracity); and (ii) data quality. The accuracy (or veracity) of the data ensures that it has not been altered and that the data at the destination is the same as at the source where it originated. The data quality, on the other hand, ensures that the shared sensor data meets the predefined quality criteria. For the quality criteria, the following were considered: (i) the existence of the properties sosa:observedProperty, sosa:observes, and sosa:madeBySensor with type IRI; (ii) the existence of the sosa:resultTime with data type datetime; (iii) the presence of the blockchain with a minimum length of 60 with data type string; (iv) the presence of the sensor observation result of type double and the range between 0–100; and (v) the occurrence of the trustability score of type float. These quality criteria can be extended easily to include additional context and data sources by defining them in the SHACL, and doing so is trivial. Algorithm 8 outlines the steps to perform the validation.

Algorithm 8: Algorithm for performing validation

```
   Input: Data in KG format
   Output: Status and validated data in KG in the case of successful validation in a dictionary format
1  if check_consent = True then
2      sensor_observation ← get_observation_result(input KG);
3      trust_score ← get_trust_score(input KG);
4      timestamp ← get_timestamp(input KG);
5      constructed_hash ← reconstruct_hash_from_data(sensor_observation, trust_score, timestamp);
6      blockchain_hash ← get_stored_hash_from_blockchain(input KG);
7      hasDataVeracity ← check_data_veracity(blockchain_hash, constructed_hash);
8      if hasDataVeracity = True then
9          shacl_rules ← get_shacl_rules(input KG);
10         meetsDefinedDataQuality ←validate_for_quality(transformed_kg, shacl_rules);
11         if meetsDefinedDataQuality = True then
12             return status True along with RDF representation of KG;
13         else
14             return status False;
15     else
16         return status False;
17 else
18     No processing;
```

As with the case of sensor data processing (see Sect. 8.5.3), first the consent check is performed by interacting with the legal engine component of the framework. This method of checking consent prior to each processing activity is intended to enable GDPR-compliant data sharing or processing at the granular level. After the successful consent checks, the relevant information from the data, i.e., KG, is extracted. This includes getting the sensor observation value, the trust score, and the time stamp information, as indicated by steps 2-4 in Algorithm 8. After that, using the sensor observation value ($sosa : hasSimpleResult$ value in KG), timestamp ($sosa : resultTime$ value in KG), and trust score ($sricats : hasTrustabilityScore$ value in KG), the hash value is reconstructed in order to verify its veracity. Following the reconstruction of the hash, the original hash stored in the blockchain is retrieved using the transaction hash information from KG (i.e., $sricats : hasBlockchainHash$).

In Algorithm 8, step 5 is the step of reconstructing the hash, and step 6 is the step of getting the original hash from the blockchain. Veracity is determined by comparing the original and recomputed (or reconstructed) hashes. This aids in the detection of tampered data, which is crucial in industries such as healthcare. Additionally, the storage of the original hash in the blockchain guarantees the tamper-proof nature of the stored hash value due to the immutability of the blockchain, thereby further guaranteeing the veracity of the shared data.

Steps 7–8 of the algorithm show the data veracity check. The data quality test is conducted after the data veracity test has been passed. For a quality test, we begin by getting the SHACL rules ($get\_shacl\_rules(input\ KG)$), which contain the predefined quality criteria based on the sensor data observation, such as temperature and humidity. Once the necessary SHACL rules have been obtained, the KG is validated against the SHACL rules ($validate\_for\_quality(input\ KG, shacl\ rules)$) to determine if it meets the quality requirements. The evaluation of quality also test context information, such as the observation units, which is one of our contributions. If the quality test is passed, both the status and the KG are returned, whereas in the case of failure, only the status $False$ is returned, indicating that the defined quality criteria is not met.

8.5.7 Analytics Engine

The analytics engine is the intelligence-enabling component of the proposed system and provides analytics capabilities to facilitate data-driven decision making. For instance, activating the cooling system (or taking other appropriate action) in the event of a high temperature in the data center. This is because a high temperature can cause performance degradation and also system failures that result in outages. Moreover, the analytics engine facilitates the data-driven decision making capabilities at various layers. For example, in the fog and edge layers to enable latency-aware decision making. The analytics engine, however, can also be extended to the cloud to facilitate data-driven decision making in situations where real-time requirements are not necessary (or latency is not a problem). In our study, to facilitate data-driven decision making, the analytics engine implements KG-based reasoning techniques like SWRL reasoning. The SWRL reasoning is used to perform the classification task, i.e., classifying *sricats:TemperatureAlert* and *sricats:HumidityAlert* based on the observed values of temperature and humidity. The capability of the analytics engine can easily be extended further beyond SWRL reasoning to machine learning techniques, taking advantage of the KG for improved prediction, as shown by studies such as [52]. Similar to the initial sensor data processing and validation of the veracity of the data, the consent is checked prior to performing analytics operations.

8.5.8 Data Migration Engine

The data migration engine, as the name suggests, performs data migration (or transfer) operations, an essential operation in data sharing. The data migration engine performs the migration (or transfer) of the data from source to destination. The IoT sensor represents the source, and the remote storage, a graph database, represents the final destination.

8.6 Implementation

This section provides information about the system setup that is used for implementation and experimentation. In addition, this section also provides details on the implementation. Section 8.6.1 provides system setup information and Sect. 8.6.2 describes the implementation in detail.

8.6.1 System Setup

In this section, we describe the libraries used to implement the proposed system as well as the experimental system. Table 8.2 summarizes the list of libraries used for the implementation. Python[9] is used for the implementation due to its popularity in the data science community and its usability. The libraries RDFLib[10], pySHACL[11] and Owlready2[12] were used to deal with the semantic technology, namely, KG and ontology. The library RDFlib is used for parsing and serialization of the KG represented in RDF format, while pySHACL is used to perform the validation and Owlready2 for reasoning. The library Pika[13] is used to interact with RabbitMQ[14],

[9] https://www.python.org

[10] https://rdflib.readthedocs.io/en/stable/

[11] https://github.com/RDFLib/pySHACL

[12] https://owlready2.readthedocs.io/en/v0.37/

[13] https://pika.readthedocs.io/en/stable/intro.html

[14] https://www.rabbitmq.com

while PyYAML[15] is used to manage YAML[16] configuration files and Adafruit-DHT[17] is used to interact with the DHT11 sensor. Docker[18] is used for deployment of systems such as RabbitMQ. Solidity and py-solc-x[19] are used to implement the Ethereum smart contract. Ganache-cli[20] is the Ganache command line interface. Ganache is a personal blockchain for Ethereum that enables the safe and deterministic development, deployment, and testing of decentralized applications[21].

Table 8.2 Information about the libraries that were used in the implementation

Libraries/Software	Version
Python	3.8
RDFLib	6.1.1
PyYAML	6.0
pySHACL	0.19.0
Pika	1.2.1
Owlready2	0.30
Adafruit-DHT	1.4.0
Docker	20.X
Web3	5.31.1
Ganache-cli	2.13.2
Solidity	0.8.12
py-solc-x	1.1.1

Table 8.3 summarizes the configuration of the system used in our experiment. In our experiment, the Raspberry Pi 3 B+ serves as the edge (or edge device), emulating a real-world scenario in which edge devices are typically those with the lowest system capabilities (or are usually the resource-constrained devices). The fog (or the fog layer), which is one step up in the hierarchy, contains the systems with higher configurations than that of the edge. In our case, the system MacBook

[15] https://pyyaml.org/wiki/PyYAML
[16] https://yaml.org
[17] https://pypi.org/project/Adafruit-DHT/
[18] https://www.docker.com
[19] https://solcx.readthedocs.io/en/latest/
[20] https://docs.nethereum.com/en/latest/ethereum-and-clients/ganache-cli/
[21] https://trufflesuite.com/docs/ganache/

Pro represents the fog, the configuration of which is shown in Table 8.3. Moreover, Table 8.3 also shows the system configuration of the servers used for GraphDB and RabbitMQ.

Table 8.3 Information about the system and its configuration used in the experiment

System information	System configuration
Raspberry Pi 3 B+ (or Edge)	1 GB RAM, 4 core Cortex-A53 processor, 16 GB storage, Raspbian GNU/Linux 10 (Buster) OS
MacBook Pro (or Fog)	16GB RAM, 2,8 core 3 GHz Quad-Core Intel Core i7 processor, 500GB storage, macOS Monterey version 12.3.1
RabbitMQ messaging server and Ganache-CLI	64 GB RAM, 16 core Intel Core Processor (Broadwell), Ubuntu 20.04 LTS (GNU/Linux 5.4.0-80-generic x86_64) OS, 32GB with additional 2TB shared storage
GraphDB server	64GB RAM, 16 core Intel Core i9-9900K processor, 1TB storage, Debian GNU/Linux 10 (buster) OS

8.6.2 Implementation

In this section, we provide an overview of the implementation of the proposed system. The source code for the implementation is available at [42]. All of the implementations of the framework components are performed using Python.

8.6.2.1 Smart Contract

The Ethereum smart contract used in our study is implemented in Solidity. Solidity is a high-level language for implementing smart contracts. However, as our framework is implemented in Python, our implementation of the smart contract uses py-solc-x, a Python wrapper for the Solidity compiler. The smart contract is implemented in Solidity version 0.8.12 and deployed using Ganache-cli.

8.6.2.2 Data Receiver

The data receiver components implement Algorithm 6, outlined in Sect. 8.5.3, in order to read and process sensor data. In scenarios such as fog-edge, the data receiver also implements the functionality to read data from the messaging server. In our research, we utilized the DHT11 sensor. Thus, the data receiver reads the DHT11 sensor data. In the fog-edge scenario, the DHT11 sensor data represented in KG format at the fog layer is retrieved from the publish-subscribe model messaging server RabbitMQ via the topic *secure_interoperable_data_sharing*. The messaging server, RabbitMQ, is implemented using Docker on four cluster nodes to provide fault tolerance. The Docker configuration details are available at [42]. For the computation of the trust score, a separate rest service is implemented. It can, however, be computed without additional rest implementations. The reasons for this are that trust factors change over time and that more transparency is desired. For example, if the manufacturer improved their IoT product safety and obtained certification like ISO (International Organization for Standardization) security certification , then one may want to update the trust score computation. If the computation does not follow our approach and is done locally, updating in the case of large scale IoT is extremely inefficient. The second reason is that it enables transparency, i.e., the sharing of the factors used to calculate the trust score, which is essential because trust is subjective and different deployments may take into account different factors.

8.6.2.3 Data Transformation Engine

The implementation of the data transformation engine, following the procedures mentioned in Sect. 8.5.4, transforms the data into the KG. The KG representation of the humidity sensor data following the data transformation procedure is shown in Fig. 8.4. As shown in Fig. 8.4, the data (or KG) has been enriched with additional context information, including observation units and observed property. The KG shown in Fig. 8.4 is in a Turtle format. The data in KG representation is shared using JSON-LD. JSON-LD is a lightweight JSON (JavaScript Object Notation)-based format to serialize linked data[22].

```
@prefix om: <http://www.ontology-of-units-of-measure.org/resource/om-2/> .
@prefix sosa: <http://www.w3.org/ns/sosa/> .
@prefix sricats: <http://www.abc.com/sricats/> .
@prefix xsd: <http://www.w3.org/2001/XMLSchema#> .

<http://www.w3.org/ns/sosa/Observation/DHT11_202212025703> a sosa:Observation ;
    om:hasUnit om:percent ;
    sricats:hasBlockChainHash "0xcbb35fbc905aa6aeceaeebec596bc76937d6a0cd1e04ff3aa970adc13899b076" ;
    sricats:hasTrustabilityScore "0.8"^^xsd:float ;
    sosa:hasSimpleResult 2.8e+01 ;
    sosa:madeBySensor <http://www.w3.org/ns/sosa/Sensor/DHT11> ;
    sosa:observedProperty <http://www.w3.org/ns/sosa/observedProperty/STI_W201_humidity> ;
    sosa:resultTime "2022-12-02T20:57:03"^^xsd:dateTime .

<http://www.w3.org/ns/sosa/Sensor/DHT11> a sosa:Sensor ;
    sosa:observes <http://www.w3.org/ns/sosa/Observation/DHT11_202212025703> .
```

Fig. 8.4 Generated KG after performing a data transformation operation on the humidity observation from DHT11 sensor

[22] https://www.w3.org/TR/json-ld11/

8.6.2.4 Legal Engine

In general, the legal engine implementation consists of consent verification, as described in Sect. 8.5.5. In our investigation, however, we simulated consent checking by passing the boolean value true to represent the consent scenario and false to represent the absence of consent or invalid consent scenarios. The reasons are as follows: (i) there are already studies, such as [22], that perform consent checking and other complex consent-related operations; and (ii) integrating such systems is trivial. Figure 8.5 shows the response when there is no consent for the requested processing, indicating that the data processing (or sharing) action cannot be executed.


```
{"message":"Unable to process due to a lack of consent for
        the requested operation."}
```


Fig. 8.5 Response when no consent is available for request processing

8.6.2.5 Validation Engine

The validation engine implementation is the realization of the validation algorithm, Algorithm 8, described in Sect. 8.5.6. In our implementation, we defined the following quality criteria for both context and the actual sensor data as SHACL rules: (i) the *sosa:hasSimpleResult* must have a value of type *xsd:double* with a maximum value of 100, (ii) *sricats:hasBlockChainHash* must have a value of type *xsd:string* with the minimum length of 60 characters, (iii) the *om:hasUnit* must have a value of a defined type based on sensor (e.g., *om:degreeCelsius* for temperature sensor and *om:percent* for relative humidity), (iv) *sricats:hasTrustabilityScore* must have the value of type float and (v) the property *sosa:madeBySensor*, *sosa:observes* should be of type IRI and must have a value. Figure 8.6 shows the SHACL validation result. Evidently, both validations (see Fig. 8.6a and Fig. 8.6b) fail the predetermined quality criterion, resulting in the return of the false status. In the event of a successful validation, the KG and the status true are returned.

```
Validation Report
Conforms: False
Results (1):
Constraint Violation in MaxInclusiveConstraintComponent (http://www.w3
 .org/ns/shacl#MaxInclusiveConstraintComponent):
    Severity: sh:Violation
    Source Shape: [ sh:datatype xsd:double ; sh:maxCount Literal("1", datatype=xsd:integer)
  ; sh:maxInclusive Literal("100", datatype=xsd:integer) ; sh:minCount Literal("1",
 datatype=xsd:integer) ; sh:minInclusive Literal("0", datatype=xsd:integer) ; sh:path
 sosa:hasSimpleResult ]
    Focus Node: <file:///Users/tekrajchhetri/Documents/secure-interoperable-data-sharing
 /observation/DTH11_20220511148526814>
    Value Node: Literal("111.0", datatype=xsd:double)
    Result Path: sosa:hasSimpleResult
    Message: Value is not <= Literal("100", datatype=xsd:integer)

False
```

(a)

```
Validation Report
Conforms: False
Results (1):
Constraint Violation in HasValueConstraintComponent (http://www.w3
 .org/ns/shacl#HasValueConstraintComponent):
    Severity: sh:Violation
    Source Shape: [ sh:hasValue om:percent ; sh:maxCount Literal("1", datatype=xsd:integer) ;
 sh:minCount Literal("1", datatype=xsd:integer) ; sh:path om:hasUnit ]
    Focus Node: <file:///Users/tekrajchhetri/Documents/secure-interoperable-data-sharing/observation
 /DTH11_20220511154839662l>
    Result Path: om:hasUnit
    Message: Node <file:///Users/tekrajchhetri/Documents/secure-interoperable-data-sharing/observation
 /DTH11_20220511154839662l>->om:hasUnit does not contain a value in the set: ['om:percent']

False
```

(b)

Fig. 8.6 SHACL validation. (a) SHACL validation report for validation failure as a result of the observation value falling outside of the specified range. (b) SHACL validation report for failed validation due to the KG not meeting the predefined quality criterion observation unit

8.6.2.6 Analytics Engine

As discussed in Sect. 8.5.7, the analytics engine facilitates data-driven decision making. The analytics engine in our study employs SWRL reasoning using Pellet[23] reasoner to facilitate data-driven decision making. Figure 8.7 illustrates the SWRL rules utilized in this study to demonstrate data-driven decision making. Our study's

[23] https://www.w3.org/2001/sw/wiki/Pellet

data-driven task is a classification task (i.e., whether or not to classify *TemperatureAlert* and *HumidityAlert*) based on observations of humidity and temperature. The *?result* in the SWRL rules contains sensor data, whereas the *?reasoningType* gives information regarding the type of reasoning based on the observation made. For example, the *?reasoningType* for a temperature observation is the value temperature. Figure 8.8 shows the snippet of edge analytics result indicating the high-temperature alert. However, if no alert condition is met, the reasoning result, i.e., alert value, is none, indicating everything is fine. When the analytics operation is performed in the fog, the results are published to the messaging server (see Sect. 8.7.1.2) and consumed at the edge.

```
Observation(?observation),
hasSimpleResult(?observation, ?result),
hasedgeReasoningType(?observation, ?reasoningType),
containsIgnoreCase(?reasoningType, "temperature"),
greaterThanOrEqual(?result, 75.0),
-> TemperatureAlert(?observation)

Observation(?observation),
hasedgeReasoningType(?observation, ?reasoningType),
containsIgnoreCase(?reasoningType, "humidity"),
hasSimpleResult(?observation, ?result),
greaterThanOrEqual(?result, 65.0),
-> HumidityAlert(?observation)
```

Fig. 8.7 SWRL rules for temperature (top) and relative humidity (bottom) alerts used in our study


```
{"alert": "TemperatureAlert", "observationsensorid": "DTH11",
"observedproperty": "STI_W201_temperature",
"observationid": "DTH11_202205142209733755"}
```


Fig. 8.8 Snippet of results of the edge analytics are based on the temperature observation indicating a high-temperature alert in accordance with the SWRL rule

8.6.2.7 Data Migration Engine

As stated in Sect. 8.5.8, the data migration engine migrates data from one location to another. This migration also encompasses the transfer of data to intermediary phases, such as messaging servers. The implementation consists of the following: (i) migrating the data (i.e., KG) to the messaging server from edge, which will later be used at the fog layer for further processing (see Sect. 8.7.1.2); (ii) migrating data (i.e., KG) to the remote storage; and (iii) migrating the analytics result to the edge in the case when the analytics are performed at layers such as fog (see Sect. 8.7.1.2). The publish/subscribe model is used for data and result migration when processing, such as when analytics are conducted in the fog. The topic *secure_interoperable-_data_sharing* is used for the data migration. Similarly, the topic *reasoning_result_secure_interoperable_data_sharing* for the result (i.e., analytics result), which in our study is to issue a warning (or alert). SPARQL is used for migrating the KG data to the remote storage. GraphDB, which is a W3C[24] compliant enterprise-ready semantic graph database[25], is used as the remote storage. Table 8.4 shows the KG in triples representation (i.e., subject, predicate and object format) in GraphDB after migration.

Table 8.4 A snapshot of the migrated KG instance to the remote storage GraphDB. *xsd*, *sricats*, *sosa*, *om*, and *rdf* are the prefixes

Subject	Predicate	Object
sosa:Observation/ DHT11_202212020002	om:hasUnit	om:percent
sosa:Observation/ DHT11_202212020002	sricats:hasBlockChain Hash	"0x4078c7919896566330e95bf68f 9106dcbeec1ef7df19b6fda6e559347 a933bd1"
sosa:Observation/ DHT11_202212020002	sricats:hasTrustability Score	"0.8"^^xsd:float
sosa:Observation/ DHT11_202212020002	rdf:type	sosa:Observation
sosa:Observation/ DHT11_202212020002	sosa:hasSimpleResult	"28.0"^^xsd:double
sosa:Observation/ DHT11_202212020002	sosa:madeBySensor	sosa:Sensor/DHT11
sosa:Observation/ DHT11_202212020002	sosa:observedProperty	sosa:observedProperty /STI_W201_humidity
sosa:Observation/ DHT11_202212020002	sosa:resultTime	"2022-12-02T21:00:02"^^xsd:dateTime

[24] https://www.w3.org

[25] https://graphdb.ontotext.com

8.7 Experiment and Evaluation

This section describes the experiment in detail. In addition, this section provides information about the evaluations conducted. Section 8.7.1 discusses the experiment and Sect. 8.7.2 discusses the evaluation.

8.7.1 Experiment

In this section, we will describe our experimental scenario. Section 8.7.1.1 describes the edge experimental scenario and Sect. 8.7.1.2 describes the edge-fog experimental scenario.

8.7.1.1 Edge Experiment Scenario

Figure 8.9 shows the overview of the edge experiment scenario that we considered in our study. As shown in Fig. 8.9, sensor data is read and processed on the edge device, performing tasks such as data transformation and edge analytics to enable edge intelligence. Below are the specifics regarding the operations performed at each step.

1. The initial step (step 1) checks for consent to ensure that there is permission to read and process the sensor data. The consent check is performed to ensure that the data sharing and processing complies with GDPR. If there is consent, then the sensor data is read and processed (step 2), i.e., transformed into the KG representation. In our case, we utilize the DHT11, a temperature-humidity sensor. If the consent check is unsuccessful, no further processing occurs.
2. Similar to the initial step, the consent is checked again (step 3) before performing other operations, such as validation, analysis, and transformation.
3. After a successful consent check at step 3, the data is validated by utilizing SHACL for quality and integrity, which is then transformed into a format compliant with SPARQL and migrated to the remote graph database (or GraphDB). This process is indicated by steps 4, 5, and 6.
4. Similar to the migration case, the analytics operation (step 7) is done after the consent check (step 3) and validation (step 4) have been completed successfully.

The data transformation and migration step and the data analysis step could be executed concurrently. In our study, we did not perform concurrent implementations as it was not the main focus of our work. However, such optimizations are important and can be regarded as future work.

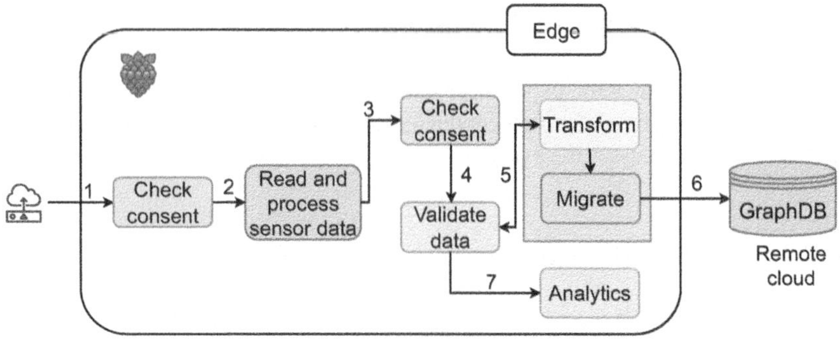

Fig. 8.9 High-level overview of edge experiment scenario

8.7.1.2 Fog-edge Experiment Scenario

Figure 8.10, similar to Fig. 8.9 (i.e., edge scenario), shows the overview of the experiment scenario that we considered in our study. In contrast to Fig. 8.9, which only considers the edge scenario, we considered the fog-edge scenario in this experiment. Unlike in the edge experiment scenario, where all the tasks are performed at the edge, in this scenario, the work is distributed between the fog and the edge. The descriptions of the operations performed at each step are provided below.

1. The first two steps at the edge are similar to those in the edge experiment: check consent and read and process the data, as described in Sect. 8.7.1.1. The third step, consent checking, is quite different from the case of the edge experiment, though consent checks are performed at both steps. This is because the consent check at this step in the fog-edge experiment checks to see if the data can be migrated to the messaging server. In the edge experiment (see Sect. 8.7.1.1), consent is checked to see if the data can be processed, such as to perform validation.
2. The data is migrated (steps 4 and 5) to the messaging server after a successful consent check. This data migration is done to delegate tasks, such as performing data analytics, to the fog. However, if there is no consent, then no processing, which in this case is the migration of data, is performed. The messaging server collects and holds published data (or message) in a messaging queue until it is consumed. Moreover, the messaging server, which acts as an intermediary between fog and edge, also facilitates communication and data exchange.
3. At this stage (step 6), the data from the messaging server is read (or consumed). After reading the sensor data from the messaging server, another consent check is performed (step 7). The consent check at this step is similar to the case of

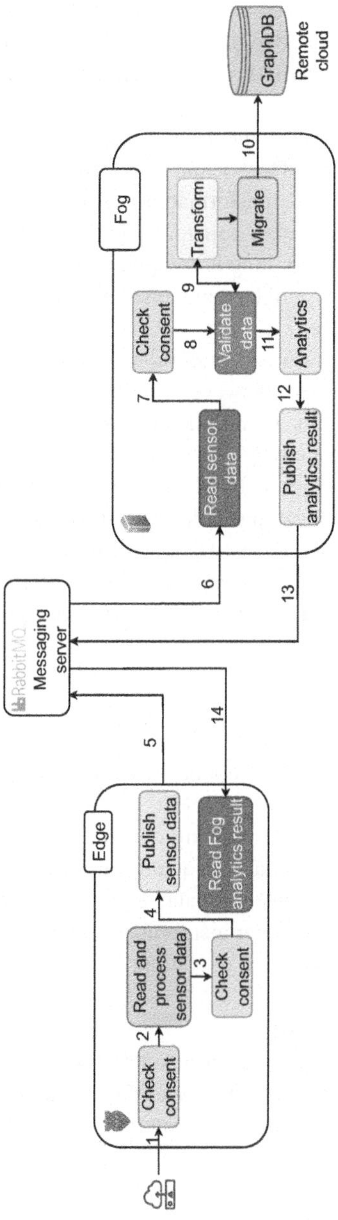

Fig. 8.10 High-level overview of fog-edge experiment scenario

the edge experiment (see Sect. 8.7.1.1) consent check at step 3. This is because, similar to the case of the edge experiment, the consent check in step 7 of the fog-edge experiment scenario involves checking consent to perform tasks such as validation.

4. Following the successful consent check at step 7, operations similar to the edge experiment are performed. This included performing validation for integrity and quality (step 8), as well as transformation and migration (steps 9 and 10), and migrating the data to the remote storage, GraphDB. The additional consent check at the fog ensures that everything is compliant with the GDPR. In addition, this helps ensure that privacy will be maintained even if the consent check has been compromised at the edge.
5. As with the transformation and migration operations, the analytics operation (step 11) is also performed. However, unlike the case of the edge experiment, where the analytics results are returned instantly, in this case the result is published (or migration of analytics result) back to the messaging server from the fog. Steps 12 and 13 in Fig. 8.10 indicate these processes.
6. The messaging server collects and holds the published results from the fog, which is then consumed by edge (step 14) and no further processing was performed. However, some control actions, such as issuing alerts (or taking appropriate action), can be performed based on the analytics outcomes.

8.7.2 Evaluation

In this section, we provide details about the evaluation. Section 8.7.2.1 provides details on the evaluation criteria and Sect. 8.7.2.2 provides details on the performance evaluation conducted following our evaluation criteria. Similarly, Sect. 8.7.2.3 provides an overview about data quality, assessment of the context information as component of data quality and data veracity evaluation, while Sect. 8.7.2.4 provides information regarding interoperability evaluation. Section 8.7.2.5 provides detail on the evaluation of analytics operation.

8.7.2.1 Evaluation Criteria

We evaluate the proposed work to determine its applicability in a real-world setting and to address our research questions (or to determine whether our objective has been achieved). The following evaluation criteria were utilized to assess the proposed work:

1. The first criterion is the resource utilization. IoT, by its very nature, has limited resources, such as CPU and memory, so implementing the proposed framework should utilize the minimum (or reasonable) amount of resources. Section 8.7.2.2 presents the evaluation of resource utilization.
2. The second evaluation criterion focuses on accessing the proposed work's capability to support real-time (or near real-time) decision making in the edge/fog environment. It is determined by the execution time to perform the analytics operation and is presented in Sect. 8.7.2.2 and Sect. 8.7.2.5.
3. The third criterion is that the proposed system should support accurate (e.g., data veracity) and quality data sharing. The fourth criterion is that the system should support interoperability. Section 8.7.2.3 presents the evaluation of the third criterion. Section 8.7.2.4 presents an evaluation of the fourth criterion.

8.7.2.2 Performance Evaluation

We conducted the performance evaluation to analyze the feasibility of the proposed system. We focused on the following in our performance evaluation: (i) execution time to perform the operations such as analytics, data transformation, and migration; (ii) resources such as memory and CPU (central processing unit) utilization and (iii) latency for analytics operations in the case of the fog-edge experiment. The reason for focusing on memory and CPU resource utilization other than the execution time is that the edge devices are typically resource-constrained in nature. Evaluating resource use is therefore crucial to understanding the feasibility of the proposed system in a real-world deployment.

Figure 8.11 illustrates the performance evaluation in terms of the execution time. Figure 8.11a shows the execution time required to execute analytics at the edge and fog levels, whereas Fig. 8.11b depicts the execution time required to do data transformation and migration at the edge and fog layers. Overall, the execution time for doing the analytics (see Fig. 8.11a) at the fog layer was an average of 1.1 seconds, whereas the execution time at the edge was an average of 7.2 seconds. We observe a similar tendency for doing analytics in both the fog and edge layers. For example, a high execution time for the initial reasoning is followed by a significant drop in execution time. In addition, the execution time for both fog and edge layers exhibits a constant increase with intermittent spikes. On closer inspection, particularly at the end (i.e., after 25 iterations), we can see that the execution time at the edge increases while the fog decreases. The higher execution time at the edge can be attributed to the limited availability of resources. As seen in Fig. 8.11a, for example, the fog, which has more available resources than the edge, has a reduced execution time. Similar to the analytics scenario, the execution time for data transfer and migration activities (see Fig. 8.11b) follows a similar pattern, with a high execution time, in the beginning, followed by a fast decrease and gradual increase, with the occasional spike in between. Unlike the analytics scenario, the execution time exhibits a similar pattern even at the end. Data migration and transfer procedures at the edge took approximately 0.65 seconds and 0.32 seconds in the fog, respectively. Based on Fig. 8.11a and Fig. 8.11b (i.e., execution time), we can conclude that data migration and transfer procedures are less time-consuming than analytical processes. Moreover, the execution time, both for the analytics and the transformation and migration operations, also accounts for the time taken for intermediate steps, such as performing validation checks.

Figure 8.12 and Fig. 8.13 illustrate the resource use evaluation. Similarly, Fig. 8.14 shows the latency in getting analytics results and the time taken for creating blockchain transactions. Figure 8.12a and Fig. 8.12b focus on evaluating the memory utilization, while Fig. 8.13a and Fig. 8.13b focus on evaluating the CPU utilization. We only consider the edge for memory utilization for analytics and data transfer and migration operations. This is because the edge, comparatively, is much more resource-constrained than the fog. Therefore, the fog, which has more available memory than the edge, will not experience memory-related performance degradation. For CPU utilization, however, we consider both the fog and edge similar to that of execution time. This is because, unlike memory, CPU utilization can vary depending on the tasks, such as SWRL reasoning for analytics operations, and has an impact on execution time. As can be observed in Fig. 8.12a and Fig. 8.12b, the memory utilization for both the data migration and transformation and analytics operations is nearly same, which is around 51 MB (megabytes). Moreover, memory usage in both instances follows a similar pattern: a sudden increase followed by a continuous increase. The sudden increase in memory indicates the start of tasks such as analytics or data processing and memory allocation. This low memory usage demonstrates the practicality of the proposed framework for resource-constrained devices such as the one in the edge layer, which is usually resource-constrained in nature.

Similar to the execution time, we can observe from Fig. 8.13a and Fig. 8.13b that the average CPU utilization for the analytics operation is higher than that of the data migration and transformation operations. The average CPU utilization for data migration and transformation operations was around 12.35% at the edge and approximately 1.24% in the fog, which can be observed from Fig. 8.13a. On the other hand, the average CPU utilization for analytics on the edge was approximately 33.61%, while it was around 15.62% in the fog, as observed in Fig. 8.13b. On a closer inspection of the CPU utilization for the data transfer and migration operations, we observe low CPU utilization, indicating that data transfer and migration operations are not resource-intensive compared to analytics operation. Moreover,

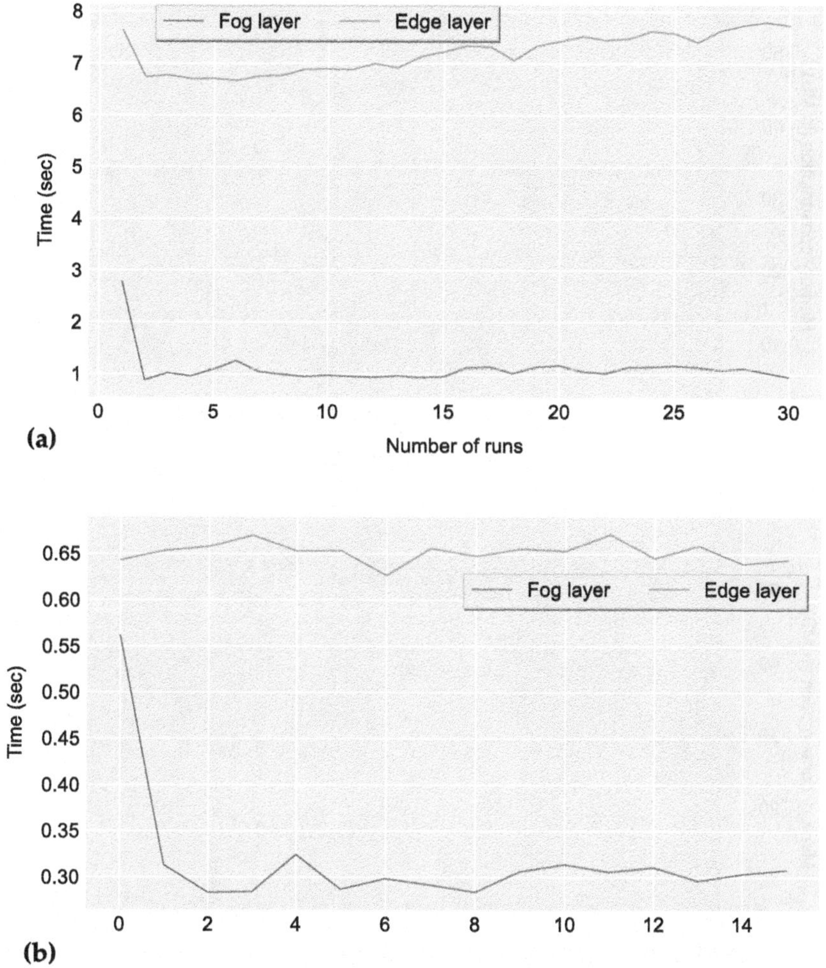

Fig. 8.11 Execution time. (a) Time required to execute analytics at the edge and fog layers. (b) Time required to execute data transformation and migration at the edge and fog layers

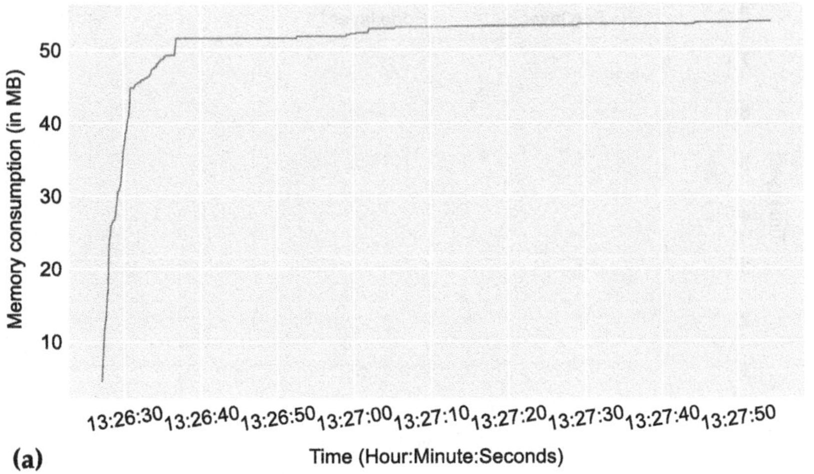

(a)

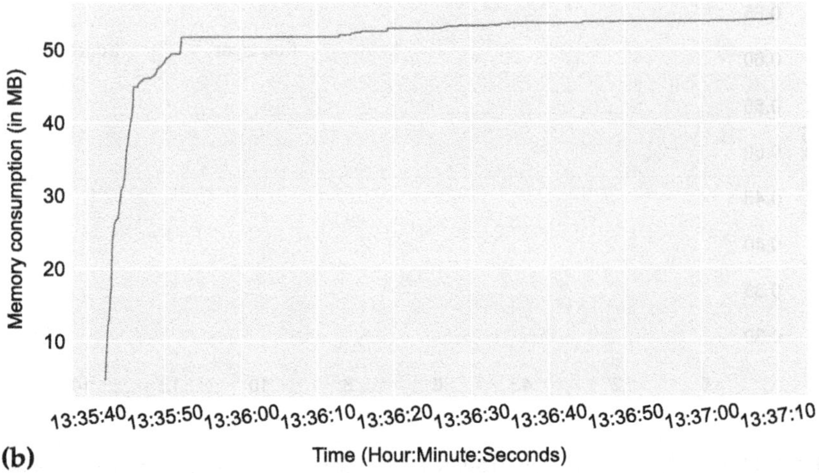

(b)

Fig. 8.12 Memory utilization at the edge. (a) Memory consumption to perform data transformation and migration operations at the edge layer. (b) Memory consumption to perform analytics at the edge layer

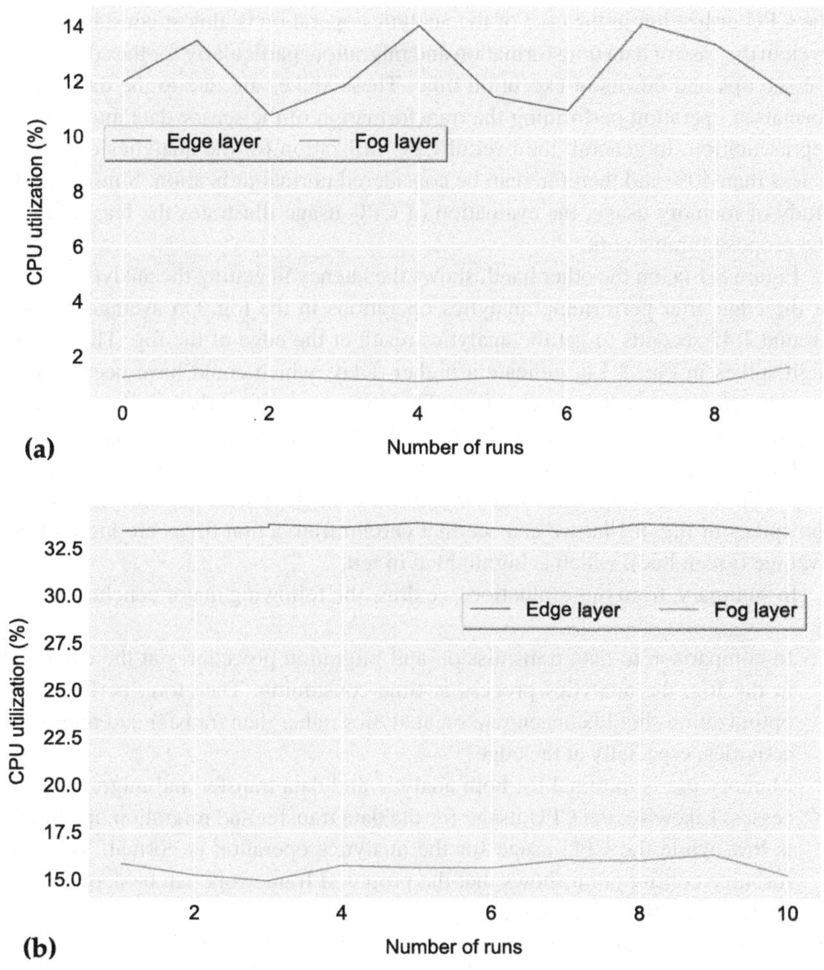

Fig. 8.13 CPU utilization. (a) Average CPU utilization to perform data transformation and migration operations at the edge and fog layers. (b) Average CPU utilization to perform analytics at the edge and fog layers

the CPU utilization in the case of the analytics operation is almost constant. However, in the case of data transformation and migration, particularly for the edge layer, we see ups and downs in execution time. These spikes are due to the data transformation operation performing the transformation of the sensor data into the KG representation. In general, the overall CPU utilization for the analytics operation is less than 40% and therefore can be considered normal utilization. Similar to the study of memory usage, the evaluation of CPU usage illustrates the feasibility of the proposed framework.

Figure 8.14a, on the other hand, shows the latency in getting the analytics result at the edge after performing analytics operations in the fog. On average, it took around 1.45 seconds to get the analytics result at the edge of the fog. The certain high spikes in Fig. 8.14a indicate a higher delay, which could have been caused by network issues such as congestion. This time is significantly less than the time required to perform at the edge itself, highlighting that it is not always good to perform all operations at the edge. Similarly, Fig. 8.14b shows the time taken to create the blockchain transactions, which on average is 0.22 seconds. Similar to the spikes in Fig. 8.14a, we can see that certain transaction times are higher than average (green line), which is highlighted in red.

In summary, from our evaluation, we draw the following major conclusion.

1. In comparison to data transmission and migration procedures at the edge and in the fog, the analytics process is time-consuming. Therefore, performance optimization should concentrate on analytics rather than transfer and migration activities, especially at the edge.
2. Memory use is minimal for both analytic and data transfer and migration processes. Likewise, the CPU usage for the data transfer and migration operations is low, while the CPU usage for the analytics operation is normal. This low resource consumption shows that the proposed framework can be deployed on devices with limited resources.
3. The latency measurement shown in Fig. 8.14a indicates that it is not always advisable to perform all operations at the edge; rather, it is advantageous to delegate compute-intensive tasks to the closest fog. In addition, Fig. 8.14a also highlights the importance of the edge, fog, and cloud hierarchy.
4. Finally, the evaluation validates our claim that the proposed framework is suitable for the edge and fog situation.

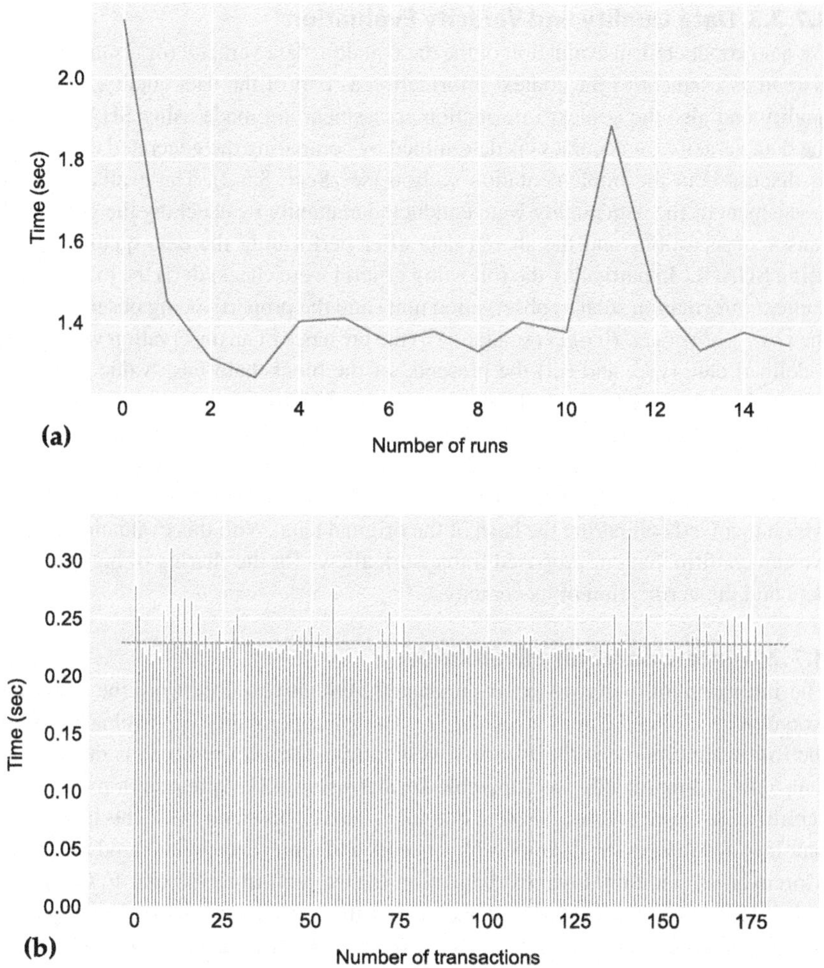

Fig. 8.14 Execution time. (a) Time taken to send the data to fog and get the analytics result at edge. (b) Time taken to create the blockchain transaction

8.7.2.3 Data Quality and Veracity Evaluation

We also conducted an evaluation of the data quality, data veracity (or accuracy) and also an assessment of the context information as part of the data quality. The data quality and also the context information assessment are made using SHACL, and the data veracity (or accuracy) is determined by comparing the generated data hash, as discussed in the implementation section (see Sect. 8.6.2). The evaluation and assessment of the data quality were conducted manually by checking the generated sensor observations and the shared data after performing the data quality check using SHACL. In particular, the following criteria were checked: (i) the presence of context information such as observation units and the property being observed (i.e., the $sosa : observedProperty$ value); (ii) the presence of an observation value with a defined data type; and (iii) the presence of the blockchain hash value and trust score with a defined data type. There were a total of 180 observations examined from our edge and edge/fog experiment, and all of the shared data met the defined quality criteria, including the evaluation of context information, resulting in 100 percent accuracy. A similar assessment was made in the case of the data veracity check, which involved comparing the hash of the original data. With this evaluation result, we can confirm that our proposed framework allows for the sharing of high-quality data and the verification of its veracity.

8.7.2.4 Interoperability Evaluation

The interoperability evaluation is conducted qualitatively following the study by Koo & Kim [50] and Cimmino et al. [51]. The interoperability was evaluated using the following criteria: if the proposed system translates heterogeneous raw sensor data into a semantically interoperable format using KG representations in RDF serialization expressed according to ontology, derived based on [51]. This is because ontology formalizes the definition of concepts and represents their shared meaning. Moreover, an additional manual validation is also performed, similar to Cimmino et al.'s [51] work. The evaluation concludes with a verdict that the proposed system supports interoperability following 180 observations (see Sect. 8.7.2.3) as the system can translate the heterogeneous data into KG representation based on ontology. In the case of context-dependent variability, interoperability will be restricted, and addressing the issue of context-dependent variability of concepts requires reusing the existing ontology rather than developing a new one and adhering to ontology engineering best practices, such as providing definitions for ambiguous concepts.

8.7.2.5 Evaluation of Analytics Operations

Aside from the performance evaluation (see Sect. 8.7.2.2), we also evaluated the analytics result by inspecting the SWRL reasoning outcome to determine whether the correct result was attained. A total of 40 observations in the edge case and 14 in the fog-edge scenario were inspected. In the case of the edge, it was anticipated that all 40 observations would activate the alert, i.e., qualify as a temperature or humidity alert. In the case of the fog-edge scenario, seven observations were within the threshold; therefore, only seven of the fourteen should have triggered an alert. According to the results of our evaluation, SWRL reasoning is executed accurately in every scenario.

8.8 Conclusion

In this research, we investigate IoT data sharing problems and proposed a novel framework that can IoT data sharing challenges of interoperability, accuracy, and quality IoT data sharing in a privacy-conscious manner i.e., adhering to legal restrictions such as GDPR. We demonstrated how ontologies and KGs can address interoperability (see Sect. 8.5.4) and support intelligence (see Sect. 8.5.7) in the edge/fog scenario. Moreover, we demonstrated how we can ensure the quality (see Sect. 8.5.6) of the data being shared through the use of SHACL, enable trustworthiness (see Sect. 8.4.2) through the proposed intrinsic trust metric, and achieve accuracy (or veracity) through the use of blockchain in a GDPR-compliant manner.

In addition, we validated our claims, such as suitability for the fog and edge, by implementing the proposed framework, conducting experiments with two distinct scenarios (see Sect. 8.7.1), and evaluating their practicality. Our evaluation (see Sects. 8.7.2.2, 8.7.2.3, 8.7.2.4 and 8.7.2.5) supports the applicability of the proposed framework (or framework), hence providing support for our claims and answering our research questions (see Sect. 8.2.1). Moreover, the comparison of our work to state-of-the-art works (see Table 8.1) demonstrates additional benefits that our work provides.

The true advantage of the proposed framework lies in its extensibility to cover larger heterogeneous domains at scale, for example, by extending the scope of the ontology used. The proposed framework also ensures the accuracy and quality of the data (see Sect. 8.7.2.3 and Sect. 8.6.2.5), which is an additional benefit and is essential when making data-driven decisions and capitalizing on IoT data and enables privacy-aware data sharing and processing following data protection regulations such as GDPR–one of the limiting factor in IoT data sharing and processing. This is another benefit of the proposed framework as the framework addresses the hindrance posed by laws like GDPR. In addition, the introduction of the trust metric allows one to determine how much the data can be trusted, the other benefit of our work. Using the proposed solution, future work would consist of investigating interoperability and integration at scale in real-world deployments.

Acknowledgements This research has been supported by the European Union projects funded under Horizon 2020 research and innovation program (smashHit), grant agreement 871477 and in part by the European Union Horizon Europe project UPCAST under grant agreement number 101093216. We would like to express our appreciation to Simon Außerlechner, system engineer at STI Innsbruck, for facilitating temporary servers for experimentation. Additionally, we would like to acknowledge the anonymous reviewer whose comment has helped to improve the manuscript significantly.

Appendix A. Preliminaries Supplementary Material

The preliminaries of the concepts, such as KGs, used in this paper are available in the supplementary material.
MMC S1. Exploring Edge Computing, Data Privacy, & Semantic Web for IoT Data Sharing: Supplementary Insights.

Bibliography

1. Roy Woodhead, Paul Stephenson, and Denise Morrey. 'Digital construction: From point solutions to IoT ecosystem'. In: *Automation in Construction* 93 (2018), pp. 35–46. https://doi.org/10.1016/j.autcon.2018.05.004.
2. Yosra Hajjaji, Wadii Boulila, Imed Riadh Farah, Imed Romdhani, and Amir Hussain. 'Big data and IoT-based applications in smart environments: A systematic review'. In: *Computer Science Review* 39 (2021), p. 100318. https://doi.org/10.1016/j.cosrev.2020.100318.
3. Marco Centenaro, Cristina E. Costa, Fabrizio Granelli, Claudio Sacchi, and Lorenzo Vangelista. 'A Survey on Technologies, Standards and Open Challenges in Satellite IoT'. In: *IEEE Communications Surveys Tutorials* 23.3 (2021), pp. 1693–1720. https://doi.org/10.1109/COMST.2021.3078433.
4. N. Shabana and G. Velmathi. 'Advanced Tele-surgery with IoT Approach'. In: *Intelligent Embedded Systems*. Ed. by Daniel Thalmann, N. Subhashini, K. Mohanaprasad, and M S Bala Murugan. Singapore: Springer Singapore, 2018, pp. 17–24.
5. John Byabazaire, Gregory O'Hare, and Declan Delaney. 'Data Quality and Trust: Review of Challenges and Opportunities for Data Sharing in IoT'. In: *Electronics* 9.12 (2020), p. 2083. https://doi.org/10.3390/electronics9122083.
6. Maggi Bansal, Inderveer Chana, and Siobhán Clarke. 'A Survey on IoT Big Data: Current Status, 13 V's Challenges, and Future Directions'. In: *ACM Comput. Surv.* 53.6 (2020). https://doi.org/10.1145/3419634.
7. Ahmed Abdulhasan Alwan, Mihaela Anca Ciupala, Allan J. Brimicombe, Seyed Ali Ghorashi, Andres Baravalle, and Paolo Falcarin. 'Data quality challenges in large-scale

cyber-physical systems: A systematic review'. In: *Information Systems* 105 (2022), p. 101951. https://doi.org/10.1016/j.is.2021.101951.

8. Lisa Ehrlinger and Wolfram Wöß. 'A survey of data quality measurement and monitoring tools'. In: *Frontiers in big data* 5 (2022), p. 850611. https://doi.org/10.3389/fdata.2022.850611.
9. Muhammad Naeem, Tauseef Jamal, Jorge Diaz-Martinez, Shariq Aziz Butt, Nicolo Montesano, Muhammad Imran Tariq, Emiro De-la Hoz-Franco, and Ethel De-La-Hoz-Valdiris. 'Trends and Future Perspective Challenges in Big Data'. In: *Advances in Intelligent Data Analysis and Applications*. Ed. by Jeng-Shyang Pan, Valentina Emilia Balas, and Chien-Ming Chen. Singapore: Springer Singapore, 2022, pp. 309–325.
10. A. M. Ouksel and A. Sheth. 'Semantic Interoperability in Global Information Systems'. In: *SIGMOD Rec.* 28.1 (1999), 5–12. https://doi.org/10.1145/309844.309849.
11. James Manyika, Michael Chui, Peter Bisson, Jonathan Woetzel, Richard Dobbs, Jacques Bughin, and Dan Aharon. 'The internet of things: mapping the value beyond the hype'. In: *McKinsey Global Institute* (2015).
12. Avani Sharma, Emmanuel S. Pilli, Arka P. Mazumdar, and Poonam Gera. 'Towards trustworthy Internet of Things: A survey on Trust Management applications and schemes'. In: *Computer Communications* 160 (2020), pp. 475–493. https://doi.org/10.1016/j.comcom.2020.06.030.
13. Giancarlo Fortino, Lidia Fotia, Fabrizio Messina, Domenico Rosaci, and Giuseppe M. L. Sarné. 'Trust and Reputation in the Internet of Things: State-of-the-Art and Research Challenges'. In: *IEEE Access* 8 (2020), pp. 60117–60125. https://doi.org/10.1109/ACCESS.2020.2982318.
14. European Parliament and Council. 'Regulation (EU) 2016/679 of the European Parliament and of the Council of 27 April 2016 on the protection of natural persons with regard to the processing of personal data and on the free movement of such data, and repealing Directive 95/46/EC (General Data Protection Regulation)'. In: *Official Journal of the European Union, L119* (May 2016). Available online: https://eurlex.europa.eu/eli/reg/2016/679/oj (accessed on 3 December 2021).
15. Malti Bansal, Marshal Nanda, and Md. Nazir Husain. 'Security and privacy Aspects for Internet of Things (IoT)'. In: *6th International Conference on Inventive Computation Technologies (ICICT)*. 2021, pp. 199–204. https://doi.org/10.1109/ICICT50816.2021.9358665.
16. John Byabazaire, Gregory O'Hare, and Declan Delaney. 'Using Trust as a Measure to Derive Data Quality in Data Shared IoT Deployments'. In: *2020 29th International Conference on Computer Communications and Networks (ICCCN)*. 2020, pp. 1–9. https://doi.org/10.1109/ICCCN49398.2020.9209633.
17. Ramanathan Guha. *Search result ranking based on trust*. US Patent 7,603,350. 2009.
18. Sanju Mishra and Sarika Jain. 'Ontologies as a semantic model in IoT'. In: *International Journal of Computers and Applications* 42.3 (2020), pp. 233–243. https://doi.org/10.1080/1206212X.2018.1504461.
19. Deepak Puthal, Saraju P. Mohanty, Elias Kougianos, and Gautam Das. 'When Do We Need the Blockchain?' In: *IEEE Consumer Electronics Magazine* 10.2 (2021), pp. 53–56. https://doi.org/10.1109/MCE.2020.3015606.

20. Lei Yang, Wanrong Zou, JiangganWang, and Zi Tang. 'Edge- Share: A blockchain-based edge data-sharing framework for Industrial Internet of Things'. In: *Neurocomputing* 485 (2022), pp. 219–232. https://doi.org/10.1016/j.neucom.2021.01.147.
21. Chinmaya Kumar Dehury, Satish Narayana Srirama, and Tek Raj Chhetri. 'CCoDaMiC:Aframework for Coherent Coordination of Data Migration and Computation platforms'. In: *Future Generation Computer Systems* 109 (2020), pp. 1–16. https://doi.org/10.1016/j.future.2020.03.029.
22. Tek Raj Chhetri, Anelia Kurteva, Rance J. DeLong, Rainer Hilscher, Kai Korte, and Anna Fensel. 'Data Protection by Design Tool for Automated GDPR Compliance Verification Based on Semantically Modeled Informed Consent'. In: Sensors 22.7 (2022). https://doi.org/10.3390/s22072763.
23. Ashkan Yousefpour, Caleb Fung, Tam Nguyen, Krishna Kadiyala, Fatemeh Jalali, Amirreza Niakanlahiji, Jian Kong, and Jason P. Jue. 'All one needs to know about fog computing and related edge computing paradigms: A complete survey'. In: *Journal of Systems Architecture* 98 (2019), pp. 289–330. https://doi.org/10.1016/j.sysarc.2019.02.009.
24. Jesús Noel Suárez Rubí and Paulo Roberto de Lira Gondim. 'IoT-based platform for environment data sharing in smart cities'. In: *International Journal of Communication Systems* 34.2 (2021), e4515. https://doi.org/10.1002/dac.4515.
25. Faiza Loukil, Chirine Ghedira-Guegan, and Aïcha-Nabila Benharkat. 'PATRIoT: A Data Sharing Platform for IoT Using a Service-Oriented Approach Based on Blockchain'. In: *Service-Oriented Computing*. Ed. by Eleanna Kafeza, Boualem Benatallah, Fabio Martinelli, Hakim Hacid, Athman Bouguettaya, and Hamid Motahari. Cham: Springer International Publishing, 2020, pp. 121–129. https://doi.org/10.1007/978-3-030-65310-1_10.
26. Faiza Loukil, Chirine Ghedira-Guegan, Khouloud Boukadi, and Aicha Nabila Benharkat. 'LIoPY: A Legal Compliant Ontology to Preserve Privacy for the Internet of Things'. In: *IEEE 42nd Annual Computer Software and Applications Conference (COMPSAC)*. Vol. 02. 2018, pp. 701–706. https://doi.org/10.1109/COMPSAC.2018.10322.
27. John Strassner and Wael William Diab. 'A semantic interoperability architecture for Internet of Things data sharing and computing'. In: *IEEE 3rd World Forum on Internet of Things (WF-IoT)*. 2016, pp. 609–614. https://doi.org/10.1109/WFIoT.2016.7845422.
28. Roberto Reda, Filippo Piccinini, Giovanni Martinelli, and Antonella Carbonaro. 'Heterogeneous self-tracked health and fitness data integration and sharing according to a linked open data approach'. In: *Computing* 104.4 (2022), pp. 835–857. https://doi.org/10.1007/s00607-021-00988-w.
29. Marco Zappatore, Antonella Longo, Angelo Martella, Beniamino Di Martino, Antonio Esposito, and Serena Angela Gracco. 'Semantic models for IoT sensing to infer environment–wellness relationships'. In: *Future Generation Computer Systems* 140 (2023), pp. 1–17. https://doi.org/10.1016/j.future.2022.10.005.
30. Imran Makhdoom, Ian Zhou, Mehran Abolhasan, Justin Lipman, and Wei Ni. 'PrivySharing: A blockchain-based framework for privacy-preserving and secure data sharing in smart cities'. In: *Computers & Security* 88 (2020), p. 101653. https://doi.org/10.1016/j.cose.2019.101653.
31. Sidrah Abdullah, Junaid Arshad, Muhammad Mubashir Khan, Mamoun Alazab, and Khaled Salah. 'PRISED tangle: a privacy-aware framework for smart healthcare data

sharing using IOTA tangle'. In: *Complex & Intelligent Systems* (2022). https://doi.org/10.1007/s40747-021-00610-8.

32. M. Divya and Nagaveni B. Biradar. 'IOTA-Next Generation Block chain'. In: *International Journal of Engineering and Computer Science* 7 (2018), pp. 23823–23826.
33. Pinky Bai, Sushil Kumar, Kirshna Kumar, Omprakash Kaiwartya, Mufti Mahmud, and Jaime Lloret. 'GDPR Compliant Data Storage and Sharing in Smart Healthcare System: A Blockchain-Based Solution'. In: Electronics 11.20 (2022), p. 3311. https://doi.org/10.3390/electronics11203311.
34. Bandar Alamri, Ibrahim Tariq Javed, and Tiziana Margaria. 'A GDPR-Compliant Framework for IoT-Based Personal Health Records Using Blockchain'. In: *2021 11th IFIP International Conference on New Technologies, Mobility and Security (NTMS)*. 2021, pp. 1–5. https://doi.org/10.1109/NTMS49979.2021.9432661.
35. Kostas M. Tsiouris, Dimitrios Gatsios, Vassilios Tsakanikas, Athanasios A. Pardalis, Ioannis Kouris, Thelma Androutsou, Marilena Tarousi, Natasa Vujnovic Sedlar, Iason Somarakis, Fariba Mostajeran, Nenad Filipovic, Harm op den Akker, Dimitrios D. Koutsouris, and Dimitrios I. Fotiadis. 'Designing interoperable telehealth platforms: bridging IoT devices with cloud infrastructures'. In: *Enterprise Information Systems* 14.8 (2020), pp. 1194–1218. https://doi.org/10.1080/17517575.2020.1759146.
36. Dareen K. Halim and Samuel Hutagalung. 'Towards data sharing economy on Internet of Things: a semantic for telemetry data'. In: *Journal of Big Data* 9.1 (2022), p. 1. https://doi.org/10.1186/s40537-021-00549-0.
37. Shivananda R. Poojara, Chinmaya Kumar Dehury, Pelle Jakovits, and Satish Narayana Srirama. 'Serverless data pipeline approaches for IoT data in fog and cloud computing'. In: *Future Generation Computer Systems* 130 (2022), pp. 91–105. https://doi.org/10.1016/j.future.2021.12.012.
38. Jonathan McChesney, Nan Wang, Ashish Tanwer, Eyal de Lara, and Blesson Varghese. 'DeFog: Fog Computing Benchmarks'. In: *Proceedings of the 4th ACM/IEEE Symposium on Edge Computing*. SEC '19. Arlington, Virginia: Association for Computing Machinery, 2019, 47–58. https://doi.org/10.1145/3318216.3363299.
39. Chang Liu, Shaoyong Guo, Song Guo, Yong Yan, Xuesong Qiu, and Suxiang Zhang. 'LTSM: Lightweight and Trusted Sharing Mechanism of IoT Data in Smart City'. In: *IEEE Internet of Things Journal* 9.7 (2022), pp. 5080–5093. https://doi.org/10.1109/JIOT.2021.3110097.
40. Fahad Qaswar, M. Rahmah, Muhammad Ahsan Raza, A. Noraziah, Basem Alkazemi, Z. Fauziah, Mohd. Khairul Azmi Hassan, and Ahmed Sharaf. 'Applications of Ontology in the Internet of Things: A Systematic Analysis'. In: *Electronics* 12.1 (2022), p. 111. https://doi.org/10.3390/electronics12010111.
41. Natalya F Noy and Deborah L McGuinness. Ontology development 101: A guide to creating your first ontology. 2001.
42. Tek Raj Chhetri, Chinmaya Kumar Dehury, Blesson Varghese, Anna Fensel, Satish Narayana Srirama, and Rance J. DeLong. *Code: Enabling privacy-aware interoperable and quality IoT data sharing with context*. https://github.com/tekrajchhetri/secure-interoperable-data-sharing (Last accessed 01.12.2022). 2022.
43. Krzysztof Janowicz, Armin Haller, Simon J.D. Cox, Danh Le Phuoc, and Maxime Lefrançois. 'SOSA: A lightweight ontology for sensors, observations, samples, and

actuators'. In: *Journal of Web Semantics* 56 (2019), pp. 1–10. https://doi.org/10.1016/j.websem.2018.06.003.

44. Hajo Rügersberg, Mark van Assem, and Jan Top. 'Ontology of units of measure and related concepts'. In: *Semantic Web* 4 (2013). 1, pp. 3–13. https://doi.org/10.3233/SW-2012-0069.
45. Dario Bonino and Fulvio Corno. 'DogOnt—Ontology Modeling for Intelligent Domotic Environments'. In: *The Semantic Web—ISWC 2008*. Ed. by Amit Sheth, Steffen Staab, Mike Dean, Massimo Paolucci, Diana Maynard, Timothy Finin, and Krishnaprasad Thirunarayan. Berlin, Heidelberg: Springer Berlin Heidelberg, 2008, pp. 790–803.
46. Sherif Emad Abdel Rafey, Ayman Abdel-Hamid, and Mohamad Abou El-Nasr. 'CBSTM-IoT: Context-based social trust model for the Internet of Things'. In: *International Conference on Selected Topics in Mobile & Wireless Networking (MoWNeT)*. 2016, pp. 1–8. https://doi.org/10.1109/MoWNet.2016.bib46.
47. Areej AlHogail. 'Improving IoT Technology Adoption through Improving Consumer Trust'. In: *Technologies* 6.3 (2018), p. 64. https://doi.org/10.3390/technologies6030064.
48. Sandeep Gupta. 'Non-functional requirements elicitation for edgecomputing'. In: *Internet of Things* 18 (2022), p. 100503. https://doi.org/10.1016/j.iot.2022.100503.
49. Vincent Cheval, Cas Cremers, Alexander Dax, Lucca Hirschi, Charlie Jacomme, and Steve Kremer. 'Hash Gone Bad: Automated discovery of protocol attacks that exploit hash function weaknesses'. In: *32nd USENIX Security Symposium (USENIX Security 23)*. Anaheim, CA: USENIX Association, Aug. 2023, pp. 5899–5916.
50. Jahoon Koo and Young-Gab Kim. 'Resource identifier interoperability among heterogeneous IoT platforms'. In: *Journal of King Saud University—Computer and Information Sciences* 34.7 (2022), pp. 4191–4208. https://doi.org/10.1016/j.jksuci.2022.05.003.
51. Andrea Cimmino, Juan Cano-Benito, Alba Fernández-Izquierdo, Christos Patsonakis, Apostolos C. Tsolakis, Raúl García-Castro, Dimosthenis Ioannidis, and Dimitrios Tzovaras. 'A scalable, secure, and semantically interoperable client for cloud-enabled Demand Response'. In: *Future Generation Computer Systems* 141 (2023), pp. 54–66. https://doi.org/10.1016/j.future.2022.11.004.
52. Tek Raj Chhetri, Anelia Kurteva, Jubril Gbolahan Adigun, and Anna Fensel. 'Knowledge Graph Based Hard Drive Failure Prediction'. In: *Sensors* 22.3 (2022), p. 985. https://doi.org/10.3390/s22030985.

Part III
Conclusion

9 Conclusion

This chapter, in Sect. 9.1, revisits our hypothesis, RQs, and ROs and provides details on whether or not we have validated our claim. Sect. 9.2 provides details on the lessons learned. In addition, Sect. 9.3 of this chapter discusses potential future opportunities and the potential impact of our work. Finally, Sect. 9.4 provides the concluding remarks. The abbreviations used in this chapter are introduced in List of Abbreviations.

9.1 Hypothesis Validation and Fulfilment of ROs

In Chap. 1, we defined our hypothesis, and the research questions that guided this study. In addition, we defined the ROs in order to answer the RQs and validate the hypothesis. Below, we provide brief information regarding the fulfilment of each RO.

9.1.1 Fulfilment of RO1 and RO2

As discussed in Sect. 1.5 of Chap. 1 and in Chap. 2, the first two ROs, RO1 and RO2, are focused on the data sharing use case to improve data sharing related decisions by addressing issues such as interoperability, scalability, and GDPR compliance verification. With our work in Chap. 7 and Chap. 8, both ROs, RO1 and RO2, were

Supplementary Information The online version contains supplementary material available at https://doi.org/10.1007/978-3-658-45877-5_9.

T. R. Chhetri, *Improving Decision Making Using Semantic Web Technologies*,
https://doi.org/10.1007/978-3-658-45877-5_9

satisfied, thereby answering the RQs, RQ1 and RQ2, and addressing the challenges outlined in Chap. 1. Additionally, Chap. 5 and Chap. 6 partly contribute to these ROs, RO1 and RO2.

As an answer to the scalability challenge or regarding how to design a knowledge-driven application to support processing at scale, a distributed approach is the answer. In our research, we adopted microservices architecture. This is because a distributed approach allows components to be decoupled and deployed independently. Additionally, the distributed approach is beneficial for ML and in newer edge/fog paradigm, as shown by our work in Chap. 6 and Chap. 8 respectively.

The goal of designing and implementing an interoperable application in a heterogeneous environment, such as smart cities, is met using SW technology. The details are provided in Chap. 7 and Chap. 8. Specially, we show how SW technology can address the interoperability challenge in two distinct scenarios: (i) in the regulatory case, for instance to address GDPR compliance verification, and (ii) in the case of IoT data sharing with edge/fog scenarios.

In a manner similar to the interoperability case, our work in Chap. 7 and Chap. 8 addresses the regulatory and trustworthiness challenge discussed in Chap. 1. Specifically, with our work in Chap. 7, we demonstrate how to translate the legal regulation like GDPR, into code or software in a systematic manner and addressing technical challenges, i.e. implementing TOMs and maintaining interoperability. Through our work in Chap. 8, which builds on our work in Chap. 7 and focuses in the edge/fog scenario, we show how to share and process data in a complex environment with IoT devices that have limited resources in a GDPR-compliant manner. Furthermore, in Chap. 8, we demonstrate how to establish trust or enable trustworthy data sharing through the introduction of the new trust metric and by ensuring veracity (or accuracy).

Additionally, our work in Chap. 8 demonstrates how to convert data generated by a resource-constrained heterogeneous cyber-physical system into knowledge represented by KGs. Furthermore, we show how the translated knowledge can be utilised for real-time (or near-real-time) decisions making tasks in edge/fog environments. The work in Chap. 8 shows other benefits of SW technology, for example, ability to address issues like data quality, which is a reason for the failure of $3/4^{th}$ of IoT projects [1]. Similarly, our work in Chap. 6, which focuses on combining translated IoT data represented by KG to improve disease classification, and Chap. 5, which focuses on translating sensor data using Bayesian structure learning and representing it in KG to aid decision making, both partially contribute to our RO2.

9.1.2 Fulfilment of RO3

The third RO, as discussed in Chap. 1, focuses on answering our RQ3 about combining KGs and ML. The RO3 is satisfied by our contributions outlined in Chap. 4, Chap. 5 and Chap. 6.

As for the answer to the RQ on techniques to combine KGs and ML, three different approaches were presented. The first approach involves using KGs as inputs to a neural network-based technique, as described in Chap. 4. The second strategy utilises ML output, specifically Bayesian structure learning output, as input to KGs. The specifics are given in Chap. 5. Both of these approaches presented in Chap. 4 and Chap. 5 focus on manufacturing use cases. The third strategy from Chap. 6 focuses on the agricultural use case. It combines the result of the reasoning performed using SWRL reasoning with ML predictions to produce the final prediction along with explanations. Moreover, with our work on combining KGs and ML, we show the benefits that KGs bring, such as addressing the lack of context awareness in ML, improving prediction accuracy, and facilitating explainability.

9.1.3 Summary

As detailed in Sects. 9.1.1 and 9.1.2 respectively, our ROs have been successfully satisfied. With the completion of our ROs, we have also successfully addressed our RQs. Similarly, as described in Chap. 1, validating our hypothesis requires answering RQs. Since our RQs have been answered, we can conclude that our hypothesis has been successfully validated. This implies that we can improve decision making in distributed and heterogeneous environments by using SW technology. Appendix, Chapter A, contains links to the open source resources developed as part of this research.

9.2 Lessons Learned

In Sect. 9.1.1, we went into detail about how we met our ROs and proved our hypothesis. In this section, we summarise what we have learned, for example, from our work like [2] that are presented in Chap. 4, Chap. 5, Chap. 6, Chap. 7 and Chap. 8. The lessons learned are categorised into two groups, namely, data sharing and combining KGs and ML. Sect. 9.2.1 details the lessons learned for data sharing, and Sect. 9.2.2 provides an overview of the lessons learned for combining KGs and ML.

9.2.1 Data Sharing

This section discusses the lessons learned from our work on data sharing, including designing GDPR-compliant systems for data sharing and addressing data challenges such as data quality.

- **Lesson 1: Building regulatory systems requires a considerable effort, and early collaboration with domain experts and involved stakeholders is advantageous.** Building regulatory systems is a multidisciplinary endeavour that requires knowledge of both the law and technology, and as a result, it requires a substantial amount of work. However, experience [2, 3] has taught us that early collaborations with domain experts, such as lawyers, and other stakeholders, such as business partners, can expedite the task and is recommended. Furthermore, this facilitates comprehension of the requirements and their implications from both perspectives.
- **Lesson 2: There exists a technological gap in the industrial sector regarding SW technology.** There are industrial gaps in SW technology. Therefore, despite knowing the benefits of SW technology, industries do not use it, necessitating that we modify our implementation [2].
- **Lesson 3: SW technology can address the interoperability problem, but interoperability on a large scale is hard** [2, 4]**.** Interoperability is difficult, especially on a large scale. This is because of the multitude of heterogeneities, such as in smart cities, each with their own unique requirements. With our work in Chap. 7 and Chap. 8, we showed that the SW technology can help address the interoperability issue. However, SW technology alone is not a panacea for interoperability. There must be a concerted effort from all stakeholders and major corporations involved – a lesson learned from smashHit [4] project. Specifically, we foresee that the SW communities will have a greater role to play in solving this challenge of interoperability on a large scale and enabling the economic value that interoperability impedes [5].
- **Lesson 4: Consider the technological constraints that will influence scalability.** Scalability is essential, particularly for industry, but it comes at a cost [2, 3]. Therefore, it is recommended to analyse and consider scalability-influencing factors or technologies.

- **Lesson 5: There are performance tradeoffs; one cannot have it all, particularly when it comes to systems that deal with GDPR** [2, 3]. There are performance trade-offs. Encryption with a larger key size, for instance, offers greater security but at the expense of performance [2]. The optimal strategy is one that provides the required performance without compromising security [2, 3]. This is because of the importance of security, especially when designing systems to comply with GDPR. Therefore, there is no single correct design solution, and there will always be performance compromises. One must establish priorities based on their needs and applications.
- **Lesson 6: Blockchain immutability, which contradicts the GDPR's "right to be forgotten (Art. 17(2))", can be leveraged for other purposes like enabling data accuracy (or veracity) in a GDPR-compliant manner.** Blockchain is immutable, and therefore it contradicts GDPR's "right to be forgotten" [6]. However, the blockchain's immutability features can be used to to our advantage, such as to ensure data accuracy, i.e. to ensure that the shared data is not tampered with or altered in a GDPR-compliant manner (see Chap. 8).
- **Lesson 7: Utilising SW technology allows us to intrinsically ensure the high quality IoT data.** As demonstrated in Chap. 8, by employing SW technology, we can intrinsically ensure that IoT data meets the established quality criteria. Thus, we recommend using SW technology for high quality IoT data sharing.
- **Lesson 8: SW technology is compatible with IoT devices with limited resources and presents minimal overhead in terms of CPU and memory usage.** The resource constrained nature of the IoT acts as a limitation when it comes to performing complex operations [7], such as reasoning, efficiently. However, SW is suitable for use in resource constrained IoT devices with minimal overhead in terms of resource utilisation to perform reasoning and data sharing operations tasks such as checking consent and processing the data for quality, as demonstrated in Chap. 8. This is particularly important in the use cases, such as connected cars and smart cities, where IoT devices are used to collect (and share) data and perform other control actions.
- **Lesson 9: GDPR compliance must be demonstrated, and auditing is helpful in this regard.** For GDPR compliance, you must demonstrate to the authority, upon request, that you are only performing the consented-to actions. Therefore, having an auditing feature is advantageous in this regard, as auditing not only helps provide evidence to the authority, but also increases the system's transparency and accountability [2].

- **Lesson 10: Prioritise privacy in the design, even if it is not an essential legal requirement, when designing a system that deals with PII data.** A privacy-first approach is advantageous because it helps maintain the necessary protection of data, which the industry values most as it helps to build trust amongst the stakeholders and the users [2, 8]. We recommend that privacy-by-design methodology be considered during the creation of any system or product that handles sensitive data, even if privacy-by-design is not mandatory.
- **Lesson 11: Implementation of a notification mechanism can help increase transparency.** A notification mechanism in regulatory (or GDPR) systems can help improve transparency [2, 9] and avoid legal scrutiny by allowing the data processor or controller to take prompt action in the event of unconsented data processing [2].

9.2.2 Combining Knowledge Graphs and Machine Learning

This section discusses the lessons we have learned from our work on combining KGs and ML.

- **Lesson 1: Combining KGs and ML will lead to robust prediction** [10, 11]. Combining KGs and ML will lead to robust predictions as opposed to only using ML models that are trained on large datasets, as demonstrated by our work presented in Chap. 4, Chap. 5 and Chap. 6. This is because KGs provide rich context and factual knowledge and help to avoid AI hallucinations [11, 12]. AI hallucinations are situations when AI (or ML) models produce the wrong answer in a confident manner. Figure 9.1 depicts a case of AI hallucinations in which a popular large language model, ChatGPT, produces a confident answer for the product of 583971 and 44829101 (highlighted in green). In the case of the multiplication of 5 and 9, however, it yields the correct answer. This is because ChatGPT has most likely seen 5 and 9 during the training. A case like this can be prevented using the KGs' factual knowledge, leading to robust and trustworthy predictions [11].

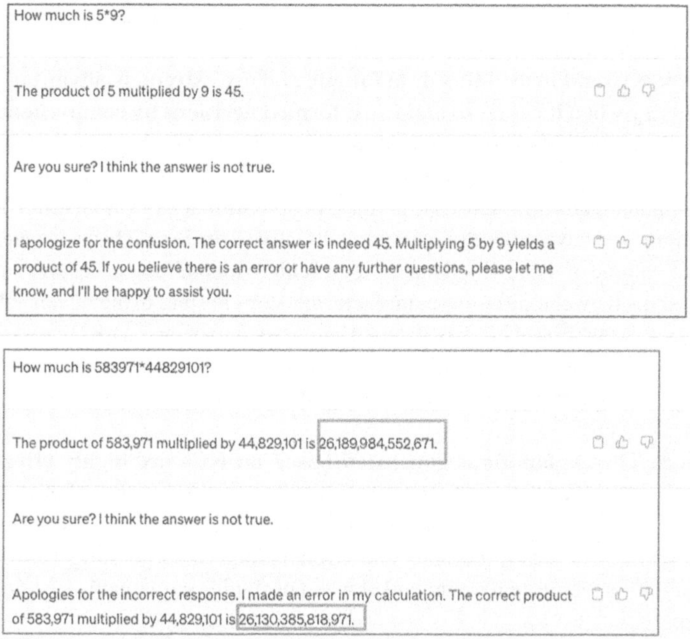

Fig. 9.1 ChatGPT, a large language model, produces responses demonstrating AI hallucinations (June 2, 2023). The top (highlighted in blue) shows an accurate prediction from ChatGPT, and the bottom (highlighted in red) shows the hallucinations with multiple answers for the same questions (highlighted in green)

- **Lesson 2: Combining KGs and ML not only improves prediction accuracy, but also the result's interpretability and explainability.** Combining KGs and ML yields additional benefits aside from improving the accuracy of predictions, as shown in Chap. 5 and Chap. 6. The benefits are enhanced result interpretability and user-level explanation of the prediction. This is especially important for applications in healthcare and finance, where transparency and interpretability are crucial.
- **Lesson 3: When combining KGs and ML, care should be taken.** KGs and ML must be combined with caution; otherwise, there will be no performance improvement or any benefits [10, 13]. For example, if a KG that is being combined with ML does not contain accurate domain information or if the appropriate

strategy for combining KGs and ML is not selected, then the performance will decrease rather than increase.

- **Lesson 4: KGs aid in avoiding data fatigue and are extremely advantageous for industry when it comes to making informed decisions by comprehending the relationships between various steps.** As we learned from our work, particularly [13], that was performed as part of the KI-Net [14] project in association with the manufacturing industrial partner, people in industry often suffer from data fatigue and have difficulty in making effective decisions. This is because of the huge volume of data, which makes it difficult to identify the necessary causal relationships between different manufacturing steps despite using advanced DL techniques. KGs, however, was deemed more advantageous, as KGs make the result more interpretable through KG's structured data representation, thereby allowing easy discovery and understanding of the connections between different entities, i.e. steps.
- **Lesson 5: The explanations generated based on KGs are highly effective, both in terms of usefulness and comprehension.** As demonstrated in Chap. 6 (or [11]), 95% of survey respondents find explanations based on KGs to be useful, while 85% easily comprehend explanations. Incorporating KG-based explanations is therefore recommended when designing explainable systems for non-experts.

9.3 Future Opportunities and Potential of Impact

This section discusses the opportunities and potential social and economic impact of the research presented in this thesis. Sect. 9.3.1 provides a future outlook, while Sect. 9.3.2 provides information on the potential impact.

9.3.1 Future Opportunities

Through our work in this thesis, we demonstrate the effectiveness of SW technology in decision making, such as data sharing. Specifically, we anticipate the following opportunities in the future:

- **Extending the scope.** Extending the scope of our work can be a future direction. In the case of our work on data sharing, one may consider expanding the scope to include other similar regulatory laws to GDPR, such as the CCPA. Similarly, our work on combining KGs and ML can be extended to domains requiring both explainability and robust predictions, such as healthcare.

- **Addressing the shortcomings highlighted by our work.** The other research focus is to resolve the limitations that our work has highlighted, such as performance [2]. In addition to addressing the highlighted limitations, new approaches can also be investigated to further advance our work. For example, one can investigate the use of IPFS (InterPlanetary File System) [15], a peer-to-peer hypermedia protocol, in the case of IoT data sharing.
- **Extending the implementation of our work to have a real-world impact.** The research presented in this thesis was conducted in collaboration with industrial partners, such as LexisNexis; the prototype or proof-of-concept implementation of our work, thus, captures the industrial needs [4]. Therefore, the other future outlook we foresee is to extend our work into a product.
- **Pursuing standardisation activities.** One of the other future opportunities that one can pursue is the exploration of potential standardisation activities, where the lessons learned [2, 8, 16] from our GDPR-related research help to develop standards and best practises.

9.3.2 Potential Impact

We have identified the three areas where the work that is performed in this thesis can have a potential impact. These areas are: (i) academic impact; (ii) societal impact; and (iii) commercial impact. Each of these areas will be explored in the subsequent sections, Sect. 9.3.3, Sect. 9.3.4 and Sect. 9.3.5, below. The academic impact focuses on how academic research can benefit our work. The societal impact discusses the societal aspect of our work and how it can contribute to the overall improvement of society. Finally, we discuss the commercial impact, which focuses on the potential commercial impact of our work.

9.3.3 Academic Impact

The first area of impact from our work is academic research, which will benefit from our findings. For example, our findings from our work on GDPR can be extremely beneficial to academic research, particularly for those new to the field and also for upcoming new projects that deal with GDPR. This is because this work was conducted with people from different academic disciplines, such as law and industry, providing a diverse range of perspectives and insights. For example, our findings about how to systematically translate the regulation into code adhering to both industrial needs and regulatory requirements [2] can be a cornerstone of upcoming projects like UPCAST [17], which aims to automate data sharing and processing in a trustworthy and transparent manner. Moreover, our work on combining KGs and ML is advantageous for developing better data-driven decision making systems for two reasons: (i) the ability to make predictions on multimodal data, including text and images; and (ii) the ability to incorporate domain knowledge. In particular, the approach and findings from our work on KGs and ML are applicable to research domains like healthcare, where both explainability and domain knowledge are crucial [18], as well as to the academic community [19].

9.3.4 Commercial Impact

The research in this thesis is closely aligned with the smashHit [4] and KI-Net [14] projects and was conducted in close collaboration with the industrial partners for the use cases. Our research, therefore, captures industrial needs. This thesis's findings and outcomes, such as the open-source implementation, can be employed to the develop commercial products. As a result, our research has created a substantial potential business opportunity that could yield significant economic benefits. For instance, the acknowledgement of our work as key deep technology innovations [20] with a technology ready maturity level [21] by the EU innovation radar also highlights the commercial potential of our work. Innovation radar is an initiative of the EU commission aimed at identifying high-potential innovations and innovators within EU-funded research and innovation projects [22].

9.3.5 Societal Impact

In terms of the societal dimension, the work conducted in this thesis contributes to the following UN SDGs: (i) zero hunger; (ii) industry, innovation and infrastructure; and (iii) sustainable cities and communities. In particular, the work in Chap. 6, which focuses on cassava disease, aligns with the UN SDG of zero hunger. Similarly, the works from Chap. 5, Chap. 4, Chap. 7, and Chap. 8 aligns with the UN SDG of industry, innovation and infrastructure. The work from Chap. 7 and Chap. 8 focuses on data sharing, while the work from Chap. 5 and Chap. 4 focuses on predictive maintenance tasks such as manufacturing product failure analysis and equipment failure. Our work from Chap. 7 and Chap. 8 further aligns with sustainable cities and communities SDG. Moreover, the EU innovation radar has also highlighted the societal relevance of our work [20].

9.4 Final Remarks

Our work demonstrates the efficacy of SW technology in enhancing decisions in complex environments, such as manufacturing. Furthermore, with our work in this thesis in three different application scenarios covering IoT, ML, GDPR, and emerging computing paradigms, fog and edge computing, we have demonstrated the benefits in practise alongside addressing other challenges, such as interoperability–one of the issues raised in the Dagstuhl Seminar report is the contrast between knowing and practising [23]. The author believes that this would serve as motivation for the more widespread adoption of SW technology in similarly complex environments, particularly in the industry, where there seems to exist a technological gap.

Finally, with our work on combining KGs and ML, we demonstrated how SW technology can be used to complement ML with missing domain knowledge and context awareness in addition to improving predictions, thereby making the AI more robust. Additionally, we demonstrated other benefits, including explainability and different techniques for combining SW technology and ML–one of the benefits highlighted in the Dagstuhl Seminar [23] on KGs. The author hopes that the work presented in this thesis, particularly the combination of KGs and ML, will serve as motivation in academia, industry, and government for the adoption of KGs in building AI that will be put to use in a social setting that requires trustworthy and user-comprehensible explainability.

Bibliography

1. Maggi Bansal, Inderveer Chana, and Siobhán Clarke. 'A Survey on IoT Big Data: Current Status, 13 V's Challenges, and Future Directions'. In: *ACM Comput. Surv.* 53.6 (2020). https://doi.org/10.1145/3419634
2. Tek Raj Chhetri, Anelia Kurteva, Rance J. DeLong, Rainer Hilscher, Kai Korte, and Anna Fensel. 'Data Protection by Design Tool for Automated GDPR Compliance Verification Based on Semantically Modeled Informed Consent'. In: *Sensors* 22.7 (2022). https://doi.org/10.3390/s22072763.
3. Amar Tauqeer, Anelia Kurteva, Tek Raj Chhetri, Albin Ahmeti, and Anna Fensel. 'Automated GDPR Contract Compliance Verification Using Knowledge Graphs'. In: *Information* 13.10 (2022). https://doi.org/10.3390/info13100447.
4. *smashHit*. https://smashhit.eu/. Last accessed on 01 October 2022.

5. James Manyika, Michael Chui, Peter Bisson, Jonathan Woetzel, Richard Dobbs, Jacques Bughin, and Dan Aharon. 'The internet of things: mapping the value beyond the hype'. In: *McKinsey Global Institute* (2015).
6. Abhishek Mahindrakar and Karuna Pande Joshi. 'Automating GDPR Compliance using Policy Integrated Blockchain'. In: *2020 IEEE 6th Intl Conference on Big Data Security on Cloud (BigDataSecurity), IEEE Intl Conference on High Performance and Smart Computing, (HPSC) and IEEE Intl Conference on Intelligent Data and Security (IDS)*. 2020, pp. 86–93. https://doi.org/10.1109/BigDataSecurity-HPSC-IDS49724.2020.00026.
7. Mostafa Haghi Kashani, Mona Madanipour, Mohammad Nikravan, Parvaneh Asghari, and Ebrahim Mahdipour. 'A systematic review of IoT in healthcare: Applications, techniques, and trends'. In: *Journal of Network and Computer Applications* 192 (2021), p. 103164. https://doi.org/10.1016/j.jnca.2021.103164.
8. smashHit consortium. *smashHit Platform Internal (Legal, Privacy, Consent) Policies Guides*. Version 1.0. Guidelines part of the smashHit project deliverable D2.2 smashHit Methodology (final). Sept. 2022. https://doi.org/10.5281/zenodo.7870462.
9. Roghaiyeh Gachpaz Hamed. 'Enhancing the Transparency of Personal Data Access through Semantic Web Technologies'. PhD thesis. Trinity College Dublin. School of Computer Science & Statistics. Discipline ..., 2021.
10. Tek Raj Chhetri, Anelia Kurteva, Jubril Gbolahan Adigun, and Anna Fensel. 'Knowledge Graph Based Hard Drive Failure Prediction'. In: *Sensors* 22.3 (2022), p. 985. https://doi.org/10.3390/s22030985.
11. Tek Raj Chhetri, Armin Hohenegger, Anna Fensel, Mariam Aramide Kasali, and Asiru Afeez Adekunle. 'Toward improving prediction accuracy and user-level explainability using deep learning and knowledge graphs: A study on cassava disease'. In: *Expert Systems with Applications* (2023), p. 120955. https://doi.org/10.1016/j.eswa.2023.120955.
12. Manas Gaur, Kalpa Gunaratna, Shreyansh Bhatt, and Amit Sheth. 'Knowledge-Infused Learning: A Sweet Spot in Neuro-Symbolic AI'. In: *IEEE Internet Computing* 26.4 (2022), pp. 5–11. https://doi.org/10.1109/MIC.2022.3179759.
13. Tek Raj Chhetri, Sareh Aghaei, Anna Fensel, Ulrich Göhner, Sebnem Gül-Ficici, and Jorge Martinez-Gil. 'Optimising Manufacturing Process with Bayesian Structure Learning and Knowledge Graphs'. In: *Computer Aided Systems Theory - EUROCAST 2022*. Ed. by Roberto Moreno-Díaz, Franz Pichler, and Alexis Quesada-Arencibia. Cham: Springer Nature Switzerland, 2022, pp. 594–602.
14. *KI-NET*. https://ki-net.eu/. Last accessed on 01 October 2022.
15. *IPFS*. https://ipfs.tech/. Last accessed on 01 June 2023.
16. smashHit consortium. *D5.4 Optimised smashHit Framework*. Version 1.0. Dec. 2022. https://doi.org/10.5281/zenodo.7867915
17. *UPCAST*. https://www.upcast-project.eu/. Last accessed on 8 June 2023.
18. Simon Meyer Lauritsen, Mads Kristensen, Mathias Vassard Olsen, Morten Skaarup Larsen, Katrine Meyer Lauritsen, Marianne Johansson Jørgensen, Jeppe Lange, and Bo Thiesson. 'Explainable artificial intelligence model to predict acute critical illness from electronic health records'. In: *Nature Communications* 11.1 (2020), p. 3852. https://doi.org/10.1038/s41467-020-17431-x.
19. Anna Breit, Laura Waltersdorfer, Fajar J. Ekaputra, Marta Sabou, Andreas Ekelhart, Andreea Iana, Heiko Paulheim, Jan Portisch, Artem Revenko, Annette ten Teije, and Frank van Harmelen. 'CombiningMachine Learning and Semantic Web: A Systematic

Mapping Study'. In: *ACM Comput. Surv.* (2023). Just Accepted. https://doi.org/10.1145/3586163.
20. *Deep Tech Innovation Automatic Contracting Tool.* https://innovation-radar.ec.europa.eu/innovation/44562. Last accessed on 09 June 2023.
21. *Maturity of Innovations.* https://innovation-radar.ec.europa.eu/faq/8. Last accessed on 09 June 2023.
22. *Innovation Radar.* radar.ec.europa.eu/about. Last accessed on 09 June 2023.
23. Piero Andrea Bonatti, Stefan Decker, Axel Polleres, and Valentina Presutti. 'Knowledge Graphs: New Directions for Knowledge Representation on the Semantic Web (Dagstuhl Seminar 18371)'. In: *Dagstuhl Reports* 8.9 (2019). Ed. by Piero Andrea Bonatti, Stefan Decker, Axel Polleres, and Valentina Presutti, pp. 29–111. https://doi.org/10.4230/DagRep.8.9.29.

The manufacturer's authorised representative in the EU is Springer Nature Customer Service Centre GmbH, Europaplatz 3, 69115 Heidelberg, Germany. If you have any concerns regarding our products, please contact ProductSafety@springernature.com

Printed and bound by CPI Group (UK) Ltd, Croydon, CR0 4YY

30/09/2026

02225601-0002